New Writing from Mexico

Edited by Reginald Gibbons

A special issue of *TriQuarterly* magazine

TriQuarterly Books

Northwestern University / 1992

TriQuarterly 85

Fall 1992

Editor
Reginald Gibbons

Co-Editor
Susan Hahn

Managing Editor
Kirstie Felland

Executive Editor
Bob Perlongo

Assistant Editor
Gwenan Wilbur

Special Projects Editor
Fred Shafer

Design Director
Gini Kondziolka

Readers
Timothy Dekin, Campbell McGrath

TriQuarterly Fellow
Deanna Kreisel

Editorial Assistants
**Matthew Kutcher, Sarah Kube,
Susan Rooney, Hans Holsen**

Advisory Editors
**Hugo Achugar, Michael Anania, Stanislaw Baranczak,
Cyrus Colter, Rita Dove, Richard Ford, George Garrett,
Michael S. Harper, Bill Henderson, Maxine Kumin, Grace Paley,
Michael Ryan, Alan Shapiro, Ellen Bryant Voigt**

TRIQUARTERLY IS AN INTERNATIONAL JOURNAL OF WRITING, ART AND CULTURAL INQUIRY PUBLISHED AT **NORTHWESTERN UNIVERSITY**.

Subscription rates (three issues a year)—Individuals: one year $18; two years $32; life $250. Institutions: one year $26; two years $44; life $300. Foreign subscriptions $4 per year additional. Price of single copies varies. Sample copies $4. Correspondence and subscriptions should be addressed to *TriQuarterly,* **NORTHWESTERN UNIVERSITY,** 2020 Ridge Avenue, Evanston, IL 60208. Phone: (708) 491-3490. The editors invite submissions of fiction, poetry and literary essays, which must be received between October 1 and April 30; manuscripts received between May 1 and September 30 will not be read. No manuscripts will be returned unless accompanied by a stamped, self-addressed envelope. All manuscripts accepted for publication become the property of *TriQuarterly*, unless otherwise indicated. Copyright © 1992 by *TriQuarterly*. No part of this volume may be reproduced in any manner without written permission. The views expressed in this magazine are to be attributed to the writers, not the editors or sponsors. Printed in the United States of America by Thomson-Shore, typeset by Sans Serif. ISSN: 0041-3097.

National distributors to retail trade: Ingram Periodicals, 1117 Heil Quaker Blvd., La Vergne, TN 37086 (800-627-6247, ext. 4500); B. DeBoer, 113 East Centre Street-Rear, Nutley, NJ 07110 (201-667-9300). Distributor for West Coast trade: Bookpeople, 2929 Fifth Street, Berkeley, CA 94710 (415-549-3030).

Reprints of issues #1–15 of *TriQuarterly* are available in full format from Kraus Reprint Company, Route 100, Millwood, NY 10546, and all issues in microfilm from University Microfilms International, 300 North Zeeb Road, Ann Arbor, MI 48106. *TriQuarterly* is indexed in the *Humanities Index* (H. W. Wilson Co.) and the *American Humanities Index* (Whitson Publishing Co.).

Contents

A Note on the Art in This Issue

*Cover design by Gini Kondziolka; cover painting by
Alejandro Romero (Nuestros dioses/Our Gods,
22″ × 30″ watercolor and pen and ink, collection of
Frank Aguilar Padrón).*

*The graphic art reproduced in this issue was curated by
Alberto Ruy Sánchez. The artists are Mónica Castillo,
Miguel Castro Leñero, Laura Cohen, Javier de la Garza,
Rocío Maldonado, Lucía Maya, Dulce María Nuñez,
Georgina Quintana, Adolfo Riestra, Gerardo Suter,
Germán Venegas and Nahúm B. Zenil.*

The map of Mexico on the following page is reprinted with permission from Cadogan Guides: Mexico *by Katherine and Charlotte Thomson,* © *1991. Published by The Globe Pequot Press, Old Saybrook, CT 06475.*

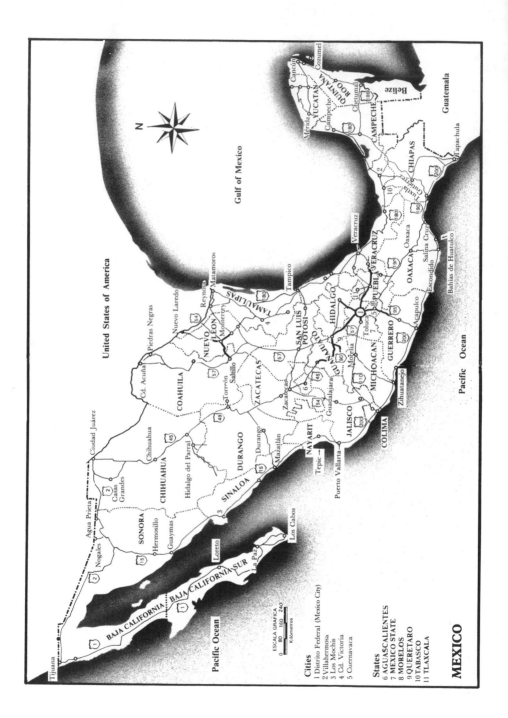

MEXICO

Cities
1 Distrito Federal (Mexico City)
2 Villahermosa
3 Los Mochis
4 Cd. Victoria
5 Cuernavaca

States
6 AGUASCALIENTES
7 MEXICO STATE
8 MORELOS
9 QUERETARO
10 TABASCO
11 TLAXCALA

ESCALA GRAFICA
0 80 160 240
Kilómetros

Pacific Ocean

United States of America

Gulf of Mexico

Pacific Ocean

Guatemala

Belize

Introduction: Borders

Reginald Gibbons

The border between our country and Mexico lies not only along the physical frontier but also within each country, within U.S. cities or Mexican suburbs, between the two languages that most (but not all, in either country) speak, between cuisines and ecosystems, between differences in habits, trade, travel, artisanry and manufacture. So, first of all, we might say that between Mexico and the U.S. there are many borders. If within our own country we seek an expression of life along these borders, we find it in Chicano writing (whether in Spanish or English) and in the work of a few anglo writers whose experience of borders has informed their sense of life and language.* If we look to Mexico, we find in fiction and poetry a startling variety of expression of what is "Mexican" (a variety almost as heterogeneous as writing in the twentieth-century U.S., for in Mexican writing we see the traces of several contests of cultures similar to what we now take for granted in our own several, even many, "Americas"). But we also find traces of the contest between the cultures of Mexico and the cultures of the U.S., traces of many crossings of these borders. (I am deliberately referring to our nation as the U.S., because our use of the word "America" is an arrogation,

---

*For a very full bibliography of Chicano writing, see Marc Zimmerman, *U.S. Latino Literature: An Essay and Annotated Bibliography* (MARCH/Abrazo Press, 1992). Arte Publico Press and Bilingual Review Press have published an extraordinary range of Chicano and other latino works. For book-length collections, see the anthology of fiction by both Chicano and anglo writers, *North of the Rio Grande: The Mexican-American Experience in Short Fiction*, edited by Edward Simmen (Mentor, 1992).

however unwitting, of a word which in Spanish means the entire hemisphere, and is often used in the plural.)

In a volume like this, the borders between these two national cultures also include the moment when we read, for these particular new works of fiction and poetry are now translations out of the language in which they were felt, conceived, labored over, polished and let go, into a language whose forms of expression and literary evolution are quite different.

Every place in the New World seems a confluence of cultures, with a residue—even if only in the etymologies of certain words still in use—of contest. In what is now the United States, indigenous peoples were drastically affected by contact with Europeans and then mostly destroyed; in what is now Mexico, they were conquered militarily, and, when not actually enslaved, they were kept impoverished. The cultural domains of English, Spanish and French settlement shifted according to treaties and wars which left ordinary people, both settlers and native peoples, rarely the framers or signatories of treaties nor the planners of military expeditions, in zones of cultural ambiguity, instability and transition. Present-day cultural borders are in part the legacy of these earlier stages of social and political evolution, including wars. There is no simple or single legacy or heritage, on any side, but rather a contradictory heterogeneity, not always acknowledged as such.

And even though the present political boundaries are long-established and policed, it is not always the nature of human custom to pay much attention to political borders when language is concerned. Because of the economic forces that steer life so powerfully, English-speaking persons have carried English words south across the political border into Mexico, and Mexican immigrants to the U.S., or their descendants, have carried them, too, when they returned to their homeland. Meanwhile, Mexican persons speaking Spanish have remained or come (back) into the U.S., carrying Spanish words into the stream of English. Many Mexican immigrants to the U.S., along with immigrants from other Spanish-speaking countries, have kept their language alive here (even though their children have often experienced a double loss, when, as Mexican-American poet Luis Rodríguez has said, first their Spanish is taken away from them in schools where they are not allowed to use it, and then they are not taught English). So the linguistic dimension of the cultural border between Mexico and the U.S. is indistinct, various, evolving.

Thus, to read imaginative writing from Mexico, especially recent

10

work, is not only to be shown the variety of what is characteristically "Mexican" in literary expression, but also to be reminded often that "Mexican" does not mean something homogeneous and identifiable by easy contrast with, for example, (caution!) "American." Mexico itself is the site of an evolution of mutually influencing differences of custom and culture, including indigenous peoples still strong in their social practices whether old or new; of Spanish-language habits of mind, speech and institutional heritage; of the effect of many immigrants into Mexico not only from Spain but also from other European countries and elsewhere; and of the cultural and linguistic pressure from our side of the political border, which influences habits and ideals of personal aspiration, common belief, politics, governance and economic regulation, entertainment, food, language, the treatment of the natural environment. . .

On this mostly English-speaking side of the border, we also receive and, depending on where we live, are affected, even changed, by Mexican influences, not only because of the presence of immigrants from Mexico—some of us are Mexican-American; some of us, as in northern New Mexico, go back to a time long before there was a United States—but also because of the cultural strength and energy of Mexico itself, over there, over here, across the many borders.

All too often, on this side of the borders, we start our definition of what is Mexican with the clichés of Mexico as seen by us gringos: the vacation spots along the coasts; bottles of Dos Equis and Corona and Tecate; some baseball players in the major leagues; ranchero music on the radio stations; restaurants; bilingual classrooms in our schools; negative images from commercial culture, from news media, from social conflicts.

Maybe, if we have been inside Mexico, we know a little about the exuberance of the Day of the Dead; the great personal generosity and warmth of Mexicans; the confused dirty cities, especially the behemoth Mexico City, smothering in poison; the ruins, the astonishing artifacts, the glyphs and documents and belief-systems of the ancient peoples; corruption, and the inertia and political monopoly of the Institutional Revolutionary Party (the PRI); the great question mark of the coming free-trade pact; and the paradoxes of an everyday life just as contradictory as our own: In Mexico City, a friend told me of two eagles living in treetops in the Coyoacán district, presumably surviving, even in that suffocatingly polluted air, by preying on the decrepit and diseased street cats and dogs. At stoplights one sees the clowns and jugglers and fire-breathers perform in front of the cars for whatever coin may be tossed to them; a suburb of Monterrey is said to be the richest on the continent. The tropics and mountains and deserts abound in extraordinary natural life, and man-made toxic wastes are rampant. Ways of understanding of how all such elements combine, with many more, to make up something incalculably complex, rise piecemeal but with imaginative vigor, whether of pathos or playfulness, out of fiction and poetry, and so this anthology is meant to provide not only pleasures and excitements of reading, but also a portrait of some part of what Mexico is like, and what is Mexican.

Over the last two years, reading Mexican books and journals, attending a few literary gatherings and events in Mexico City and Guadalajara during short visits, I have reminded myself to try to notice in what ways writers and writing, readers and reading, and the literary works themselves, are different from what we in the U.S. are more accustomed to. Mexican short stories and poems often seem to me, more noticeably than I had ever thought of most English-language writing in the U.S., not only individual works of creation and individually expressive, but also miniature sites of the many evolving contests—which do not always need to be characterized as either hostile or friendly—of historical heritages and differences of custom, sometimes defined by contrast across a border.

I am thinking, for example, of the use by Spanish-speaking Mexican writers of indigenous materials, on the one hand, and their way of addressing materials from the U.S., on the other. (For an exemplary illustration of these two poles in this volume, note how Juan Villoro situates his confused young couples at an ancient, pre-Conquest ruin, and how Luis Humberto Crosthwaite writes of both the cutural and the political borders between Mexico and the U.S.)

By comparison, the literary moment in the U.S. makes me wonder: Are our own many cultures keeping more to themselves, each one producing its writers and other artists, each one jealously guarding its heritage and experience and putting up along its borders signs that read "EVERYBODY ELSE KEEP OUT"? Are we exploring as well as our Mexican contemporaries the borders, barriers, confusions and possibilities between and among our own many cultures? Are our models of fiction and poetry more constrained in this way than those available to the Mexican writer? Are Mexican writers more aware of, and interested in exploring, the contests and mutual influences of the variety of heritages in Mexico? Do we seem a little timid, by contrast?

An example: I have noticed how common it is for Mexican poets to make apparently unselfconscious and authoritative reference to aspects of indigenous cultures—especially ancient places and surviving words (such as for the flora and fauna of the tropics—see poems by José Luis Rivas, Elsa Cross, Elva Macías, and Efraín Bartolomé). I wondered how either white or Native American "America" would have reacted if a U.S. poet of the stature of Octavio Paz, and as remote as he in terms of his personal heritage from the indigenous cultures, had made such surprising, but authoritative and wholly capable, use of some Native American artifact analogous to the Aztec calendrical sunstone, which for Paz became the subject of his best-known and most ambitious poem.

Perhaps this was possible for Paz, and for the Aztec sunstone, because it is so important to Mexico's sense of itself as a nation that it is a *mestizo* nation—a mixture of indigenous and European peoples—in ways that the U.S. never was nor will be. There are indigenous populations in Mexico, still, of far greater size than those in the U.S. The major indigenous cultures of Mexico built with stone, and while those civilizations are gone, their monuments and artifacts remain a part of the living sense of Mexican heritage as our Native American heritage does not, for most people in the U.S. There are living indigenous traditions, however evolved over time and through contact with people of European descent and the modern world, everywhere in Mexico, and they are absorbed into the texture of culture in many ways, from cheap exoticism and tourist kitsch to a kind of high-minded anthropological chauvinism to fabled attempts to decipher Mayan glyphs to the poem I mentioned earlier, Octavio Paz's "Sunstone" (which by the way was first translated into English by Muriel Rukeyser, another inhabitant of borders and one to contest fiercely anything expected or routine).

Yet my guess is that many white American readers and fellow-writers could well consider a poem like Paz's—relying on an artifact of a gone world—patronizing or merely exotic or irrelevant, or at best hopelessly idealizing, as if their own sense of the world had superseded everything as remote as that. And confronted with a successful, even a famous poem, that raised such an artifact and sense of life to the mythic center of the heterogeneous cultural identity of the U.S., some Native Americans might feel culturally ripped off, as if they owned a kind of exclusive right to mention or make imaginative use of their own heritage.

This is not to say that anyone's poem using such an image or artifact is, simply by virtue of such use, a good poem, by any of the great variety of standards by which "good" is judged in a country like ours. I am suggesting that some contemporary Mexican writing can be read as an argument for imaginative freedom, and against proprietary cultural nationalism; it may show us that we, in our many cultures, could be more open to, more curious about, more indebted to each other, in artistically productive, even liberating, ways.

Thus one of the possibilities of imagination for a Mexican writer seems to be to draw more freely than we do on both indigenous and European (Spanish) heritages for adequate symbols for states of being, for feeling, for both social and psychic movement and change, for conveying what it is like to live across borders. (And the Spanish heritage is itself richly heterogeneous: I find very interesting the traces of Islamic heritage alive in the poems by Coral Bracho and Jorge Esquinca, even when these traces are only aids to imaginative exploration, not themselves the deep subjects of poems.)

If what I have tried to characterize above, as I see it, may be called the psychosocial context of Mexican writing, then the sociological context, too, of writing, publishing and reading in Mexico is much different from what most of us encounter in the U.S.

In Mexico, as in Spain, writers are regarded and cubbyholed in terms of not only their published work but also their chronological "generation"—a word we scarcely use in speaking of U.S. writers. One implication of this is that generations are expected to be different from each other, and another, more constraining, perhaps, is that the members of a generation are expected to resemble each other somewhat as artists.

Writers of poems and short stories are accustomed to seeing these, along with their cultural journalism, published in newspapers, many of which have sizable literary sections. This means that the dissemination of at least some literary works, especially in cities (and above all in Mexico City) is far more widespread and less rarified than in the U.S. The market for literature in Mexico includes the readers of newspapers, while in the U.S. literature is a "niche" inside a media business much more oriented than its Mexican counterpart toward revenue, "product," mass scale, and sound bites and slogans. (This is not at all to say that language in Mexico is immune to corruption by political usage.)

In Mexico, the sorts of jobs that writers take include many more of what here we would call "arts administration" positions in cultural institutions of various sorts. There seem to be groups of writers formed around specific cultural institutions. Yet, in Mexico it's hard to find books—good bookstores are few and the system of book distribution seems haphazard—and because writers are already grouped in genera-

14

tions and also around literary and cultural institutions, from little magazines and writing workshops to Octavio Paz's independent magazine *Vuelta* to the Instituto Nacional de Bellas Artes, the dissemination of new work seems somewhat based on personal acquaintance.

Compared to the philanthropic support of literature in the U.S., in Mexico a lot more government money goes to literary institutions and publishing; private donations from individuals to literary institutions are fewer (although there are still instances in Mexico of individual patronage of individual writers or artists); and corporate support of literature is much greater (as it is in many countries).

As María Luisa Puga notes in her essay, literary success and reputation have been till now, and still are, mostly tied to being at the center of Mexico, in Mexico City. There is not the wide geographical dispersion of writers, presses and literary magazines, writers' colonies, and so on, to which we are accustomed in the U.S. Mexico City, which both produces and consumes the great majority of cultural products of all kinds, is an intellectual and artistic center more dominant over the nation as a whole than New York in our country. For that very reason, the attempt by some writers outside Mexico City to take the measure of their own provinces and to make an artistic career outside the center has been getting stronger, and is both interesting and impressive. (Outside Mexico City, Guadalajara is the next largest, and perhaps only important, literary center in the country; and by comparison to Mexico City it is small.)

The publishing scene is not nearly as commercialized yet as in the U.S., principally, one would guess, because the reading public is not yet able to consume much writing. About half of Mexico's population of eighty million is said to be impoverished and to a great extent illiterate. What is called a best-seller in Mexico may have a print run that is very small by U.S. best-seller standards. The short-story collection seems to be a more publishable form in Mexico, year in and year out, than in the U.S., where its strength is somewhat at the mercy of commercial hunches and fashions. Print runs of collections of short stories are about the same size as those from small presses in the U.S.; and of poems, also about the same—which means they are rather larger, proportionally, in Mexico, than they are in the U.S.

The criteria for the selection of the works in this volume were that all the short stories (excerpts from novels were excluded) and poems had to offer not only something that seemed to answer in part the question, "What is Mexican?" but also a freshness of conception and execution

15

that would allow for convincing and authoritative translation. It was not my intention to produce a documentary volume that "surveyed" Mexican writing—that would be a more academic goal. I sometimes found myself more interested in works than in writers; I wanted to achieve a certain variety, including expressions and representations of provincial life; and I have included a few works by writers who even in Mexico are not yet well-known, since the pleasure of discovery has always been at the heart of *TriQuarterly*.

The year 1968 divided contemporary Mexico from its past—in October government troops shot and killed students demonstrating in Mexico City. The social and psychological effect on Mexico was far greater than that of the Kent State killings on the U.S. in 1970. The cataclysm of 1968 shifted awareness and thinking, consciousness and expressive goals. Although one does not see 1968 itself as a subject of much work here (it does figure in a few works), this collection takes 1968 or thereabouts as a defining beginning date of the contemporary, and so it includes, with only a few exceptions, Mexican writers born around the year 1945 and afterward—that is, it begins with writers who as young women and men were part of 1968, and of whom 1968 remains a part, and it comes far enough forward in time to include a few writers who were only children at the time of the killings. The exceptions to the 1945 date are two writers, María Luisa Puga and Jesús Gardea, who for several reasons belong with this rather than an earlier generation.

If there has had to be a certain amount of arbitrariness of circumstance in limiting the size of this anthology—trying to get books, to find out about writers, always yields somewhat haphazard results—there has not been, I hope, any arbitrariness of judgment. Yet undoubtedly another editor would choose differently. In Mexico over the last twenty years there is just as great an increase in the number of writers as in the U.S.

The main design of this anthology includes several sorts of writing. A great range of experience, and sometimes stylistic experiment as well, have been brought into fiction and poetry by women writers such as Carmen Boullosa, Ethel Krauze, Mónica Mansour, Silvia Molina, Bárbara Jacobs, Carmen Leñero, Silvia Tomasa Rivera, and other women included in this volume. The folk element has been superbly manipulated, like a painter's palette, by Angeles Mastretta, Jesús Morales Bermúdez and Ricardo Elizondo, in a way for which equivalents in our writing are few. The provincial, sometimes tropical setting, has been richly explored and exploited artistically by Luis Arturo Ramos, Carlos

16

Montemayor, Gloria Velázquez, Severino Salazar, Dante Medina, Jesús Gardea and others.

There are the works of socially and politically sophisticated urban experience, like the fiction by María Luisa Puga and Héctor Manjarrez, and poems of the metropolis by Manuel Ulacia, Fabio Morábito, Héctor Carreto and others. Hernán Lara Zavala shows Mexico City and the provincial town in contrast to each other—each, in the face of violence, with its characteristic loneliness of being. Experiment—formal or conceptual—informs Guillermo Samperio's Chinese-box stories; Carlos Chimal's extraordinary protagonists (alley cats) and manipulation of point of view; the satire of Oscar de la Borbolla, Enrique Serna and Alvaro Uribe; Alberto Ruy Sánchez's modulations of tone; and Fabio Morábito's arch fable of translators. The work of some writers pushes toward new subjects—Juan Villoro's drifting young couples, Luis Zapata's tentative male whores, Luis Humberto Crosthwaite's vision of Elvis.

But these categories are only a poor and provisional sorting of the rich variety of new Mexican writing, and leave out works less easily typified—such as the elegant poems of Alberto Blanco, Luis Miguel Aguilar, Víctor Manuel Mendiola, David Huerta and others.

There are only two essays; each pertains to writing and each raises questions and controversies—as she travels, María Luisa Puga keeps a journal on provincial education and contemporary literature; the most apparent cultural border between Mexico and the U.S. is Chicano life and culture, hence the inclusion in this anthology of one Mexican writer's perspective on Chicano literature—Martha Robles's.

And as my purpose here is not to characterize each writer's work but rather the scope of the volume as a whole, there are more contributors to this volume whom I have not mentioned. And there are many more writers of these younger generations, and *many* excellent writers born earlier than 1945, who also deserve translation into English. I hope that this anthology will stimulate more curiosity among readers and more work among translators to bring that work into English as well. We will offer readers of *TriQuarterly* a continuing series of Mexican stories and poems, by writers of all generations, in future issues.

So here is one answer—provisional, time-bound, and lying across several borders—to the question of what is Mexican. May it provoke many questions and at least a few more attempts at answers.

* * *

I wish to express my thanks to Annette Cowart for her assistance in preparing this issue; to María Cristina García Cepeda for her encouragement and to the Fondo Nacional para la Cultura y las Artes for essential and generous financial support, without which this project could not have been completed; to the Fund for Culture/Fideicomiso para la Cultura (in turn funded by Fundacíon Cultural Bancomer and the Rockefeller Foundation), for additional financial support; to John Dwyer and Robert Earle for their assistance and enthusiasm; to the translators for their devoted and excellent labors, and especially to Cynthia Steele, who made a number of very helpful suggestions regarding the contents of this volume; and to Argentina Erdman and Olivia Maciel Edelman, who helped answer many difficult questions of translation.

I am also thankful for the goodwill, aid and hospitality of many writers and friends of writing in Mexico. When a literary journal undertakes a project as large as this—even after all the unfortunate but necessary omissions of stories and poems for which there isn't sufficient space—it can come to seem too large to be completed successfully or paid for. But what can happily overcome these obstacles—as happened in this case—is the dedication of many people for whom fiction and poetry are among the essentials of a full life, including fellow readers and writers, financial donors and, most especially, my fellow staff at *TriQuarterly*.

Except where indicated otherwise, translations of the poems are my own.

From *Big-Eyed Women*

Angeles Mastretta

Angeles Mastretta (Puebla, Puebla, 1949) is a journalist, poet and fiction writer. Mastretta's work has established itself as part of Mexico's "new realism" genre. Her fiction is historical, political and feminist. Her well-known novel, Arráncame la vida *(1985), won the Mazatlán prize for literature in 1985.*

Aunt Natalia Esparza

One day Natalia Esparza, she of the short legs and round tits, fell in love with the sea. She didn't know for sure at what moment that pressing wish to know the remote and legendary ocean came to her, but it came with such force that she had to abandon her piano school and take up the search for the Caribbean, because it was to the Caribbean that her ancestors had come a century before, and it was from there that what she'd named the missing piece of her conscience was calling to her without respite.

The call of the sea gave her such strength that her own mother could not convince her to wait even half an hour. It didn't matter how much her mother begged her to calm her craziness until the almonds were ripe for making nougat, until the tablecloth that they were embroidering with cherries for her sister's wedding was finished, until her father understood that it wasn't prostitution, or idleness, or an incurable mental illness that had suddenly made her so determined to leave.

Aunt Natalia grew up in the shadow of the volcanoes, scrutinizing them day and night. She knew by heart the creases in the breast of the Sleeping

21

Woman and the daring slope that capped Popocatépetl.* She had always lived in a land of darkness and cold skies, baking candies over a slow fire and cooking meats hidden beneath the colors of overly elaborated sauces. She ate off of decorated plates, drank from crystal goblets, and spent hours seated before the rain, listening to her mother's prayers and her grandfather's tales of dragons and winged horses. But she learned of the sea on the afternoon when some uncles from Campeche passed through during her snack of bread and chocolate, before resuming their journey to the walled city surrounded by an implacable ocean of colors.

Seven kinds of blue, three greens, one gold, everything fit in the sea. The silver that no one could take out of the country: whole under a cloudy sky. Night challenging the courage of the ships, the tranquil consciences of those who governed. The morning like a crystal dream, midday brilliant as desire.

There, she thought, even the men must be different. Those who lived near the sea which she'd been imagining without respite since Thursday snack time would not be factory owners or rice salesmen or millers or plantation owners or anyone who could keep still under the same light his whole life long. Her uncle and father had spoken so much of the pirates of yesteryear and those of today, of Don Lorenzo Patiño, her mother's grandfather, whom they nicknamed Lorencillo between gibes when she told them that he had arrived at Campeche in his own brig. So much had been said of the calloused hands and prodigal bodies that required that sun and that breeze, so fed up was she with the tablecloth and the piano, that she took off after the uncles without a single regret. She would live with her uncles, her mother hoped. Alone, like a crazed she-goat, guessed her father.

She didn't even know the way, only that she wanted to go to the sea. And at the sea she arrived, after a long journey to Mérida and a terrible long trek behind the fishermen she met in the market of that famous white city.

They were an old man and a young one. The old man, a talkative pot smoker; the youth, who considered all of this madness. How would they return to Holbox with this nosy, well-built woman? How could they leave her?

"You like her, too," the old man had told him, "and she wants to come. Don't you see how she wants to come?"

Aunt Natalia had spent the entire morning seated in the fish stalls of the market, watching the arrival of one man after another who'd accept

---

*Popocatépetl: volcanic peak near Mexico City

anything in exchange for their smooth creatures of white flesh and bone, their strange creatures, as smelly and beautiful as the sea itself must be. She lingered upon the shoulders and gait, the insulted voice of one who didn't want to "just give away" his conch.

"It's this much or I'll take it back," he had said.

"This much or I'll take it back," and Natalia's eyes followed him.

The first day they walked without stopping, Natalia asking and asking if the sand of the seashore was really white as sugar, and the nights as hot as alcohol. Sometimes she paused to rub her feet and they took advantage of the chance to leave her behind. Then she put on her shoes and set off running, repeating the curses of the old man.

They arrived on the following afternoon. Aunt Natalia couldn't believe it. She ran to the water, propelled forward by her last remaining strength, and she began to add her tears to the salty water. Her feet, her knees, her muscles were aching. Her face and shoulders stung from sunburn. Her wishes, heart and hair were aching. Why was she crying? Wasn't sinking down here the only thing she wanted?

Slowly, it grew dark. Alone on the endless beach, she touched her legs and found that they had not yet become a mermaid's tail. A brisk wind was blowing, pushing the waves to the shore. She walked the beach, startling some tiny mosquitoes that feasted on her arms. Close by was the old man, his eyes lost on her.

She threw herself down in her wet clothes on the white bed of sand and felt the old man come nearer, put his fingers in her matted hair and explain to her that if she wanted to stay, it had to be with him because all the others already had women.

"I'll stay with you," she said, and she fell asleep.

No one knew how Aunt Natalia's life was in Holbox. She returned to Puebla six months later and ten years older, calling herself the widow of Uc Yam.

Her skin was brown and wrinkled, her hands calloused, and she exuded a strange air of self-confidence. She never married yet never wanted for a man; she learned to paint and the blue of her paintings made her famous in Paris and New York.

Nevertheless, her home remained in Puebla, however much, some afternoons, while watching the volcanoes, her dreams would wander out to sea.

"One belongs where one is from," she would say, painting with her old-lady hands and child's eyes. "Because like it or not, wherever you go, they send you back home."

Aunt Leonor

Aunt Leonor had the world's most perfect belly button: a small dot hidden exactly in the middle of her flat, flat belly. She had a freckled back and round, firm hips, like the pitchers of water she drank from as a child. Her shoulders were raised slightly; she walked slowly, as if on a high wire. Those who saw them tell that her legs were long and golden, that her pubes were a tuft of arrogant, reddish down, that it was impossible to look upon her waist without desiring all of her.

At age seventeen she followed her head and married a man who was exactly the kind one would choose, with the head, to accompany one through life. Alberto Palacios, a wealthy, stringent notary public, had fifteen years, thirty centimeters of height, and a proportionate amount of experience on her. He had been the longtime boyfriend of various boring women who became even more tiresome when they discovered that the good notary had only a long-term plan for considering marriage.

Destiny would have it that Aunt Leonor entered the notary office one afternoon accompanied by her mother to process a supposedly easy inheritance which, for them, turned out to be extremely complicated, owing to the fact that Aunt Leonor's recently deceased father had never permitted his wife to think for even half an hour in her lifetime. He did everything for her except go grocery shopping and cook. He summarized the news in the newspaper for her and told her how she should think about it; he gave her an always sufficient allowance which he never asked to see how she spent; he even told her what was happening in the movies they went to see together: "See, Luisita, this boy fell in love with the young lady. Look how they're gazing at each other—you see? Now he wants to caress her; he's caressing her now. Now he's going to ask her to marry him and in a little while he's going to be abandoning her."

The result of this paternalism was that poor Aunt Luisita found the sudden loss of the exemplary man who was always Aunt Leonor's daddy not only distressing but also extremely complicated. With this sorrow and this complication they entered the notary's office in search of assistance. They found him to be so solicitous and efficacious that Aunt Leonor, still in mourning, married notary Palacios a year and a half later.

Her life was never again as easy as it was back then. In the sole critical moment, she had followed her mother's advice: shut your eyes and say an Ave María. In truth, many Ave Marías, because at times her immoderate husband could take as long as ten mysteries of the rosary before arriving at the series of moans and gasps culminating the circus which inevitably began when, for some reason, foreseen or not, he placed his hand on Leonor's short, delicate waist.

Aunt Leonor lacked for nothing a woman under twenty-five should want: hats, veils, French shoes, German tableware, a diamond ring, a necklace of unmatched pearls, turquoise, coral and filigree earrings. Everything, from underdrawers embroidered by Trinitarian nuns to a tiara like Princess Margaret's. She had whatever she chanced to want, including her husband's devotion, in that little by little he began to realize that life without exactly this woman would be intolerable.

From out of the affectionate circus that the notary mounted at least three times a week, first a girl then two boys materialized in Aunt Leonor's belly. And as only happens in the movies, Aunt Leonor's body inflated and deflated all three times without apparent damage. The notary would have liked to draw up a certificate bearing testimony to such a miracle, but he limited himself to merely enjoying it, helped along as he was by the polite and placid diligence which time and curiosity had bestowed upon his wife. The circus improved so much that Leonor stopped getting through it with the rosary in her hands and even began to thank him for it, falling asleep afterward with a smile that lasted all day.

Life couldn't have been better for this family. People always spoke well of them; they were a model couple. The neighbor women could not find a better example of kindness and companionship than that offered by Mr. Palacios to the lucky Leonor, and their men, when they were angriest, evoked the peaceful smile of Mrs. Palacios while their wives strung together a litany of laments.

Perhaps everything would have gone on the same way if it hadn't occurred to Aunt Leonor to buy medlar fruit one Sunday. Her Sunday trips to market had become a happy, solitary rite. First she looked the whole place over, without trying to discern exactly from which fruit came which color, mixing the tomato stands with those that sold lemons. She walked without pausing until she reached an immense woman fashioning fat blue tacos, her one hundred years showing on her face. Leonorcita picked out one filled with pot cheese from the clay tortilla plate, carefully put a bit of red sauce on it, and ate it slowly while making her purchases.

Medlars are small fruit with intensely yellow, velvet-like skin. Some are bitter and others sweet. They grow together on the branches of a tree with large, dark leaves. Many afternoons when she was a girl with braids and agile as a cat, Aunt Leonor climbed the medlar tree at her grandparents' house. There she sat to eat quickly: three bitter ones, a sweet one, seven bitter, two sweet—until the search for and mixture of flavors became a delicious game. Girls were prohibited from climbing the tree, but her cousin Sergio, a boy of precocious eyes, thin lips and a determined voice, induced her into unheard-of, secret adventures. Climbing the tree was among the easiest of them.

She saw the medlars in the market, and they seemed strange; far from the tree yet not completely apart from it, for medlars are cut still on the most delicate, full-leafed branches.

She took them home, showed them to her children, and sat the kids down to eat, meanwhile telling them stories of her grandfather's strong legs and her grandmother's snub nose. In a little while, her mouth was brimming with slippery pits and velvety peelings. Then suddenly, being ten years old came back, his avid hands, her forgotten desire for Sergio, up in the tree, winking at her.

Only then did she realize that something had been torn out of her the day they told her that cousins couldn't marry each other, because God would punish them with children that seemed like drunkards. And then she could no longer return to the days past. The afternoons of her happiness were muted from then on by this unspeakable, sudden nostalgia.

No one else would have dared to ask for more: to add—to her full tranquility when her children were floating paper boats in the rain, and to the unhesitating affection of her generous and hardworking husband—the certainty in her entire body that the cousin who had made her perfect navel tremble was not prohibited, and that she deserved him for all reasons and forever. No one, that is, but the outrageous Leonor.

One afternoon she ran into Sergio walking down Cinco de Mayo Street. She was walking out of the church of Santo Domingo holding a child by each hand. She'd taken them to make a floral offering, as on every afternoon that month: the girl in a long dress of lace and white organdy, a little garland of straw and an enormous, impetuous veil. Like a five-year-old bride. The boy, with a girlish acolyte's costume that made him even at seven feel embarrassed.

"If you hadn't run away from our grandparents' house that Saturday, this pair would be mine," said Sergio, kissing her.

"I live with that regret," Aunt Leonor answered.

That response startled one of the most eligible bachelors in the city. At twenty-seven, recently returned from Spain, where it was said he had learned the best techniques for cultivating olives, Cousin Sergio was heir to a ranch in Veracruz, another in San Martín, and one more in nearby Atzálan.

Aunt Leonor noticed the confusion in his eyes and in the tongue with which he wet his lips, and later she heard him answer:

"If everything were like climbing the tree again."

Grandmother's house was on 11 Sur Street; it was huge and full of nooks and crannies. It had a basement with five doors in which Grandfather spent hours doing experiments that often soiled his face and made him forget for a while about the first-floor rooms, occupying himself instead playing billiards with friends in the salon constructed on the rooftop. Grandmother's house had a breakfast room that gave onto the garden and the ash tree, a jai-alai court that they'd always used for rollerskating, a rose-colored front room with a grand piano and a drained aquarium, a bedroom for Grandfather and one for Grandmother; and the rooms that had once been the children's were various sitting rooms that had come to be known by the colors of their walls. Grandmother, sound of mind but palsied, had settled herself in to paint in the blue room. There they found her drawing lines with a pencil on the envelopes of the old wedding invitations she'd always liked to save. She offered them a glass of sweet wine, then fresh cheese, then stale chocolates. Everything was the same at Grandmother's house. After a while, the old woman noticed the only thing that was different:

"I haven't seen you two together in years."

"Not since you told me that cousins who marry each other have idiot children," Aunt Leonor answered.

Grandmother smiled, poised above the paper on which she was sketching an infinite flower, petals upon petals without respite.

"Not since you nearly killed yourself getting down from the medlar tree," said Sergio.

"You two were good at cutting medlars. Now I can't find anyone who can do it right."

"We're still good," said Aunt Leonor, bending her perfect waist.

They left the blue room, just about to peel off their clothes, and went down to the garden as if drawn by a spell. They returned three hours later with peace in their bodies and three branches of medlars.

"We're out of practice," Aunt Leonor said.

"Get it back, get it back, because time is short," answered Grandmother, with a mouth full of medlar pits.

Aunt Jose

Aunt Jose Rivadeneira had a daughter with eyes like two moons, as big as wishes. The first time she was placed in her mother's arms, still damp and unsteady, the child opened her eyes and something in the corner of her mouth looked like a question.

"What do you want to know?" Aunt Jose asked her, pretending to understand that gesture.

Like all mothers, Aunt Jose thought there had never in the world been a creature as beautiful as her daughter. Aunt Jose was dazzled by the color of her skin, the length of her eyelashes and the serenity of her sleep. She trembled with pride imagining what her daughter would do with the blood and chimeras that pulsed through her body.

Aunt Jose devoted herself to contemplating the girl with pride and joy for more than three weeks. Then unassailable fate caused the child to fall ill with a malady that within five hours had turned her extraordinary liveliness into a weak and distant dream that seemed to be sending her back toward death.

When all of her own curative talents failed to make the child any better, Aunt Jose, pale with terror, took her to the hospital. There they tore her from Aunt Jose's arms and a dozen doctors and nurses fussed over the child with agitation and confusion. Aunt Jose watched her child disappear behind a door barred to her, and she let herself sink to the floor, unable to control herself or bear that pain like a steep hill.

Her husband, a prudent, sensible man (as most men pretend to be), found her there. He helped her up and scolded her for her lack of hope and good sense. Her husband had faith in medical science and spoke of it the way others speak of God. He was disturbed by the state of foolishness into which his wife had settled, unable to do anything but cry and curse fate.

They isolated the child in intensive care. A clean white place which the mothers could only enter for half an hour daily. So it filled up with prayers and pleas. All the women made the sign of the cross over their children's faces, they covered their little bodies with prayer cards and holy water, they begged God to let them live. All Aunt Jose could do was make it to the crib where her daughter lay, barely breathing, and beg: "Don't die." Afterwards she cried and cried without drying her eyes or moving an inch until the nurses told her she had to leave.

Then she'd sit down again on the benches near the door, her head in her hands, without appetite or voice, angry and surly, fervent and desperate. What could she do? Why should her daughter live? What could she ever offer her tiny body full of needles and catheters that might interest her enough to stay in this world? What could she say to convince her it would be worthwhile to make the effort, instead of die?

One morning, without knowing why, enlightened only by the ghosts in her heart, she went up to the child and began to tell her tales about her ancestors. Who they had been, which women wove their lives together with which men before she and her daughter were united at mouth and navel. What they were made of, what sort of work they had done, what sorrows and frolics the child now carried as her inheritance. Who sowed, with intrepidity and fantasies, the life it was up to her to extend.

For many days she remembered, imagined, invented. Every minute of every available hour Aunt Jose spoke ceaselessly into the ear of her daughter. Finally, at dawn one Thursday, while she was implacably telling one of these stories, the child opened her eyes and looked at her intently, as she would for the rest of her long life.

Aunt Jose's husband thanked the doctors, the doctors thanked the advances in medical science, Aunt Jose hugged her daughter and left the hospital without saying a word. Only she knew who to thank for the life of her daughter. Only she knew that no science was capable of doing as much as that element hidden in the rough and subtle discoveries of other women with big eyes.

Aunt Concha Esparza

Near the end of her life she cultivated violets. She had a bright room that she filled with flowers. She learned how to grow the most extravagant strains, and she liked to give them as gifts so that everybody had in their houses the inescapable aroma of Concha Esparza.

She died surrounded by inconsolable relatives, reposing in her brilliant blue silk robe, with painted lips and with an enormous disappointment because life didn't want to grant her more than eighty-five years.

No one knew why she hadn't tired of living; she had worked like a mule driver for almost all of her life. But those earlier generations had something that made them able to withstand more. Like all earlier things, like the cars, the watches, the lamps, the chairs, the plates and pots of yesteryear.

Concepción Esparza had, like all her sisters, thin legs, huge breasts and a hard smile, absolute disbelief in the plaster saints, and blind faith in spirits and their clownish jokes.

She was the daughter of a physician who participated in the Revolution of Tuxtepec, who was a federal deputy in 1882, and who joined the anti-reelection movement of 1908. A wise and fascinating man who filled life with his taste for music and lost causes.

However, as fate likes to even the score, Concha had more than enough father but less than enough husband. She married a man named Hiniesta whose only defect was that he was so much like his children that she had to treat him just like another one of them. He wasn't much good at earning money, and the idea that men support their families, so common in the thirties, didn't govern his existence. To put food on the table, keep house and buy coverlets for the beds, to pay for the children's schooling, clothe them and take care of other such trifles, was always up to his wife, Concha. He, meanwhile, schemed up big business deals which he never pulled off. To close one of these deals, he had the bright idea of writing a check on insufficient funds for a sum so large that an order was given for his arrest and the police arrived looking for him at his home.

When Concha found out what it was all about, she said the first thing that popped into her mind:

"What's happened is that this man is crazy. Totally nuts, he is."

With this line of reasoning, she accompanied him to his trial, with this line of reasoning she kept him from mounting his own defense, which might have really done him in, and with this line of reasoning she kept him from being thrown in jail. Instead of that horrible fate, with this same argument Concha Esparza arranged for her husband to be put in an insane asylum near the pyramid of Cholula. It was a tranquil place, run by friars, at the foot of the hills.

Grateful for the medical visits of Concha's father, the friars agreed that Mr. Hiniesta could stay there until the incident of the check was forgotten. Of course, Concha had to pay for the monthly maintenance of that sane man within the impregnable walls of the asylum.

For six months she made an effort to pay for his stay. When her finances could allow no more, she decided to retrieve her husband, after first having herself declared his legal guardian.

One Sunday she went to get him in Cholula. She found him breakfasting among the friars, entertaining them with a tale about a sailor who had a mermaid tattooed on his bald spot.

"One wouldn't look bad on you, Father," he was saying to the friar with the biggest smile.

While Mr. Hiniesta was talking, he watched his wife coming down the corridor to the refectory. He kept talking and laughing for the whole time it took Aunt Concha to arrive at the table at which he and the friars were talking with that childish joy that men only seem to have when they know they're among themselves.

As if unaware of the rules of a gathering such as this, Concha Esparza walked around the table in the clickety-clacking high heels she wore on occasions she considered important. When she was in front of her husband, she greeted the group with a smile.

"And you, what are you doing here?" Mr. Hiniesta asked her, more uncomfortable than surprised.

"I came to get you," Aunt Concha told him, speaking as she did to her children when she met them at school, pretending to trade them the treasure of their freedom in exchange for a hug.

"Why?" said Hiniesta, annoyed. "I'm safe here. It's not right for me to leave here. What's more, I'm having a good time. There's an atmosphere of gardens and peace here that does wonders for my spirit."

"What?" asked Concha Esparza.

"What I'm telling you is that for now I'm fine right where I am. Don't worry. I have some good friends among those who are sane, and I don't get along badly with the loonies. Some of them have moments of exceptional inspiration, others are excellent speakers. The rest has done me good, because in this place even the screamers make less noise than your kids," he said, as though he'd had nothing to do with the existence of those children.

"Hiniesta, what am I going to do with you?" Concha Esparza inquired of the empty air. Then she turned and walked toward the exit with its iron grill.

"Please, Father," she said to the friar accompanying her. "You explain to him that his vacations cost money, and I'm not going to pay for one day more."

One can only guess what the father told Mr. Hiniesta, but in fact that Monday morning the latch on Aunt Concha's front door made a slow sound, the same leisurely noise it used to make when her husband pushed it open.

"I came home, Mother," Hiniesta said, with a mourner's sadness.

"That's good, Son," answered his wife without showing any surprise. "Mr. Benítez is waiting to see you."

"To offer me a business deal," he said, and his voice recovered some liveliness. "You'll see. You'll see what a deal, Concha. This time you'll see."

"And that's the way this man was," Aunt commented many years later. "All his life he was like that."

By then Aunt Concha's guesthouse had been a success, and had provided her with earnings that she used to open a restaurant, which she closed some time later to get into real estate, and which even gave her the opportunity to buy some land in Polanco* and some more in Acapulco.

When her children were grown, and after Mr. Hiniesta's death, she learned how to paint the waves at "La Quebrada," and how to communicate with the spirit of her father. Few people have been as happy as she was then.

That is why life really infuriated her, leaving her just when she was beginning to enjoy it.

Translated by Amy Schildhouse

---

*Polanco: an expensive district in Mexico City

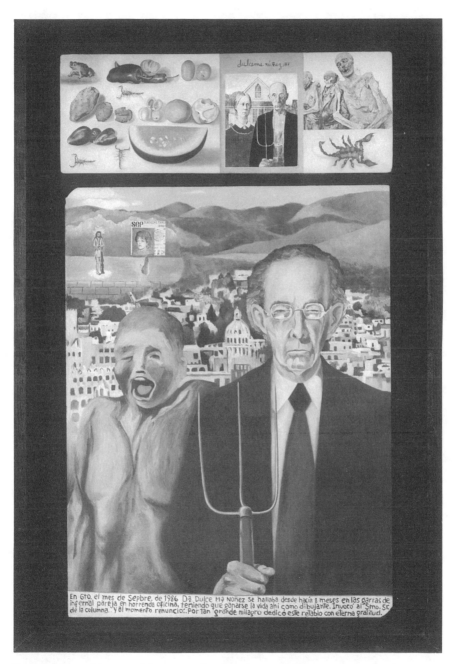

Dulce María Nuñez, *Mexican Gothic* (1987, oil on copperplate)

Sunday

Luis Arturo Ramos

Luis Arturo Ramos (Minatitlán, Veracruz, 1947), has been director of the University Press at Veracruz State University, where he also taught creative writing. He has also taught at UNAM's branch in San Antonio, Texas, and recently was a writer-in-residence at the University of Missouri. He is the author of two novels, Intramuros *(1983) and* Este era un gato *(1988), and he has published essays and short stories, including* Los viejos asesinos *(1981) and* Domingo junto al paisaje *(1987).*

for Roberto and Charo

I

The rumbling of the tram jolted him. He stayed in a midway state in which only the awareness of the difficulty of abandoning it seemed real and permanent. Seconds later, the noise took possession of the space. It occupied defined places, remembered places, until a street appeared in his mind. Then the warmth of the light made itself felt. It reached the bed and obliged him to throw back the blanket. He stayed there, attentive to the reverberation of the tram, until it faded into the soft, vulnerable light of morning, into the certainty that everything was beginning again.

Sitting on the bed, he devoted himself to contemplating his legs. He looked at the feet abandoned on the wooden floor like two objects without an owner, ruined by use like a pair of scuffed shoes. He compared the tone of his skin, the structure of his bones with those that would be shown to him, protected by the lack of reserve of someone

34

who undresses out of necessity. *Whores and sick people have something in common*, he said and realized that it would have been a good line.

The light curved over the bed. It drew a dense odor from the rumpled blanket, an inheritance from the highlands and as useless here as the phrases that filled his head. He rubbed his thighs to bring some color back into them. With his hands he measured their thickness. They could pass for those of an overgrown child if it weren't for the color, the flabbiness.

The groans snapped him out of his musing. He glanced toward the door and strained his ears to catch the sound of breathing or of some telling movement. She was alive. She was still alive and he didn't even venture to say to himself that's good or that's bad. She was there, curled up in spite of the heat, gathering strength to complain about the light that was now burning that body so similar to his own.

Still in his underwear he went to the sink and rinsed all traces of sleep from his face. The sensation of the sea struck his skin and gave him the impression that nothing had happened. He pictured himself abandoning the sea just as the first light was gilding the surface. His slow stroll reduced the dawn to little more than a brief interval between the sea of sleep and the vigil of that bed pungent with heat. Day and night separated by something more than a little light. Another skin perhaps. Or the gift of prophesy. But night only had meaning for vampires and werewolves. For other mortals, it was only the momentary confusion of seeing yourself with another face, the daily duty that forces you to change your shirt or look for an extra blanket. Or perhaps the awareness that the time to return had come.

The clattering of the second tram moved along the street. He felt the vibration of the floorboards beneath his feet. He noticed the cracks quiver against his skin as if he were treading on a live body. The smell of the wood occupied the space that the cold water had just cleaned. *The awareness that it is time to return.* And he had returned. Older and more compromised. And just like prostitutes and sick people, calling on a cliché to explain his suffering. Worse perhaps, since in his case it all sprang from an unquestionable truth. The truth of a sick woman, of the practice of his profession, of his return.

He went to the window and leaned out onto the balcony. Half hidden by the curtains, he tried to anticipate the approach of the next tram. But he only heard the doors, the voices of children saying: "Goodbye, goodbye," with the hypocritical courage of someone who bids farewell only to return four hours later. He had lasted longer.

Nevertheless he returned in spite of that farewell he had thought definitive but which kept gnawing away at him over the years. He had returned in spite of his promise and of the disgust he was bound to feel for this city.

But in the final analysis the goodbyes promised by the children had managed to make him happy. And he even thought he'd found, somewhere among the shouting and the rushing footsteps, an aftertaste of the old hope that made every day a little shorter. Or at least the momentary happiness permitted by the pretense that it is oneself who is leaving; oneself who utters that shameless goodbye that would take one far from the gray of the sand dunes, from the white coral houses, from the age-old light that, as weak as it was, still managed to break through the darkness. But the almond trees and the flame trees remained. Duty remained. That illness against which there is no inoculation.

He became aware of the rumbling of the tram, and the clock in his head announced a quarter to seven. He imagined the tram moving along, solemn and swaying, inventing a street merely by passing through it, like a bloated and bored Adam going around naming things. He returned to the room and put his ear to the crack in the door. He listened to the deliberate rhythm of the asthmatic breathing. He went back to his bed and, while he was putting on his pants, he hummed an old melody as the tram slowly faded into the distance.

II

At that other time he opened a similar door, the one responsible for making him think that all closed doors are always the same one. But this time he opened the appropriate one and confirmed that everything remained the same. The rise and fall of that labored breathing was there. Vital and awkward, pushing him to confuse the time and the circumstance. So it was as if he were returning to the past. As if today he were to repeat, one more time, just like every morning, the old return of three years before.

"Mother. . . . It's time for your medicine."

There was no reply. He waited the length of time required by the ceremony and repeated what he had said.

"Mother. . . . The medicine."

The bulk stirred. A mass of yellow hair appeared and slowly regained the whiteness of ash as it moved away from the light. The woman smiled at him from the blankets.

"Aren't you hot?. . . It's almost seven. . . . Aren't you hot?

The whisper of his voice restored to its original dimensions that room which the morning brightness made deep and limitless. She answered him that she felt well. That the heat helped her.

The woman sat up until she was leaning back against the head of the bed. She smiled once again, conscious of the triumph of her movements, of the momentary defeat of pain.

"Do you want me to move you closer to the window?"

He knew that she would tell him no. In the adjacent square, the leaves of the almond trees were accumulating brilliant reflections in the dampness of their curved forms. The woman shook her head and her grimace let him know that the action was painful for her. Why doesn't she speak? he asked himself. Why does she like pain? But he knew it wasn't true. Voice becomes useless when there are just two people. You had to leave words for larger groups.

While he was measuring out the drops in the glass, while he was selecting the pills and pouring the water into another receptacle, he observed her in the dressing-table mirror. He looked at her long and equine profile. Her tightly drawn and ungiving hair formed a halo in which not a single strand broke the clear, solid outline. The hair that was once flowing, responsive to the slightest hint of a breeze, had been transformed by time and immobility into a helmet of old and fluted silver. And he was still smiling at the memory when a sudden flash, the reflection of light against the mirror, destroyed that placid image, exploding it into luminous and writhing waves. At that point his mother turned her head and met his gaze in the glass. She smiled and it was as if her lips took on the form of the expanding waves into which her head was dissolving. He saw her smile and he felt afraid of the face in the mirror.

He stirred the liquid in an attempt to rid himself of the vision. The smell of the medicine reached his nostrils. The rhythmic clinking of the spoon forced him to look down. The water in the glass was changing before his eyes. Green became red and then settled into a violet. This time he didn't blame the light. Everything seemed to be changing in spite of the stillness of the air.

He approached the bed with the two glasses in his hands. Holding the pills in the last three fingers of his right hand. His mother looked him in the eye as if she feared a mistake. While she drank from one glass and then swallowed the pills with the water from the other, she kept her eyes on her son's, expecting some revealing sign. At least that, he thought. Does she think that I could really poison her? he asked himself again.

His mother had told him as much. Many years before she had said to him, "If I were a doctor, I would attempt the perfect crime. . . Don't you think that doctors are granted the possibility of killing without having to account for it?" They laughed. Everybody there had laughed at the idea. But she, with the glass in her hand raised for the toast, protected at that moment by the act of bringing it to her mouth, looked at him pretty much as she did now. She looked at him and smiled with a gesture that could have been a challenge or an insinuation. Then he, without avoiding her stare, replied that for some, writers perhaps, the possibility became an obligation.

By that time her hair had already acquired its strange consistency, that luster that dazzled with its total whiteness, and nobody knew if it was from tinting or that lineage of which she was so proud. Family heritage, premature graying was a distinctive characteristic of the women of her family. "If you had been born a woman, you would already have white hair," she used to say to him.

But he hadn't been born a woman. And the one who was leaning against the head of the bed, hardened by immobility and the years, was by now another person. Different though the same; just as one closed door looks like another.

She gave him back the two glasses and as she did so she touched the back of his hand.

Staring at the window, she let her eyes fall on the branches of the trees with the same disinterest with which she forgot her hand on her son's. He stayed there, calm, holding his breath without knowing why. He looked at the now innocuous profile of his mother and then at what she seemed to be staring at. They stayed perfectly still, until slowly, like a voice that was calling them from afar, the parsimonious vibration of the tram reached them and grew insistently.

"Seven o'clock, Mother."

He drew back his hand. A sense of emptiness and freedom flooded over him. Rarely did she touch him, and when she did it there remained that difficult feeling, a mixture of relief and helplessness. *He felt weightless, certain that he would have been able to fly had he wanted to*, he wrote mentally and immediately regretted it.

"Are you feeling any better?" he asked, by way of penance for what he considered a betrayal.

The woman nodded her head but didn't even smile to thank him for his interest. He left the bed to place the glasses on the dressing table and he heard the knocking at the door. Almost running, he left her bedroom and headed into his own. Then he crossed the room that served as his office and opened the door. The abruptness of his action produced in the woman a comical shudder that went through her body and ended up in the hands carrying the tray.

"Breakfast, Doctor," she said as if it to beg his pardon.

She tried to step inside but he blocked her with his body. He stayed there, filling the doorway, an immense presence before the surprised eyes of the waitress. The woman looked at him somewhat surprised and shifted her head, attempting to see what he seemed to be hiding. Then, with a gesture of indifference, she deposited the tray in the hands of the doctor.

"What are you going to want tomorrow?" she asked him with a suggestion of protest.

It seemed stupid to him but listening to her he realized the important thing was to get her away from there. This discovery filled him with perplexity and an overwhelming sense of the ridiculous. He became aware of himself there, face to face with her, holding a tray that was beginning to burn his hands, suffocated by the steam coming from the eggs and the refried beans, but with a growing sense of certainty that he had to get her out of there to make space for that day that was beginning to turn out different, even if things were falling into place with a terrifying similarity.

"What are you going to want?" the waitress insisted.

"The same as always," he said hurriedly. "What day is tomorrow?"

"Monday," the waitress replied, visibly perturbed. He didn't know whether she was telling the truth or not. Anyway, what did it matter? Every day was the same day, just as one door is like another.

"O.K. . . . well . . . bring the same thing," he added, aware of the improbability of the dialogue.

"And your mom, how is she?" the woman dared to inquire in an obvious attempt to slip inside even if just through the noise of her words.

"I'll pay you tomorrow," he said.

He took two steps backwards and closed the door with his foot. Could she be thinking that I have killed her? he asked himself. Had it been another day he would have stayed with his ear at the door in order to listen to the muttering of the woman, or the melody that, in feigned indifference, she was immediately beginning to sing in order to convince herself that it didn't matter to her at all anyway.

He spent a couple of seconds mentally reserving for himself the chipped cup. Then he placed the one fork on his mother's side. When he went into the bedroom the woman had already changed position and had her back to the door. Facing the window, the profile of her body was outlined vividly by light. He knew that she was not asleep. That she was watching him from within her silence in order to make him say the first words.

"Breakfast, Mom."

She preferred "Mother"; nevertheless he called her "Mom" in an attempt to overcome her distance. The strategy had the desired effect. The woman rolled over in her bed and slowly began the process of changing. He witnessed her transformation. He saw her move against that light like a pitiful, clumsy wave. He watched her remaking her body in front of his eyes like an ambiguous being who was evolving over millions of years in only a few seconds. She punished him with her pain, her movements, with the thousand changes that surfaced on her abused and dried-out body. She punished him without words or groans because she was a perfect portrait of pain and loneliness. Just being there and making it known to him was enough.

He contemplated the spectacle with dignity and fortitude. He stood facing her, the tray in his hands, like a friend welcoming someone who has been gone for a long time.

"Why didn't you pay her?" she asked him when they were facing each other.

He smiled as he remembered the waitress's amazement. The expression that reproached him for the irrationality of his behavior. He knew right then that, in spite of some indications to the contrary, the new day was already taking shape and for some reason that still wasn't clear, it was becoming special for him.

III

" . . . like the almond and the flame trees."

"What did you say, Mother?"

"I said like the almond and the flame trees."

"What about them?"

The woman was looking through the window. Very close to her, so close that she might have touched some of them, the leaves of the almond tree were soaking up the afternoon light and converting it into tiny geometric figures. Figures that then, when the wind shook the branches, rolled over the depressions in the other leaves, broad and dark.

40

"I said they are like people. Or rather, that people should be a little like them."

He looked at the leaves and tried to see them as ordinary and common. Eaten away by insects and age. But he couldn't. They were beautiful. The luster of the almond. The flower of the flame tree. In this way he had turned out like his mother. He loved the fresh green of the leaves after a rain. The acid taste of the tiny leaves of the flame tree. The violent contrast of the two trees that were growing so close together that their branches were entwined. He didn't reply. He continued wrapping up the fine white powder in pieces of brown paper, heaping them carefully on the corner of the table.

"Do you remember the story of Medusa?. . . As a child you liked me to tell it to you over and over again."

He got up. He brushed the traces of the medicinal powder from his hands and his shirt. He walked to the window and leaned out. The square was deserted. He judged the light and concluded that he had two more hours. There were no clocks in the room. His mother did not allow them. That would be an official stamp on her confinement. In the absence of clocks, and using a little imagination, they could live with the illusion that he had just arrived, that she had just lain down, that she was only taking a nap to shed the weariness after a hectic morning.

"Do you want me to take you out onto the balcony?"

The woman shook her head and half-closed her eyes, waiting for the pain to diminish. Why does she do that? he asked himself. Why does she have to do it in front of me?

"It's a beautiful afternoon," he said, gazing steadily out the window.

". . .You really enjoyed the story about the mane of serpents. What could a woman with serpent hair be like? you used to say to me. Then I would take you by the hand and lead you to the patio. Look at the flame tree, look at the almond."

He closed his eyes. He refused to remember.

"Why did you have me put wheels on your bed then?"

". . .You used to die with laughter when you imagined people in the act of turning into stone. And did they eat and go to the bathroom, and did they itch and not be able to scratch, you used to ask."

He realized how memory distanced her from pain. It helped her move her body so that his wouldn't block out the miniscule landscape of almonds and flame trees.

"If the only thing you want is to be right there. . ."

"Then we had the idea of showing you what the inside of the human body is like. . . and your father and I used to explain to you. . . this is for breathing, this is for pumping the blood through the body."

"Mom, Mom, what are you talking about?"

But she had found her way and was coming back with that voice that reverberated against the walls of the room, became mixed with the scratching of the leaves against the window, and the dull gasping of the wind against the panes.

". . . and we told you how nice it would be if you were a doctor just like your father and your grandfather and just as I could never be because I got married to have you and to take care of you the way you're taking care of me now . . . "

He went back to the table. He hid his fear behind the frantic exercise of sealing little envelopes with tape. He tried to dispel the sound of that voice that was bent on making him pay for the guilt of his departure.

"Be quiet, Mom. . . . Please be quiet."

He realized that the light was accumulating on her face and erasing all traces of pain. It was restoring the luster and freshness so that he, from the darkness of his closed eyes, amid the smell of the powder, might sense the resurrection of that face so similar to his own. He knew that the woman was smiling behind his back, framed by the waves of her hair that was recovering its glossiness and softness.

He got up. He overturned the table. The envelopes scattered a powder that burned the nostrils. From the middle of the room he howled in an attempt to silence that voice that was whispering out his history.

"Then I'll pull the wheels off, Mom. It's not right for you to stay in one place only."

But she continued in the same whispered tone, without taking her eyes off the trees. Letting them know that she was grateful for the leaves, the light, the dampness that they reserved for that old lady driven crazy by immobility and neglect.

". . . tied by their roots to the land, the land of their people. Tied by their roots like people are tied down by memories.

". . . Mom, Mom, if we carry on like this we're going to go crazy."

IV

He listened to the murmuring. Beyond the door, the sound of shuffling feet and voices was growing. In front of him, piled in exact, meticulous pyramids, the brown paper envelopes protected the magic of the powders. He looked at the clock on his desk and while he waited for the minute hand to reach twelve, he sensed the shadow in the threshold of a door that he didn't hear open. The smell of the body forced him to look up. It was a woman too fat for her age and size. Then he realized that he was dealing with something more disgusting than a simple premature obesity. From her breast hung a bundle that the woman sheltered with her shawl. Their eyes met and in hers he discovered fear. The woman opened her shawl and showed, as an excuse, the reason for her daring. Attached to her, almost part of her body, he noticed the shape of a baby who seemed to be asleep.

"Do you have an appointment?" he asked her, forgetting the time and the place. As if, between the time when such remarks had meaning and the present, where it was all superfluous, twenty-three years had never existed.

The woman did not answer. She abandoned the doorway and came forward until she was touching the edge of the desk with her body, with the body of the child. A sour stench (*sweat and weariness intermingled; the dust of the road and drowsiness*, he could have written) obliged him to get up. In the doorway, the frightened faces of the patients awaited a violent gesture. The restitution of the order destroyed by the sudden presence of the woman.

"Come in . . . sit down."

The woman placed the body of the child on the desk. She did it carefully, as if it were a sharp-edged object. In spite of the delicacy of her movement, she jarred one of the carefully constructed pyramids. And as if that brief cataclysm anticipated the future, doctor and patient abandoned everything to follow with their eyes the collapse of the brown-paper construction. The woman smiled. She smiled, conscious of her clumsiness and of what this might cause. But the doctor was already moving towards the door and slamming it so hard that the floorboards shook and the recently flattened pile quivered like a spider's web buffeted by the wind.

He opened the child's clothes and leaned over his body. He considered the child's color. He was astonished by the baby's indifference. He noted the strangeness of that skin, flaccid and tight at the same time. The child was dead. He had just died, for he was only just beginning to stiffen. Died perhaps while waiting. Alive just a few minutes before, nurtured by the heat absorbed from his mother's body during that crowded journey through the dust and the faded green of the drought-stricken countryside. He thought about his own mother. About the woman who two doors away was staring at the bone-dry almond and flame trees.

"He's dead," and he gestured like someone rejecting a useless object.

The woman seemed not to hear him.

"He's dead," he repeated, close to losing control. What pained him was not the disappearance of a useless child, but rather the emptiness he felt at that moment. And to fill it with something he demolished with a sweep of his hand the rest of the medicinal pyramids. The woman was startled and this time dared to break the silence which she had respected even at the death of her son.

"Forgive me," she said, feeling a guilt she was unable to name.

The doctor burst out laughing. The woman picked up her son and wrapped him in her shawl. He didn't see her leave; but this time he heard the noise of the door and then the expectation of the patients hit the back of his neck like the breath of an animal.

"Next," he called out.

(*They come in nervously. They admire the flasks, the shining, nickel-plated instruments. The prints of bodies cut in cross-section from head to toe, the enormous posters that depict the human body from the epidermis to the bone. They scrutinize the amber-colored liquids, the collection of stones of renal architecture. They stop before the pair of fetuses returning their gaze from the curved wall of the glass vessel, and end up smiling under the jubilant luster of the glass that protects his medical diploma, knowing that they have reached the promised land.*)

V

He opened the door. Another, though always the same. (*All doors are alike*, he could have written). And in spite of the fact that his mother feigned surprise at seeing him there, fastened to the ground by the two stuffed suitcases that hung from his hands, she wept real tears. She cried on his shoulder for a long while, obliging him to hold his head at a painful angle in order to avoid the hard and prickly mass of her hair that was uncomfortable against his face. There he was, hearing her groan down there, feeling the weight of the cases stretching his arms, raising his eyes to the ceiling of the apartment just like any martyr in a cheap print.

"You've come home, my son. . . . I knew that you would come back . . . I always knew it."

And he remembered, beyond the pain in his shoulders, beyond the impossibility of finding a place to put down the suitcases, the times that he'd furiously crossed out phrases like those *because nobody says things like that anymore.* (I missed you so much . . . A mother always forgives . . . The Virgin was also a mother and knew about suffering.) Because nobody had ever said things like what his mother was now repeating.

He resisted the embrace and those tears, inexplicable since barely two weeks before he had been there, in that very room, to tell her that it was O.K., that he would return.

"Not to help you die well, Mother . . . I am coming back because I've had enough."

And his mother detached herself from his body to lead him to the bedroom and ask him to close his eyes so as not to see what he was already guessing he would see. He got rid of the weight of the cases and took on the other weight, which was lighter, scarcely perceptible, after the martyrdom of the first one. He sensed the finely molded finish of the picture frame, the stench of camphor. He sensed on his closed eyelids the warmth of his mother's gaze and, over his whole face, the proximity of that smile which was spreading before him, beneath his frozen expression.

"Open your eyes, son."

He saw the doctor's diploma. The bombastic signatures. The seals and coats of arms. He turned the frame over to confront the second part of a scene already played out. (*When you feel yourself faint-hearted — that's what she said: "faint-hearted" — read what it says on the other side and you will not falter.*)

"Art is long, life is short." Hippocrates. The timely idea that prompted applause and commentaries during the toast. Then the talk on the omnipotence of the doctor. The perfect crime. Control over life and death. "For writers, the possibility of death becomes an obligation" — he said that or something similar and she responded with a look that has been the same ever since.

He let himself be hugged again as he thanked her for her deference and her care. The frame began to weigh heavy in his right hand. It brought back the memory of the suitcases, of his return, of the twenty-three years away from that city. He imagined his doctor's diploma to be the shackles that anchored him to that tranquil and docile territory: but he regretted it instantly. It was too trite. Such comparisons were out of style. Nevertheless there they were, within reach of life but not of literature.

Six stories over twenty-three years. Six stories published in second-rate papers and third-rate magazines. Each story bearing the name of a day of the week. Stories that began on Monday and ended on Saturday. Published and republished over and over again while the grants just evaded him and editors invited him to wait the three years stipulated for every beginner. And in shunning those three years he became mired in a never accepted wait that lasted twenty more. Until the loneliness of his widowed mother degenerated into suffering, and you can avoid duty in search of wealth but not when sickness strikes.

And there was the oath, Hippocrates.

"When you feel fainthearted" (*Nobody says things like that anymore, Doctor*, they said to him and he believed it) "read the other side and you will not falter."

And in spite of his return. Of the magic formulas. Of the fetishes on the office walls, his mother abandoned her meanderings through the apartment to prop herself up briefly in a wheelchair and then in that bed besieged by almond and flame trees. Her hair acquired the consistency of sand, and then crystalized into a cap that had the swirls of a shell.

Her head grew on the pillow filled more with memories than with sufferings. And now it weighs heavy on the shoulders of life because it no longer does on the shoulders of her body. He laughed. There's nothing funnier than realizing that your own story turns out to be your best literature.

VI

The villager bares his stomach and accepts the auscultation. The hand presses the greenish surface. He takes note of the interior life revealed in convulsed and recurrent movements. He examines the existence of the poor man reeking of animals, who watches his eyes with a gaze eaten away by fear. He mutters in a low voice, conscious that the man is struggling to translate his grunts. He frightens him even more by shaking his head in a condemning negative.

He resorts to the stethoscope. He tells him to sit down, to breathe deeply, to cough, to say something.

"What should I say?"

"Whatever you want."

The man mumbles an "I don't know what's wrong with me," and the doctor retrieves through the instrument an echo that he doesn't manage to interpret, just as he has already failed to translate the stirring of the man's intestines into anything concrete.

"Get up. Get dressed . . . Next!"

And each one peels off his clothes and his smile, and the fear appears along with the wait for his words. The orders that will regulate the lives of these fools and their toothless women and their skeletal children and their repulsive old folks who nevertheless pay. And not exactly with piglets or turkeys as in some folktale.

"It's nothing. Don't worry. Take this. Buy what I'm putting down for you here."

And they smile because he guarantees them life although he does not know what they will die of nor when. He realizes that he is deceiving with impunity and even with pride. He deceives like one who tells stories or writes them. *Your characters don't have a life of their own. . . . You condemn them in advance. You hand them over from the very first lines. There is no surprise for the reader.* If surprise exists. Life is only the repetition of the same acts endorsed by identical words. Take off your clothes. Lie down. You have cancer. You are going to die. There's nothing wrong with you. Tomorrow it will be gone. Next. . . . Next!

VII

She decided that they would stay there. The office in the first room. In the room where she had embraced him in welcome. Here his bedroom and hers opening onto the balcony alongside the almond and flame trees.

"When it's hot we can push the bed onto the balcony and it will be like a day in the country. I will be able to touch the leaves just by reaching out my hand," she said.

From that moment she gave herself over to the task of pretending that time had not passed. They went around to secondhand stores, markets, pharmacies. With other people's possessions she regained part of what his past could have been. His mother decorated the stage with the attention to detail of an expert director. She arranged the flasks in the glass cabinet. The enormous charts loaded with swollen livers and scarred lungs. She pointed out the best place for the jar with the twins. Two bodies fused into one single mass. Without ceasing to be one, prevented from becoming two.

"There . . . beside the poster," she said, and she helped him position the shelf. The twins would receive the newcomers and nothing would escape their gaze.

"Imagine, if nobody can resist the gaze of the dead, what will happen with the stare of those who never lived?" she added.

And she forced him to look at the jar. The slimy mass that was swimming in the formaldehyde and rotating gracefully until it touched the rounded wall with its forehead. Then she stretched out her arms in an expressive gesture and spun around again in the middle of the office like a newlywed who steps into her home for the first time. Rejuvenated, conscious of the empire that was growing around her, she invited him to contemplate the universe of which he was to form the center.

"Here you will write the best of books . . . Make each prescription a chapter of a biography."

He typed out the announcement for the newspaper. *Appointments from eight to two and from five to eight, Monday through Saturday . . .*

"Your first publication in the city of your birth," she said to him when they read the paper and she smiled again with that old smile that began the day of the toast and that still hadn't stopped.

"I can't do it," he told her finally.

She carried on as though she hadn't heard. With the newspaper in her hand she took a few steps towards the light. She contemplated with pleasure the five lines that established the location and conditions.

"Mom . . . ," he repeated, his voice softened, "I can't trick them."

She looked him straight in the eyes. On the other side of the window the branches of the trees were buffeted by the wind. The hair on the woman's head was somewhat disturbed. It crackled in time with the wooden windows.

"You can do anything. . . You're not short on words."

She hugged him to her and this time her hair did not hurt his face. But he insisted again in the same damp, softened tone:

"Mom . . . please. I can't even cure you."

"Have faith . . . fortitude . . . you are all I have left."

That night she lulled him with words. She told him of her loneliness, of the twenty-year wait. The slim hope that his sporadic visits would become permanent. It couldn't be any other way. What would they live on. Daily practice would bring back his skill, his knowledge of the bodies of others. You will begin to write a new chapter in your life, she told him.

The following day he awoke to the certainty that nothing remained of his rebelliousness. He had returned and he was staying.

" . . . the almonds, the flame trees."

VIII

He went down to the restaurant on the first floor and ordered two meals instead of one. He saw the waitress looking at him from the order window between the dining room and the kitchen. Then he watched her follow all his movements. He figured that she never imagined "the lady's son" would be like this. The portraits in the living room of the upstairs apartment displayed a different face (The lady's son receiving his degree. The lady's son saying goodbye from a bridge. The lady's son in a Mexico City bookshop.) Just perhaps the slimness of the body, those limbs whose joints made one think of a badly set hinge, scarcely preserved even a fleeting similarity. But there he was, defeating by his presence any intention to call the woman's stories lies. That son existed. It was he, and he had returned. So there was a past that had been put in doubt and lost in a moment of bad luck.

She watched him order the meals and offer to pay right then as if he were a casual customer and not a regular. He insisted on it and said that he would pay daily for what they delivered to him at his office. It seemed to everyone that he wanted to leave it very clear that he might depart at any moment. Then he walked out with the certainty of having constructed behind himself that past in which no one had believed.

That was when they went around to attics and flea markets. Awnings that smelled of bat dung, in search of that past that urgently needed to be recovered. The past which he, sidetracked by the dream of telling stories of others, had not been capable of constructing himself. They acquired a set of instruments, obsolete but incredibly beautiful in their shape and sharpness. They chose a glass cabinet that was taller than he and in which, with his mother's help, he set up a display that gave privileged position to the receptacles filled with anonymous internal organs, having neither memories nor issue. He was amazed by the constant transformation of those little brothers who looked at him so seriously, cradled too late by the amber liquid that lulled them.

And every afternoon, when he returned tired and sweaty from his long journeys through the histories of other people, he looked at the woman in the restaurant, who was expecting some greeting or smile from him. He noticed the shock produced by his purchases and he imagined her composing in her head the universe that was being born on the second floor. Crammed now with mountain ranges and peninsulas, with rivers and wetlands; transforming itself to receive those who were beginning to tear themselves away from failing villages and farms in an attempt to take shelter in that territory that was free of illnesses.

And every morning also she was there to confirm with incredulous delight the well-behaved line of patients stationed at the foot of the stairway. The slow climb up the staircase. The sweaty and earthy breathing of those men and women accustomed to the flatlands and the free-flowing wind.

And between two and five o'clock, the halls and stairs, empty, he used to listen to her coming up laboriously, struggling with feet and hands to maintain her balance, the tray and the food. He was aware of her pausing behind the door waiting for the rhythm of her breathing to allow her to reconstruct her smile. Then, the three gentle and spaced knocks, doubtless meted out by the toe of her shoe.

He would open the door and confront her smiling face. The sweat that glistened in the cool but dank half-light. Her respectful and provocative "Here you are, doctor." He would leave her there, with the weight of dinner for two still held chest-high, blurred out by the steam rising from the hot *atoles** and stews, maintaining a smile that little by little began to give way to weariness. He would leave her there to study shamelessly that strange mixture of dryness and sweat. He observed her parched gaze and then her tongue as it licked her lips. The muscles that trembled from the effort, the smile that flickered uncontrolled and turned her mouth into a dark, pink amphibian.

He would reach forward and put in her apron pocket a handful of coins without taking his eyes off her face and gauging in this way the effect of his hand brushing her body under the cloth, discovering the elastic of her panties, the depression of her navel, and caressing with a motion not lacking in tenderness the lean, drawn skin.

"Here you are. . . Count it if you want to, but it's all there."

"Thank you, Doctor."

And he smiles as he recognizes in the voice of the waitress the same submissiveness of his patients.

In the back room, his mother was losing ground, distracted by her insistence on maintaining at all cost the starched whiteness of his medical gowns, the pristine state of his moccasins. She really began to die; or at least that's the way it seemed to him. The laughter and activity of the first months obliged her to spend long periods resting in the rocking chair and then in the bed. She accepted her exhaustion with the certainty that it had a more distinguished purpose than the straightforward, vulgar one of keeping her immobile. She realized that her son's staying depended on her confinement and she bore it with the strength

---

atole: a hot thick drink made with corn flour

50

of a martyr. She smiled at her suffering. She blessed it and became strong in her sickness. But she missed the gentle swaying of the flame trees, the color of the light on the almond leaves. She requested and got her son to adapt little wheels for the legs of her bed so that her body could be moved around at her will. She crisscrossed the floor of her room until she settled in one corner. From there she could bask in the light, see the tops of the trees, and the city that crackled below with heat and trams, sand and sudden gusts of wind.

IX

"Why did you come back?" asked the woman.

"I have a sick mother," he replied, knowing full well that his words oozed affectation. That the gesture that accompanied them suited perfectly the insubstantial, peeling room that only seemed to be held together by the weak thread of light from a bulb burning in the midafternoon.

"You came home to cure her?"

"To help her die well," he said and he turned over to look at her. Under stiff sheets grayed by use, as attentive to her face as she was to his words, he realized that the woman was reliving in her imagination a scene from a cheap movie.

The woman squeezed his hand and came closer to kiss his cheek. It was an act watered down by the light from that bulb that had always been there, that none of the transitory tenants had ever bothered to turn off, as if they were certain that the existence of the universe depended on it. He resisted the touch of her lips under his ear, her caressing hand that seemed to be inviting him to make love again.

"You poor thing," said the voice at his ear.

Her commentary brought to his mind the eternal criticism of his friends (*You seem to write for maids*). And it had to be true because beside him the woman was crying in an act that in the light from the bulb became repulsive and theatrical. Nevertheless she seemed calm, knowing that it was easier to share sorrow than love. Knowing that on this rests the strength and the punishment of lovers.

He moved her aside gently. He feigned the need to look out the window and got up to turn off the light in an attempt to provoke chaos. But nothing happened. The curtain billowed with natural light and he realized that from the other side the brightness was eating away at the walls. It was an enormous bird that pecked at the whitewash and the

51

stones. He opened a crack between the curtains and looked out at the port. The rigging of the ships, the scrap iron on the corners of the quays. The distant sea, turned into an apparition by the brilliance of the afternoon.

He turned his back to the light and looked at the woman's face. As she leaned against the head of the bed, her tiny breasts disappeared into her body. Scarcely more than two purplish spots that could be mistaken for bruises. *A sorrowful body beaten by life.* In his mind, he scratched the sentence out. How could he evoke this vision emerging from the soiled sheets, propped up against the brass frame with the shame of a saint cheapened by the faith and stupidity of her devotees? The woman misinterpreted his gaze and opened her arms in an invitation to closeness. If not to love at least to closeness. How could he name those arms if not with the same words as always?

"Let's go . . . it's late."

It was the last time. There was no point. And in reply she took her revenge three times a day in the repetition of the same meal, with the insult which in her eyes (and in those of his mother) was implied in the chipped cup, the pewter spoon, the impossibility of finding a fork to spear the pieces of meat. The only thing that stayed the same was the formal manner of speech which she could never bring herself to drop either in love or in war. No one had ever called him by his name. He was among those who warranted a special treatment (Son, Doctor, Sir) as if everybody understood his distance, his fragility, and the fact that all it would take to crack him was a little shove.

X

The whole day he had resented the silence on the other side of the closed door. Seated behind his desk he missed the bustle of the passage and the stairway. He spent a long time looking at the empty chairs, the Chinese decor of the office. This place, where every day of the week people squeezed in, had flung into his eyes the warm, hollow breath that remains in spaces used to crowds. But this was the day that God rested, even if he himself was not disposed to. There was still a lot to do. So much that he decided to undermine time just as before he had attempted to turn the world upside down in that hotel on the waterfront. He would add another day to the office sign, to the announcement in the paper. He would add another slot in the week because the world does not wait. It was there on the other side of the door, ready for him to give it a name, just like an indefatigable god, less creative perhaps but certainly more persevering. A world baptized to the rhythm of illness and neglect. Run through from pole to pole by the anemic light of the bulb in a flophouse, measured by a week without the parenthesis of a day off.

He got up from the desk and walked towards the window. He contemplated the throbbing of the night, certain that the long-awaited day was just around the corner. Close by him, the smallest things began to shake and then, seconds later, he felt on his skin the reverberations of the last tram. Perhaps it was Monday again. The jar on the shelf, the grains of sand on the windowpanes shook. Behind the other door, the slow rasp of the breathing began its painful task. He turned his face to confront his world: the glint of the instruments, the posters showing the intimacy of the human body, the haze enveloping organs and gelatins, the unlikely curved flasks. The inseparable twins who, from their restricted suspension, were presiding over the arrival of that first day already beginning to materialize.

He walked to the door and waited a moment. His mother's breath was struggling laboriously in that bed that he imagined rumpled and warm. He opened the door and turned on the light. Her eyes were open. He watched her looking at him as if she knew what he was going to do. What he was set on.

"Mom . . . there's no point anymore . . . I'm going to take the wheels off the bed."

He didn't notice if she nodded or pretended she hadn't heard him. He crouched down beside the bed. It would be easy. He wouldn't even have to get her up to do it. He smiled inwardly as he imagined the dull thud of the bed leg as it struck the floor. The sudden jolting of the mattress. Her shocked face. He knew that she was now incapable of moving. Blanketed from time to time by the sunlight when it would reach the top of the bed, floating between the sheets like the twins in their flask of formaldehyde.

Translated by Tim Richards and Judith Richards

She Lived in a Story

Guillermo Samperio

Guillermo Samperio (Mexico City, 1948), author of eighteen books, has won several important literary awards. His collections of short stories include Lenin en el fútbol (1978); El hombre de la penumbra: el hombre de las llaves (1985), from which "She Lived in a Story" is taken; and Miedo ambiente y otros miedos (1986). His book of short prose pieces, Cuaderno Imaginario (1990), contains "Free Time" (see page 378).

to Fernando Ferreira de Loanda

When we believe we are dreaming and we awake,
we experience vertigo of the mind.
—Silvina Ocampo and Bioy Casares

During the evening hours, the writer Guillermo Segovia gave a lecture at the Preparatory Academy of Iztapalapa. The students of esthetics, under the direction of the young poet Israel Castellanos, were enthusiastic about the detailed presentation by Segovia. Professor Castellanos did not neglect to thank the lecturer and praise his work in front of the students. The one most pleased was Segovia himself; even though, before beginning, he felt a little nervous, when he began explaining the notes he had prepared two days before, his words flowed with strength and ease. When a young man asked about the creation of characters inspired by real people, Guillermo Segovia was secretly disappointed that the emotion and confidence that had filled him had not been displayed before a more sophisticated public. Such a vain idea had not kept him from enjoying a certain giddy taste for creative and sharply defined words, that space in which his theory and examples converged in a dense and, at the same time, simple discourse. He allowed the phrases to intertwine without being too conscious of them; the interaction of terms produced an obvious dynamic, independent of his voice.

Guillermo Segovia had just turned thirty-four; he had three books of stories, a novel and a series of newspaper articles published domestically and abroad, especially in France, where he had received his degree in literature. Returning to Mexico six years before his speech at the Academy, he had married Elena, a young Colombian researcher, with whom he had had two children. On his return, the writer took a job at a newspaper, while his wife worked at the National University of Mexico. They rented a small house in old Coyoacán,* where they lived comfortably.

Now on his way home, driving an '82 VW, Guillermo could not remember several points from the end of his presentation. But it didn't bother him too much; his memory was prone to sporadic lapses. However, he was excited about one part that he did remember and that he could use to write a story. It had to do with that witty comparison that he had made between an architect and a writer. "From the creative point of view, the designing of a home invariably takes place within the realm of the fictitious; when the bricklayers begin to build it, we are now witnessing the fulfillment of that fiction. Once finished, the owner will inhabit the house and the fiction of the architect. Extending this line of reasoning, we might say that cities are fictions of architecture; for that reason the latter is considered an art form. The architect who lives in a house that he designed and built himself is one of the few persons who may live in his own fantasy. From his own perspective, the author is an artificer of the word, he designs stories and sentences so that the reader may live in the text. A house and a story should be solid, functional, necessary, lasting. In a story, one might say, movement demands fluidity, from the living room to the kitchen, or from the bedrooms to the bath. No unnecessary columns or walls. The different sections of the story or of the house should be indispensable and created with precision. Literature is written and homes are built so that man may live in them in comfort."

"To live in a text," Guillermo went on thinking while his car traveled through the night down Iztapalapa Avenue. He paid attention only to the stoplights, without noticing the sordid panorama of that part of the city. Not even when the traffic became heavier around Calzada de la Viga did he notice the change in direction. "To live in a text," he insisted, despite

Coyoacán: a middle-class part of Mexico City, centered on an historic village containing sixteenth-century buildings

55

his mental blanks. The idea of inhabiting words overwhelmed him; all of a sudden he wanted to create a story around that idea. Imagining the way to frame it, he thought he would try to avoid the literary solutions of similar problems. Out of the blue, he said to himself that a woman would be the appropriate character. In a clouded manner he visualized a woman living in a story created by him. "She lived in the text" was the first transformation. "Now I'm already in the domain of the story; the sentence itself is literary, it sounds good."

He remembered several women, far and near, but none of them met his requirements. He went back and began by imagining her activities. He created a small catalog of professions and tasks, finally leaning toward actresses. He wondered about the reasons for his selection as his car sped away from the Country Club neighborhood and headed toward Miguel Angel de Quevedo in order to cross the Tlalpan bridge. He gave full rein to his thoughts in search of an answer or a justification. "In one way or another actors live in the text. They live the part they were given to play and they also live the text; they do not embody anyone at all. In the theater they live in literature for a brief moment. In motion pictures, some of their moments endure with a tendency toward the infinite. Dramatists have written plays in an attempt to approach the ancient dream of the fiction writer: that human beings live in their texts. Thus, artistic creation transcends the imaginary level in order to achieve reality. In regard to my own concept, the movement is reversed; that is, reality moves toward the imaginary."

Guillermo Segovia's car turned onto Felipe Carrillo Puerto, advanced a block and turned toward Alberto Zamora; thirty meters farther along he came to a stop. As he shut off the engine, he decided that the woman in this story would be a young actress whom he admired, for her performances and her extraordinary beauty. Furthermore, the actress somewhat resembled the painter Frida Kahlo, who painted herself in the dreams of her paintings, another way to live in one's own fiction. Even though Segovia did not give a title to his works before writing them, on this occasion he had an urge to do so. "She Lived in a Story" would be the title of his tale; the woman's name, just like the actress from reality, would be Ofelia.

Guillermo got out of the VW; he went into his house; passing through the modest living room on his left, he entered his study. A small room, the walls of which were covered by book shelves from floor to ceiling. He turned on the light, he took his typewriter out of its case, he put it on the desk, at the other end of the room, next to the window, through which could be seen a few plants in the small garden. He turned on the radio of his sound system and tuned in *Radio Universidad*. When he opened the top desk drawer, Elena appeared in the doorway.

"How did it go?" she said, walking toward him.

"Fine," Guillermo answered, moving in her direction.

They kissed; Segovia caressed her hair and hips. They kissed again, and when they separated, Elena said again:

"How did the people react?"

"They were quite interested. I realized that the boys had read my stories. Which, of course, I owe to Castellanos... during the discussion an interesting idea came up," he explained, heading for the desk.

"The children just went to sleep... I was reading a little...don't you want something to eat?"

"No... I would prefer to start writing..."

"O.K. I'll wait for you in the bedroom."

Elena left the room, blowing a kiss toward her husband off the palm of her hand. Guillermo Segovia settled down in front of his typewriter; from the drawer that he had left open, he took out several sheets of blank paper and inserted the first one. He typed the title and began to write.

She Lived in a Story

That day, the cold wave intensified in the city. Around eleven o'clock at night, more or less, a fog settled in, brought on by the low temperature and the smog. The darkness was more intense than usual and it gave an eerie feeling even to the brightest areas. The old streets of the center of Coyoacán were reminiscent of scenes from centuries past. Even the light coming from streetlights and cars seemed shadowy; it penetrated only slightly that ancient space. Only a few people, dressed in topcoats or thick sweaters and scarves, walked along hugging the walls, trying to ward off the cold. They looked like silhouettes from another time, as if from this Coyoacán, a Coyoacán from the past had emerged and the people, failing to recognize their own century, were heading for places they would never find. With Plaza Hidalgo at her back, down narrow Francisco Sosa Avenue, Ofelia was walking. Her slender figure was dressed in gray woolen slacks and a thick black sweater which because of its bagginess seemed to hang from her shoulders. A violet scarf encircled the woman's long neck. The white skin of her face was a tenuous light that stood out against her dark hair, which brushed her shoulders as she moved. The sound of her black boots on the flagstones was barely noticeable.

Although it was impossible to ascertain from which direction, Ofelia sensed that she was being watched. On the corner of Francisco Sosa and Ave María she stopped while a car turned to the right. She took advantage of this instant to look behind her, thinking that she would discover who was watching her. She only saw an old couple that walked out of a doorway and headed for the Plaza. Before crossing the street, she felt vulnerable; then she experienced a slight shudder. She thought that perhaps it would have been better if someone had been following her. Despite being alone, she started walking again, certain that the night was watching her movements. She became a little frightened, and instinctively began to walk faster. She rubbed her hands together, looked toward the trees in front of her and then all the way down the avenue that faded into the foggy mist. "It would have been better if I'd let them give me a ride," she lamented as she was about to cross Ayuntamiento Street.

Just minutes before, she had been in the old structure of the Center for Dramatic Arts, watching the dress rehearsal of a work from the Middle Ages. When the rehearsal was over and after going out into the street, one of the actresses offered to take her home; Ofelia came up with the excuse that she had to visit a friend who lived right around the corner, on Francisco Sosa. The truth was that the strange, gray atmosphere of Coyoacán had made her feel like walking; furthermore, for her the foggy atmosphere was a continuation of the staging of the play and it brought to mind the time she had spent in England. She said goodbye and started walking, while all the others got into their cars.

She first felt the impression of being watched while walking down the avenue. Now, realizing that nothing special was happening to her, she found no real reason to be afraid. The phenomenon should have had an explanation, but for the moment she couldn't figure it out. This idea was comforting and, somewhat more encouraged, she warmed her hands by blowing on them. Nevertheless, this sudden ease of mind heightened her perceptive abilities. There were, no doubt, eyes attempting to look inside her; eyes whose function seemed to be of a tactile nature.

Fine, it was impossible for her to separate herself from life's experience, but she still wanted to understand. Were these feelings new and therefore as yet undefined? What were those searching eyes after? Seldom had she experienced the feeling of being threatened: she accepted a certain amount of insecurity given the violence of Mexico City. She moved cautiously; now that she really was exposing herself, no one was threatening her. The people in the few cars that were passing by paid no attention to her at all. Then she remembered the intensely lit spaces on the stage, when the glare of the spots prevented her from seeing the audience, who in turn were looking at her. She knows that a multitude of eyes are out there in the dark, moving to the rhythm that she establishes; lots of eyes, a great concealed eye, a giant eye fixed on her body. Trying to bolster herself with the memory of this, Ofelia told herself that perhaps it had to do with her skin's memory, foreign to her mind; in that murky landscape, perhaps it had returned to her body and was gradually possessing it. Eye-network, eye-space, large eye coming toward her, growing eye; Ofelia wanted to escape the sensation by shaking her head. The effort, she knew all along, was useless; now devoid of strength, she abandoned herself to her fate and felt herself sinking into the depths of night. All of a sudden she found herself walking in total darkness, losing her sense of place, still with some certainty that she was facing no danger.

When she turned into the alley where her house was, she could feel the enormous eye on her hair, her face, her scarf, her sweater, her slacks. She stopped and felt a kind of dizziness similar to what you experience in a dream where you float unsupported and without any way of coming down. Ofelia knew that she was only a few meters from her house, in Coyoacán, in her city, on the Earth, but at the same time she could not avoid the sensation that this was a dream, and while she experienced vertigo, it was a pleasant feeling because a dreamer, in the end, knows that there is no danger and he throws his body into the darkness like a zeppelin that descends when it is watched. Ofelia remained standing in the alley, trying to understand; in a quiet voice she said to herself: "This is not a fainting spell nor a psychological problem. This does not come from me, it's something outside of me, beyond my control." She moved slowly toward the wall and leaned her back against it. The sensation became heavier in her thin body, as if the fog in the alley were resting on her. "It's not that they're still watching me; it's something more powerful." She raised her hand to her forehead and repeatedly passed her fingers through her hair; alarmed, suddenly understanding the situation, she said to herself: "I'm inside the eye." She lowered her arm slowly and, following the idea in what she had just said, she continued: "I'm inside the gaze. I'm living inside a stare. I'm part of a way of seeing. Something forces me to walk; the fog has descended and its murky fingers reach out toward the windows. I'm a silhouette from the past sticking to the walls. My name is Ofelia and I'm opening the wooden gate to my house. I enter, to my right shadow-theater figures appear in the garden, and from among the plants out jumps Paloma, eagerly greeting me. Her white coat is like an oval ball of cotton suspended in the darkness. She barks at me timidly, comes up to my legs and rubs against my calves; then she stands on her two hind legs inviting me to play. I pet her and gently push her aside; she growls mournfully, but I am already walking among the plants along the path made of stones from the river. The entryway light is on; I open the door, I close it. I want something to eat and I head for the kitchen. I stop and I feel obliged to retrace my steps, I continue on toward the living room. I turn on the floor lamp, I open the bar, I grab a glass and a bottle of cognac. Without closing the bar door, I serve myself and, after taking the first drink, I realize that I still want something to eat, but the taste of the cognac captivates me and, against my will, I decide not to eat. When I lift the glass to my lips a second time, Plácida appears, she greets me respectfully and *asks me if she might get me something. I tell her she should go to bed, explaining that tomorrow we have to get up early. Plácida leaves with a slight bow of the head, and I finish my drink. Between my fingers, I am carrying the bottle and the glass; with my free hand I turn off the lamp and, in the dark, I cross the living room and climb the stairs. The door to my bedroom is open and I enter. I turn on the light, I approach my dressing table, I place the bottle and glass on it. I sit on the seat, open the drawer, take out my notebook, a fountain pen, and I begin to write what is happening to me."*

I know very well that I still live inside the gaze. I hear the sounds that are generated deep within it, like the noises of the city that rise to the top of the Latin-American Tower. I have had to move with precision and calm. My fear is disappearing; I'm surprised, but without any desperation. Now, all of a sudden, I'm upset, angry; I must write a protest. Yes, a protest, gentlemen. I protest! Men of the world, I protest. I write that I am an inhabitant, I write that my anxiousness has left me; I stop writing. I served myself a shot of liquor and downed it in one gulp. I really like my old Montblanc pen, it has a good nib. My body's burning up, my cheeks are red. I'm afraid I can't stop living in two worlds; Francisco Sosa Avenue, which seems so far away from me now, is two roads, just one large eye. In the streets of this ancient Coyoacán that I love so much, there exists another Coyoacán; I was walking through two Coyoacáns, two nights, double fog. At this moment of precipitous revelations, there are people like me who live in both Coyoacáns; Coyoacáns which coincide perfectly one with the other, neither under nor above, just one center and two worlds. Someone, perhaps a man, at this very moment is writing these very same words that are appearing in my notebook. These very same words. I stop writing; I have another drink. I feel a little tipsy; I'm happy. As if there were lots of light in my bedroom. Paloma barks at two invisible moons. It occurs to me that I should write that likely the man's name is Guillermo, he has a beard, a long straight nose. It could be Guillermo Segovia, the writer, who at the same time lives as another Guillermo Segovia. Guillermo Segovia in Guillermo Samperio, each inside the other, a single body. I insist on thinking that he writes with his typewriter precisely what I write, word upon word, only one discourse and two worlds. Guillermo writes a story that is too pretentious; the central character could have my name. I write that he writes a story that I live in. It's already past midnight and the writer Guillermo Segovia is tired. He stops writing, he scratches his beard, he twists his mustache; he stands up, he stretches his arms and then, lowering them, he leaves the study. He goes up to the bedrooms on the second floor. He enters his bedroom and sees that his wife is asleep, with an open book on her lap. He approaches her, kisses her on the cheek, takes the book from her and puts it on the night table; before leaving, he glances once more at his wife. As he goes downstairs, he senses that he is being watched, although he cannot determine from where. He stops and turns, thinking that his youngest son has gotten up, but no one is there. "This is probably a suggestion that comes to me from my own story," he thinks while still trying to figure it out. He goes on down and the sensation becomes more intense. This change bothers him because he understands that the next step is to know that he is not being watched, but that he lives inside a gaze, that he is now part of a new way of seeing. Standing at the foot of the stairs, he thinks: "That gaze could be Ofelia's." From my way of thinking, in what I write with my beautiful Montblanc, I feel like I'm disinhabiting Guillermo Segovia's story. And he cannot pretend that my text might be entitled something like "Guillermo Lived in a Story"; now I write that Segovia, already scared out of his wits, moves toward his study at the same time that I begin to live in just one Coyoacán, while he gradually inhabits two, three, many Coyoacáns. Guillermo picks up the fifteen pages he has written, a half-written story, full of mistakes; he picks up his lighter, lights it and touches the flame to the corner of the pages and they begin to burn. He observes how the flames rise from the tale he had prematurely entitled "She Lived in a Story." He throws the half-burned manuscript into the small garbage can, believing that when it finishes burning the "suggestion" will cease. But now he hears the sounds generated deep within my steady gaze, like the sounds of the city that rise to the top of the Latin American Tower. He sees the smoke rise from the garbage can but his fear does not diminish. He wants to go to his wife so she can comfort him, but he senses that this would do no good. Standing in the middle of the study, Guillermo does not know what to do. He knows that he lives in his house and other houses, even though he is unable to visualize them. He goes to his desk, he sits down in front of his typewriter, he opens the second drawer. Overcome by the urgent need to halt his own disintegration, without knowing exactly what or whom to kill, he takes out his old .38 Colt that he inherited from his grandfather. He stands, walks toward the door; he's holding the gun at ready. As he crosses the living room in the darkness, he feels as though he is about to lose consciousness, still holding fast to the idea of the moment that he is living. Finally, in this state of confusion and anguish, he returns to the second floor. The room at the back is still lit; he heads in that direction.

Stopping in the doorframe, he does not recognize the bedroom; his eyes are unable to tell him what they are seeing even though they do see.

61

Through his index finger the cold reality of metal begins to flow; he senses the trigger and the grips. A pale light appears in the background of his perception, helping him to recognize the elements of his situation. He distinguishes shapes, shadows of some reality; he looks at his extended arm and raises his eyes. In front of him, seated on a pretty little bench, a woman is looking at him. Segovia slowly lowers his arm and lets the Colt drop, which produces a muffled sound as it hits the rug. The woman stands and tries to force her thin lips into a smile. When Guillermo realizes that he is not facing any danger, his fear subsides, leaving his body slightly numb. Without thinking about it, he decides to move closer; with this movement of his legs, he finally achieves lucidity. He stops next to me; in silence, accepting our fatal destiny, he takes my hand and I am willing.

Translated by Russell M. Cluff and L. Howard Quackenbush

Rocío Maldonado, *Heads* (1989, ink on rice paper)

Man with Minotaur on Chest

Enrique Serna

Enrique Serna (Mexico City, 1959) has published two novels, El ocaso de la primera drama *(1986) and* Uno soñaba que era rey *(1989). "Man with Minotaur on Chest" is from his first book of short stories,* Amores de segunda mano *(1991).*

to my sister, Anamaría

> *My love of the ornamental exists, undoubtedly, because I sense in it something identical to the substance of my soul.*
> —Fernando Pessoa, O livro do desassossego
> [The Book of Disquiet]

I am going to tell the story of the boy who asked Picasso for an autograph. As everyone knows, at the beginning of the fifties, Picasso was living in Cannes and used to sunbathe every morning on La Californie beach. His favorite pastime was to play with the children building sandcastles. A tourist, noticing how much he enjoyed the children's company, sent his son to ask him for an autograph. When he heard the boy's request, Picasso cast a scornful look at the man who had used the boy as an intermediary. If he detested anything about fame, it was that people would buy his autograph and not his paintings. Pretending to be captivated by the boy's charm, he asked the father's permission to take him to his studio so that he could give him a drawing. The tourist consented with the greatest of pleasure, and half an hour later saw his son return with a minotaur tattooed on his chest. Picasso had granted him the

63

autograph he'd wanted so much, but tattooed on the boy's skin, in order to prevent him from selling it.

This is, *mutatis mutandis*, the anecdote told by the biographers of the Malagan painter. They all celebrate the incident, believing that Picasso taught the art dealers a lesson. I should have refuted them long ago, but it wasn't wise for me to reveal the truth. Now I can't keep quiet any longer. I know they're using secondhand information. I know they're lying. I know it because I was the boy with the tattoo, and my life is an irrefutable proof that commercial exploitation triumphed over Picasso.

To begin with, I want to make it very clear that my father was not a tourist, nor did he take any vacation while I was living with him. Both he and my mother were born in Cannes, where they worked as caretakers at the home of Mrs. Reeves, a fiftyish millionairess, obese and North American, naturally, who used to spend the summers on the Côte d'Azur, and during the rest of the year divided her leisure time — so much leisure time that a single city couldn't accommodate it — among Florence, Paris, Valparaíso and New York. We were a practicing Catholic family to whom God gave a child each year, and as our income, indifferent to the biblical precept, neither grew nor multiplied, we endured a misery that, as time went by, began to border on malnutrition. My father had seen Picasso's photo in the newspaper and thought he could make money with his autograph. The painter's joke didn't discourage him. When Mrs. Reeves came home he ordered me to show her my chest. She was an art collector and when she saw the minotaur, she was astounded. In a surprising fit of tenderness, she took me in her arms, crushing my ribs with all the force of her four hundred pounds, and without asking my parents' permission, she organized a gala dinner in order to exhibit me before her friends.

I was one of those antisocial children who'd refuse to say hello to adults. I'd grumble when my mother's friends would fuss over me in public and I always tried to be covered with mud so I wouldn't have to put up with their kisses. I decided to boycott my debut into society. Reluctantly, I allowed them to dress me in a stupid sailor suit and to smear my hair with something gummy, like the day of my first communion, but I didn't agree to let them imprison my feet in those ridiculous patentleather shoes that Mrs. Reeves subsidized along with the rest of my outfit, in order to appropriately frame her pictorial jewel. Bunkered in under the bed, I could hear my mother's scoldings and Mrs. Reeves's attempts at bribery, as she offered me a bag of candy in exchange for my going down to the parlor where a select group of bons vivants were impatiently awaiting my appearance. I would have stayed under there all night, unsociable and rebellious, if my father, hearing the racket, hadn't come to drag me out of my hiding place.

If God and hell exist, I wish him the worst of torture. Ever since Picasso tattooed his signature on my chest, I stopped being my father's son and became his business. I remember his eyes glittering when Mrs. Reeves, puffed up like a newly wed elephant, led me, with my chest uncovered, into the center of a circle of professional parasites and aristocrats who'd come down in the world; they leaned over to see the tattoo with that nun-in-ecstasy face that snobs put on when they feel they're standing in front of masterpieces of Art with a capital A.

"Isn't it gorgeous?" asked the fat woman, in English, resplendent with satisfaction.

"Oh, yes, it's gorgeous," replied the chorus of guests.

At the table, I sat in the place of honor. Afraid that I'd catch a chill, my mother tried to put a shirt on me, but Mrs. Reeves stopped her with an energetic gesture. A famous auto racer took a picture of my chest, managing to position the camera in such a way that my face—lacking in artistic value—wouldn't spoil the photo. His girlfriend, who was then a protest singer and is today one of Lockheed's major stockholders, was giving me winks of complicity, as if insinuating that she really understood Picasso's joke and looked down on those idiots for taking it seriously. I got along better with the more proper guests, particularly a countess who had Parkinson's disease, and nevertheless, out of maternal instinct or her desire to annoy the hostess, began to feed me. None of her trembling spoonfuls made it to my lips, but many fell on my left nipple, soiling the minotaur's brow. Although Mrs. Reeves tried to minimize the mishap with a benevolent smile, I noticed a spiteful gleam in her eye when she asked my father to clean the spot with some cotton moistened with warm water. I didn't understand why they treated me with so much delicacy, but something was clear in the midst of the confusion: that day I was in charge. That's why when my father leaned over to clean the minotaur's horns, I spilled a bowl of boiling soup on his pants.

With her dinner, Mrs. Reeves achieved great social success. It was something like her doctorate in sophistication, the proof of refinement that she needed to enter the grand world of which she'd only known the outskirts. I opened the gates of paradise for her, and when summer ended she wanted to keep me at her side like an amulet. I vaguely recall a closed-door discussion between my parents, Mama's crying when she packed my suitcases, the farewell on the dock with all my brothers and sisters waving white handkerchiefs. Then, I didn't really know what was going on. I believed Mama's compassionate lie: my patronness was taking me on a vacation on her yacht because she'd grown fond of me. I confess I didn't miss my family during the Mediterranean crossing. Besides feeding me with generous servings of steak (a dish unknown to my anemic child's stomach), Mrs. Reeves let me zoom around the deck like a bullet, play pirates with the crew, and torment Perkins—her spoiled cat—by lighting matches under his tail. In exchange for so much freedom, she only prohibited me from exposing my chest to the sun in order to avoid peeling, which, according to the big hypocrite, could be damaging to my health.

I opened my eyes too late, when we took the plane to New York. On the stairway, Mrs. Reeves bid me goodbye with a laconic "Take care," and two of her servants lifted me off the ground, taking me delicately by the armpits, like a fragile and valuable object. At this point, I already felt like a little king and I thought that they were going to carry me into the jet. And so they did, but not into the first-class cabin, as I expected, but into the animal hold, where they wrapped me in a thick strip of foam rubber to protect the minotaur against possible scratches. Perkins meowed vengefully when they installed me next to him. In his cage, he seemed much freer, and more human, than I. Then I understood that they'd sold me. Then I cried.

It wasn't, after all, a blatant sale—Mrs. Reeves's attorneys tricked the French authorities by representing the agreement as a lifetime stipend. She committed herself to cover my expenses for food, clothing, housing and education in exchange for my permission to exhibit the tattoo. My father rid himself of a mouth to feed and obtained fifty thousand francs in a single business deal. I don't know in what crack in his Christian conscience he was able to hide that despicable act.

Hardened by pain and humiliation, I decided to take advantage of my new situation and forget forever the home I had lost. I was a slave, yes, but a slave ensconced in silk sheets. With Mrs. Reeves, I accustomed myself to comfort and pleasure. As soon as I arrived at her Park Avenue apartment, she made me a list of privileges and obligations. She wanted to be a mother to me: I would have private tutors for English, piano, horseback riding, and fencing; the best toys; the most expensive clothing. She only requested that in front of visitors I imitate the silence of the furniture. She assigned me a prominent place in the living room, between a Goya lithograph and a miniature version of Rodin's *Mercury*. My job—if you can call it that—consisted of standing immobile while guests contemplated the minotaur. Soon I began to hate the word *gorgeous*. Mrs. Reeves's friends couldn't manage to say anything else when they saw the tattoo. But the most unbearable of all were the "connoisseurs" who, after the obligatory exclamation, expounded their personal readings of the work.

"The minotaur is a symbol of virility. Picasso has created his yearning for rejuvenation on the boy's chest, using the tattoo like one of Ariadne's threads, which will permit him to exit his interior labyrinth for the sunnier space of flesh and desire."

"Say what they will, Picasso's theme was always the human figure. It's natural that his interest in man has led him to dispense with canvas and paint directly onto man's skin, in order to fuse the subject and object of his artistic expression."

The comments of these idiots made me hate Picasso and, along with him, part of my own person. At that time I couldn't understand what they were talking about, but I had already begun to feel like nothing, invisible, diminished by the tattoo that merited more attention and more respect than I. Some guests didn't bother to look at my face: they fixed their gaze on the minotaur as if I were a flesh-and-bone frame. If it hadn't been that Mrs. Reeves, when she wasn't playing the part of the cultured hostess, showed tenderness and affection toward me, I think I would have committed suicide before losing my baby teeth. Ingenuousness saved me. I didn't know that works of art needed maintenance. With her maternal poses, with her pretense of selflessness and human warmth, Mrs. Reeves was doing nothing other than protecting her investment. Just as she preserved her Munch and Tamayo oils from humidity, she treated me with love in order to conserve a life which—whether she liked it or not—formed part of the work.

I was sixteen years old when my hormones declared war on contemporary art. A spot of black fuzz first covered the legs of the minotaur, climbed upwards from my navel to where the bull's head began, and wound up burying the drawing under a dense tangle of hair. Mrs. Reeves hadn't foreseen that her property would convert itself into a man with hair on his chest. Desperate, she tried to shave me with a razor, but she desisted when she made a little nick that—to her dismay and my delight—erased the o from Picasso's signature. After slapping me as if I were guilty of what my glands had done, she calmed her nerves with a strong dose of tranquilizers. Various experts in the conservation of paintings came to her aid. For them the problem wasn't technical but esthetic. They could always remove the hair with wax, but did they have the right to interrupt the evolution of a work conceived to transform itself over time? Would Picasso have utilized human skin if he hadn't wanted the hair to conceal the tattoo as I grew? A poet who boasted of his friendship with the painter settled the question. In his opinion, the hair fulfilled the same function as Metro tickets and matchboxes in the synthetic cubist-period paintings done in collaboration with Braque. To eliminate it would be a crime against culture, a stupidity as horrible as shaving Marcel Duchamp's mustachioed *Mona Lisa*.

Fearing they'd call her an enemy of culture, Mrs. Reeves agreed to leave the minotaur covered with hair. I thought that the moment of my liberation had arrived. Who would be interested in an invisible Picasso? I hadn't considered that the less the riffraff of the art world enjoyed a work, the more they extolled and mythicized it. If the naked minotaur had caused a sensation, covered in hair it obtained spectacular success. Arrogant, Mrs. Reeves compared herself with Mme. de Guermantes: she gave three cocktail parties a week and even then she had a waiting list of hundreds of socialites who were fighting for the privilege of NOT SEE-ING the tattoo. Now the *gorgeous*'s were insane, euphoric, and some guests, who weren't content with praising the nonexistent, caressed the hair on my chest, arguing that Picasso's intention had been to create an object to be touched. I defended myself from the masculine caresses with kicks and shoves, but my outbursts made the victims more enthusiastic instead of placating them, and there were some who demanded, with Mrs. Reeves's permission, that I hit them again, harder.

"When the boy strikes," exclaimed a critic from the *New Yorker*, bleed-ing from the nose and mouth, "the protest implicit in the minotaur is directed onto the spectator, making him feel the esthetic experience in his own flesh."

That difficult period, when I didn't know whether to restrain or unleash my aggression, ended fortunately when Mrs. Reeves suffered an embolism which carried her off to the next world. Allow me to pause here in order to spit on her memory. Even after her death she continued to mock me. I didn't expect much from her will, just a modest annuity for all my years of service, but I never imagined that she would include me among her assets. And on top of that, she tried to play philanthro-pist. I was donated to a museum in her hometown (New Blackwood, North Carolina), "with the desire that my contemporaries be acquainted with the most significant works of modern art," according to what she wrote in a letter to city officials.

This betrayal marked the end of my patience. I was certain that they would never grant me my freedom if I didn't seize it myself. Mrs. Reeves's notary deliberately delayed the formalities of the donation in order to display to his friends the work he had in his custody. He was a vulgar, despicable person. Not only did he wound my human dignity by crudely shaving me, but with him sophistication was worthless: he also injured my artistic pride. After having alternated with important works in Mrs. Reeves's living room, I couldn't stand the company of his middle-class junk: I, a Picasso, next to a reproduction of Salvador Dali's *Last Supper*!

I escaped from his house with my sensibility quite battered. Wandering aimlessly around the streets of Manhattan, I arrived in Greenwich Village, where I made friends with a Puerto Rican pickpocket, Franklin Ramírez, who offered to show me his trade if I would be his assistant. We worked the subway cars at rush hour. I would drop some coins and Franklin would let loose his agile fingers in the pockets of the innocents who would help me pick them up. With him I spent the happiest days of my life. Finally someone was treating me like a human being. I was free, I had a friend to share adventures with, I was earning a living doing something more fun than posing like a luxurious doll. The most admirable thing about Franklin was his overwhelming sincerity in matters of painting. He didn't like the minotaur. He said that the bull's head was poorly drawn, that it looked deformed, like a child had drawn it, and as an example of artistic quality he offered his own tattoo: an open-legged blond that a San Quentin artisan had drawn on his shoulder. Franklin gave me twenty percent of the take and paid my room and board. In his way, he was more generous than Mrs. Reeves, but he was still a hoodlum. He pretended to believe that I was an orphan recently let out of the reformatory (I invented that false story in order not to arouse his greed) while he investigated my true identity. Poor Frank, I don't blame him. When the newspapers announced the reward for anyone offering information regarding my whereabouts, he thought he would make the first honest deal of his life. At dawn, the police arrived at the West Side flophouse where we had our hideout. When I saw that my buddy wasn't in the room, I knew he had betrayed me. I was too grown-up to cry. I did something more intelligent: I accused him of corrupting the morals of a minor. They detained him when he went to pick up the reward. Poor Frank. He'd behaved like Judas, but I was no Jesus Christ.

We both went to jail. Franklin returned to San Quentin and I was transferred to a more obscene jail, the New Blackwood museum, where they'd reserved a glass cage for me with a sign giving credit to Mrs. Reeves for her generous donation. Now they called me *Man with Minotaur on Chest*. The title suggested that not only the tattoo, but also I, its unfortunate bearer, were creations of Picasso. For rebelling against this barbarism, I gained the dislike of the director of the museum, a stingy gray functionary to whom my demands for humanitarian treatment were nothing more than the caprices of a starlet. "What are you com-

69

plaining about," he would say, "when you earn your living without moving a finger?" Alleging a tight budget, he rationed my food. His was a democratic museum, he couldn't spend more on me than on the other pieces. Democratically he wanted to force me to remain immobile for hours, to smile when the visitors photographed me, to tolerate, without sneezing, the humiliating feather duster of the old man who did the cleaning. Being there against my will, I didn't feel any obligation to cooperate with him. I assumed a rude, rebellious attitude. I covered my showcase with steamy breath, I went on covered-chest strikes, I exposed my member to the highschool girls and I made fun of their art-history teachers, interrupting their lessons with insolent shouts—Don't pay attention to this cretin: *Guernica* is a piece of junk, *Les Demoiselles d'Avignon* were whores just like you!

Complaints about my conduct reached the ears of the town mayor, who submitted my case to public opinion. The editor of the local newspaper thought that no work of art, however important it might be, had the right to insult its spectators. Considering that if Picasso was an atheist then I could very well be the anti-Christ, the head of the Methodist church demanded my immediate expulsion from New Blackwood. The liberals were opposed: never would they permit a fanatic to destroy the artistic treasure of the people. To please the opposing factions, the mayor resolved that they would have me chained and gagged. Not even the beasts in the zoo were treated this way.

It's true what people say: the more bitter our adversity, the closer we are to salvation. News of my capture in New York had put all the museum thieves on notice. The New Blackwood museum was poorly protected. They broke in at night, after easily disabling two watchmen who were dull and rusty from years of inactivity. When the thieves illuminated me with their flashlights, I couldn't contain a shout of joy. Politely, I helped them disconnect the showcase alarm and offered myself in their service: "Take me wherever you want, but get me out of here. I'll find my own buyer, I won't be any trouble." My willingness to be stolen did not move them. I felt a blow on the nape of my neck and a pricking of my arm. The world leaned down on my eyelids. . . .

I woke up forty-eight hours later in a foul-smelling basement. I suppose they gave me dose of sedative that would have put a camel to sleep. I never saw the faces of my assailants. Afraid that I would identify them, when they brought me food they wore Donald Duck masks. Lying on a louse-ridden cot, I listened to the raindrops, the ringing of a telephone, the distant noise of streetcars. More than the discomforts, what tormented me was not knowing what my fate would be. Would they ask a ransom from the New Blackwood authorities? Would they tear off my skin to sell it on the black market?

I recovered my tranquility when one of the kidnappers had the kindness to inform me that I was in Hamburg. My theft was a job ordered by the German magnate Heinrich Kranz, better known as the Snow King because of his limited participation in the international traffic in cocaine. Kranz ordered them not to take me out of the basement until the day of his wife's birthday, so that he could surprise her. With my eyes blindfolded, I was driven to a castle in the Black Forest—Kranz's country home—where the party took place. In a huge salon, illuminated with the pyrotechnics of a discotheque, were gathered the most exquisitely corrupt of the European jet set. Horrified, and scarcely recovered from my initial dizziness, I contemplated some engravings which would later become familiar. The straightest of the guests had hair painted green. A septuagenarian Boy Scout was caressing the buttocks of a boy who could have been his grandson. On a circular platform three hermaphrodites were dancing a rumba. Next to the dance floor was a pit full of mud in which naked couples were rolling around.

With a glass of champagne that someone put in my hand, I moved around the salon. Cocaine was circulating generously. A transvestite in a nun's habit kissed me with impunity. The real women—nearly all of them beautiful—would bite their lips when I passed by them, as if inviting me to fornicate right in front of their husbands. Their conduct was as obscene as the decor of the castle. The Kranzes had an impressive collection of painting and sculpture, but they deliberately mistreated their treasures, for which they felt not the least bit of appreciation. Gauguin's *Yellow Christ* was hanging upside down, as in a black mass, and had a rubber penis stuck in its mouth. There were some *Women in Bronze* by Henry Moore dressed as whores, with transparent panties and sequined brassieres. I saw one barbarian putting out a cigarette on a Rembrandt self-portrait, another who emptied his glass onto a fourteenth-century Russian icon. To what use would they put my tattoo?

I didn't want to find out. I ran in search of an exit. When I tried to jump out the window, ready to break my spinal column if necessary, a Chinese bodyguard grabbed me by the neck. "The rady is waiting fol you," he grunted, threatening me with a revolver. I had to accompany him to the Greco-Roman room. It was decorated like a fourth-class dive. A red light, brothel-style, illuminated statues of Olympic athletes, busts of Trajan and Marcus Aurelius, Etruscan amphoras that served as spittoons. A jukebox was playing inane country-music songs. It looked older than the thousand-year-old antiques. The Chinese fellow ordered me to sit down at a table with mismatched legs occupied by an emaciated, dissipated bar girl wearing false beauty marks on her cheeks and a T-shirt that read *Fuck Me and Leave Me*. She was my new owner: the perverse Uninge. She greeted me in the manner of Caligula, with an artful squeeze of my testicles.

"Welcome to the Art Desecraters' Club. You don't know how much you mean to my collection. You're something different. I was getting tired of inanimate works. As much as I hate them, one gets tired of stomping on them."

"Why do you hate art?" I asked, intimidated by her tender greeting.

"How marvelous. Besides being good-looking you're innocent." The perverse Uninge looked at me with a mixture of compassion and scorn. "Do you think that your flimsy tattoo deserves some respect? No, my love, not here. I laugh at Picasso and people who admire him, beginning with your former owner, may she rest in peace. The poor whale. She thought she was cultured and sublime. I'm beyond all that. We're in the age of the fraud, dear. Art died as soon as we put a price on it. Now it's a pretext for playing the market. I move a finger and the painting that was worth one hundred dollars in the morning is quoted at fifty thousand by evening. If I work those miracles, don't you think I can also take away the value of art? That's what I've dedicated myself to for the past few years. Heinrich could buy me everything I wanted, but I have a weakness for stolen works. It's the first step in desanctifying them in order to remove the halo of dignity they have in museums. Afterwards comes the fun part: to spit on them, get them dirty, wipe the floor with them. And you know why, luscious? Because when I do that, I destroy myself, because I no longer believe in anything, not even in my little game of desecration that drives these idiots crazy but no longer satisfies me. I want someone to treat me like I treat the pieces in my collection. That's why I need you. Punish me, baby, hit me, destroy your whore!"

The perverse Uninge cried on my knees, like a fallen woman who at the point of death repents of her sinful life. I confess that her speech had moved me. Since I was a child I had been putting up with everything Uninge denounced. The art dealers had destroyed my childhood. Picasso had designed the tattoo to insult them, and they, instead of being offended, had demonstrated, at the cost of my happiness, that even his jokes were worth a fortune. I wiped away Uninge's tears with a handkerchief. Poor woman. At heart she was a moralist, like all great libertines. I held her tenderly against my chest, to tell her without words that I understood her and respected her. It was an unpardonable error.

Her moment of weakness had passed and she thought I was trying to blackmail her emotionally. In her eyes the spark of rancor gleamed anew.

"Li Chuan, come here!" The Chinaman came running. "Take him to my room and make him undress. I hate people who feel sorry for me. Get ready, doll, because you're going to get to know the perverse Uninge."

In her bedroom I lost even the last trace of chastity. It would be naive to say that she reduced me to the category of a sexual object, because the truth is that my body didn't matter to her. All her refined lust was concentrated on the tattoo. She pinched it, she scratched it, she licked it until her tongue was dry, smearing it with apple jelly when she got bored with the taste of my skin. I made love to her with a hood over my head because she didn't want to see my face. As I was inside her body and yet didn't exist for her, my first amorous venture left me with an aftertaste of frustration. Afterwards came the lashes, not given to me, of course, but to the minotaur, to Picasso, to Uninge's own conscience. I was the one who bled, but not the one who received the punishment. She sprinkled my wounds with lemon juice, mounted me again and, as the moment of orgasm approached, she stuck a pin in my chest. The pain was so intense that I lost consciousness, but Uninge administered some smelling salts to prolong the torture. Facing the bed was a Chagall that occasionally moved towards the right, revealing a hole undoubtedly meant for a voyeur. Could it be Heinrich Kranz or one of Uninge's lovers?

When I no longer had the strength to even beg for mercy they took me to a dungeon where I was locked up for three days. On the walls were photos of famous iconoclasts: the savage who defaced the *Pietà* with a hammer shared a sort of altar with the old lady who threw sulfuric acid on *Las Meninas*. Drawings of doves abounded. Uninge adored them, not exactly because they were symbols of peace, but for their excrement, which destroys the facades of cathedrals.

My stay in the dungeon annihilated my rebellious urges. The perverse Uninge had me in her power and I had nothing to gain by opposing her whims. When I got out, I was disposed to obey her in everything, and as she, for the moment, had tired of me, I was ordered to satisfy her friends. I admit that I fulfilled my duties with pleasure. Anyone who thinks my behavior is shameless or cynical should take into account the fact that I was an adolescent in the throes of full sexual awakening. If I participated enthusiastically in orgies and group sex, if I saturated Uninge's friends with pleasure, if I let them urinate on the tattoo, and slapped them, and dressed myself as a minotaur to fulfill their fantasies, it was because I was in the springtime of my sexuality. I regret nothing, except having permitted them to use me as an intermediary so they could go to bed with Picasso.

Uninge and Heinrich belonged to the elite of the international underworld; that is, they rubbed elbows with bankers and heads of state. It's not easy to escape morally undamaged from an environment like that. I learned to lie, to steal jewels from my lovers, to blackmail them, to play the gigolo so they would give me good tips. I became—let's be honest—a common prostitute. And it was as a prostitute that I had the idea of obtaining the rights to exploit the minotaur. I followed the example of professional soccer players who when they're unhappy with their club buy back their contract in order to sell themselves to the highest bidder. Why should I stay on Uninge's team if I was the natural owner of a tattoo in such demand?

Escaping from Germany wasn't difficult, but once I was free, I needed to shake off the New Blackwood authorities who would undoubtedly try to make me return to the fold. I prepared a double cross with intelligence and ease. First I took Rubens's *Venus* out of the Black Forest castle and hid it in an abandoned cabin. Nobody noticed its absence. Uninge had summoned her satanic tribe to a party that would last all weekend. I gave the tip to the police, who arrived around midnight, when everybody's noses were full of coke. Since I was still a minor, I was the first to get out of jail. Outside, two detectives were waiting for me. The mayor of New Blackwood had sent them when he heard of my capture. Over the telephone I proposed an agreement: I'd give them the Rubens *Venus*, a piece worth much more than the minotaur, in exchange for my freedom and ten thousand dollars. The cheapskate refused to pay the financial compensation, but agreed to the exchange.

I took the first plane to Paris, determined to get rich with the tattoo. Thanks to my knack for public relations, I quickly got together a clientele of eccentric millionaire women who paid exorbitant sums to go to bed with a masterpiece of contemporary art. I moved into a luxurious apartment in Saint-Germain. I'd entertain two or three women a night, putting them in different bedrooms, like a dentist who sees several patients at the same time. I wound up charging an extra fee for taking off my T-shirt, and I prohibited those women inclined to scratch from touching the tattoo. How they suffered: going to bed with me was as prestigious as wearing a Coco Chanel original. When I made my first million dollars I planned on buying a house in Cannes, preferably the house I'd grown up in, so that my father could die of fury at seeing me so prosperous. I didn't count on the damned inspectors from the Ministry of Culture.

They knocked on my door one Sunday, in response to a call from a spiteful customer who couldn't afford my fee. I went through a long interrogation. They'd discovered that my father's transaction with Mrs. Reeves had been inhuman and unconstitutional. So what else is new, I told them, indignant at the crude way they'd forced me to show them the tattoo. They asked me to reconstruct the trials of my life from the time of the sale in Cannes up to my prostitution in Paris. I told them a melodramatic story, punctuated with sobs, in which I always played the role of the victim: society was to blame for all my misfortunes, I'd been treated worse than a slave, et cetera. I moved them to tears. In a fit of vulgarity the Chief Inspector begged my pardon in the name of the human race.

As I suspected, the French government, despite its humanitarian mask, sank their teeth into me at the last minute. They were deeply sorry that unscrupulous persons had used the tattoo, and consequently my body, in order to make a profit, causing me injury of a moral and psychological order. And so, as a minimum compensation for my misfortune, they offered me a scholarship to prepare for a technical career. But after all, a Picasso is a Picasso, and three times a week I would have to pose in the Georges Pompidou Center, where naturally they would respect me in my capacity as a human being.

I signed up to study industrial engineering with the illusions of anyone starting a new life. I wanted to be normal, to go out with girls my own age, to work at something useful. I showed up punctually at the Pompidou Center, forcing myself to be friendly to all the visitors, including those detestable Picasso fans who would stand in front of the tattoo for entire afternoons. The most annoying one was a Marxist professor of esthetics who tried to use me in order to support his doctoral dissertation on the manipulation of taste in bourgeois society. My case demonstrated the force of the merchandise-money-merchandise cycle in the political economy of artistic production. Not even for him was I simply a mortal human.

I would have put up with him and a thousand more cretins if I hadn't gone crazy shortly after becoming a common citizen. It happened that my new life, a healthy, hardworking, simple life, left me with a profound inner emptiness. Believing that I needed a girlfriend, I tried to make friends with my classmates from the Polytechnic, who knew nothing about the tattoo, and I discovered with fright that I couldn't return their affection. I expected from them the inhuman treatment I'd gotten used to in my long career as an artistic object. Not only was I an incorrigible exhibitionist, but I had developed an inferiority complex towards the minotaur, a morbid complacency at being the shameless complement of the gem that I wore on my chest. And those girls didn't even see the tattoo. They loved *me*, the man who could offer them nothing because of his complete lack of the most elemental self-esteem.

I failed not only at love, but also at my studies. They say that art is useless or it isn't art, and my character proved it. Incapable of any sustained mental effort, used to relaxation and leisure, in class and out I dedicated myself to *dolce far niente*. Given that my only vocation was repose, I preferred to exercise it in the Pompidou Center, where they paid me overtime at a rate of three hundred francs per hour. I needed to be on exhibit in order not to be depressed, but the remedy was worse than the disease, since, when I fled from productive work, I fell more and more into my deplorable condition as an ornament. That contradiction drove me to drink. I drank alone or in company, in the middle of the street or in the restrooms of the Pompidou Center; I drank cognac, beer, rum, bleach, aftershave, vinegar. I had terrifying hangovers, deliriums in which I saw Picasso struggling with God. Which of the two was the Almighty? Death, compared with that depressing life, seemed like a desirable step, a happy solution. In tribute to the cliché, I was at the point of throwing myself into the Seine, but at the last minute I chose Nembutal. I'd taken four when I had a brilliant idea. In the last few weeks, pathetically impoverished, I'd been drinking turpentine. I took a bottle and poured some on a piece of burlap. Rubbing vigorously I first diffused the colors of the tattoo. My hand was trembling, I had to give myself courage with a drink of the turpentine. The contour of the drawing disappeared after a thousand painful rubbings. Finally, ignoring the irritations and burns, I assassinated, with painstaking care, the signature of Picasso. I had broken the chains. I was myself.

Feeling naked, revived, promethean, I ran to show my chest to the inspectors at the Ministry. I wanted to boast, haughtily, of my misdeed, showing them who had won the battle. But they still had an ace up their sleeve: the sixth clause of the third paragraph of the Law of Protection of Artistic Heritage. This charming clause calls for a sentence of twenty years in jail for anyone who destroys works of art which, because of their recognized value, would be considered national property. "And what happens when a work destroys a man?" I asked them, furious. "Who would have been punished if I had died on account of the tattoo?" They crossed their arms in reply to show I had no way out. They drove me in an armored van to this prison, where for the past few months I have devoted myself to the Kafkaesque pastime of writing letters to the Secretary-General of the UN, pleading with him to intercede on my behalf in the name of Human Rights. As the Secretary-General has not yet deigned to reply, I've decided to publish this account so that the public will know of my situation.

I demand the freedom to make use of my own body!

No more crimes in the name of culture!

Death to Picasso!

Translated by Judith de Mesa

Germán Venegas, *Vertigo* (1988, charcoal on paper)

The Stone at the Bottom

Manuel Ulacia

Manuel Ulacia (Mexico City, 1953) received his bachelor's degree in architecture from the Universidad Nacional Autónoma de México and his master's and doctorate degrees in literature from Yale University. He has been a professor at both universities and has published La materia como ofrenda *(1980) and* El río y la piedra *(1989), both books of poetry; a critical study entitled* Luis Cernuda, escritura, cuerpo y deseo *(1986); and a translation in collaboration with Eduardo Milán entitled* Transideraciones *(1987).*

As my father's breathing
fails little by little,
the probes and needles
and oxygen mask removed—
between systole and diastole,
on the stage of memory
one after another
the images like lived photos.
The trip to school at eight A.M.
with its enigmas
of the Yellow River,
the gardens of Mesopotamia,
the Great Wall and Newton's apple,
and later, at recess,
while talking with other children
in the cool shade of tall trees,
the image of my father transformed
into the author of heroic feats,

and at home again,
the family reunited,
my father tells of the thousand and one discoveries
of his laboratory,
essence of rose, musk, lavender,
and the adventures of his mother as a child,
on the revolutionary trains
from Campeche to Mexico City,
the cockfights
that his father liked so much,
the excursions to mountains and rivers,
the forgotten image of his grandfather
who painted fans in Valencia,
his brief childhood in an immense garden,
stories of immigrants of almost a century ago
who left behind
the gothic tower, the olive grove and the cattle
and who never returned.

And at the end of the day
I watch how my parents get ready
to go to a party,
and after the goodnight kiss,
lost in the movie
on the black-and-white television
I imagine that life is like this,
and that my parents are dancing
on a moonlit terrace,
to a waltz by Augustín Lara,*
and that my father is a movie star,
a pirate in a sea-battle,
Tarzan in the Amazon jungle,
and that someday I too will be big
and I will smell the scent of violets
on a girl's neck
and I will embody my fate
the way they explained to me.

———————————

*Augustín Lara: popular Mexican singer of the 1940's

As my father's breathing
fails little by little
and his pulse slows,
between systole and diastole
time extends outward
like the concentric circles that form
when a stone is thrown into the mirror that water makes.
Every instant is an hour,
every hour a lifetime.
The time that goes by, brief.
Those sunny days in the country,
the weathered walls of the house,
the stable, the corral,
the dam for the watering pond
with its reflections of moving clouds,
where one day my father showed me
how to measure the water's depth
by the time it takes
a tossed stone to reach bottom.
And the woman who shells the corn
as if she were shelling the seeds of time.
Into what waters do we fall
when we go, if time does not exist?

What is the depth of heaven?
Where was the germination of the hours we live?
And then at dusk,
together in a dimly lit room,
in the loud steam of hot irons
over white sheets
my father told me
that in the next room
his father had just died:
first image of finite time,
a falling stone,
immense measuring that we disavow,
the sharp profile of my father's face,
the white sheet that shrouded his father,
the secret glance between the two ironing-women,
the hand and the clock that take the pulse.
My father sits up in bed

and asks, What time is it?,
and without listening he says, Tomorrow at the same time.
Shaking with cold his body begins
to give birth to another body,
an invisible butterfly with white wings
that awaits the precise hour
when out of him it will take flight
for its wedding with the void.

As my father's breathing fails,
an anguish revives—
a sharp-edged stone in the throat.
Those meals, in my youth,
when the only sound one heard
was the clink of porcelain serving dishes;
the sidelong glances
that hid the blushing
of fleshly passion
and my secret games in the bedroom;
while the wounding light coming in through the window
lit up the clouds on the pitcher,
the empty plates, the crumbs,
because, awakened in my lascivious dreams,
my singular desire had been revealed to me.

Now I would not be the image of the hero
dancing with a girl on the movie screen
nor the captain of industry
nor the man of discretion of whom society approves
nor the prey of virginities lying in wait for me
nor the father who perpetuates the species.
And later the quarrels—
freedom does not make men happy,
my mother says, *it only makes them men.*
My father is silent:
indifference is fragile armor.

My father lives inside the ideogram of his world,
he constructs other dreams
without thinking about the finitude of time,
about the stone, and its falling,

about the dark bedroom.
Tomorrow, tomorrow, always tomorrow
and the house grows larger,
while my mother's hair turns gray,
and in the mirror my sister discovers
her beginning breasts,
and my grandmother becomes a child again.
Tomorrow, tomorrow, always tomorrow.

As my father's breathing
fails little by little,
I want to tell him
that the only thing I wanted
was to live truly the truth of my loving,
but now he hears nothing,
he says nothing,
silence has taken over his body,
the body of my mother,
the circle that formed around their bed,
the dark room,
the clear mirror of water
where the stone keeps falling
in the fragile gravity of this instant.

As my father's breathing fails,
the image of the window, like a photo, reminds me
that outside there is the world.
I contemplate the brightly lit city,
the cars going by,
the teenager who meets
his girlfriend on a corner,
the passing bicyclist,
the athlete running across the park meadow.
Pondering the fragility of time
I contemplate the world,
the window again,
the reunited family,
and I am thinking that my father no longer speaks
or sees or hears,
that his dead senses
are beginning to perceive the theater of the world

through us,
that the only memory of his life
is what lies in the fragments of our memory:
an immense puzzle with missing pieces.
What must he be thinking about as he leaves himself behind?
My mother's skin?
Newsreels from the Second World War?
First communion and the commandments?
The tumors spreading through his body?
My father, stammering,
says he has a stone in his throat,
it won't fall,
he's going to fall with it.
To where? In what place?

As my father's breathing fails him,
he seems to begin to forget everything:
the chemotherapy and the welts,
the waiting rooms and operating rooms,
the portrait of his grandmother and the young legs
of girls,
stone from Oaxaca and the song of the canary,
the red rattle and first cry.
Or, in his forgetting—
the last dream that time will devour—
perhaps he goes down a road
looking for his father.
But already that road is another road,
the house another house.
His life fits into one instant, now.
All the parts are reconciled.
A single sun shines in his consciousness,
a frozen fire that the world consumes.
In the mirror of water
the last wave is traced.
The stone, falling,
has hit bottom.

Letter to the Wolf

Carmen Boullosa

Carmen Boullosa (Mexico City, 1954) is a poet, playwright, editor, short-story writer and novelist. Known for her feminism, she has published short stories, including Las Midas, a children's story; two novels, Mejor desaparece (1987) and Antes (1989); theatrical works, including Cocinar Hombres (1985) and Totoles (1985), a work based on a traditional Náhuatl story; and poetry, including Abierta (1981) and La salvaja (1988), from which "Letter to the Wolf" is taken. In 1990, Boullosa was a distinguished visitor at San Diego State University, where she taught a course on twentieth-century Hispanic poetry. Presently she lives in Mexico City with her husband and two children.

Dear Wolf:
I've reached here by crossing the open sea of forest,
the vegetable sea you inhabit,
the clearing of rage in the darkness and the light stealing
    across it,
in its dense, uninhabitable night full of howling that prevails
                    even in the daytime or in silence,
a sea of leaves
that fall and fall and grow and sprout, all at the same time,
of intertwined grasses,
swells of birds,
waves of hidden creatures.

I've come here by crossing the bridge that connects the fearful
                    world to your house,

this inhospitable place
made hostile by its sea of inhabitants,
inhabited like the sea.

There is treachery in everything because everything is alive . . .

For instance, that thing over there, though it looks like a
        shadow from here,
where will it walk to when it wakes up?
It will charge like a beast when I pass it,
enraged at the sound of my steps.

That's true of everything I see.
There's treachery in everything
. . . that was the path, wolf,
the route that led me to you . . .

Listen to my faint voice, so very close.
I'm already here.

Pick what you like out of what I've brought.
You can barely look at it,
as insignificant as it is,
lost in the thicket you inhabit.
I'm here to offer you my neck,
my fragile virgin's neck,
a pale hunk of flesh with little, very little, to gnaw on,
take it, take it.
Hurry up with your attack!
Will the banquet delight you?
(I can't run away, I have nowhere to go
and I don't know whether you'll look me in the eye
when you bite into me.)
Aware I'm a prisoner
and convinced there's nothing so great as a
                        virgin's neck submitting to you,
and no greater goodness than that inscribed in your
                        painful,
                        slow,
                        endless

and cruel,
loving attack,

I'll seal this letter.
Sincerely yours,

      Carmen.

Translated by Cynthia Steele

Episode in Al-Qayrawān

Jorge Esquinca

Jorge Esquinca (Guadalajara, 1957) studied communications at the Instituto Tecnológico de Estudios Superiores de Occidente; he was a member of the writing workshop led by Elías Nandino. His works include La noche en blanco *(1983) and* El cardo en la voz *(1991).*

> [O]ne of the holy cities of Islam [. . .] As a result of Bedouin incursions in the 11th century, the decline of steppe cultivation in favour of nomadic life, and the rise of Tunis as capital, Al-Qayrawān declined into an isolated market town for nomads.
> —Encyclopedia Britannica

The whole sea fits in the eye of a needle.

Through the night the enormous seabirds sleep in the shelter of the ancient walled city.
  Against their steely beaks, the desert wind sharpens itself sliding along them like the instrument of some augury, a dagger, a reptile. . .

I was cataloging the dunes of the desert, ocean waves dispersed and imaged in the feathers of the great birds.
  Everything was passing through the eye of a needle that stood straight up in the center of my dream like a diamond minaret,
  so that I could separate the colors of the spectrum and show them to the nomadic shepherds who were crossing the pastures.

87

Then with the rain came my mother's voice to wake me. "Search among the orange-tree roots for the elusive stone of your dream."

I was looking at my mother's face in the eye of the needle and it was an island surrounded by the water of the sea that had come in with the birds.

Nettles grow along the city walls. The merchants put up tents as white as summer salt.

And the crying of their wares is whiter than salt.

To tell the story of the caravans it is enough to invoke the eye of the needle, its flashing brilliance, its serene levitation.

"The line of the horizon is the pilgrim's prayer, it always wants to rise but it is patient."

In my dream her gentle voice made its way like a cloud over the desert.

Lifted up against the sky, returning there, my hand is an insignificant little pool. Before I bathe, even before I drink, I raise my face to the sun and the day begins with a beating of wings.

"Guard your flocks, for there exist no thoughts more perfected than the stones."

I drink the sea from the palm of my hand and its taste is good. Between the turquoise liquid and my lips burnt by the motionless midday sun nothing intervenes.

"Enter the mosque slowly, for its expanse does not disown the desert."

In the afternoons some egrets fly over the battlements, majestically they descend toward the great fountain and just before touching the water they dissolve.

"Love only that which robs you of sleep, for only that is destined to endure" — her voice had said.

I was cataloging the ships I have never seen. The fertile ports I will not visit, the wide bays bordered by palms where children gather to invent stories like this one;

I was the heart of the needle through which flowed a luminous filament and the supplication of a woman whom I have called mother

so as not to unveil the mystery of her eyes, as hypnotic as the traders' amber;

I was the fish caught in the resin, this murky moon which on the walls keeps watch over the breathing of the city.

We have seen the silhouette of the caravan disappear before nightfall. At first it seemed to be coming toward us, the sound of its passing reached us from time to time. Then, in the blink of an eye, the infinite silence of the sands.

Later—at the hour when bonfires are lit—I will tell you of the sea.

I learned of you through the eye of the needle, through the enchanted wheat-ears that spring up at the mouth of the irrigation ditch.

I learned of you from the shifting line of the dunes, from the wind that traces with them a new version of your fate.

I learned of you, my fugitive twin, when I least understood and I was walking at your side between the desert and your absence.

Later—at the hour when bonfires are lit—I will tell you of the sea.

The palm of my hand—lifted up against the sky, returned there—gives birth to a mirror.

The Huapango*

Luis Miguel Aguilar

Luis Miguel Aguilar (Chetumal, Quintana Roo, 1956) comes from a remote area of Mexico that borders Belize and Guatemala. He is the editor of the magazine Nexos *and has published* Medio de construcción *(1979) and* Chetumal Bay Anthology *(1983).*

I've seen something in your eyes
That to you I'm not going to say;
And to you I'm not going to say
What it was I've seen in your eyes.

I saw you arrive one day
And we went out somewhere;
And then in those eyes of yours
I saw something I'll never say.

When we came back at night
It was you my mother told me about;
Not to her either did I say
What I saw in your eyes that day.

This girl I saw next morning,
I thought that she was you;
But in her eyes there was nothing
Like what in your eyes I saw.

---

*Huapango: Mexican folk dance of Veracruz

There will be a lot of men;
And want you for themselves, they may;
Please never show to them
What I saw in your eyes that day.

Gerardo Suter, *Codices: Coatlicue* (1991, silver gelatin print)

The Last of the Tribe

Fabio Morábito

Fabio Morábito was born in 1955 in Alexandria, Egypt, and moved with his family to Mexico in 1969. Morábito studied Italian literature at the Universidad Nacional Autónoma de México and literary translation at the Colegio de México. He has published three books of poetry, including Caja de herramientas *(1989) and* De lunes todo el año *(1992), which won the Aguascalientes prize in 1991. He has also published a book of short stories entitled* La lenta furia *(1989), from which "The Vetriccioli" is taken; a children's book,* Gerardo y la cama *(1986); and a book of essays,* El viaje y la enfermedad *(1984).*

I was born far
from my country, in a
city founded
on the outskirts of Africa,

for on every continent,
in every country, however small,
there is something extra
that does not belong there

or that faces away from the rest,
and this is almost always a port.
Almost always it is full
of Europeans and Jews.

I was born in the midst of a battle
between languages and origins

that only ends
farther inland, in the desert;

perhaps it's because of this
that something of the unreal nourishes me,
something of eternal farewell;
and irony isn't enough—

nor heartiness nor art—
to keep me from being
someone who everywhere he goes
feels like a stranger.

Unreal Alexandria—
that's the city I mean—
princess of trade,
port of entry for every

pleasure, I remember
only the embankment
along one of your avenues:
an old breakwater,

a cold afternoon, date unknown,
and below, my mother and me
on a beach filthy
with oil from ships,

with sea urchins and algae,
at the moment when
above us the streetlights
came on, down the causeway.

Patient Alexandria,
sensual and purpled a bit,
privileged and mild
like an old slave woman

who from being so defiled
and spent by the centuries

has become strangely
pure, almost mystical.

Isn't that the most human
journey of the flesh,
the beautiful leavening
of the invulnerable?

Why does everything Arabic
put me in my thoughts
and make me wish for
a complete asceticism

like that simple life
depicted on a pack
of Camels?—the palm tree,
the camel, the desert.

Arabia of journeys,
name torn
whole from my mouth
like a hard stone,

indivisible and pure
for those pilgrims
who travel to Mecca
in tumultuous throngs

and recover there
the oily gestures
of trade, the delights
of oral existence.

Has the hour come for me, too,
Alexandria, to return to you,
and for us to settle our accounts?
I know: my time of life—

already near its first crisis,
its first serious

battle, which is gathering
force and urging itself on

while I'm cleaning my house
so that there won't be any misunderstandings—
also requires some
pellucid pilgrimage.

And those of my relatives
who want to recall Alexandria
are fewer and fewer, and the Arabic
that the family spoke

in so many expressions
of rejoicing and jokes
is scarcely heard
in our table talk.

The cold of old age,
the death of some,
the remoteness of others,
and hard indifference

have weakened you, Egypt,
and you're nothing but a name,
just another symbol
of youth and pleasure,

only some photos
I look at once in a while,
I, the youngest, the furthest removed,
the last of the tribe.

Voices of the Water

Alberto Ruy Sánchez

Alberto Ruy Sánchez (Mexico City, 1951) is the director of Artes de México, *the major fine-arts magazine in Mexico. A disciple of Octavio Paz, Ruy Sánchez served as editorial chief for a number of years at the cultural magazine* Vuelta, *which Paz founded in the early 1980's. He has published essays, novels and poetry, and lectured in many countries. His works include the essay* Introducción a Octavio Paz *(1990), which won the José Fuentes Mares Award; a book of poems entitled* Lo inaccesible *(1990); a novel entitled* Los nombres del aire *(1987), which won the Villaurrutia prize; a book of tales entitled* Los demonios de la lengua *(1987); and most recently,* Tristeza de la verdad *(1991), a study of André Gide. City Lights Books will publish* Los nombres del aire *as* Mogador.

for Margarita

Men walk along various paths. Whoever follows and compares them will witness the emergence of strange figures. These figures are part of the secret writing that permeates everything and can be perceived in everything: on unfolding wings, on eggshells, in the motion of clouds, in snow, in crystals and petrifications, on frozen waters, on the inside and outside of rocks, plants, animals, men, in the nocturnal sparkle of the stars, on one glass surface rubbed and stuck to another, resinous surface; in the arc filings form around a magnet and in the surprising coincidences of chance. Visible in all these figures is the key to a hidden writing, its grammar, but this visibility does not mean it can be reduced to fixed forms, and it resists being turned into a lasting key. One might say that a universal solvent—the alchemists' alkahest—had been spilled over men's senses. Their desires and thoughts seem to congeal only for a moment or two. Then their premonitions surge, and a moment later everything before their eyes becomes confused once more, as it was before.

—Novalis

The rain suddenly breaks the dry calm of the afternoon. Its thousand voices pursuing and succeeding one another thoroughly drown out all conversation. They simultaneously stop a dogfight and a couple making love outdoors. The windows cry out, the rooftops cry out, the trees howl as their leaves sway, and on the ground water falls on water like one tempest trampling another.

The afternoon had turned to confused music and through it runs a woman like a beam of light rushing into a pool of water. The joy in her face not only makes her more beautiful, it makes one think that this woman isn't worried about getting wet. She runs, but not to get out of the rain; something else calls her. She is like a narrow river that enters a wider river and crosses it almost without mingling.

She makes her way through the rain, passes through it. One might also say she looks down at it, for her hurried steps kick the reflection of the rain she sees on the ground. Now and then a few drops slide past her head, and her hunched shoulders carry them down the length of her back where, following the same course, they enter a deeper riverbed. Then she shudders once or twice, a reminder that even deep inside her it is raining.

The packet of papers she is trying to protect with her arm and hands is a bunch of letters poorly wrapped in a yellow envelope, together with other pages written in the same washed-out, nearly illegible hand. She sees his name is abandoning the paper, she can almost see it floating on the water. A small piece remains in her hands: her thumb squeezing a drop of water against the letters and the half-drowned ink seeping from either side. So too the sheets of paper were slipping from the packet, and so from her skin an impatient legion of nanny goats was emerging, hoping to feed on the words imprisoned in those letters.

And now, to clarify what wave it was that moistened her movements, I should explain that before reading the letters, she opened the door with a single turn of the key, looked at the table, and carefully poured paper over wood. In so doing, she rapidly laid down a beach where her impatient glance might finally settle. To one side, four letters written on various kinds of paper. To the other, a more plentiful packet of pages that says on the first page: voices of the water.

First letter. The most yellowed sheet of the paper. The most elated penmanship. Updated. At the top, his name, legible only to her.

The December afternoon when we gathered a thin caress of dark earth on the skin of our backs, just a few yards from our braided bodies the lower bank of the cemetery was beginning to be eaten away, as it was every night by the amorous advance of the waves. Five slender crosses revealing submerged graves seemed to scratch at the surface of the water, which, as the day slowly drew to a close, took on the irritated shade of reddened skin. By then the wind was similarly abusing our nakedness. Its chilly whistle hastened us to unravel arms and legs and put an end to the little candescent death to which we offered ourselves.

Before the black line of the horizon could spread itself over the whole of the sea and sky, we gazed at a white sail that was flapping violently in the distance. The shifting crew members were barely distinguishable. The sail seemed to be sinking but would escape from sight only to spring up again from its invisible hiding place, tinted by the advanced twilight. It was an image whose outline shimmered: at first a bright goose feather stuck in the belly of the tide, suddenly it was floating dragon vomit. The white blaze lasted three blinks of an eye. We thought the vessel had gone down following the movement of the night, but as we later learned, it reached—needle on cloth—the shelter of the dock.

As the cold insisted on sealing our pores, we got dressed. Abandoning the cemetery, we found ourselves surrounded by a thousand luminous specks nibbling at the night—crab eyes and fugitive phosphorous from the graves. The fragile black veil with its intermittent lights unwittingly illustrated the inconstancy of our emotions: there was something in us, too, mute and blinking, that seemed to have escaped from those graves, moving toward another life. We shivered as if the wind had lodged in our clothes and wanted to deposit its turbulence in our bones and guide our steps.

Embracing one another, we walked until we could no longer see the silhouettes of the graves. We began to wet words in a café-bar in the port. We simulated a boiling waterfall to drive off the intrusive wind and make our bodies' new riverbed our own. A burning sensation slicked our throats. We slid down the drinks—a two-mouthed skin-flask—as if our swift lubrication were fueling a fire.

Second letter. Various sheets of paper of different sizes. A long stain on the first page. The writing becomes illegible toward the end. The date is written two times, one over the other.

After so many months of silence, I send you at last the long letter you were asking me for. If I began on the previous page by describing to you one of the last moments we spent together, it wasn't to celebrate any eruption of my memory, even as its infectious fluids moisten the sheets you hold in your hand like cheap perfume. I would like to tell you calmly of the chain of accidents and obsessions that, little by little, have cornered me this time. Of course, you might see all this as just a bunch of excuses and justifications for not having written to you sooner. But it is, moreover, an awkward attempt to tell you, almost in your ear and with unavoidable clumsiness, of the songs, bellowings and stampings of a strange force that dances through this kind of confinement. And if I should mention again the last afternoon we spent in the Séte cemetery, by the sea, it is only because that is where the obstinate, haughty sensation that pounds in me to this moment first began to inhabit me.

When I found myself in the knot of our bodies, gently rolling around among dry flowers and gravestones of sand, my eyes were pummeled by rage, objects, memories. I shuddered for the first time when I thought how we were, that afternoon in Séte, like something that dies and turns into something else: a parody. I know this isn't very clear, but I can't say it in just a few words because I myself still don't understand what it might mean to have the sensation of acting out a macabre mockery of all I had lived and desired up to that point.

It was as if each minute in time were not succeeding the previous one, but paralyzing it. As if all things were transforming themselves, laughing at what they had been before. It was like believing that the butterfly learns to fly in order to mock the self-absorbed caterpillar, or that the foam of a wave falling on the sand is the laughter caused by the withdrawal of the previous wave. Ice wants to point out water's clumsiness and steam, its bad temper. An erect penis is the stuck-up laughter at its moment of limpness, while a flaccid penis mocks the stiff one with more expressive mimicry.

Here in Mogador, they say the world was created in bursts of laughter, that it was made by nine gods with three heads each. The nine gods were making fun of each other, as usual, when it occurred to one of them to create a strange thing that was a caricature of its victim. The insulted god responded with a new freak that quickened the hilarity of the other gods. Then one would respond by creating a consumptive cat or a bat-frog that was no longer simply the grotesque portrait of one of the gods but a mockery of the previous caricature as well—that is, of the previous creation. Suddenly the nine gods were creating strange, foul plants, dry planets, black holes in the universe, axolotls, viruses, tiny edible dogs. Successive mockeries that have given us the illusion that certain animals derive directly from others or are their lovely evolution, when everyone here knows that man is nothing but a badly made monkey with the ridiculed profile of one of the gods. This scene of the final creation ends, as they tell it, with an explosion of euphoria of which it is known only that laughter interfered with breathing and turned a few faces purple. The three heads of each of the nine gods all began to parody each other, then each of their appendages, and still later, they were laughing down to their most minuscule particles. As the world continued to grow amidst this turbulent confusion, it soon became impossible to distinguish who was imitating whom and where motion began.

Suddenly I could see the farcical kinship between all things, and on occasion, I even find my own skin harboring altered machinery. Something has inhabited me since that night and it is never the same inhabitant. Things happen in me, deteriorating in order to take on forgettable formations. Against my will, I am exposed to the incessant passage of a watery snake with a thousand successive bodies. It shapes me from within, differently every time, and leaves without the slightest pretext, inserting itself, inserting me into any other body whatsoever, penetrating a pair of eyes or a couple of words, spreading itself over the cracks of pavement, racing down lines of sight, compelling me to hold images of myself I had never suspected.

What I wanted to describe to you is this sensation of fluid in a thousand forms, of vast permeability. The passage of time—and of the world through time—as endless parody is merely the visible form of this flow, its crudest face.

If I could maintain the same mood, at least while I write, you would receive not several letters but a single, stable one in which I would calmly describe for you the small, trivial incidents which, from that afternoon in the cemetery through this morning, have allowed me to recover what I am now sending you together with these letters.

Third letter. This is the penultimate series of small pages in the first packet. The paper is of two colors. Each character is round and stable like that of a manuscript copied several times over. The date is recent and indicates the passage of more than a month since the previous letter. To look at each page is to experience a state of tranquility that allows one to think of certain landscapes and certain movements.

Only two or three unsettling dreams still make me feel as I did when I wrote what you've read up to now. I begin again, but with simpler objectives. I think those sensations are fading now. I say this because I am slightly ashamed at the elation of the previous pages.

100

We said goodbye that night in Séte and the next day I embarked on the Agadir, the Moroccan boat that would take me to Mogador. I was dwelling on your image as I boarded, and there in the boat it merged with what I least expected. I need not explain how the gestures of the French from the port contrasted with those of the Arab sailors. I recognized something familiar in them, yet at the same time, very distant. I don't need to explain to you how extremely comforting their gaze, their proximity, the casual manner of their labyrinthine intimacy, were to me.

Dinner was the only thing lacking that night to add to the mood I had carried in me from the cemetery on the beach, the pleasure of the tiny explosions that accompany a strange spice. The subtlest of disturbances entered through my mouth and through my mouth it would leave, finally taking the form of silence. It was dawn when we entered the Gulf of Lions. I was with several other passengers in a sailor's cabin, listening to a long tale of transactions and tongue twisters, when I had my first premonition that the phantom of the Gulf—seasickness—had leapt to my tongue. I don't remember my tongue having ever been so surprised. The contractions continued to squeeze my stomach although it no longer held even the idea of a single damp crumb. Even the memory of food had been left afloat on the choppy, open sea. Minute particles lost in the jaws of the waves that seemed to bite us. I tried to reach my place in the boat, assisted somewhat by a sailor who was also on the verge of overflowing.

As I was traveling third-class, we descended six long flights of stairs, far below the boat's waterline. Then he left, just as the smell rising from my passenger compartment hit me. We were close to eighty people in a room full of rows of semi-reclining seats. Obviously there were no windows. A blanket bearing the name of the boat was folded on each seat. It was like a movie theater with neither screen nor emergency exit.

Nearly all the passengers there were Moroccan workers returning home after having worked a long time in France. I thought I was the only one whose tongue was horrified, but when I reached the compartment I realized that I was one of those least harmed. People were running to the only bathroom and never getting there in time. When people did make it, they found the bathroom as overflowing as they themselves were. You had to lie on the floor because the queasiness in your mouth increased when you stood up. Lying on the floor, under and between the seats, it hardly mattered where you put your face. It was so difficult to stay in one place that even the pills and suppositories a doctor gave us refused to stay in our bodies. Some said it was colder

101

than in any blizzard. The cold never relented; nothing gave off warmth, not even for an instant, and since we were right in the prow where the boat took the brunt of the waves, we absorbed the blows of the tormented sea almost directly into our bodies. Nor did the motion ever cease: each blow was the inevitable notification of the next.

Then there was the smell, the greatest cause of the delirium of food-stuffs. Furthermore, I still remember with horror the exceedingly Arab manner in which my companions sang out their troubled self-confidence without inhibition. I can remember in detail the mass of slow and excessive belches that would begin with a dry blast and end with a repeatedly fluid one. No one held back a sound; no one could have.

Several men were crying with their children in the back of the compartment. Two tattooed women were shouting out their prayers, as if wanting to conquer the insistence of the waves with the harshness of their words. Knees and forehead touching the floor, they would lift up their heads and whip them back against the floor. The people watching these women shut their eyes, but even their eyes could not remain in one position for long.

It's hard for me to go on telling you about that night. Imagine that it lasted so many hours that the moment arrived when time no longer mattered. No one could sleep, stay warm or keep from smelling or hearing the clamor of mouths mimicking the sea. We were submerged in that intestinal storm, which seemed to be shaking the sea rather than vice versa. It was an abdominal contraction that stretched frightfully into the world. It was the world stirred up by the turmoil of a few "intestinal snakes" deposited in the most fragile corner of a boat.

Sleep did not arrive with the night that time: it was more of a generalized faint that came over us. We didn't fall asleep; we practically fell unconscious. The contractions continued. The women praying in Arabic continued hitting the floor and we could feel their blows even in our eyelids, despite our efforts to keep them closed.

Dawn didn't follow either. Day doesn't follow night in a pit. Rather, it was as if something else had begun: something like the arrival of someone you've been expecting for some time. When I opened my eyes, everyone in the compartment was calm. Who could say how many hours had passed? Everyone knew each other's most primal responses and now glances intertwined in recognition. We had all sung and were now gathering up our grains of voice scattered among the others.

In the back of the room, a circle had formed around a man. Eight or nine people were listening to him. He was moving his arms and the dance of his fingers was so eloquent it almost allowed me to guess a few details of descriptions in Arabic. Now and then the people listening to him would hesitantly utter a word and he would shake his head or nod in approval. I asked someone to explain the story to me and bit by bit I was given the rough outline of a brief sea epic. It concerned a strange boat which our narrator, Ibn Hazam, swore he had seen two years earlier on this same passage after a great storm.

This man had his listeners knitting their brows on the periphery of his tale. If I understood correctly, there was a time when the cities of the Mediterranean expelled everyone who didn't fit the logic laid out by the streets. City dwellers would pay sailors to take these people away and throw them into the sea. On occasion, after weeks at sea, since the logic of the ocean was contrary to that of the streets, it would become difficult to distinguish between the people who had been expelled and the crew. And so, once of those boats came to hold only those whom the Arabs called "people without corners." The people living in the ports then began to speak of a boat they referred to crudely as "the ship of loons." Ibn Hazam said he had seen the ship emerge from the horizon issuing a shrill, monotonous music. Everyone pressed him for details. I don't know if I understood what he was saying or what I preferred to understand. But certainly I inserted my own images into his. I liked the remote story of the ship.

But in less than an hour the prayers broke loose again in response to the disquieting litany of building waves. Imagine everyone's horror when they saw that what they thought was over had begun again. This time the jolting was gentler but the passengers' torment and wailing were greater. A woman and her two children tied themselves about the waist with a length of cord so as not to be separated when the boat broke up. A pallid boy came down to the compartment swearing at the top of his voice that he had seen the captain and his assistant very seasick and in tears. The two women began again to whip themselves against the floor in distress and the few men who could still articulate a few words joined them.

Also on board was a guilt-ridden missionary—Christian, of course—who wished to give a sermon relating the life of the holy Portuguese nun who, in the midst of a storm, saved the crew of a ship that was carrying thirty women to the Barbary Coast to pay a large ransom for their husbands. He told how they flung a handkerchief full of relics belonging to the holy woman into the sea and that the floating bundle was immediately surrounded by a halo of tranquil water. The halo grew and grew and by the time the bundle reached the horizon, harmony reigned over all the sea and all the sky. And suddenly the sun came out and land was sighted, as if joyfully welcoming the vessel.

The more the missionary sweetened the ending, hoping to instill optimism in the passengers and crew, the more desperate they got. Everyone was talking at the top of their lungs and it was just as well they couldn't hear him, for they might have thrown him into the water, relics and all, to see if it was true.

I lost consciousness more quickly than before, and only remember hearing people shouting insistently that we were becoming the very ship Ibn Hazam had described. I know I thought a good deal about this before my eyes gave out.

I awoke in the ship's infirmary. The sunlight, filtered and refracted through a bottle of serum knocking against the metal window frame, scratched me. I know you can't trust everything you see, but there in the distance was an orange canvas sail and a tall topmast covered with foliage. A clown with bells tangled in his hair was climbing the mast to untie a roasted chicken that hung from its branches. It was the tree of knowledge of good and evil, Ibn Hazam had said, but I saw in addition four goats perched in the tree, grazing on its leaves. The ship was crammed full of people and it was difficult to see how it remained high in the water. I wanted to go up on deck to get a better look at it with the others but it was out of my sight in an instant. The last thing I remember is the bright color of a long plank emerging from one end of the ship, which a gluttonous monk and a singing nun supported on their legs as if it were a table. Piles of cherries rolled down the plank, crashing at last into the sea.

The ship's doctor came to calm me down. I found his assurance insulting. He said that it was all my imagination, afire from the weakness of my body, and he left the hospital cabin saying in a loud voice, accompanied by rhetorical, operatic gestures: Oh, *great sea endowed with deliria!* And he slammed the door after nearly shouting at me: *The wind is on the rise . . . You must try to live!*

Eight other people on the boat had seen the ship. But the nine of us gave very different and even contradictory testimony of what we believed we had witnessed. I can understand that it must have been difficult to believe us at the time. I thought then that while we were indeed all very weak and perhaps inclined to delirium and while the ship might be a phantom, she certainly sails, if only on an imaginary sea that extends to wherever any of us who saw her might be.

Her voyage, suspect and less personal than I imagined at the time, was part of the journey that began for me the afternoon at the cemetery and which, somehow or other, ends as I send you the packet of impossible chronicles of the ship's passage and the voices issuing from it, which you should find together with these letters.

104

I have experienced this journey of the things and people that touch me inside as confluence, magma, confusion. When I desired you and evoked your image, a thousand phantoms emerged to inhabit this new region of invocations. The nights in the boat extended the boundaries of this region until I lost it over the horizon. Perhaps my need to travel from port to port collecting everything people would tell me about the ship was a way of touching once more that lost territory over which, directly or indirectly, you reign. Beyond that, I can explain nothing. What is certain is that in completing my collection of voices, I felt like someone who traces a circle in the air and, to close the circle, I needed you to read all of this.

Arriving at the port of Mogador—I'll tell you later of my amazement when I entered this walled city, magical and inaccessible as you are—I was surprised that so many people spoke to me of the ship. At the slightest instigation, they would start to tell me what they knew of her, and I noted everything down and later assembled each of the stories that follow. Almost everyone spoke to me of the ship's crew. It struck me as odd that they should know about their lives in such detail. But one woman explained it to me very clearly: "Here, before seeing the boat you speak of, we hear it. The sea breeze carries a tangle of noises to the coast, by which we know that it is passing close by. Those who hear it for the first time are frightened; the others run to climb the tower of the fortress in order to hear better, or stand at the end of the dock. And when in the distance a speck appears, those with good eyesight say that the people on the boat all have their mouths wide open, that they approach shouting out the stories of their lives, of their sorrows. Everyone talks at the same time. Thus, the stories intermingle. That's why the stories that reach us are already well worn. But given that each person hears the story he or she can catch, and catches the story he or she prefers to hear, one is always more or less content when the boat passes by."

Translated by Mark Schafer

The Mule Going Round the Well

Ethel Krauze

Ethel Krauze (Mexico City, 1954) was raised in a world of many different languages, including Russian, Polish, Yiddish, Spanish and Náhuatl, a native Mexican-Indian dialect. She has published fourteen books including short stories, poetry, novels, essays and plays. "The Mule Going Round the Well" comes from her book of short stories entitled Intermedio para mujeres (1982). Other short-story volumes include Nana María (1987) and El lunes te amaré (1987). Among her collections of poetry are Para cantar (1984) and Fuegos y juegos (1985). Krauze is involved in Mexican cultural television programs. She gives literary workshops and also coordinates public relations for the national literary program of the Consejo Nacional para la Cultura y las Artes.

"Where are we going?"

He laughs and doesn't answer. Is he going to take me somewhere to do that? Who does he think he is? Is he trying to intimidate me? And what if I don't feel like it? What—does he think a woman is always supposed to feel like it, with him? It's annoying. Let's wait a while, I tell him, and I really mean it. Let's try doing something else first, I don't know, maybe just be nice to each other for a while, who knows. Because I really don't understand what's going on with me. What if I don't get wet enough? Yesterday he asked me to do it to him, well, he didn't ask me directly, he insinuated it, but it seemed like he was looking down on—was it himself or me? Should I do it or not, I thought, do I want to or not, I don't know if I want to or not. Well, I say O.K., he comes on me, he fills me up good and then cool, real cool, he leans back on the steering wheel. Is he happy? And what about me? It sort of disgusted me; and what about me?

106

He falls asleep, I think, for a minute, he turns on the radio, lights a cigarette, I smooth my hair, dry off my—not exactly my sweat, what sweat, after all; is it really true that you sweat when you do it? He doesn't say a word. For a moment his eyes sparkle. He starts the engine; should we go?; sure, why not, you've already started the car; I don't care where we go, let's just go!

"Weren't we going to have a cup of coffee or a drink?"

"What?"

"Yeah, that's why we stopped in front of the bar, wasn't it?"

"Well, we're already here; I thought, well, what you told me."

"Yeah, I know—what I told you."

"So I guess you're not ready yet."

"No, it isn't that; I don't want to lay any trips on you; just give me some time."

"O.K., O.K., O.K., that's fine."

Fine? What's fine, for me to cut them off? To somehow castrate myself? Does that seem fine to you? I'll be damned! And to think that I'm doing it for this beast, to see if we can have something and not end up castrating each other so fast without getting anything out of it. But I like his skin. He's an accountant or an engineer or whatever, but I don't give a shit what he is, at this point I don't give a shit what any of them are. I find him attractive; he's tall, real tall, with tanned arms, lots of body hair, and gray eyes. He's immense, enormous, almighty. I feel tiny beside him, as if people on the street were laughing at how we look together. And I love how he laughs and then he seems to look at me out of the corners of his eyes and then something glows inside him; that's the only time I think or feel or suppose I'm really interested. And he's affectionate, because he's also a gentleman, not like the snotty-nosed boys that have hung around me all my life, every single day of my life. Damn! I hope he's interested in me, I hope he's really interested in me. . . . But then he comes out with some shit; I'm not sure exactly what, but I don't give a damn; I'd like to fall in love with him and have him fall in love with me; I'd like to swoon and make him swoon. I hope I'm not going to blow it this time. Do you want it, baby? Sure, but let's do it right; sure, but it takes effort, you have to show some grace, some real desire.

"So there isn't any problem, is there? If you come home late and all that."

"Well. . ."

There isn't any problem? You already did it, didn't you? All because of that time Irma introduced us at the bar and we were talking on and on with those girls you picked up, till four in the morning, then we got rid of the poor things and only Irma, me, you and your friend were left. How great, how fantastic! But I'm not going to blow it this time, I swear!

"Well, there won't really be a problem, but I don't want to do it until I feel like it. Why?"

"No, just in case we're late."

"Oh. . . and I don't suppose you live at home anymore, do you?"

"I still go there to sleep, but I'm getting an apartment with some friends."

"Oh yeah? And I suppose you've got a job."

"Well, right now I'm still a student."

Right now, always right now; it's all bullshit; we don't know how to talk about anything but sex. If we leave out sex for the time being, everything is left out, it's all provisional, fleeting, useless, unimportant. He's already asked for the check; now he's going to take me to the car, make me do it so he won't have to go home in pain, so he won't have to pay money for what he's already bought with other things, and he'll be able to sleep like a baby after he comes a few minutes from now. And what about me? Who gives me orgasms and puts me to sleep all worn out?

It's definitely better to be a man. They come onto you, they have the power to call you when they feel like it and tell you to go to hell when they're tired of you. And they have that tiny but definite pleasure of their ejaculation, the freedom to always be what they are. But don't you dare take the initiative with them or they'll think you're desperate and easy, that you're spreading your legs wide for their sweet whip; but don't turn them down either, or they get tired of waiting. "You won't give it to me whenever and however I want it? Get lost, sweetheart; I've got another twenty girls waiting in line; it's up to you." And what do they give you in exchange: a little saliva, an incoherent grunt, a whitish secretion to toss in the toilet. And what about the magnificent orgasm? It stayed in there, stuck to your skin, or hidden deep inside you.

"We're going to do it today," I tell Irma.

"Really? You finally made up your mind?"

"Don't be silly; what do you think? I've seen him five or six times now, and I've already drawn it out to two weeks."

"Yeah, that's already a record, isn't it?"

"Uh huh, but I think if I drag it out any longer I'll spoil it. The other day I told him we should wait a while, that day I told you about when he asked me why we didn't make love. What love? Since when do we love each other, I say, just out of curiosity, you know? So he said O.K., let's wait till you feel like it. He didn't get it at all, but I didn't want to lay any of my trips on him, but I've had it with getting really hung up on the first hunk I meet, because I swear—and you and I have already talked about this—I swear that I go home afterwards and feel like shit, ugly, stupid, empty, useless, because what do I get out of it, hell, just tell me what I get out of it. So I tell him to be patient, let's wait and see, O.K.? Let's wait and see if we do it or not, let's see if it's worth it. All right, fine, he says. I tell you he didn't get it at all; that's why he waited five days to call me again, supposedly because he had exams and was studying day and night and who knows what."

"O.K., O.K., but you said that now you've made up your mind."

"What choice do I have? Look, I really do want to now, I admit it, I want to, why not, I've been waiting for months and you know it; how much longer can I wait? And this guy I like comes along, he sort of gets stuck on me, I tell you he's been hitting on me for two weeks already, and I like him, I really like him, he's fascinating, I don't care but he's fascinating, so it's time, isn't it? If not now, when? It's all going to be ruined, you know?"

"Yes, come to think of it, if I had waited that long with that idiot I told you about, maybe things would have worked out for us, who knows."

"Look, I don't care if we break up, but let's get it over with; I'm fed up now, completely fed up!"

Today's the day. Shit. The marvelous day. And what if nothing happens? And what if he tells me to go to hell? And what if he doesn't turn me on anymore? And what if I don't feel anything? Well, it doesn't matter anymore; I already committed myself; we're on our way. Insurgentes Avenue at five P.M., the Manacar Theatre, San Angel, the university, the shitty high school, Tlalpan, where are we going? Down the old highway to Cuernavaca, what horrible places, how incredible the highway looks at this hour. And isn't this beast ever going to talk to me? He's content, on his way to paradise, and I feel like I'm on a nonstop flight to the slaughterhouse to find my mother. He looks at me, smiles, now I'm smiling too; you're going to get it in a minute, don't worry; all I ask is that you take a good look at it, that you see that mine is different, it's mine; it may not be very round or very good, but it's marvelous. And how can I get you to see this; now I don't know how to hand it to you on a silver platter, because if you don't see it, it isn't your fault. I don't know how to make you feel like mine is worth more than all the rest of them, because maybe it isn't worth it anymore, maybe it's never been worth it. Useless, imbeciles. Now we're arriving.

"What do you think? Nice, huh?"

"It isn't bad. I like that yellow skylight; it gives the place an atmosphere of. . . I don't know."

"Want a drink?"

"No."

". . .Because we could order room service."

"Yes, I know we could order room service."

"Well. . . "

"What are you laughing at?"

"I don't know; all the high drama struck me as funny."

"What high drama?"

"Yeah, all the complications, when we know it's all going to lead up to this. Who was it that said that? I can't remember."

"But that's the whole point, isn't it?"

"There you go; exactly. And do you know why I'm laughing so hard?"

"You're really on my case."

"I'm nervous as hell—how stupid, how dumb can you be? But don't just stand there looking at me like that. Do something, big guy, do something; take my clothes off. . ."

Come here, my love, I want to feel your burning skin and have you pour me out, light and wet, and make me feel so nice and thick, and everything the poets say when they turn into lovers. This is all so difficult. Come here, cover me with saliva, the enormous weight of your body, yes, please destroy me, my love, I don't know how to tell you anymore, what to call you, since you really aren't mine. How awkward I am. And you aren't surprised, you don't suffer, don't scream; you only spill yourself out slowly, like you're doing it on demand. I don't know whether to touch you—where? And you, why don't you move across my body from head to toe, sweetly, you're going about your business, doing what you need to do, and I don't know how to stop you so we can look at each other first, so I can kiss you with all my heart. What am I saying! Come on in, then, let it hurt me, like a bull in heat, you seem to be coming closer and looking for me between my lips there, yes, yes, yes, more, your delicious fingers, you're doing it right, right, right, I'm sinking sinking, sweet cold sinking in the amazing heat of your crotch, sinking in seas, rivers of bellowing foam, no, no, no, wait, wait, wait you son of a bitch, don't go off yet, don't leave me like this, and now you're happily coming, hunched over your bitch's back with your little doggie's whimper, and me wiping off my belly button and my eyes and my legs. . . . Your pitiful drops, oh your goddamn love, why are you doing this to me?. . . . Go ahead and smoke, you bastard, enjoy what you think you've achieved.

"Don't you want a cigarette?"

"No."

"Did you come?"

"I don't suppose I need to ask if you did, do I?"

You laugh; you're so cool. But it doesn't matter; I'll learn; I'm patient. I like to feel your skin; I'm satisfied with that for now, that you've enjoyed yourself; and I should tell you so! And I should say it without loving you, let you learn to love me, let me learn to love you and let us make some sort of sense of all this, and I've done it all for you, you believe that you've waited for me, that you've been patient with me, but you don't know anything about my patience. Waiting for you to discover that you can love me, then making me discover that I can love you. Patience to learn not to hate you, not to hate myself. And now you're coming again. And afterwards it's the same thing all over again, always the same, not knowing what we're doing or why.

"I'm going to take a shower."

"Yeah, let's take a shower!"

"Don't tell me you're going to take a shower; you can't go home with your hair wet. No, you wait here; I won't be long."

I can go home however I feel like it, wet or dry, and I almost always go home dry, and if I wanted to get my hair wet I'd know how to do it. You don't even let me enjoy what comes afterwards, because it all ends here, as if you had cleaned me off of you and here I haven't even gotten dirty yet, I'm still an immaculate virgin!

"And like I was saying, Irma, like I told you before, he wasn't even going to call me. We said goodbye as if nothing had happened; I was beside myself all the next day—should I call him or not, I don't understand how he can not call me the day after, to be polite if nothing else, he might at least thank me, don't you think? But no, on Thursday I finally called him because I couldn't stand it any longer; he wasn't home so I left him a message. And I waited. . . . I think I was falling in love with him. I didn't go to school all week, I just couldn't, and that bastard acted as if nothing had happened; he didn't give a shit about me, Irma. He tossed me aside as if I weren't worth a damn! So then I said, This guy can go to hell. And it keeps happening to me again and again, like a mule going around a well, and it just isn't worth it. And tell me, please tell me where I went wrong, where I blew it. I waited. Be careful, I told myself, no kidding, and I didn't take the initiative, or talk dirty to him, believe me, I was even careful about that, I was patient. I wanted us to have something, and it was useless, don't you see, it was useless again. And me like a jerk, as if nothing had ever happened, there I was left high and dry, am I going to keep ending up there all my life? And what do you know, as if that wasn't bad enough, two weeks later the phone rings, and I'm all involved in other things by then. . . .

"Hello?"

"Hi! How about that, you're finally home."

"Oh, it's you."

"I called you a bunch of times but you were never home and I've been tied up with exams; they're really breaking my. . ."

"Yeah, I know, they're breaking your balls, uh-huh."

"They told me you called the other day. . ."

"Did I? I don't remember. Oh yeah, it was that day I got shit-faced, it was really something."

"Well, they gave me your message, but like I say, I've been busy as hell, especially the last few days, 'cause I'm going out of town over Easter vacation."

"That's great. I'm thinking about making some plans of my own."

"Yeah, I'm going to Cancún with some buddies."

"All right! You're gonna have pussy coming outta your ears."

"Don't be silly; what's wrong with you?"

"And blond pussy, the kind that knows how to give great blow jobs. Far out!"

"Hey, what's with you?"

"Nothing, I really laid one on, it isn't worth talking about, it's really really awesome. Jesus!"

"Well, we should get together sometime."

"Right on; damn straight. Fuckin' A!"

Translated by Cynthia Steele

Four Poems

Elva Macías

Elva Macías (Tuxtla Gutiérrez, Chiapas, 1944) was one of the first Spanish instructors to teach children in China. She studied Russian language and literature at the State University of Moscow, and has traveled the world, giving lectures on poetry in the United States, Canada and Bulgaria. Her books of poetry include Los pasos del que viene (1975), Círculo de sueño (1975), Imágen y semejanza (1982) and more recently Lejos de la memoria. Presently she directs two series of literary recordings for the Universidad Nacional Autónoma de México entitled "Voz Viva de México" and "Voz Viva de América Latina."

"For Aries" is a companion poem to "On Capricorn," balancing Capricorn (Macías) with Aries (Macías's husband of twenty-five years, the writer, actor, politician, and consummate chiapaneco storyteller Eraclio Zepeda, who fought in the Cuban Revolution, was a deputy for the United Socialist Party of Mexico [PSUM] and has played Pancho Villa in a couple of movies, including Reed: México Insurgente).

On Capricorn

You take care of me;
you don't want me gathering pebbles
from the cliff,
crowning my braids with thistles,
feeding on nettles.
You're afraid I'll nurture vermin
or levitate over the roof.
But you can decipher ashen cartographies
inside my skirts.
You know about cobwebs that cure wounds
in my loins.

You've seen the thread of blood
that gushes from my index finger
when I write.

You've realized.
Let our eyes sleep, then,
in different equinoxes.

For Aries

Over here your serene excess
your sprawling leopard's habit.
Over there your admiralty,
your great chivalry.
Over here protection from the bonfire,
your laughing dialogue
with those who are gone.
Over there your lichens
caressing my drift.
Overhead, constellations,
and over your slumbering skin
our land.

Open House

to Roger Brindis

In the stable the beasts are panting;
they have brought in the orchard's bounty:
an aroma of fresh-cut grapes
invades the courtyard.
In the garden
the peacocks, the stone-curlews, the *pijijis** are strutting
among almond trees, tamarinds, roses. . .
Bare feet lavish coolness on the corridors.
Over the table seasonal fruits are spread,
everything hastened by chores or idleness.
Each morning
the doors open wide;
in the foyer the madman and beggar find respite,
and travelers, without picking any locks,
escape the midday sun.

**pijiji*: a reddish-brown, aquatic bird, similar to a duck, native to the marshes of Southeastern Mexico and Central America

Tulijá River

In the rain forest
a peacock drags
his tail of water
in a series of leaps
swaying foam
shaking the sun
multiplied eyes
blue
green
water
blue
hoarding steps.

Translated by Cynthia Steele

Laura Cohen, *Spas I* (1985, silver gelatin print)

Three Poems

Mónica Mansour

Mónica Mansour was born in Buenos Aires in 1946 and moved to Mexico in 1954. She has published poetry; short stories, including the book Mala Memoria *(1984), from which "In Secret" is taken (see p. 148); and a novel entitled* En cuerpo y alma *(1991). She has also published a number of essays on contemporary Latin-American writers. Presently she writes and works as a translator in Mexico City.*

the street doesn't understand what I say
when I press the soles of my feet against its hard flesh
or when I stop touching it
or speak in stuttering stops and starts
it only pushes on
even though I stay, beside the night,
smeared on any old wall along the road

*

there are lovers who appear
when there's no time for anything but hating
like that day in '68
when a strange man put his hand
up into the deepest part of me
and pulled out a tight knot
tiny and damp
for five thousand
dark secret pesos
a hand stirred around in my body

and I was depopulated
I only had time for hating

now we're sitting here
feeling love you wouldn't recognize
what do you know about knots and other people's hands
who remembers the five thousand pesos and fifteen years
this isn't a day in '68
and we are still alive
smiling
over this table

*

women — for example, three women —
who mean to recover the words
for the body   for loves and hatreds
for lost memories
three women who have known
the same men   the same rain
are drinking around a table
are talking

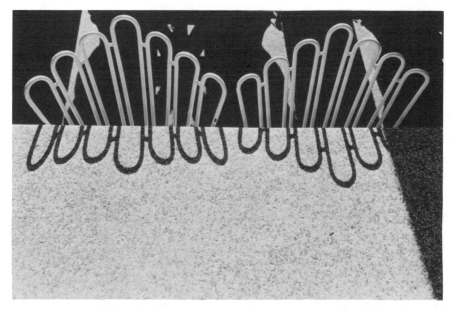

Laura Cohen, *Spas II* (1985, silver gelatin print)

In the Darkness

Hernán Lara Zavala

Hernán Lara Zavala (Mexico City, 1946) studied engineering and literature at the Universidad Nacional Autónoma de México. He did his postgraduate work in England, where he wrote his thesis on English novelist Henry Green. Currently, Lara Zavala teaches philosophy at the Universidad Nacional Autónoma de México, where he is also the director of literature and cultural affairs. Among his works are a book of short stories entitled De Zitilchén (1981) *and* El mismo cielo (1987), *which won the Latin-American Colima prize for writing in 1987.*

for E.Y.

Angela leaves her father's house prepared to leave Zitilchén forever. Lugging two large suitcases, she makes her way along the long, rocky, unpaved street leading to the town square. As she walks along she remembers that Saturday in October when she saw the village for the first time: it was a night thick with stars; the moon was rising, immense, amber-colored, surrounded by a broad halo of color. Most of the people were strolling around the square; others stood chatting in small groups. Round faces would pause an instant to stare. There was a little of everything: from farm workers and chicken ranchers who came down from the hills, to the Amaro, Baqueiro and Carpizu families, who came all the way from Mérida and Campeche to spend the weekend in Zitilchén. Despite their differences, they all looked cool, freshly bathed, neatly dressed: the men with their shirts untucked, the women in simple, bright, one-piece dresses. The young people laughed, clapping their hands, calling out rapid greetings to each other, while the old people watched, sitting on park benches or on chairs set out in front of their houses. Along with the music announcing the next show, a murmur permeated the festive atmosphere of Saturday night in town. At the café under the arcades, next to the station, men were laughing and playing dominoes. Shouts, dominoes, Havana cigars. The music was interrupted every now and then by a voice announcing the movie: "Avoid the crowds; the Peón Contreras Theater invites you to come see. . . ." Amid the commotion of the square, you could make out the grillwork of the atrium and, in the back, the church towers, flat, smooth and bulky.

Ever since her arrival, Angela had attracted attention, even though she was too slender for those people's tastes: simple men with a single idea of what a woman should be. They were attracted by her serious, almond-shaped face with its light brown, slightly sunken, clear eyes; her long nose and full lips which would suddenly break into a sweet, melancholic smile, like a Xtabentún flower. Angela had left Mexico City in a big hurry on the eight-o'clock plane. It stopped in Veracruz, in Ciudad del Carmen, and finally reached Campeche at about three P.M. From the airport she took a taxi into the city, to the bus station. She had something to eat and waited for the next bus to Zitilchén, which left at around five P.M.

When she reached Zitilchén she looked in vain for her father, scrutinizing the faces of the people, who kept staring at her—maybe because of her miniskirt—and familiarizing herself with the town. He had agreed to wait for her there. Angela had only seen her father sporadically, most recently about three or four years ago. She decided to sit down at a table in the café to wait. Surrounded by all sorts of street vendors—mostly children and *mestiza* women—she was distracted by the curious singsong of one of them who was shouting: "egg ta-cos, egg ta-cos." Someone touched her back.

"Angela, is it you? I hardly recognized you! How do you feel? Your mother sent me a telegram telling me you had left. I phoned her immediately to find out what was going on. Tell me, what happened to you?"

"I'm O.K., Dad, I'm O.K. The army came into the university, attacked the Polytechnic Institute, and even though the soldiers left Monday, there was a horrible slaughter. They're arresting a lot of students. I was scared."

"Take it easy; don't worry. You'll be all right here, you'll see. There's no one to bother us here. Come on, let's go home."

In the darkness no one moved. From the roof, across from the Business building, you could see the esplanade like a small forest, occupied by an army poised for combat. The bonfires shone brightly in the night. In the distance you could make out the School of Medicine; on the other side stood the Science tower; further along was the administration building, looking dead if it weren't for the red light bulbs that kept on blinking insanely. The library was a black mass against an even blacker background. Gathered around a bonfire, several soldiers were trying to warm their hands with comical gestures. Two of them, with their green coats and their rifles slung over their shoulders, went through the pantomime of standing guard. An officer gave instructions here and there. Arturo, Chano and Angela, motionless, observed them from a building next to the university. Chano, tall and hefty, couldn't contain himself and, cupping his hands to his mouth, yelled,

"Soldiers!" His cry produced an echo that made the air repeat, *diers!* "Listen! *sen!* You're killing your own people! You're bigger victims than we are! *we are!* Unite! *nite!*"

"Quit hiding in the dark!" responded an officer. "Cowards!"

"I'll hide in your fucking mother!" answered Chano, with the veins standing out in his neck and his face red. The air repeated, *mother!*

They were very close and were able to make out the officer's orders. Arturo pulled Angela toward him and, turning to Chano, said, "Let's get out of here, they're coming this way!"

They hurried past some propane tanks and headed for a laundry room. Arturo opened the metal door. They went in: first Angela, then Arturo, and finally Chano, who cautiously watched the door to the roof.

"Close the door, lock it, and lie down on the floor," Arturo called from the wall, turning off the light.

Lying on the cold tile, huddled against the wall, they waited. Arturo whispered into Angela's ear:

"Now can you see why I don't like you coming with me?"

Angela, fearful, said in a barely audible voice, "Through thick and thin," and pressed her body against his. They heard the soldiers' boots coming up the stairs, their hobnail boots ringing, tac-tac-tac.

"This is where they were!" an officer's voice could be heard on the roof, "Find them!"

You could hear the soldiers' footsteps as they spread out. One of them struck the gas tanks, and the vibrating sound lasted for a few seconds. They kept silent, lying still on the floor. Three blows from a rifle butt resounded on the metal door.

"Open up! We know you're in there! You goddamn fags!"

Angela hugged Arturo and held her breath. You could hear the ringing of the soldiers' hobnail boots against the cement, and further rifle blows on the doors of the other laundry rooms. The officer gave a distant order and the soldiers went down the stairs in a rush.

"Don't move," Arturo said. "It could be a trap."

122

Angela and the two young men stayed put. Then they heard the distant crying of a woman saying over and over again: "Don't take them! They haven't done anything!"

Her father's house turned out to be much bigger than she had expected. From the street you could see two tall, broad, maroon-colored doors; old and rather weather-beaten. One of them opened into a small parlor, obviously reduced from its original size, with only a couple of rocking chairs and a wooden sofa. The house was just one story. While her father went to look for his wife, she entertained herself looking at two small paintings hanging on the wall. One showed the different stages in the development of man and the other of woman, over a period of ninety years. Life was thus represented as a pyramid with stairs. Each level summarized a ten-year period and over each of them was an illustration alluding to the corresponding age, with a simple, badly rhymed verse for a legend: "Between twenty and thirty / he finds a wife and security."

To the left of the parlor was the bedroom they had prepared for her, which prior to her arrival had been occupied by Rafael – nicknamed Rach – the oldest of her half-brothers. The bedroom opened onto the street – that same unpaved street she was now walking down – through an enormous, colonial-style window with grillwork. A pink hammock with a mosquito net had been hung for her, in case, because of the heat, she preferred to sleep there rather than in the only bed in the house. Beyond the parlor was a large space containing the dining room with large arches overlooking an immense patio full of weeds, with a chicken coop at the other end. To one side of the dining room was the bathroom and, on the other, the kitchen: dark, rustic, exhaling a strong fragrance of oranges and cacao beans.

The other outside door led directly to the bedroom occupied by her father and his wife. Adjoining this bedroom was Enrique's bedroom; her younger half-brother, who – as she later found out – would share his room with Rach while she was living in the house. Amira, her father's first cousin and now his wife, was tall, stocky, gray-haired. She was about the same age as her mother but wasn't any more beautiful.

The building was full of students. The soldiers knocked on the doors of all the apartments and ended up taking away two young men who seemed clearly suspicious: they had long hair. One of them studied economics, the other architecture. From the building where they lived, they were led with their hands up to the university, to the Business School, prodded on by rifle butts. They were deposited in front of the captain, a dark-skinned, short man with a thick mustache, flanked by two soldiers. When he saw them coming, the officer took off his helmet and belt and ordered the taller of the two to approach.

"Hey you, big guy," he told him defiantly, "repeat what you yelled at me a while ago."

"I didn't say anything," the young man replied, gravely.

The captain slapped him. The young man's expression remained the same; he stared at the floor.

"Come on, you bastard, let's see what you can do," the captain told him, on guard and with his fists cocked. "I'm not armed and my men won't interfere."

The young man stayed put, his face down.

"A fag, like most big men," the captain said, straightening up. He went up to him and touched his face.

The young man slapped the hand away. One of the soldiers caught him by surprise with a swift kick in the testicles that left him fallen on the ground.

"Hey you," the captain told the other student. "Come here and let's see if you're any more of a man." The young man cautiously approached. Without warning, the captain slugged him in the pit of the stomach, knocking the wind out him. He grabbed him by the hair and kneed him in the chin. The young man fell down next to his companion.

"Take them away," ordered the captain as he put his belt back on. "That will teach you to be patriotic and have more respect for the military. Oh," he added, "and cut that goddamn hair."

(It isn't that I need to justify myself to you, but I think I should explain. . . . It was, let's see. . . in 1950. I left town headed for Mexico City, hoping to strike it rich. I was young and, as a good Carpizu, I was also ambitious. I was eighteen. I left the family, the agave plantation where I worked with my father, and Amira, who was my girlfriend at the time—hoping to get ahead.

I started out working for a notary public. It was hard, tedious labor of the sort I wasn't used to. You can imagine. . . from seven in the morning till seven at night, transcribing records into massive notebooks. For me, it was especially hard to be shut in all day; I, who had spent my child-hood and adolescence outdoors around chicle crews; bees, chickens and zebues; cornfields and agave leaves.

At seven, when I got off work, I would hole up in a small apartment in the Colonia San Rafael that I shared with a group of boys from Campeche and Yucatán who were in the city like me, some of them working,

124

others studying, but all of them trying to dig out of a hole. Our reaction to the alienation of the city and the overwhelming work load was to spend most of our salaries in low-life cabarets. Often at night we would end up wandering the streets longing for a shot of rum, a dance-hall girl. Eating in Chinese cafés and run-down greasy spoons. Every now and then we would get some relative to invite us over for dinner. But those relatives were frightened by how regularly we visited and by our voracious appetites, and they started avoiding us, putting us off, little by little closing their homes to us. Still, every Saturday after the first payday of the month, we would pool our funds and cook up a big pot of pork and beans; then we would sit up drinking mercilessly till dawn, singing Yucatecan songs, drunk with anguish and nostalgia.)

Going along that same road, Angela remembers how her father's accent had spread to his wife and then the whole town, even infecting her. Her luggage forces her to walk slowly. She has made very little progress. Her hands feel numb. Unable to bear the weight any longer, she sets her bags down at the side of the road and rests. She flexes her hands. Then she picks up her luggage again, ready to continue walking down the long, unpaved street. With each step, she feels a sharp blow against her legs, which makes her movements slow and painful. She feels someone watching her and turns around. It is the staring, weightless eyes of Aunt Estela, which, from her wheelchair, motionlessly watch Angela. On many an afternoon, Angela had taken her to the park, to the plaza or the boulevard, giving her a change from the eternal scene of the neglected, solitary street where she lived. Aunt Estela would spend entire days and a good part of the night watching. She liked to see the *mestiza* girls go by with their washtubs of tortilla dough balanced on their heads; the children playing; the men on their way to the hills. They would greet her with respect. She was a descendent of the Negrón family and had married a Carpizu. A stroke had left her paralyzed on one side, unable to talk. So her existence had become concentrated in the senses of sight and hearing. Life as contemplation. She slept very little and her eyes, used to seeing so much by now, were as deep as those of a nocturnal bird, with the same touch of wisdom and disdain. On many afternoons, in fact, Angela had talked to her aunt as she would only have spoken to a confessor or a psychoanalyst—if she had confided in one of those. Aunt Estela's vacant, green eyes (a color that ran in the Negrón family), worn-out by now, had observed her amid that other dark abundant greenery of the laurel trees along the boulevard in the solitary, hot, static atmosphere of Zitilchén afternoons. Angela would sit down in front of her, on one of the cement

125

benches, talking to her, making an effort to recognize a spark of affection or warmth, of anger or complacency, while she would tell her about her past: "At the university I met a group of kids. I identified with them and we started hanging out together. We would show movies at the film club, throw parties, organize roundtable discussions, that sort of thing. When the student movement started, we changed our activities. We spent all our time collecting contributions to defend the struggle, publishing bulletins, distributing fliers, organizing graffiti parties, and standing guard at school, until this wave of repression came and they arrested a lot of *compañeros*. One of them was Arturo. It was incredibly painful and humiliating."

Or her impressions of Zitilchén:

"Amira treats me like I'm her own daughter. Every morning she asks me what I want to eat; at five P.M. she has several buckets of water heated so I can take a bath; at night she hangs up my hammock and puts up the mosquito net. Papá spoke with cousin Aidita, principal of the elementary school, so I could teach classes in the morning; if not, imagine how tedious it would be, doing nothing all day.

"Rach and Enrique are far-out. At first Rach struck me as sullen and unpleasant. But he's a really good person, a hard worker. Every Monday morning bright and early, he sets out for the sawmills and beehives he has in San Benigno. He spends three or four days there and comes back tired and dirty. The next day he sleeps in, then goes off to the Ramal or the Cometa to have a beer with his employees. He has introduced me to all the cousins that I wouldn't have been able to meet otherwise. There are so many of them. Now I go along with them on their outings to the villas, the haciendas. Some weekends we go to Mérida or Campeche, to dance at the Tulipanes or the Baluartes. They're a lot of fun. Enrique is my constant companion. We go together to buy fruit at the market or biscuits at the Alpuches' store, and at night I go with him or with Rach to visit the relatives, to the movies or just to chat in the park."

Without moving, she felt the breeze swinging her hammock, cooling her off. Her heart beat faster and, amid the sounds generated by the night—crickets' chirping, wood creaking, the crackling of leaves and the breathing of people sleeping—she could make out a few glimmers of silence, even as her face was bathed in the light of the full moon. She had been dreaming and, when she woke up, she realized her body had gone numb, especially her hands. She opened her eyes and saw, horrified, that the air in the room was turning red, then gradually it started vanishing and finally disappeared. She turned over, and looked toward the window. She felt the beating of her heart and a throbbing in her ears. Through the cracks in the wood shutters, she saw a star so bright that she supposed it must be Venus.

She walks past the Muñoz's makeshift shop. They must be about ready to close, without any visits from their few customers, who would be buying only blocks of chocolate and *cocoyoles** in heavy syrup. Drowsing on the counter, Don Pepe Muñoz doesn't even see her go by. How many nights they had stood chatting in the shop, while the bats flitted around the dim light bulb of the depressing little room that served as a store. And how can she forget that night when Don Pepe had a cat brought in:

"Pay close attention to what's about to happen," he said as he deposited the cat on the ground.

The motionless cat had begun following with its eyes the movements of a bat fluttering around the light bulb. Without budging from its spot, the cat attracted the bat to it, with fixed gaze until the bat inexplicably started losing altitude in a tragic spiral that brought it into the cat's paws.

She wanted to cry but something prevented her: fear, the kind of fear that won't even let itself be shown. Arturo had opposed her coming. Angela had insisted.

"Remember what happened to us the other day across from the university."

"This is different. That time we caused it ourselves. Today it's just a meeting."

"The government is scared; anything could happen. They're prepared to go to great lengths."

"I don't think they'll dare do anything. There's a lot of reporters from the international press; it would be terrible publicity."

"You don't know them: sons of bitches. We're a country of apathetic people, of amnesiacs, of bastards."

That afternoon she herself had seen several young people fall to the bullets. When the first shots were fired, it was total chaos. She stood paralyzed until Chano pulled her, dragged her over to where she was now: once again, stretched out on the floor, in the apartment of two elderly ladies at whose door they had knocked at random, desperately, insistently. The two good women took pity on them and let them in. How surprised they were to find lots of young people lying on the floor.

---

*cocoyoles: palm-tree fruit

127

She and Chano were led to one of the bedrooms, which was filled with that stuffy smell typical of old people's houses. Little by little, as the number of students grew, that smell started vanishing, giving way to another: the odor of sweat and mud, of bodies exhaling rage, anguish, impotence and silence. The young people on the floor reached the living room by now. The only empty space was in front of the door. The old women themselves were lying down, comforting each other. Someone had kept knocking on the door, but they had refused to open it. The house had filled up with students scattered over the floor. The pleading voices had had to find another refuge or simply surrender to soldiers, riot police or cops. It was nearly eight P.M., and the gunfire wasn't letting up. In tragic and shameful silence the ambulances and paddy wagons wove in and out, throwing off red reflections.

(A year later, with a little that I had put aside, along with some money my father had sent me from Zitilchén, I managed to buy an old junker. It was a Studebaker 40, I still remember. I changed jobs and became a traveling salesman for a pharmaceutical laboratory.

I definitely preferred the constant traveling to the endless days behind a desk. I'd go to Puebla, Oaxaca and Chiapas. In Puebla I met your mother and, shortly afterward, married her. I couldn't stand living alone anymore. A little while later, you were born, and I found I had to work harder and harder. I was promoted and they gave me the Southeastern route. That allowed me to return to the village after being away for years. Nothing had really changed, or nearly nothing; simplicity and a slow way of life were still typical of Zitilchén. The chicle industry had collapsed, but my brothers had earned more money in a year than I had during my entire time in Mexico City. And without trying too hard. Only one of my cousins, Flavio, had gone bankrupt, taking his whole family with him. My brother Daniel wasn't rich, but he had rented the movie theater from one of our uncles, and he was helping him manage the ice factory and the nixtamal* mill. He was doing better than I was.

The first time I went through Zitilchén after being away for so long, I stayed there for almost a week. Every day I invited my brothers and all our cousins to get drunk with me, and I never let anyone else pay a red cent. I saw Amira, the girl I had been in love with, again, following in the ancestral footsteps of my uncles and grandfathers, who had always intermarried. During the years I spent in Mexico City, I thought I had

*nixtamal: corn boiled in water with lime or ashes, used to prepare tortilla dough

128

managed to forget her. But no, there was still a feeling inside me that came back to life when I was in the village again, near her.)

She walks on by, weighed down by the heat, feeling her Aunt Estela's eyes on her back. Could she have heard the gunshots? Their endless chats, scattered over the sordid afternoons in Zitilchén, gave Angela a breath of hope, of understanding, and she seeks refuge in her aunt's hidden tenderness.

"Today I went with Rach to the Ocuchil Hacienda. It's really lovely. He took me to watch them sow the agave. Afterwards we went to the watering place near Holcatzín. On our way back we stopped by the part where they used to distill rum. Everything seemed so beautiful in that abandoned, defenseless state. The original stills, receptacles and pipes are still there. We were standing there chatting when Quintín, Grandfather's godson, came in, and told us a story that you probably already know but that disturbed me deeply. Maybe because he told it when he heard I was a village schoolteacher.

"Quintín told us that, about thirty years ago — maybe you remember — a group of teachers tried to organize the peasants against the Carpizus, the Negróns, the Amaros and the rest of the landowners in town. Apparently there were only a few of them, five or six, who would visit the agave plantations and the most important haciendas. They would invite the peasants to gather after work at the schoolhouse, where the teachers would talk to them about how to organize against the bosses. Quintín said that it was one of the women teachers who was in charge of going to see people at Holcatzín. He said that, at first, they took a liking to her: the novelty of a woman trying to stir up the peasants. But when some of them realized that she was more convincing than she seemed, they started trying to talk her out of it: "Don't get involved," they told her. "Stick to your classes." And she would answer, "But I'm not bothering anybody. We're just talking. Or are you afraid of a woman's words?"

"She kept going to Holcatzín and started getting to know the peasants. In order to win their confidence, one afternoon she agreed to meet with them at the distillery. They spoke, they had her speak. They took out the bottles. They drank. She agreed, willingly at first. But when she tried to say no, it was already too late. Someone had grabbed her by the shoulders and, pressing the bottle to her lips, forced her to keep drinking. They found her in the road naked, staring straight ahead, repeating, 'Look, she isn't as skinny as she seems. . . .'"

129

Stay where you are. Stop. Her body was exposed to the night. Suddenly, abruptly, the dark room filled up with an exuberant, pleasant color. She felt anxious and remembered the feel of her first nights in the town, when, in the early morning, in between dreams, she would listen to carts go rumbling past her window or hear the squeals of pigs about to be slaughtered—which gave her the wildest nightmares. She would awake, startled, in pain, only to realize who she was and figure out where she was: "Here I am, living another life, of another people," she would tell herself, hoping to go back to sleep. She intuited a shadow and, with heavy lids, let herself be caressed by the nocturnal breeze, which touched her softly, delicately.

"The Flight of the Bumblebee," announcing the next show, resounds in the clear air of the plaza. Angela manages to glimpse part of the modestly lit church, and remembers the innumerable nights she has walked by there. On Thursdays she used to play bingo next to the gas station, with Amira or with one of her half-brothers.

"Angela, eat something. How about a flan?"

"If you'll have one with me, why not."

"You go ahead and eat, you're young and slender. And just look at me. Anyway, whenever I eat a lot at this hour, I have nightmares. Since there have been thefts in town, the other night I woke up shouting at your father, 'They're stealing the chickens.' And your poor father woke up frightened, grabbed his pistol and went out in the yard. He didn't realize I was dreaming."

As she draws closer, she is gradually overcome by the desire to disappear. She wishes she could avoid the faces and stares. The nearly imperceptible sound of her suitcases bumping against her legs distracts her and she pauses, once more to rest. She can make out part of the plaza. People are already sitting in the doorways of their houses, "taking in the coolness." She picks up her luggage again and decides to walk faster. The street makes walking difficult, and she longs to pass by without being noticed.

"Fear sucks," whispered Chano, as if he were reading her thoughts.

"What about Arturo?" Angela asked quietly. "What's become of Arturo?"

"Don't worry. He can take care of himself. There's no way we could look for him in all this chaos. . . . He was upstairs, with the speakers. . . ."

"Shhh!" someone silenced them.

"Take it easy," Chano pleaded with her. "I don't think anything's wrong."

130

She could feel the silence of the apartment throbbing around her. As if it were methodically beating against her temples. It was an artificial silence, constructed out of horror, isolated from the strident noise outside. A gray darkness made the bodies lying on the floor look to her like absurd burial mounds. No one spoke. Some of the breathing seemed labored. Someone was breathing with a nasal, whistling sound. So this was the serious part of life: an absurd jumbled crowd that you can't escape. She had trouble identifying herself, recognizing herself. It was as if the person lying there were another woman, different from the one who had lived through her childhood and adolescence. It occurred to her that the world is like that. Like a dark room full of bodies where some people have more trouble breathing than others. Some of us exhale a faint whistling noise when we breathe, and we don't recognize ourselves until we find ourselves in the darkness, scared to death, piled on top of each other, together in the most abject solitude.

(On one of the many nights I stayed in the village, I was headed for my father's house. It was after ten P.M. and the electric plant had stopped functioning. I was alone. Tipsy. I decided to take a detour by Amira's house. I knocked on her bedroom door—discreetly, but insistently. She slept in one of the back rooms of the house, facing the road to Campeche, you know where it is. When she heard the noise at the door, she peered out one of the windows and started scolding me, telling me I must be crazy, reminding me what time it was. I told her it was midnight, I knew that. That for me it was a strange and marvelous midnight because I had felt an overwhelming desire to see her. She accused me of being drunk and asked me to go away, saying we could talk some other day. She tried to shut the window but I wouldn't let her. "Haven't you realized what this is all about?" I asked her. And, lowering her eyes sadly, she answered, "What do you expect me to realize?")

[Saturday night at the Lions Club. The hall is full of people. The tables, arranged all along both sides of the room, are all occupied. Music, commotion. A small band is playing up front, on a platform. The couples are dancing energetically in the middle of the hall.

Angela comes in, accompanied by Enrique, her ten-year-old half-brother. They pause in the doorway. Their eyes search the place and, from one of the tables, they see a young man wave his arm at them.

Angela and Enrique go over to the table. They sit down. Someone from the same group asks Angela to dance. The couple joins a small cluster of acquaintances who are dancing with each other.

131

From his table, Rach watches the people dancing.]

"When we sat down, a stranger, a *huach*,* approached the table. He asked me to dance. I said yes. Rach danced with one of his cousins. While we were dancing our eyes met. I smiled but he didn't smile back. I noticed the contempt on his face. When the set ended, my partner invited me to sit at his table. I accepted. I danced with him the rest of the night.

"Later I found out that, when the three boys left the Club, they had found the boys from Zitilchén waiting for them. There was a fight. They tell me that Rach was the only one who fought with the boy I was dancing with. From what they say, Rach won by a long shot, even though he was shorter." He fought Yucatecan-style, with his feet, getting strength from who knows where, they said later. Rach didn't say anything to me about it."

(I returned to Mexico City and went on with my normal life. I wanted to forget that night. When I went through Zitilchén, about six months later, I listened with apprehension to some rumors that were going around town: Amira was expecting.

One Monday morning I set out from Mexico City in my car, as usual, heading for Villahermosa. I had dinner in Catemaco and, just before Ciudad del Carmen, I stopped to see some friends and in town I gave away all my medicine samples. Between there and the city, infected with a spirit of liberation, I drove along tossing out the car window all the printed advertisements from the lab I worked for. Not all at once. I would grab a few sheets of paper and let the wind carry them away, let them fly off and end up lying alongside the highway. I spent that night in Ciudad del Carmen and rested as I hadn't in a long time. I went into Zitilchén never to leave again. I wrote your mother a long letter explaining everything; I would keep supporting her but wouldn't return either to the laboratory or to live with the two of you. It wasn't easy for anyone, believe me. Not for your mother, or for Amira, or for me. I don't imagine it was for you either.)

[Angela, in a white nightgown, eating an orange in the kitchen. Barefoot. She wanders absentmindedly around the house and, when she reaches a door, she sticks her head in. Someone is asleep in one of the

---

Huach is a Mayan word used to designate an outsider, a Mexican who was born in another state (other than Yucatán or, in this case, Campeche). It has come to refer especially to someone from Mexico City.

132

hammocks. The other one is empty. Angela goes up and watches. She shakes the hammock lightly by one end. *"Rach, wake up. Lazybones."* He wakes up. He stretches. *"What time is it?" "Real late. It's nearly ten. Get up."* She tugs on the sheet. Rach covers himself.

"Go away," he had said. *"Go sit down to breakfast and I'll be with you in a minute."*

"Lazy. Get up," she had responded, tugging on his sheet. He covers himself again.

"I said, don't be a lazybones," she had told him, tickling him so he would let go of the sheet. He turns over in his hammock, laughing. *"Wait, wait."* Infected by his laughter, Angela keeps tickling him: *"Get up, get up,"* she repeats with a nervous laugh, playing around.]

She felt imprisoned by an immense helplessness. Her abandoned body let itself be carried along by the swinging hammock. She heard a creak, noises, footsteps. She half-closed her eyes and felt her body. The hot touch of hands took her by surprise. She lay still, with her eyes closed, her mouth open, feeling like she was falling toward herself the way a languid autumn leaf returns to the earth. The hands sought for her desperately, blindly. She let herself be kissed. All at once she saw two eyes like burning embers and heard the shots; she felt the hot blood mixed with sweat and with saliva, her bodily flesh and the bat's downward spiral, her chest burning and the soldiers firing on the students and her own tears in the midst of the shouting and the confusion of the night.

She is in front of the little, illuminated church. She turns right, toward the station, next to the theater. She passes the green foyer of the Baquieros' house, which always stood open. She looks toward either end of the park and recognizes the houses of the Negrón family and of Uncle Leandro, the Armenian's clothing store, the Alpuche family's corner shop, Don Armando's drugstore, and she can't hold back the tears once again falling freely down her cheeks.

Angela walks along with her eyes fixed on the station. It is nearly eight and the bus should be there any time now. The vendors come around to everyone. She waits standing up. At last a pair of lights appears along the main street that connects with the highway. The noise of the passenger bus interferes with the sound of the movie-theater loudspeakers, which, in her nervousness, she has stopped listening to. Some passengers get off: no one she knows. The ticket vendor asks her where she is going. It sounds like a joke. "Mérida," she finally replies. She nods, watching how they mark her luggage. The singsong of the vendors returns, like an echo across time: "Can-dy, o-ran-ges. . . ."

The driver is drinking a soft drink while she attentively waits in her seat. From the window she takes in the town with her eyes, looking at the dark little faces with lively eyes and the park full of innocuous labyrinths lined with flowers and bushes. How many nights has she strolled there. Sometimes she had gone with Rach to play bingo, and when there was some movie that appealed to her they would go to the theater, hurrying afterwards so they would get home by ten, when the village turned dark. One year. She had gotten used to the people, to their irony, to taking baths in the afternoon and dressing up every night. "The Flight of the Bumblebee" pulls her out of her reverie. People are still gathering in the plaza. The driver starts the bus's engine, unleashing a powerful, dry noise. Angela knows that, in this place she is leaving, her name will remain linked to the mysterious events of a night in Zitilchén. How she cried when they carried him away, bleeding, to the doctor, hearing the confused, anguished voice of her father saying over and over, "*This was an accident; don't worry, Rach; you're going to pull through,*" and then, turning toward her, reproaching her, "*I don't know how you dared do this to me. . . .*"

The bus leaves, crossing half the plaza, then heads up the street leading to the Mérida highway. It passes by the telegraph office, the Lions Club, the gasoline station, the last little straw huts, white and fragile, then it disappears into where the road is dark.

Translated by Cynthia Steele

Starting Over

Silvia Molina

Silvia Molina (Mexico City, 1946) has published short stories, novels, essays and children's books. Among her more recent works are: Dicen que me case yo *(1989),* Imagen de Héctor *(1990),* Campeche, punta del ala país *(1991) and* La leyenda del sol y de la luna *(1991). In 1990 Molina took part in the International Writing Program at the University of Iowa.*

to Saúl Juárez

One day I woke up with the question already on my lips. I asked my husband, as I threw off the covers:

"Santiago. Santiago, wake up! Are you happy with what you are?"

He pulled the covers up again and turned his back to me.

"Just tell me if you're happy with your life, happy with what you are right now."

"What a way to wake somebody up!" he countered.

"I want to know if you like being an accountant's assistant. Have you ever thought that you yourself might be the agency accountant? Have you ever thought of being something else? Of being different?"

At that moment the Santa Rita bell rang, for the six-o'clock mass. You see, we never had to buy an alarm clock. Santiago got up to bathe, leaving my questions hanging in the air. But I followed him into the bathroom and, while sitting on the toilet, I hit him with everything I could think of:

"Well, I'm not, Santiago. I'm not satisfied with myself. Since I've been sick and incapacitated I've realized that I don't like anything, not even my work: always teaching the children the same things, the 'important' dates of Mexican History, Article 123, the location of the states . . . putting up with that insufferable principal and the envy and gossip of the other teachers. You know what? I don't intend to return to that school. I dreamed that I didn't want to die without having done something I really enjoy."

The only thing my husband thought of was to ask if I was feeling well. Then he said:

"You look pale, go lie down and rest."

"It has nothing to do with resting. I want to change, to be someone else, the person I always wanted to be and couldn't be."

He stuck his head out from under the shower head and looked at me sitting there, such a poor little thing. Perhaps he was surprised by my complaint.

"For example?"

"For example," I answered, "I'm a teacher because it was the quickest degree I could get, so I could support my mother. But now I'm willing to admit that I never liked it. And I couldn't even support her, because my entire check used to fall into the hands of the man who was going to be my stepfather. I wanted to be a biologist, to look through a microscope and see bacteria moving around, microbes dyed blue, yellow or green. To draw amoebas like we used to do in elementary school, or cells...to see how many shapes they take. But she would say, 'Those professions are for daring girls, who have more opportunities and a better education.' She always put me down. And yet, now that I've been undergoing all these tests I've realized that I envy those young women who spend their time in front of beakers, droppers and little tubes, observing strange beings that twist and palpitate when you pour something on them. I can tell you this because they let me look one time, now that they all know me so well. Don't you think that with my white robe and mask, I could take the place of any one of them?"

"Picking up other people's shit," he said with contempt.

And I told him that he was being contemptuous of me. And that I was no longer willing to go on just putting up with everything and never complaining, not speaking out when I felt like it, not demanding to be heard, not making my own decisions. That I was no longer willing to lead a colorless life, confined by the name somebody else gave me, along with a particular way to be.

"I'm that way," I assured him, "because that's the way they told me to be."

"Well, what are you?" he asked, grimacing as if he was facing a scorpion.

136

"I'm like that. Don't you know me?"

"Like what?"

"Well, always thinking that life is what I'm living, what they taught me. Without having suspected that there were other things that I could change. I wanted to have a child because I learned that that was how it had to be, because all of my friends were looking forward to the day when they would buy a little cradle, knit camisoles, embroider bibs. When they told me I would have to have a hysterectomy I was terribly frightened. How was I going to tell you? When I was going to end up only half a woman. And I felt guilty for not being able to give you that little girl you always talked about when we made love."

My husband began to shave hurriedly, ignoring what I was saying.

"I'm talking to you, Santiago, listen to me," I told him.

Do you know what he said? That he had talked to his mother, that she was coming from Coatepec to stay a few days with us, that he had told her that I was not well, that I needed help around the house, someone to keep me company in case I have to have another operation.

"That's precisely what I don't want, Santiago. I don't want your mother to come and tell me how to make chick-pea soup, how I should wash the collars of your shirts. That's what I'm trying to tell you: I'm no longer willing to put up with family dinners, to have to look into the face of that nincompoop of a brother of yours who always manages to find an excuse for lowering your paycheck. If your mother shows up I'll run her off."

My husband left the bathroom, slamming the door behind him. And, do you know what? I didn't even cry. Any other time I would have. Often, when we fought I would. And what's more, he would always say:

"Is that all you can do—cry?"

That morning I realized that I really was going to try, somehow, to change my life.

I met my husband the day he came to my school to apply for a job. Just by chance I took down all of his personal information. The principal's secretary had not come to work that day and I was in the office to help out. When I got to his physical description I said everything out loud while looking at him:

"Black, curly hair. Large, black eyes. Strong nose. Thin lips. Robust complexion. Your height?" I asked him.

"Five feet, eight inches."

"Age?"

"Twenty-six."

"Identifying marks?"

"I have a mole here," he said, pointing to his right hip.

I blushed and then smiled.

"You look prettier that way," he told me.

"Come back on Monday," I said.

He came on Monday but only to tell me that he had found a job with a travel agency that didn't require as much information as a little old school that hadn't even been accredited by the Ministry of Education. And to tell me that he had come to invite me out to dinner.

In the restaurant he asked me to begin looking for a place to live because by December, to our mutual delight, we would be getting married. I told him that he was crazy, but now you see . . .

He was always happy, refined, and had no bad habits or vices, and he was never apathetic. He would always fix the iron and the radio and the television for my mother. He'd put a nail here, a lock there, he'd take the clock apart, change the propane tank and see what was wrong with the water heater.

We got married in January and the agency gave us a trip to Taxco and Acapulco.

To tell you the truth, it didn't really dawn on me that I was getting married. I don't believe I ever thought, "I'm going to get married." Maybe I was still a little in love with the gymnastics coach. On the other hand, my mother always had plenty to say about it:

"I found this espresso pot today when I went to the market at La Lagunilla. It's for your house."

That's how she began to accumulate things for my house: sheets, a tablecloth, two blankets, a set of Vasconia dishes, some Anfora stoneware . . . all with my wages, of course; my wages that I continued to give her every two weeks.

Before that, I wouldn't have dreamed of being a bother to my mother. While my father was still living with us it was different; everyone said we were a very close family. The only time I felt the closeness, that sense of family, was when we would go to Cuitzeo. Grandpa and Tatita would throw open the doors to us. They were fishermen, you see.

Tatita, my great-grandfather, would always tell me that, since he couldn't teach me to throw the fishing net, I'd have to learn to play the guitar. Sometimes at parties he'd make me sing. We'd practice for a long time during the evenings after he came back from the lake. He'd sing harmony for me, and I could tell he was so proud . . .

Later, I hated to go to Cuitzeo because that's where my father met "the other woman." We never gave her a name, she was just "the other one." I also learned not to use her name. That's what they taught me.

You know, up till then things just happened to me, and I always accepted them.

I know that a person doesn't change overnight. On top of that, you change but other people don't understand the change, and everything just gets more difficult and more complicated. My mother, for example. Guess what she said when she came into the room after my first operation. That I should thank God because children are a real bother. I'd like to be able to tell her how much she has hurt me, but I'm afraid that not only do I lack the courage to confront her but, actually, I'd like to see some expression of love from her, even if it's just a little. Then my mother told me how tired she was, how bored, about the material she had just bought that she was going to take to her best friend so she could make her a dress.

When my husband came in the room it was an entirely different situation. It was more like an abyss, like darkness, like glass shattering into a thousand pieces. At first he remained standing, right there, looking at me, as if he didn't know what to say. Then he came over and kissed me on the forehead.

"Maybe we can adopt a child, don't you think?"

"Maybe that's not the only thing I could have given you," I managed to say before the tears began to pour out of me.

Then he told me that at the agency they were going to give him a few days off with pay and some airplane tickets so we could go to Veracruz, to the beach.

Listening to him, I was sure that he was in more pain than I was from my cancer, from my sterility, from a rebelliousness that was beginning to take shape, because of the idea that I was living a life that I hadn't chosen. As if the light that I had seen when I opened my eyes, after the operation, in the intensive-care unit had penetrated me, telling me that I could change, that there would be other things more important than motherhood. I'd have to begin searching, changing. The problem was that if I stopped being that person I didn't want to be, my husband should give up certain things that he had never admitted were wrong.

It was not in his character to want things to be different. I think I already told you that he was a very good and happy person, that he was dependable around the house and that he was tidy in all aspects of his life. I would have liked, for instance, for him to make a clean break with his family. His mother was constantly coming from Coatepec, settling into our little apartment for one or two months at a time. And even then, it wasn't that I couldn't stand her. Her presence simply meant that everything ceased being the way I liked it: we could no longer live in the buff, move around in total freedom, decide where we might go or what we might do. If you wanted to watch TV, you'd have to be content with what the lady was watching. I got tired of smiling, of buying the best plums or mangos or apples for dessert. And the lady, just to "please," would reorganize the pantry and the closet. You'd no longer know where the salt was or where to find the towels. And if you went out to feed the sparrows the feeder wouldn't be where it belonged because "there's less sun on this corner," and you'd have to explain to her but that's where the rain gutter drains from the floor above.

When I left the hospital, change became my obsession. Santiago would attack me by saying:

"How stupid! You'll never stop being María López!"

That's my name. What they named me at birth, just María López. There's nothing special about it; actually, I've really outgrown it. It can no longer resist this power that's trying to shatter it, to blow to pieces and scatter all the vowels to one side and the consonants to the other. But I dream, you know, that the letters come back together and that María López takes on a new meaning, a unique María, different. A López with a round, prolonged "O," accompanied by a distinctive, renewed María.

My convalescence proceeded as if I myself had walked out onto a high wire stretched between two poles in a circus, as if I had told myself that being up there in the air, at that height, was just kid stuff. It was like being on tiptoes on that wire, scared to death because I couldn't do the most important thing, walk.

In a certain way it was starting over like when my father abandoned us. One day he said he was going to Cuitzeo and we never saw him again. Two months later, my mother gave his clothes away to the plumber. His only suit, his dress shoes, his navy blue tie and the felt hat he always wore to work.

I wanted to stop her.

"He's probably sick and that's why he hasn't returned. What will we tell him about his things?"

"Do you think he's coming back? He's probably with 'the other one.' There's nothing in this house that he wants."

"There's nothing in this house that he wants," became an echo in my dreams. To this day, I've never forgiven him, but it has nothing to do with the hatred my mother's family has for him. Really, he had the right to look for a woman who understood him, who understood his simplicity. He wasn't a city man. He was a fisherman who couldn't adapt to working for the Ministry of Commerce as Director of Services. He had the right to return to his lake, to look forward to a bed that awaits his return. My father had a right to all of it, except forgetting that I was there in that apartment pacing desperately from one side to the other, waiting for him and trying to give some kind of shape to a future without him.

During those years we lived in Tacubaya, on Avenida Jalisco, right across from that Canada shoe store. At night, the red, yellow and blue lights of the Canada sign would go on and off in our apartment. When it would light up our building it seemed as though my bedroom would take on a warmer, roomier feeling.

My dad had the habit of coming into my room early each morning to close the curtains and readjust my bedspread. Then he'd pat me on the back or he'd lay his hand on my forehead or he'd caress my hair while kissing me. Many times, between dreams, I'd sense his presence or I'd count his steps: from my bed to the window, from the window to my bed, from my bed to the door. He loved to walk. On Saturdays, for example, we'd walk to the Mixcoac market, just for the pleasure of walking. He would point out everything.

"Look, María, the District clock, it dates back to eighteen-ninety-five. Can you see it?"

Once he took me as far as the Del Carmen church, in San Angel, so I could see the mummies. He carried me all the way back on his shoulders while I clung to his thick head of hair. He constantly interrupted our conversation to greet his acquaintances: the hardware-store owner, the man from the paper store, the butcher, the woman from the fabric store . . . to a certain extent he seemed to live in Tacubaya as if it were his own town. And you might not believe it, but he always seemed to be proud of me. He'd bring things home to me from the office: pencils; little key rings with a picture of López Mateos, the presidential candidate; little notepads . . .

Once my grandfather came to take me to Cuitzeo. By then I was seventeen years old. I didn't want to go. Why? I thought that my father would reject me again. He should have come to get me himself, don't you think? I never saw him again. He doesn't even know that I got married, that . . . . Also, I suppose he doesn't care about me—he has his other daughters nearby.

I think the greatest shock to me was after I got the test results from the 20 de Noviembre Hospital, the very same day they told me and my husband that I'd need chemotherapy treatments. And that wasn't what bothered me, since from the very beginning they had pointed out the advantages and disadvantages of the procedure. What really happened was that Santiago came home that night drunk and, like a volcano, he erupted, he spewed out all his resentments, one after another, he hurt me terribly, he hurt himself without being able to help it.

Santiago only drank socially. He could hold eight or ten rum-and-Cokes without turning into the "party clown," like the television commercial used to say. He'd just get a little happy, but he never lost his good manners even when he was drunk.

It had been a long time since we had gone out anywhere to unwind, and we weren't invited out by anybody anymore. In other words, I believe we were alone too much. At the beginning of my illness, some of my friends and one couple that Santiago knew from before our marriage would come see us. My friends from the school where I worked and from the teachers' college had agreed among themselves not to let me be left alone. They would bring me mandarin oranges, grapes, chocolate cakes, cookies, daisies and carnations. They'd tell me all the gossip from work, about the principal, about the other teachers, about friends who were not present . . . until I'd get tired and they understood that I wanted to sleep.

But as I'm sure you're aware, when an illness drags on too long, people get tired of thinking about you, they become distracted and, little by little, other things come up, such as going to the movies, to Chapultepec Park, grocery shopping, taking care of their children, they just get tired.

That night I was up till three in the morning waiting for Santiago. The worst possible disasters kept running through my mind: that he had been mugged, run over. I even wondered if I'd have to relive my father's abandonment—after all, I personally relived my mother's desperation. Santiago never did that; I mean, just go off somewhere. When he returned I was in the bathroom. My swollen stomach required me to spend most of my time there, getting rid of every single drop of water that I drank. All of a sudden I heard the door opening. At first I felt relief and then, as you can imagine, I was like a battery of rage with a fresh charge. I had never seen him like that, like a limp dishrag. Where was his enormous, firm body, his strong arms, his robust legs, his straight back that my hands knew by heart? Where was that man who, that morning, had left home in a pressed suit and a clean shirt? We never did find out where he lost his tie.

I just sat there looking at him, burning up with anger:

"Here's your dumb wife, just waiting for you to come home whenever it suits you. Just look at you . . ."

Santiago cut me off in a hefty voice, in spite of his condition:

"I'm fed up with you, with your cancer, your pride, that idiotic idea that you do everything right, your fucking talk about changing. You're going to die, María. Can't you understand that? Can't you see reality?"

"Reality?" I said. "What is reality to you? We're all going to die, Santiago. Everyone. At any moment. You yourself could die before I do, even with your good health. Death is always near. I'm not afraid, Santiago. You are. That's the difference."

"But you've already been chosen, María," he insisted.

He let himself drop to the floor and leaned his back against one of the chairs we bought at Los Hermanos Vézquez. I sat down in front of him, trying to understand his loneliness, my own. Why was he giving in before even taking up the fight?

"Stop kidding yourself, María. Let people help you. Why don't you call your own mother if you don't want mine to come?"

Poor Santiago, you should have seen him. He was pulling at his hair and moving his head from side to side. He seemed to have crumbled inside from a single blow. To put him back together would have taken a long time.

Many times I tried to convince him of the harm that my family had caused me, especially my mother. What could I expect from her when, after a fashion, she had now achieved some sort of organization in her life? How could I make Santiago understand that while I had cancer I was still alive?

"One doesn't have to have four hands to make a bed or wash eight plates. Since I can't go to work I've been thinking about how I might study here, and someday I may become a biologist, don't you understand?"

"Son of a bitch," he yelled. "Don't you understand? You're building castles in the air."

"All right, Santiago," I answered. "Let's suppose that I'm going to die. How soon? Did the doctor happen to tell you the hour, the day, the month? I'm not just going to fold my arms. I'm not going to wait for death while stirring a cup of herbal tea. If I only have four days left I'm going to live them; if it's four months, then the same. If I live for four years that would be marvelous. More time to do what I never had the opportunity to do, because of my apathy, because I always believed in what they taught me: all my life was like being in school taking dictation in a steno pad, writing down what I should and shouldn't do. I don't care if other people don't like the way I am, I don't care what they say, what they think, what they imply. Now I've opened up a huge sketch pad and I've begun to draw a line that will carry me to the very edge of it, a line that will have whatever form I give it, while I still can."

"You're really screwed, María! You're screwed!"

I couldn't change his mind. He sprawled out flat on the floor, repeating and repeating the same thing, pounding the tile with his fist.

I had no idea where all my strength and anger came from. I could see how tired he was of me, how exhausted he was, as if his impatience was going to do away with everything all at once.

And yet, for me, time and everything else had a different meaning. I no longer yearned for night to come so that I could go to bed and stop thinking, to see only one dark wall, to wait for sleep to envelope me as if I were already dead.

Nothing hurt me more than seeing Santiago that way, suffering without wanting to understand anything, without so much as recognizing me, trying to deny me this opportunity.

I wanted to take him to the bedroom, make love to him, allow María López to become a furious torrent that was dragging a half-dead Santiago to the very brink of himself. I wanted my eager hands to explore his entire body; I wanted his hands to carry me to the precipice where I would become the flow that falls in an angry waterfall to where he was. But Santiago and I remained there alone, in the quiet night.

I took my pain pills and went off to bed thinking of Tatita, you see. All of a sudden the mind jumps from one thought to another as if one had nothing to do with the other, when, in reality, they are more related than you might expect.

The last time I saw Tatita, my great-grandfather, was in Cuitzeo when I went there with my mother. At that time my father had only been "missing" for two years. My mother was going to sign the divorce papers so she could marry my stepfather. I didn't like anything about that trip. Nothing. Going to my grandfather's house had always been a very natural thing to do: to be on vacation, settle down amid the disorder, go out into the orchard to pick fruit, chase the chickens all around the patio, never get tired of looking at the lake. That particular trip we had to call ahead: not this week, but next. We took every precaution not to run into "the other woman." Once we arrived in Cuitzeo, my mother sent a message ahead: we're here now, we'll be visiting.

144

We stayed at a guesthouse, and they didn't even give me time to get reacquainted with the town—the tiled roofs, the cobbled streets, the smell of clay . . . "María, you're the same color as Cuitzeo," my father used to tell me when I was a child. And we did all that without him even being there. They told us that he had come here to Mexico City because of an "emergency," and that he had left everything signed.

My grandfather came out to meet us. Before, we would just walk in. I don't know if you'll understand me, I was very apprehensive. But he hugged me as always. He picked me up: "Just look how cute and how big you've grown, María." Then he told me to go look for Tatita so that, as he put it, he could see me.

I found him on the veranda in a wheelchair, reduced to skin and bones. His gaze was lost out on the lake and he had an innocent look on his face. The Tatita I had left behind playing the guitar until the wee hours of the morning was now only an old, withered hide.

He didn't recognize me. He told my aunt who was sitting next to him: "Put a serape around Teresita, it's cold."

"I'm María, Tatita," I told him. "I'm María. She's Teresa, my aunt. I'm María, your great-grandaughter. Have you forgotten me already?"

My aunt Tere brought her index finger up to her lips as a signal for me to be quiet. But Tatita didn't pay any attention. He turned his childlike face and lost gaze back toward the lake. Who knows what he was thinking.

That's how it was becoming with Santiago—he couldn't see me. I was talking to him about me, but he couldn't even recognize me.

One Sunday when I woke up, I realized that Santiago had not come home to sleep. Somehow, it was as if I had been expecting that to happen. For weeks he had been acting strangely, he'd arrive late, he'd hardly speak, any little thing would upset him or he'd find any reason to quarrel. But above all, every time he had the opportunity he'd leave the house upset, slamming the door.

Upset, I got out of bed. I understood that I'd have to spend the rest of my life without him.

When I looked at myself in the mirror, I realized that something was slipping through my fingers. Even though I was willing to fight the cancer, I couldn't deny the effects it had had on me. It wasn't my paleness that bothered me or even those gray bags under my eyes. It was accepting the idea that the distance that had grown between us was now reflected in my face. If earlier I did not understand why Santiago would take the slightest excuse to pull back from me, I discovered the reason for it when I looked in the mirror. I had also begun to be another person physically.

I threw myself on the bed. I listened to the street noises, the car engines, the children's shouts from the nearby cul-de-sac, and I caught myself doubting for the first time. Could I transform my fate into something miraculous, from which happiness would spring? But something made me recognize in the street sounds the persistence of life, the continuity of it, as if for a second I had grasped my death with the tips of my fingers, so that I could admire it. Perhaps just as I had done as a child in Cuitzeo, when I would examine butterflies and then let them go and watch them disappear in their uneven flight.

And while I thought about life and death, a series of memories flowed rapidly through my mind. Nighttime in our little apartment in Tacubaya, with its intermittent red, yellow and blue lights, and a single shadow, in each corner, that symbolized the absence of my father. The hope that dawn might bring him back: maybe tomorrow, next week. Then I'm going to tell him. . . . He's going to hug me. The stiff, disturbing figure of my mother sitting in the darkness of the living room.

On the other hand, I remembered my grandfather's house, the clarity of the sunlight bringing into focus the abundance of objects, of vases, of flowerpots. Each object had its reason for being, according to my grandmother, who spent most of her time in the kitchen in her starched apron. These are cloves, María. That is cumin. Tatita's voice calling me, reaching out to me no matter where I was:

"Come here, María, let me show you this. I bought you this guitar in Paracho, you have to learn to play it. The person who can't sing can't love anything. Come here, child, come here."

And I struggled to try to forget my last memory of him: his lost gaze, the smile of a child. And I wondered how my father is: "The person who can't sing can't love anything." What does his voice sound like, is he gray now, is he thin, does he wear his wide-brimmed hat? Some day, some dawn has he thought of me, his little María, the first one he carried in his arms, the first he kissed, covered up at night, carried on his shoulders along Revolución Avenue, showing her that same Mexico City that he was discovering himself? And I was filled with hate, and anger.

Then all of my friends began to march through my mind, those who worked with me at the school, those from the teachers' college, my classmates from before. A list of names of the people in whom I could not confide my doubts, my resentment, the fear of holding in my

146

hands—for the first time—my destiny, no matter how advanced the cancer may be.

I wanted one, just one woman friend, one true friend to whom I could open up as I have with you whom I scarcely know. Do you understand now? At that time I would have wanted one friend who could gently squeeze Santiago's hand, who could be the bridge that would unite us across the impassable abyss separating us, one who could listen to him, too, because I recognized that he was even more lonely than I was since, without having understood me, he had called my ideas hairbrained and ridiculous, the only ideas that I could cling to life with. I needed someone to tell Santiago that it was not a lack of love that led me to leave him, that it was not contempt that forced me to tell him not to be afraid to accept his own challenge, not to be afraid to live, to allow me to live out my own fate.

Now you know why I don't want to see him. Please don't insist. He's come to tell me that everything will be *the same as it was* between us, that his mother has come from Coatepec to stay for a few days while I recuperate, that at the travel agency they've given him a trip to the coast, that if I survive this we'll adopt a child. Tell him that the woman he's looking for is not in this room, that there is only a María López who insists on starting over a second time, in order to bring the letters of her name back together.

Translated by Russell M. Cluff and L. Howard Quackenbush

In Secret

Mónica Mansour

For a biographical note on Mónica Mansour please see page 118.

Both of us arrived on time. To get a cup of coffee and chat. Among other things: "I'm always fighting with the literature teachers" (clink) and also "My wife says . . . " (clink). He paid the check and we left (clink again). We got into the car together. "Why do you smoke so fast?" "Because I'm happy." Silence.

We saw each other from time to time over the space of a couple of months. Clandestinely, it goes without saying, but not a lot. One day he called me at nine in the morning and at ten we met in the same park as other times. That day everything seemed somewhat different, odd. We didn't sit on the grass but instead on a bench and every so often a lone wanderer would pass by. He began the chat with a great coughing fit, which he followed up with a lengthy explanation of how sick he was and how bad he felt. He had a cold and a host of other sicknesses and complaints. I felt bad, uncomfortable, because I know what all that means. And the conversation kept on for a while with lots of interruptions. That's when I understood at last how this friend had written about a lot of things, about how circumstances make couples break off, but he forgot this one: after the sicknesses you told me a brief anecdote in which the most important part was the comment of a little girl: "If we don't go after him, we'll lose him again." At that moment I grasped what I hadn't grasped before: I wasn't there when you got lost, I never searched for you, I just found you one day. This is a form of breaking off too, but no one's written of it yet.

Bolting like that, and then you keep showing up everywhere at all hours, in this damned typewriter that I can't write a thing on, where I can only ask why you're not here anymore, why I didn't let you stay, why I didn't let you love me. And I cry.

Will I go? Yes. But look, I'll be late. I'll wait for you.

Hello. Both of us timid but content. And we talked about everything we'd done that day, as if each day we made a tally. I'm hungry. Let's fix something, come on. (And I always remember the day he told me that the difference between the working class and the bourgeoisie was that workers always shared their food, while the bourgeoisie only offered you coffee. And I always remember I told him that wasn't true, because my family is bourgeois and they make a kind of equation of food with affection.) We cooked and set the table and when at last we sat down he got a satisfied look on his face, as though he'd already finished the meal, he leaned back in the chair, lit a cigarette and started to laugh. The fact is I didn't understand and I had to ask, insist that he let me in on the secret ("He who laughs to himself is remembering his ill deeds," so they say). "It's just that I haven't felt this good for a long time . . . " He put out the cigarette and we started to eat.

He began to speak to me about you and then we made love: the age-old custom always new. A love silent in words. Afterward he told me many important things: a repertoire of sensations, distinct, dispersed, but always definitive. At times I thought I wasn't there with him, while he relived what he told. But at times yes, I was there with him: when I began to participate in those anecdotes streets houses bars in other countries and cities. And afterward he again talked to me of you. Silence after, then he started to laugh. But before I could ask him why, he'd already said it: "How marvelous life is. I'd like to tell everyone. What can I do to make everyone know how good I feel?" And then, "You give me back my sense of humor." It's true, I can see it's true: I'm your laughter, but when you laugh you fill my house, you furnish it, you decorate it in a different way. (I'm getting used to your laughter and sometimes I miss it. Sometimes it hides, it slips through my fingers, and I look for it among my records, behind the books, between the guitar strings, beneath the bed, inside my shoes. And all of a sudden it enters clandestinely and looks at me from the table, watching all my movements, each detail, each effort, and when I find it it makes me laugh and I think of you when you're with me.)

First I fell in love and then I fell out and now I only fall in love every time I see you. And all that because we're a love out of context, a love that never begins and never ends. It only exists when we're together. And for that very reason we can keep inventing lives trips music and whatever pops into our heads. All those things can serve as a pretext to keep you on my mind: I remember what we invent together and what we invent apart, and sometimes there aren't enough hours in the day to remember everything I can keep inventing.

It's such a great tenderness, thick as hot fresh bread, beckoning you to bite. Nothing about it is fragile, transparent, crystalline, delicate. No, nothing. It's like fresh sourdough: warm, soft, doughy inside; hard, crusty, ordinary on the outside. Its sensible presence there in the center of the table, in the daily breadbasket, as unperturbed as the return of the sun, brings a new day to each passing moment.

"I don't want to love her, but right now I love her a lot."
And then one daybreak those drops of wine trickled out of me.
At first you put on a brave front, but afterward everything seemed enormously in doubt. No, please not that: don't forget that tears say things deeper and wider than the size of someone's eyes: age-old custom forever new. Everything you imagine is true. Don't doubt any of it.

(No, it wasn't all the same to me, because your body, vulnerable and protected, wasn't there when I let a few hours slip by. No, because that's a death. And it surely must be mine, because you're up on your feet and walking.)

How would we put it? Kind of a tall guy, well-built, big hands, thin lips, a look or bearing sometimes sad in spite of the laughter. That's right: a frank wide-open smile, I'd almost rather call it a gut-busting guffaw. Shy all the same, very shy. At times an innocent, at times afraid without realizing it, even if sometimes he does know it. But always sincere: the face, the hands, the eyes give him away. Passionate in everything, though that too sometimes frightens him. Fearful and for that reason he wants to justify himself and offers lots of explanations. When he forgets his fear, he mixes up anecdotes with sentiments, sensations with memories in every word. He's one of those for whom there aren't enough hours in the day for living, so he recounts what he's lived while he's living something else and it all snowballs into a great present memory that moves along with him and widens with each of his steps, smiles, sadnesses, loves. It's not enough. He needs more time to live because he needs more time to feel the joy of what he's lived. He talks. He likes to talk a lot and each word speaks more than he knows. And then the words snowball. Phrases, anecdotes, memories grow out of him in all directions. And when they've grown huge he bursts out laughing so that he can begin all over again. Yes, he talks. It always seems as though he walks slowly to fully feel his weight on the earth, the ground beneath his feet. That's how he walks, that's how he laughs, that's how he touches me, that's how he fumes. In truth, he is a beautiful man, one of those you can't keep yourself from embracing.

"I'll see you on Friday, it should be interesting, make sure you go." I changed a few plans, canceled the rest, and went on Friday. I hadn't been around there for quite a while, and besides, lots of things had changed since the last time. I was nervous. I didn't know what might happen. I went in. I looked around and, sure enough, the first thing I noticed was that you were nowhere in sight. So I set myself to looking at the photos on the walls. Almost at once Berta arrived, took me by the arm, greeted me with effusive kisses and hugs. "I looked everywhere for your phone number. You can see the exhibition later. Come with me, let's go somewhere where we can catch up on things." Without letting go of my arm, she steered me toward the back. We went in and there you were with the others. I stood there not knowing what to do or say, but trying to act as natural as possible. "Good evening" was all I could think of to say. "Do you all know Mónica?" And before anything else could happen I said yes, almost without wanting to look, "Hello," and went into the other room. But I did manage to see your face, just as perplexed as mine, and smiling, as if you wanted to burst out laughing. She, warming to her role, came in after me and began to tell me the story I already knew, the story you'd told me a week ago, and that had already moved me, surprised me and filled me with indignation a week ago. All the same, I listened again, while I thought about how you, on the other side of the wall, also knew that I'd heard the same story. I tried to concentrate on not giving any indication that I was familiar with the facts (you'd arrived in the morning, tired, sad, nervous, anguished, and had let that story and many others flood out over me: every one that sprang to your eyes, your hands, but couched in laughter and anecdotes). But she suspected nothing, because she was so caught up in playing her part as well as possible. At last the little talk was over and we went out. You saw me, wanted to laugh, but only smiled.

I didn't know, in fact, what might happen. A week ago you'd arrived at my house without your laughter. That day you came and told me— with an effort, yes with a great effort, but also, by the way, as will happen when someone doesn't want to tell—something I had more or less already guessed. "As you've doubtless realized I've separated from my wife." I suspected something: numerous daily incidents you told me about you were telling me about for the first time; another day you said "I'm going to see the children so they'll know they have a dad"; another day you ventured that the ideal couple really could exist in this world . . . I suspected something, but to flatly say "you've doubtless realized" was an exaggeration, because I've always tried not to think about you except when we're together.

I didn't know, in fact, what might happen when we ran into each other in plain sight of the others, your friends. And suddenly you came up to greet me. We stood there talking for a minute and you told me you were sick. You'd already told me once before that you were sick and we didn't see one another for a long while after that. Friday you told me you were sick and you were preoccupied, but it wasn't the same. Afterward you went off somewhere. And I stayed, talking with the rest, and of course with her too: you stayed just long enough to see us both and then you disappeared. I laughed to myself thinking about what you might be thinking about: the crazy world, the topsy-turvy world. The thing is, it never occurred to you that we wives and lovers always have something in common, something important. And that's why we're always curious: to discover how we're alike and how we're different. And that's also why, in general, we get along . . . as long as at least one of the parties doesn't know the score. But you alone disappeared.

We went to the hotel we'd gone to before, the one with the velvet brocade on the walls and marble in the bathroom, that hotel that doesn't look like it rents by the hour and that, besides lovers, also lodges conventioneers and provincial businessmen, that hotel where we first got to know each other, that hotel where you insinuated your jealousy, smoking like someone on the lam, that hotel with parking so hidden and disguised that we didn't know about it ourselves and left our car across the street from the front entrance: what lack of experience in this sort of secrecy . . . We went to the hotel where we'd been before and there was no room. I felt a strange mixture of amusement, shame, anger and envy. Our inexperience hadn't helped us at all. We got back into the car, reflecting on the absurdity of the circumstances; without exchanging a word, it seemed obvious to us that bowing to the force of reality was a way of accenting the ridiculousness of it all. Therefore we undertook an odyssey in search of another possible shelter for a few hours. And after another frustrated attempt, we saw a gateway leading to a parking lot. Above it hung an illuminated sign that said "Hotel-GARAGE," and to one side of the lot an old building with a small door. We went in, me walking behind. A gloomy corridor with dirty white walls, in various states of peeling, that alternated with flag-green doors, shut or slightly ajar. About halfway down the corridor a space toward the right, a little counter and its corresponding petty employee. One hundred fifty pesos, señor (the other, as I recall, the one with brocade and marble, had cost more than twice that). Walking along a corridor filled with doorways, I felt so vulnerable, and I began to imagine someone I knew would start forth from one of those doors, but of course we'd all be in the same boat, best not to think about that. They took us to a door standing ajar that was in another corridor around the corner. It was green too, and could only be shut from the inside. He went in first and decided it wasn't very prudent to turn on the light, there was always the danger of unexpected surprises. It looks clean enough, he said, and only turned on the bathroom light. We undressed, slipped into bed and protected ourselves from so many corridors and so many doors. They say green is a soothing color, above all it soothes the sight . . .

You talk about spaces. No, that's not right, you speak of a single space. But suddenly I get the impression you don't recognize it. That space isn't in a place but rather gets invented leafily around us when we're together. As if it were sun, without knowing for sure, we forge it with hammer blows, ray by ray, to walk in dawn light every day. Do I miss you? Yes, I do. But when I come to myself I close my eyes and think about a highway, wide and long, and I set out walking at once, sometimes even running, and after a while I can open my eyes again and sit down to look at the other sun. Sometimes, walking along the highway, I see a mountain a tree a sea or the color of black or red earth, knowing that you'd look at it too, but I think on your highway there's also a mountain a tree a sea and lots of black and red earth. So I keep walking. Your presence doesn't hurt me, it burns like sun and draws itself on without rest.

In my zeal to put up a wall between you and me I came to a realization. Searching out bricks or inventing them doesn't lead anywhere. Besides, I don't like walls, I've never liked them. Now I have another solution, but we'll both have to collaborate: we'll turn our backs to each other and that's that. No peeking, no laughing, no crying over someone in public. If one of us lapses, the other must remind him or her of the rules of the game.

"I don't want to love her, but right now I love her a lot."

The truth is, me neither and me too. And you say, how do you know I'm afraid? If any of my pals read this he wouldn't recognize me. Well that's O.K.: me neither and me too, so I dare to write this chronology in secret.

Once a long time ago I wrote a story out of pieces of our matings and meetings and mutenesses, and that story lacked an ending, which should have gone like this:

One day I threw a party without really wanting to. Not because I don't like parties: on the contrary, I love them. But that day a get-together had been planned by a girlfriend who was visiting in my country; and she had this notion that everyone who spoke to me was a friend who should be invited to the party. So it fell out that the most diverse people got together in my house: friends, acquaintances, strangers; some I liked fine, others so-so, some I couldn't stand. What strange mixtures: enough to make anyone drunk. And that very strange night was, besides, the first time we announced ourselves in public. Yes, we already had a few accomplices, but that's not the same thing. The upshot was catastrophic: I got drunk and danced, you felt too good and too bad all at once, you wanted to leave but you stayed. And afterward you disappeared (again). What an ending!

In reality, it didn't seem an ending nor was it.

Next chapter: You came back, you talked, you wrote letters. Yes, you came back time and again, I felt between us that dangerous and ambiguous word called *love*, pronounced just the way it sounds, but I held my own. (Every time I write the word *love* to you I feel like I'm putting on airs: it's probably because my blood starts flowing the other way.)

Today I watched you cry and only wanted to touch your hand, take you in my arms for a long time and not say a word. But it was better to leave you alone in your confusion.

Months go by: they always go by. You with your other relationship, me with my other relationship.

One night — another night — we went to dinner. We talked a lot and I almost convinced you (and myself) that couples and all that stuff are a failure, a lie: you and I could never distance ourselves from those multiple and various truths. We came back to my house and out of that thick swarm of words we strung together brilliant and intellectual conclusions about our own selves: we wouldn't make love anymore, we'd been using one another; each of us would make an effort to have our own relations, separate and apart; we wouldn't see each other anymore, except in case

154

of emergency. Wow wow wow how rational and logical, what willpower . . . !

Let's just say that I never asked and you never answered. That is, I didn't know better and I proposed a game to you:

Let's say I was a bricklayer. And I began to build a beautiful pathway bordered by lots of trees for people to walk under. The paved pathway climbed up a hill and had dirt paths forking off it, which on one side led into the woods, and on the other led to a cliff with a river at the bottom. So people could sit underneath a tree on top of a big rock to talk or look at the same things, feeling the skin of the one beside them only as a nearby warmth.

Let's say you were a carpenter and that you were making a simple, lovely bridge with great planks, for crossing stony, inopportune haps and mishaps, without any need to go around them, and one would arrive in a short time at a conversation a year ago, on the way to Ajusco, underneath a tree, on a big boulder.

Let's say that I was building a well-protected fort with massive walls and that I was furnishing it with an absence that couldn't escape. And let's say then that due to a lack of light and air, I called on my carpenter friend to make a large hole in the wall and build a doorway so absence could go out and presence could come in.

Let's say the carpenter right away brought in some furniture, a clean shirt for after work and a bottle of wine. And that we then shared it.

Let's say that afterward we left together through the new door, and went down into the aquamarine sea and then later we walked around in the dawn and lay down in the middle of a forest of sun.

Let's say that you did want to play that game with me.

Months go by: they always go by. This time they were four, without us seeing one another or speaking, as if we didn't exist. Again we happened to meet by chance. Beautiful as always. And all at once I woke up. Fears and defenses, shocks and pretexts up to my eyeballs: in the end, what were they good for. One day not too long ago I went to have tests done for something that had been bothering me for a long time, they put my blood in a jar, and when they gave me back the results your name was written in red all over them.

I almost proposed to you love and marriage and . . . Well, it's just a saying . . . And yet, here I am before you: a poor witch who can't even see into the future one instant, that of your voice on the phone, that of your face at the door, while I start to construct a world taking for granted a fundamental rock-bottom: this love so thrown out of tune at just the wrong times. Only with you do such complicated worlds, contrary and contradictory, only with you do they all tend to the sea.

And still I ask myself, by what right could I suppose that love exists here? By what right do I incorporate you into a new and imaginary world? Was it perhaps some gesture of your hands or eyes? Was it perhaps some nostalgia whose tattoo was ingrained in your skin? Or was it perhaps some memory of mine that leapt out of time and came to manifest itself casually here between my sheets?

One day long ago, on account of the anecdote of a little girl, I thought there was a fundamental place where your world and mine connected: prison and exile. And that day (guilty) I thought I never searched for you, I only found you. Now I realize you're not here and I need you like the sea. I go out into the streets with three years weighing me down, I wander through them with my eyes peeled, I ask everyone who crosses my path, but I haven't found you. People don't answer, they don't know, they don't speak. I appear at open windows, on the porches, in the faces of your friends, but I haven't found you. People don't answer. Maybe I should begin visiting the prisons, but I've never had much faith in the word of men in uniform, they wouldn't tell me what your cell's like, they wouldn't give you my messages in inoffensive words that only you and I know because we've trod their earth before writing them down. But from here, from this gray asphalt that drags me through the city, I imagine your cell and your bars. I'm sure that in many ways your cell probably resembles the one that also sheltered me so kindly. And we already know the prison sentence determines the characteristics and the decorative scheme of the cell. Our crimes were very similar, a weakness for the loss of blood allowed them to trap us. But now I'm walking through these gray streets and searching for you.

Wait for me. I know that I'll find you. Don't worry if you don't receive my messages. Soon I'll arrive with our three years on my shoulders and between the two of us we'll care for them.

Now, yes, the ending for the story: you still hurt me.
No, better phrased: now you hurt me more than ever.
Now I'm afraid of having to return to fear.
In secret.

Translated by Johnny Payne

Dulce María Nuñez, *The Hand of God* (1990, oil on fiberboard)

Miguel Castro Leñero, *Anonymous Portraits* (detail; 1990, oil on canvas)

Miguel Castro Leñero, *Anonymous Portraits* (detail; 1990, oil on canvas)

A Woman and a Man

Vicente Quirarte

Vicente Quirarte (Mexico City, 1954) writes poetry, short stories and essays. He is also a translator and a literary critic. Currently he is a professor at the Universidad Nacional Autónoma de Mexico, where he obtained a degree in Hispanic literature. Among his books of poetry are Vencer a la blancura *(1979)*, Puerta de verano *(1982)*, Bahía Magdalena *(1984) and* Fragmentos del mismo discurso *(1986). He has also published a study of the Spanish poet Luis Cernuda, entitled* La Poética del hombre dividido en la obra de Luis Cernuda *(1985).*

A woman and a man can, for example,
go into a hotel (that hidden temple
that will appear if you only invoke it)
and love each other in broad daylight.

But a woman and a man should go
beforehand to a movie even if they never notice
what's happening on screen
and he stares at the peach down on her cheek
and she squeezes his thigh when she's frightened.
Or a woman and a man can
go out for a walk and his hand seems
an extension of her waist—or vice versa—
and then the rhythm
of the woman's stride slows
(because the only thing like this
is the sailing of a deep-water ship
on certain days in spring)

or pay for the coffee that's already cold
when their eyes and hands have said yes a thousand times.
And without even touching, fixing themselves up or speaking
a man and a woman can, finally,
go into a hotel and give each other their bodies,
leave the window open so that
the hot breeze from the parks comes in, and the memory
of those leaving the movie theater,
of the clinking of spoons against cups,
of the weak voice that is saying, "Yes, that way."

[Where the conch of]
Raúl Aceves

Raúl Aceves (Guadalajara, 1951) lectures on cultural journalism and is involved in research at the Centro de Estudios Literarios de la Universidad de Guadalajara. His works include a chapbook, Cielo de las cosas devueltas *(1982), and a book entitled* Expedición al ser *(1988).*

Where the conch of
yucatán/campeche/quintana roo
turns in the deep south of Mexico

and sinks in the warm pools of the blue caribbean

where the white cities of the mayas
the green cries of the jungles
the red suns of the macaws
foretell hot winds

a geography drawn by the earth
on its long way toward the coast

toward the ransom of the treasures sunken
where what's planted by the native is himself
himself is what he harvests, himself is what he awaits

Two Poems

Rubén Medina

Rubén Medina (Mexico City, 1954) is the author of Amor de lejos *(1986) and has been living in the United States since 1978.*

Priam

How hard it is, Father, to talk to you in these times
when it seems one no longer believes in anything
not even in the odor of a November night
and only with difficulty does enthusiasm leap from one's lips.
Now, instead of going out, as you did so often, to the movies,
you raise that brandy bottle to your soul.
Now, at fifty, when the rain won't stop
and there's no umbrella for covering your bones.
Now that after so many years in the factories
one comes to love one's work and to do it wisely.
And your children have grown with their bruises
watching you love and fall all the time.
Piece of sun. Burning tree.
Dancer who could make a good partner even out of a
      traffic signal.

A man who's made thousands of mistakes.
Now that life has been so long

but is still worth dancing like a *cumbia*.*
It is I, Father, whom you made sing ridiculous songs
those Sundays when we visited family.
Who cried in Chapultepec when there were electrical storms.
And who brought you lunch every day
at Hulera Americana, Inc.
And learned about strikes, cold early mornings and scabs.
And later used to look for you in the pool halls when you were
    laid off.
It is I, Father, whom you took to see movies
in which john wayne killed apaches and the audience
    applauded.
Whom you found purse-snatching with a gang
around the edges of a Metro station.
And who went to baseball every day and admired the middle
    classes.
It is I, Father, whom you and your friends
wanted to make into a man by calling a little faggot;
and then out of rebelliousness I kissed young men.
Because dialectic also has its whims.
It is I, Father, who wandered around the city with a guitar
while the army was patrolling the streets
and you moved out and Mother almost went mad.
And who dealt in passports and loved a girl
from the other side of town the way one loves the late
    afternoon.
It is I, Father, who spoke of Cuba, Vietnam,
the Communist Manifesto, and whom you used to view with
    compassion.
And whom afterward you found writing poetry
when you came home to visit.
Who ran away from every kind of work.
And later they came looking for the wives of intellectuals
while they were planning a revenge with pure language.
It is I, Father, for whom you went looking
at a bus station when I spent weeks staring at the clouds.
And who struck you in the face at the door of the psychiatric
    hospital

---

cumbia: a popular dance from Colombia

164

while Mother was looking at me with her ruined eyes like a
    saint's.
And who said, O.K., enough, and slept for weeks.
It is I, Father, from whose eyes sand is pouring
in the supermarkets of California.
And who lives with a woman who is a river.
It is I, Father, comrade of the dawn.
It is I, Father, your eldest son.
Let's go, get up, it's time to go home.

Poets Don't Go to Paris Anymore

for José Peguero

Oh Paris—May I ask what you do with the poets
who arrive from proletarian
slums?
Do you perhaps change hatred
into the old wine
of the aristocracy,
or do you increase the aching
in their shoes,
in their pants pockets?
Do they learn, these poets, mercybocoo,
or work as extras
in sci-fi films?
Do they watch Vallejo
go walking down the Boulevard Raspail
with his loaf of bread on his shoulder
and his sad donkey eyes?
And this, my friend, is the house
where Rimbaud and Verlaine
were two phosphorescent armchairs.
Poets don't go to Paris anymore.
They go from hospital to bar,
from street to factory,
from dance hall to office,
from friend to lover,
looking for Father Monday.
Renew the day of the rabbit,
the night of the resting elephant.
They get on buses
to last night
and there's no time for cursing the job,
the son, the daughter.
(Who needs shoes, Aztec boy?)
There's no time for games with flowers
and those baby Rimbaud dreams

at twenty
and women who have even told them their names.
Poets don't go to Paris anymore.
They're down in the South
where the war's still going on.
They're up in the North
where the plague has set in.

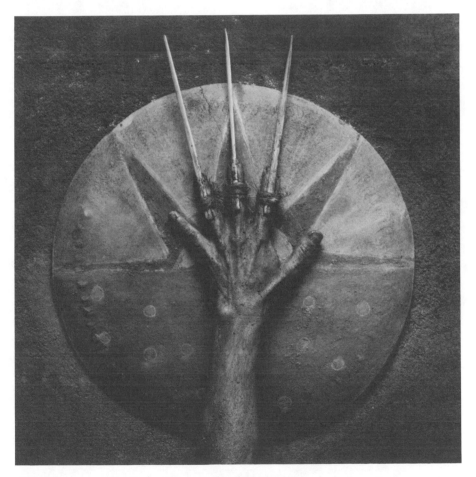

Gerardo Suter, *Codices: Tlapoyahua* (1991, silver gelatin print)

Nahúm B. Zenil, *Evangelist* (1989, mixed media on paper)

Virgins

Lucía Manríquez Montoya

Lucía Manríquez Montoya (Monclova, Coahuila, 1961), has published poems in a number of periodicals. This poem was anthologized in the 1990 poetry annual published by the Instituto Nacional de Bellas Artes.

Virgins have set up a whorehouse
in which cringing and crouching are prohibited

there is purity in the marble chambers
and the divans have about them an air
of withdrawal

on none of the women does the duration
of her continence show
nor her rank as voluntary dove

none wears the expression
of an admonished churchgoer
or feels she has to walk on tiptoe

god comes in
and they put a carnation
in his lapel

Jesus, May My Joy Be Everlasting

Severino Salazar

Severino Salazar (Tepetongo, Zacatecas, 1947) is the author of the novels, Donde deben estar las catedrales *(1984),* Llorar frente al espejo *(1989),* El mundo es un lugar extraño *(1990) and* Desiertos intactos *(1990). "Jesus, May My Joy Be Everlasting" is from* Las aguas derramadas *(1986).*

I

When Adelaida Avila died of old age, all of us in Zacatecas thought this meant the end of her house, that house up on top of that hill, forever sitting there as if exchanging glances with the city day in and day out. That house through which so many of us women had passed over the years. But no, the house had more to say on the matter. Tino González, her successor, brought new life to the house and reopened it a few months later with the savings of the deceased Adelaida Avila, who had been his mistress, though in name only. Tino González did not serve her as a man, for he had been rotting ever since his youth; he only—and this he did do—protected her and managed her business. Now the house was smelling of fresh paint and recently bought furniture; it shone once again above the same hill. And the man had given the house a new attraction: he extended the bar onto the terrace, enclosed it with windows—wide, tall windows that reached the lofty roof and looked implacably onto the city—and built an enormous dance floor of polished cement that looked like water, and a raised section for the band. On Saturdays there was music and dancing all night long; the gaiety lasted until the crowing of roosters

170

and the light of dawn began to encircle the house. By that day and age the Zacatecans knew perfectly well how to behave in a place like this. They didn't start fights or cause a ruckus: they minded their business and we all had a good time there. But suddenly, who knows from where, Don Tino González pulled out a dancer and singer, complete with husband. Some say they arrived from the north, although when they showed up in the brothel, no one cared where they were from. (The conjectures all began when the man disappeared and the woman no longer sang or danced.) From the moment she set foot on the dance floor of the house now belonging to Don Tino González, she was received enthusiastically and all the men wanted to see and hear her. She sang on Fridays, Saturdays and Sundays. The singing lasted the whole weekend, stopped on Monday, and began again the following Friday. Her fame quickly raced through the state. She attracted people like a powerful magnet no one can resist, no matter how far away you are. Zacatecas is the hub of many highways and has many attractions like its movie theaters and its awfully big stores. Which is why it wasn't long before she had to sing and dance every night. Don Tino González's house was always packed on the weekends; by midnight there wasn't even room to breathe. The girl singer's husband was a boy not more than twenty-three years old, dark, tall and thin; well-formed, sinewy muscles; large, veiny hands; large eyes as well, elongated, with a sad gaze, although he always had a smile on his lips. He didn't have eyes for any other girl, although it was not rare for the girls of the house, behind his wife's back, to try to seduce him. And he would get rid of them as if they were a necessary evil, as if he were accustomed to this happening, and would leave them with a look of boredom on his face, not letting anything disturb his inner world. There was even a woman who became obsessed with the boy—it never fails—the one named Cristina. She longed to get rid of the singer and take her place, supplant her in the world that contained the two of them, but, disillusioned that she was unable to achieve any success and certain that she could not bear to suffer seeing him every day, so close and unattainable, she decided to leave for Fresnillo, to go to another house she knew there which was frequented by young miners who looked a lot like him, to keep her life from growing sadder. And she went to search, among the men leaving the mine, for a man like the one she had set eyes on. You could see from miles off that Ildefonso—that was his name—was in love with his dancer, whom they announced every night as Terry Holiday. It seemed as though he was always thinking of her even when the two of them were together, as if imprisoned by an insatiable love, as if that woman, her music, her words, her movements, and her rhythm were forever spinning around in his head like brilliantly colored butterflies. He was looking in her direction all the time—on the dance floor, seated at a table, or wherever—while he prepared the drinks and snacks consumed there. He was the one who gave orders to the waiters and made sure that everything ran smoothly at the bar and in the kitchen. But one thing is for sure: he always had his eyes on his wife. Not as if he were watching over her, because she didn't have eyes for other men either; the looks they exchanged back and forth were not tainted with jealousy; they contained a confidence the Zacatecans found hard to comprehend. They lived in their own world and carried with them, wherever they went, invisible threads that always held them together. No one was ever able to penetrate that universe, so small and yet so large, or to break those bonds, so strong and yet so fragile, especially given the place. They lived here, in two modest rooms at one end of, and nearly detached from, the ranch house. They slept nearly the whole day through and would arrive at the dance hall just after eight, the two of them holding hands, fresh and recently bathed, the woman dressed to sing and dance three sets until four in the morning. She was tall and dark as well. Someone said they looked like twins. Along with the legend of being a good singer and dancer, another one spread that she was an incorruptible woman; perhaps that was the root of much of the fascination she aroused in those who came to see her dressed scantily and with two large, pink ostrich feathers adorning her head. I never took a liking to that woman. She seemed very distant. She would look at us as if we weren't for real, like a fish from inside its fishbowl, or from inside death itself. Who did she think she was? She never spoke to us or told us her sorrows, or let us tell her ours. As if we weren't equals, as if we didn't live off the same thing and in the same place. Her songs spoke of an inner world— violent, delicate and beautiful, fragile as the perfumed flower of a prickly pear that grows and spreads its petals onto the spines pointing up like swords—that made her body writhe on that hot, smoke-filled dance floor redolent of liquor and pierced by spotlights. Music, love, passion and gaiety were the elements that made up the atmosphere contained within Don Tino González's house, behind which passed the pilgrims who climbed the hill every night. And through Terry Holiday, it was as if each person discovered his own separate world, that world that had remained undiscovered for so long. Terry and the boy were very young—we were all very new then. They were just beginning to enjoy their lives; each had the other and the two of them were one. You could see that fate was shining magnificently on them. If anyone had asked them if they wished to be more or have more in life, they would have looked at each other in puzzlement, for they never would imagine that a human being could come to feel such tremendous uncertainty. Tino González's house was the place to be. That's the way things were until one night, when General Aniceto López Morelos appeared. Then our lives all took different paths.

172

II

(They would say to me: Florentino, tell us how General Aniceto López
Morelos turned up here, during the *cristero* rebellion.* Someone would
always ask me when we'd be standing here at the entrance to Tepetongo
and we'd see him going to Zacatecas or going back to the Víboras
Hacienda to the south. This town had the cursed luck to have suffered
him so nearby, with only a long irrigation canal to separate us from him,
and the road that skirts the canal leads right into the center of the
hacienda. Well, to fill you in on a little bit of history, there we were
fighting in the rebellion as it neared its end. First, General Montalba
arrived in a train to Calera. No sooner had he got his troops out of the
boxcars and cattle cars than he was defeated. The brainless fools
propped their machine guns on mules and fired them like that. The poor
animals, like pinwheels gone crazy, rushed at their own soldiers, firing
on them: they defeated themselves. As one might expect, they had sent
for him from Mexico City, and that's when, a little while later, Aniceto
López Morelos arrived like one of those tornadoes that brings bad
weather in its wake. He came in by the Valley side, killing people to his
heart's content, already sowing the legend of cruelty and terror that
would follow him to the grave. He was a wicked person with no remorse.
As he made his way, he burned entire towns to the ground, killed many
priests, and finally tortured the priest Juan Chorrey without mercy,
revealing what the imagination of a depraved man is capable of. He was
an example of villainy, of what the the devil himself would do, for by all
indications that man was possessed by the devil. He made us tremble
and reflect a bit on the evil running loose in the world. He came to the
Víboras Hacienda driving everything he had rustled along the way. The
last remaining daughter of the owner of the hacienda joined him. I think
it was more out of fear and to keep from losing what she had. And since
she was a woman already advanced in her years, she soon vanished from
the earth. She was buried in the beautiful Víboras cemetery, where all
her ancestors lay. Legend has it that the old man frightened her to
death. In any case, the general remained in charge of this zone, previously one of the most rebellious in the country. And he was soon feared
throughout the region. One of the men who also arrived with him was
Salvador Chávez, nicknamed "Cowboy," but he only lasted two years,
thank God. Imagine what it would have been like to suffer under two
men as evil as them, for the so-called Cowboy was like the general's twin

---

cristero rebellion: a clerical antirevolutionary uprising that began in 1926

brother, his right-hand man, just as mean and heartless. He had helped the general fight the *cristeros* and rustle the cattle with which he filled the pastures of the hacienda: dairy cattle, fierce bulls and herds of horses. There were so many cattle they were coming in from all sides: stolen, I used to say, from nearby and from very far away. General Aniceto López Morelos's appetite knew no bounds. And there would always be the person who came to claim his poor lost animals. All those people would mysteriously disappear. There are people buried all around Víboras. Nor could anyone enter the pastures: they were tightly guarded by his soldiers. From then on, his was the arm of the law throughout these parts. He installed the municipal presidents and his vote was very important in deciding who the governor would be. The prison in his barracks was empty: capital punishment was always the only sentence. He was feared throughout the region; he desolated it. There weren't even thieves around anymore. We were at peace, the truth be told, but you couldn't even take a deep breath. He was a thief himself and couldn't stand to look at one. He didn't forgive anyone anything. Miraculously, one man escaped his soldiers and tells that a mile or two behind the walls of the hacienda is a thick, black wood, and everywhere men are hanging from the trees, some nothing but bare skeletons and others with a few shreds of clothing still stuck to them. And the man who visits a landscape like that never makes it out to tell the tale. In short, this general was such an outlaw that he even stole heaven, but that's a horse of a different color. In any event, Cowboy helped him a lot in constructing his world, his empire. When we *cristeros* were finally given amnesty right there in Víboras, we came down from the hills to hand over our animals, saddles, bandoliers, rifles, ammunition and all our gear. Cowboy filled a granary with all that stuff, and we went back to our places of origin, by streets and paths. Some disappeared once more over the hills. Until one day when Cowboy was running around drunk—he too was full of vices—and like a revelation he got this hunch: the general was going to get rid of him. So, as the general was out around Zacatecas, Cowboy availed himself of his absence to steal some horses and other goods and take refuge in the sierra, declaring himself a rebel. Actually, no one ever figured out why he did it, since the general held him in high esteem; he would have forgiven him anything, for he felt a strange love for the so-called Cowboy, the kind that is only felt in prisons and between criminals. In any event, more men joined up with Cowboy every day. He would ride between Víboras and Tepetongo in the middle of the night and we would scarcely even know it. I'm sure that on those nights the general would sit up in his bed listening for him to pass by with a touch of fear and joy, going over the crazy moments of their friendship. Cowboy knew the whole state and its mountain ranges like the back of his hand. No army could have beaten him. Until one of his own men betrayed and killed him and the band broke up. Meanwhile, the general's fortune was taking on fantastic proportions. It was said he had safes brimming with everything he had stolen and now what the hacienda produced, for he made soldiers on the state's payroll work his land and take care of his cattle. Until a soldier arrived whom they called "Boss." He was a tall, thin man, with small eyes and red hair. And he certainly sized up the general. A friendship began between them that we found inexplicable. The general held him in very high esteem, for he had arrived at his moment of greatest need.)

III

By then, the general was an old man. Squat, fat and beardless, his face shone like the blackest patent leather. His hair was short and thick, graying, and so straight it lay flat; his voice was sly and shrill like a woman's. And he was unable to say more than three words in a row without sticking in another three curses. General Aniceto López Morelos had never set foot in the whorehouse despite the fact that he spent the night in a hotel in Zacatecas all the time. I had paid a visit with the sergeant and other soldiers shortly after being sent to the barracks here. What would be the point for a man like him, who could have any woman he chose at any hour of the day or night and fill his hacienda with them? But that very day we had arrived in Zacatecas in pursuit of this other woman who had left him. The thing is, that poor old guy, he couldn't even get it up anymore. She was a really pretty girl he had stolen from a store in Jerez more than two years earlier. Everyone in Víboras said that the old bugger was really in love, because he would take her wherever he went and even showed her the combinations to the safes, dumb as a doddering fool. One day he caught her in Boss's quarters and we all thought this was going to be the end of the so-called Boss and his old lady. But no, the general forgave them. And afraid that she was going to escape with the soldier, he became very friendly with the two of them. That's how we discovered Boss's real duties, why my general loved him so. But in the end, she didn't run off with Boss, but with another soldier who truly loved her—who risked everything—taking with them a bag full of money. They were nowhere to be found in

175

the hacienda when the sun rose, and they left no trail. The general ordered Boss to bring us to Zacatecas, and he put on the ring he used— so he said—to banish sadness. The diamond in it was huge. We crossed Tepetongo, Jerez and Zacatecas by jeep, followed by another truck filled with soldiers. My general was in search of a woman he loved and who had left him all alone. We didn't find hide nor hair of her. At night, since the old man was depressed and feeling sad all by himself and it was a Saturday at the end of September, he asked us to take him to Tino González's new house. "I want to remember Adelaida's empire," the old queer said. We got there around eleven at night. The place was packed with customers. All the tables were taken. Don Tino himself had to put a table practically on the dance floor where the general, Boss and three of us sat. Moments later the lights went out and the band stopped playing. A trumpet announced the singer and dancer, lit up in the middle of the floor by a spotlight of the whitest white. "Here is Terry Holiday! . . . " a smooth voice full of enthusiasm was saying into the microphone. There she stood—one arm raised over her head in a gesture of greeting to the audience, smiling, showing two rows of nearly transparent teeth, so white and perfect. She was slim and extremely tall, her height exaggerated by her high heels; her skin was smooth and the color of cinnamon, her dark hair fell in jet black waves over her shoulders, too wide to be those of a woman. Her hips were small and her breasts too, hidden by the lace of the silvery dress which hung in two strips—one in front, one in back—and barely held together by a metallic belt. She had that air women have today and it made her resemble the one who had left the general. Accompanied by the music, Terry Holiday covered the floor singing and moving her body in time to the melody, to the words of her songs. The movement of her body, her words and the music were all one and made each person's heart leap with joy inside his chest; beautiful and profound sentiments rose to the surface of our skin and all of life, in a flash of lightning, felt easy and beatific; everything suddenly became happy and full of life. The woman, singing and dancing, caused us all to look only at the good side of existence. After seeing her perform, anything could happen, as if life came into focus for a moment, like in the center of the barrel of a gun, and one could pull the trigger, die with no regrets or go on living. . . . The world of all that is distant and impossible looked close and possible; the world of fear and hate, it was like they were wiped away forever. The general was moved, he seemed beside himself; only his beady eyes where shining with sheer enjoyment. "I feel the same yearning as when I met my first wife," he told us soldiers. "You, go tell Tino that I want to have a chat with that

176

chorus girl," that dirty old man said to me, staring at the diamond on his ring as if in a trance. I waited for the artist to finish her number. Through the smoke, the reek of alcohol, the music, and the light, her body moved like the body of a fish. I went right up to where she was standing. She smiled at me and I told her that the general would be honored if she would join him for a bit. She looked at the old man's table and then at me. With her head she said yes. A while later, there she was chatting with him. But before anyone knew it, he was suddenly holding her hand. She wanted to free herself and was struggling, looking toward the bar. All of a sudden, her man leaped from behind the bar; next thing we knew he was standing in front of the old man and punching him right in the face. In less time than it takes me to tell you, it turned into the Last Judgment. Chairs and punches were flying and we were getting out from under everybody. Boss fired his gun once and somehow calm was restored. Don Tino's house began to empty, like someone letting the air out of a balloon. Everyone left except for the body that lay stretched out in the middle of the dance floor; the spotlights that previously made Terry Holiday dance, now bathed him in light, like a dead fish at the bottom of a fishbowl. The dead man's blood covered the diamond of the ring, which rolled on the floor without anybody noticing. We immediately left with the general and Terry Holiday for the Víboras Hacienda. And there were those who, from that night on, never set foot again in that house on the hills overlooking Zacatecas.

IV

Since the trip from Zacatecas to the Víboras Hacienda is long and takes nearly three hours, to pass the time I began counting the shooting stars that night. But the noise of the truck in which we were escorting the general made me drowsy. I couldn't stop thinking about Terry Holiday and what she had sung during those two hours. In my imagination, I was still seeing and listening to her, her voice so clear over the monotonous hum of the motor. It's said that she and the boy wrote her songs together. And this night, she had started to sing a new song in front of the general; it spoke of a man who is sowing and finds an untended plant thriving among the furrows of his field, with thorns that enhance its beauty. But the sower takes a stick and, full of rage, destroys the plant, just because he has heard that the sap flowing through its stem is poisonous. But the plant is there, thick with beautiful and untouchable flowers and it does no harm to anybody: not to the insect that spends its life running over the surfaces and byways of its stems and leaves, nor to the rodent or lizard taking pleasure in its shadow and protection. It adorned the landscape and was in harmony with all of nature. Then there was another of her songs, a while back, which she brought down from her house and began singing to all of Zacatecas: "A Moment's Love." It was a melody people whistled in the streets, sang in the cantinas and hummed at home. It spoke of a flower that opened its fragile, iridescent petals in the morning, as if it too were a tiny piece of the sun, and was extinguished with the day itself, with nightfall. Then it went on dying all night long, never to open again. The memory of that flower, so ephemeral, caused a suffering greater than its entire existence. The song ended with a question posed by the singer amidst desperate cries that could not be consoled: why was its death longer than its life, and why was its memory more fragrant?

That very night, Terry Holiday vanished for all of us—or did we all, along with the general, make her disappear? She vanished with her music, her movements, like the fragrance and the flower of her songs, that flower that only lasted while the day was light. Extinguished with her was her voice and the song I liked the best. The one that said that love is like building an avenue of crystal cathedrals along the pathways of the soul, and then, when it goes, we are all like the city: we carry an immense glass cathedral deep in our soul, but so fragile, perhaps so ephemeral. Later, that memory accompanies us throughout life, like the ghost of a cathedral that had stood within us.

That song made me remember how, whenever we passed in front of the cathedral, the general always had the jeep stop for a moment, and from his seat he would look at the facade and then at the towers and would say to himself, almost secretly: "What a marvel, what a marvel. . . ." And since the general was not a believer, we didn't understand what he was saying. But I did know that if he had lived during the time when the cathedral was being built, he would have been one of the slaves working to the tune of a whip. You could see from miles away that he was nothing but a thick-soled Indian.

V

It was just about dawn when we went to sleep in our tents with the novelty that an early frost was moving over the pastures and orchards of the hacienda. As we arrived with Terry from Tepetongo you could already see the irrigation canal, which almost rings the hacienda, letting off this cold vapor which the wind was sweeping slowly over the fields and which wound through dead corn stalks and the trees and gave the night a leaden, mysterious quality. The water in the troughs in the corrals had hardened. The cows and calves were lowing sadly, as if holding a mournful conversation from pasture to pasture through the darkness; the horses were stamping the ground, restless in their stables. Dawn would find the fields of oats and wheat plastered to the ground, the frost-burnt trees would drop their tiny fruit, festering water as if the whole countryside had gone slack, as if Nature had suddenly lost all her strength. . . . But that same morning—before the sun rose to melt the petrified water and make it circulate again through the canals, to animate the world, which for a moment had remained paralyzed—prompted by a sudden hunch, the general made a decision before dawn: to get rid of Boss, at any cost. He simply told him, without any explanation, to leave the hacienda and his life forever that very day and never return; that he no longer needed either a driver or an overseer.

VI

We got the news from Tepetongo: for one reason or another the general didn't like her anymore; but it didn't strike them as particularly strange over there because they knew the general was an infamous man. So the soldiers had amused themselves with her the whole night, until one of them had the idea of taking her to the dam and throwing her in the water naked. The night being very dark, they lost sight of her and thinking they had drowned her, went back to the barracks feeling somewhat disappointed because the amusement had ended so suddenly. What the people of Tepetongo found strange was that the general never had forgiven anyone before, and he had actually let Terry Holiday escape him, God only knows why. They said that something was not quite right with the poor old man. Now, many years later, she walks around Zacatecas altogether changed, asking for coins with the other beggars that scour the train station and the bus terminals. But even so, every Saturday she would come to Don Tino's house (which, even for us, wasn't the same: we were older women, ourselves; we had fewer and fewer customers). Very few people dared to make the climb up here, for it cost a lot to get drunk; also, they said they would leave the place feeling depressed. And even though a few years have passed, Terry Holiday still comes by, still visits us; she hasn't forgotten the way, the slope that leads her up here. Her bust shriveled up or she never really had one, a few long hairs have grown out on her and they're starting to spread over her chin and jaw. She still wears that dress with faded sequins and her feathers too, now discolored. And she sits here very straight for a few hours, proud and sure of herself—beautiful and mysterious like a cathedral in ruins—with a brandy on the rocks in her hands, smiling undoubtedly at her memories, as if no time had passed and she was just waiting for the moment to go out and sing on the dance floor. You can still sense in her the presence of a different kind of woman—how should I say it?—aristocratic and refined, yes, respectful, polite; but decrepitude and decadence make her a sad, poignant figure who, for those of us who watch her, shakes deep inside us the scales we use to weigh life. Sometimes, smiling, she gets up from her chair and starts to sing in that horrifying voice that lacks all tone and rhythm the story of a man who was sowing seeds and who cut the flower off a thorny plant with his stick because people said it produced poison, or the one about a flower growing in a jail cell, or the one about a city filled with crystal cathedrals. Then she sits down and looks around; her face tells us that she is looking at that other time in the past, and when she has finished her drink, the expression on her face changes, as if the drinks have brought her clarity and she realizes that she lost everything: she lost her youth, she lost her Ildefonso, she lost her love, and all this made her lose her mind. She is completely adrift, perhaps forgotten by God, if it's possible for God to ever forget anyone. It's the first time I've laid eyes on someone who had no attachments to life. And I've seen my share of people passing through this house. You can see how evil has marked her: her body is the battlefield for nothing less than the war between evil and life. She cries without the tears running down her withered face, she cries inward. And before it gets any later, she leaves the place very slowly, without saying goodbye to anyone; she goes back to the city alone, perhaps ashamed of having dared to come and rummage through her memories. She begs her way through life, collecting the necessary money to come on Saturday. And on those days she leaves me wondering: "Why get so upset? Why look for things in life that aren't there? Why go crazy over life trying to find them?" Terry and all those men who come here for my company and who frequent this house make me dizzy with their comings and goings, the way the pigeons must make the towers of the cathedral dizzy. Life, after all, is what goes on between the pigeons and the stones of the cathedral.

VII

General Aniceto López Morelos passed away one afternoon—a cloudy afternoon swept by the cold wind of late November—in a city hospital in Zacatecas, many years later. By then he had long forgotten one of his greatest crimes, one that still has not come to a close. As his misdeeds had become increasingly sporadic and less obvious, by the time he was an old man there were people who truly loved him. He died attended by nuns and doctors to whom he gave great sums of money and other favors. But in Tepetongo there was a man who never forgave him, for he had been the victim of one of his crimes. And that same man commented on the very day of his passing: "The general was such an outlaw he even stole heaven." All because he knew that at the hour of the general's death a group of nuns were praying around his bed. And from the cathedral, in the afternoon, a melody spilled out that invaded the city like a very fine perfume: a choir accompanied the organist who endlessly played "Jesus, May My Joy Be Everlasting" with all the stops out on that monumental organ. And it wouldn't be surprising if one day in the not so distant future the state came up with the idea of erecting a statue in his memory. But, fortunately, these poor eyes won't see that day.

And so Adelaida's old house and the three human beings who were bound up in its story are dying out. Many small details and doubts that were raised later, when the events had grown cold, were never cleared up. Only that, the day after they stole Terry Holiday from Zacatecas, a man arrived naked in Tepetongo very early in the morning; he was badly beaten, wounded and covered in mud, freezing to death and begging for human compassion. He was mute with terror. He surely had escaped from the Víboras Hacienda, also. Another of that old wretch's crimes, said a man named Florentino in Crescencio Montes's store.

But despite the years that pass, the house continues to emerge from the shadows every morning, like a ship floating on the rolling hills of the city drifting all night over the vast sea of the mountains of this state, propelled by gaiety, music, alcohol and our passions. And then, as it rests here quietly anchored for the day, we passengers on this ship cannot get out of our minds the awful thought that for each of us, alone, separately, sooner or later, our shipwreck will come.

The grave of General Aniceto López Morelos can be found today in one corner of the beautiful cemetery of the hacienda that was his. The grave of Terry Holiday—no one remembers exactly when she died or when she was last here in the house—is also in a corner of our personal cemetery. That place where we secretly bury all those pieces of life that die on us.

Translated by Mark Schafer

181

Georgina Quintana, *The Abyss* (1987, oil on canvas)

The Guitar

Jesús Gardea

Jesús Gardea (Ciudad Delicias, Chihuahua, 1939) is one of the most prolific and influential writers of Mexico's provinces. He began to publish later than his age-mates, and has published six novels to date; his first was El sol que estas mirando *(1981), and his most recent is* El ojo del diablo *(1989). His books of short stories include* Las luces del mundo *(1986) and* De alba sombría *(1985), from which "The Guitar" is taken. Gardea also teaches at the Universidad de Ciudad Juárez in Chihuahua.*

The man unhooked the guitar from the wall. Then he looked for a place to sit. There was only one chair, by the window. The man sat down. The sunlight struck his back. The man bent over the guitar. His hand on the guitar neck lay still, as if detached from the rest of his body. It was like a bird with long, dirty nails. Then the strings sounded. Slowly. The eye of the guitar didn't even blink: it went on sleeping. The hand that was playing flourished a tight, thin metal chain around its wrist. When the last string fell silent, the man raised his head and said to me:

"Oh, how you all forget about things. . . ."

I looked at the shape of the guitar on the wall. In the middle of the whitewash it was intensely white. My eyes traveled over the wall to the window. I could no longer see the man, but I knew that he was embracing the guitar with both arms.

"Some ten years of forgetting," he muttered.

Through the window, I could see houses scattered over the plain, their parapets neatly cut out by the round scissors of the sun. Where the walls met the earth the shadows were dripping. The shadows: like water from an earthen jar. It was one o' clock, time for my siesta. That afternoon, however, I was not going to sleep. Not with the unexpected visit. My

183

eyes left the brightness of the window and the solitude dotted with houses. A little wave of drowsiness caressed me. The guitar sounded again. The strings were strummed energetically several times. Then there was silence. I looked at the man, who was looking at me.

"They've hired me to entertain you," he told me.

I didn't notice anything unusual about him, but there was salt on his lips, a barren plain of salt in his voice. He rested the guitar on his crossed legs. After speaking, he had sat still: he was undoubtedly waiting for me to say something. I looked again at his cheap little bracelet and his dirty fingernails and remained silent. He grew impatient. He shifted position. He held the guitar vertically, resting it on his thigh. Then he warned me:

"But I'm no good at that, you know?"

The ribbon the guitar had hung from on the wall, tied to the end of its neck, was blue. I noticed it when the man returned the guitar to its earlier position. The ribbon, looped around twice, swayed slightly. It looked to me like velvet the way it had moved in the light of the room, the way heavy fabrics move. A length of twine would have traced a different movement: like a piece of string. The man, after his warning and after a short silence, threw these words in my face:

"And you—cat got your tongue?"

I understood why he said that. Because of the business about the guitar. I placed the palms of my hands on the bed and straightened myself up a bit:

"Who are you?" I asked him, and tried to harden my voice to reflect another barren plain.

"It wasn't no dog came in here, you know," he responded.

"I wasn't expecting anyone," I told him.

He, by way of answering, drummed on one of the low strings.

"And besides, it's time for my siesta," I added.

The man returned to the same thick string. I took my eyes off him and looked at the houses again, at the shadows growing toward us. The solitude of the plain is not silent. If you know how to hear it, it moans like a thirsty heart far from water.

"Did you hear?" the man asked me.

"What."

"The string. Completely out of tune. Sour. It's impossible to play a thing like this."

"Yes, it's impossible," I agreed, scanning the solitude outside, the solitude of the sky beyond the houses and the plain. But then, suddenly, the man got up from the chair and stood in front of me at the foot of the bed. He was grasping the guitar by the neck. He showed it to me.

"It has to be tuned," he said, and the instrument's eye looked at me without looking, still asleep. "I'll have to take it with me."

Then he left the room with guitar. Afterwards, I heard him talking with the people of the house. Not for long, because right away I began submerging them all in my dream.

The next day, the man didn't come back. I waited for him all morning. All afternoon. I didn't take my siesta. It was as if the shape of the guitar on the wall was calling to me and my gaze was constantly moving in that direction. But I was also looking at the chair where the man had sat with the body of the guitar in his arms. The morning sunlight filtered with the whisper of gentle liquids through tiny holes in the back of the chair. It covered the shiny chair with little dots. I didn't remember the tiny holes. Perhaps they had been made to aid the circulation of light and silence. And the clock struck one in the afternoon. And then there were voices behind the door. I didn't understand what they were saying, but they were destroying the great tranquility of the house. An hour later they were quiet. I thought it was because the man had returned. And I thought that soon he would come again to my room. But no: in his place appeared a man of the house. He came up to the foot of the bed and rested his hands on the brass pipe, as on a railing. As he looked at me, he began chewing the left side of his mustache.

"What did he say to you?" he asked me after letting go of the bristle.

The shape of the guitar was the shape of a woman. Her rump was radiant.

"What did who say to me?" I asked back.

"The man."

"Nothing."

"The two of you spoke."

"All right. He said that the guitar was dying."

"The guitar?"

"Because of your carelessness. The man didn't say it to me, but his heartbreak at finding the instrument in such condition sprang from his lips. He strummed the guitar, his loving ear glued to it."

"That man puts on airs. What else did he tell you?"

"That he was going to take the guitar."

"Where?"

"I don't know. Maybe to his house."

"His house! He has no house here."

I looked again at the shape of the guitar on the wall. The other man took hold of his mustache. He left the bed and began walking around the room. I reminded him of the chair, in his way. He ignored me altogether. He kept on walking and spitting out tiny bits of black bristle. Then all of a sudden he stopped:

"It so happens that guitar is a real jewel, Miguel," he said to me. "The man let us know the moment he was crossing the threshold to leave. We never would have imagined it. We reacted a little late. We should have stopped him. Tune it here, with us, ringed by our huge repentance, our growing love of music. But we went out looking for him anyhow. This town is hell. Solitude, the sun—they're no company, Miguel."

"I hardly ever see any of you out in the streets. That's why the sun tortures you."

"But we looked for the man in the shadows as well."

"And?"

"Even so."

"They say the shadows usually are something else. A negative of the sun, a thousand times worse than the sun itself."

"Yes. Or dirt paths overflowing with solitude. But let me tell you what I came for. We want you to say, if necessary, that the man came in to steal and that he threatened you. That he was violent with you. We intend to find him and get the guitar any way we can. Sabas thinks the instrument is worth thousands, thousands of pesos."

"The man could still come back, Saltiel."

"Of course, Miguel. It's only three and the afternoon isn't over yet."

"If that's what you want. . . ."

"One of us will stay here to receive him in case he returns."

Two days passed. The man didn't return. The house was totally silent. They had forgotten about me, forgotten to bring me food and drink. When I finished the leftovers from the last dish they'd brought me and the last drop of water, I strained and got myself up. The shape of the guitar danced for several moments in front of me. Like Saltiel, I reached for the brass tube so as not to fall. I looked through the window at the blurry houses on the plain. The air in the room buzzed in my ears. I was tempted to lie back down. I was breathing poorly. I was breathing a tiny thread of air lit up by the early morning sun. As in a dream, I supported the whole weight of my body on the brass tube and waited. Little by little, I was recovering air like a loaf of bread. I looked at the shape of the guitar. Its hips, its shoulders, its slender woman's neck called me. But I had to get myself something to eat. I staggered out of the room. Outside, in the hallway, the silence nearly suffocated me it was so deep, as if the other men had quarried it. To break it somehow, I weakly slapped the wall, said Nemesio's name, and continued on toward the kitchen. In the kitchen, I found flies and dirty dishes. The window to the outside was closed. But in the clutter on the table, I caught sight of a piece of bread and some crackers. I leaped like a bare-boned tiger, airborne, on top of my discovery. The flies fled. I sat down and began devouring the piece of bread, looking with greedy eyes at the crackers, the leftovers on the plates. I was down to the crumbs when I heard the front door open and close. The flies, as if that was all they had been waiting for, took back possession of the table. The first thing I thought of was the man with the guitar. I heard other doors as well. A fly flew by, heading toward the hallway. The noises of the house had ceased. I imagined the man sitting in the chair; his thin chain and his black fingernails. I thought I'd like to hear him play, but nothing came to mind. Someone suddenly burst into the hallway, walking slowly. He seemed to be heading toward the kitchen. Probably the man, sick of waiting for me, tired of sitting, was out looking for me, roaming through the house. But as the footsteps grew nearer, I understood. I recognized them. Nemesio was standing in the kitchen doorway. He held a small valise in his hand, his old cashmere sweater slung over his shoulder.

"Why did you get up?" he asked.

"I was hungry," I answered.

"I'm going, Miguel."

"And the others?"

"They left me here on guard, in case he returns with the guitar. They told me not to be a distraction. Here I was, sitting at the table, eating at the table, sleeping at the table. . . I'm beat. It's clear that man's not coming back. Yes, that's clear. But what about Saltiel and Sabas and Braulio? Today I went out early to walk the streets and see if I bumped into them. Nothing."

"They must be on the man's trail. Did you look, did you go into the shadows, Nemesio?"

"I'm telling you it was early."

"That's where you would find them then; when the sun rises and the shadows appear."

"No. To my mind, they've skipped town. They deceived me. They got the famous guitar back and they've sold it."

"Wait until tomorrow."

"I can't, Miguel. There's nothing left to eat. Except for those crackers. But I'm leaving them for you. You're convalescing. They'll taste delicious."

Nemesio said no more. He made a movement with the little valise as if weighing it. He turned around and left.

I didn't hear him close the door. Finding myself alone, I felt a coldness in my heart. Nemesio had made my hunger vanish. Even my willpower to get up and go back to the room. The flies walked over the crackers as if they were a pile of ruins. Two had gone down to the bottom of a plate as if into a valley and seemed to be resting. I swatted them all away. Then I stretched my hand out and took the crackers. Many of the swatted flies did loops in the air and flew back toward me to compete for the loot. So I got up. They followed me. They nibbled at me and bumped against my hand. But I wouldn't let go. The hallway, the deep silence, gathered up the din of the desperate attack. The crackers began softening from my sweat. I couldn't use my other hand because I was using it to support myself against the wall. I felt the floor rolling. The door to my room was not far; I could see it, open, bright as a frame full of light. . . . I closed it behind me. Not one fly had managed to slip into the room with me: decimated, filled with terror, they buzzed outside. Leaning back against the door, I listened to them for a good while. The sun on my bed set my white sheets afire. The brass had a hot shine. I peeled myself from the door and approaching the bed, dropped the loot. The sheets were covered with dark stains: scalloped chocolate-colored medallions. The chair was also under the empire of the sun. I decided it was better to sit than to lie down. I moved the chair so that I would face forward, looking at the shape of the guitar, half of me in shadow. I wasn't thinking of sleeping, but as soon as I sat down, sleep overcame me. In my absence, the sun got down off the bed, slid along the brass, walked slowly along the floor, over my body, until it reached the window and jumped into the street.

I woke up in the middle of the afternoon. Hungry. I remembered the crackers. I went to get them. Sleep had given me strength. The crackers still held the heat of the sun and it seemed to me it had made them even darker. Thinking about the man with the guitar and those madmen, I began eating the crackers, taking care to make them last. I was picking at the last one—there were eight of them—when someone entered the house. A few seconds later, I watched as the door to my room opened to admit Sabas. I was surprised to see him. Sabas looked at me and then looked at the shape of the guitar on the wall.

"And Nemesio?" he asked me. "He's not in the kitchen. Where did he go?"

"In search of all of you."

"Us?"

"He said you'd deceived him and that you'd run off with the guitar, far off, to sell it."

"It's not true, Miguel."

"It sounded reasonable to me, Sabas."

"I'm by myself, Miguel."

"And the others?"

"Each man is on his own, Miguel. But here: in town."

Sabas saw my mouth, my hand holding a bit of cracker.

"What are you eating?" he asked me.

"Crackers."

"They're my crackers. Who brought them to you?"

"No one."

"Nemesio?"

"I got them."

"You? You got up?"

Sabas took another step towards me. Sabas had eyebrows that tended to rise demonically at the slightest annoyance. That afternoon they were covered with dust. I found them threatening.

"We hired the guy for your entertainment," he said, his voice harsh, "on account of your great weakness."

Sabas took another step towards me. I went on the alert, almost like a shadow. But instead of touching me, Sabas walked by me, over to the shape of the guitar on the wall. Sticking his finger out, he followed its contour. He did it very slowly and when he was done, he said without turning around to look at me:

"But I don't care. It's your health. Your life, Miguel."

"Yes," I responded through my teeth.

"You'll have to replace my crackers once you've gotten better, Miguel."

I sat on the edge of the bed. Sabas and I were both looking at the wall. Then, as grieved as the guitarist, he said to me:

"What sadness, Miguel! What sadness lives inside us!"

Sabas started tracing the outline of the shape again with his finger. I looked outside. The houses on the plain looked foreign to me, as if they had never existed, as if they had descended, as Sabas and I were talking, from the afternoon sky. They shone with a yellowish color, like old bones gnawed by the sun and air. I saw a human form turn a corner. He had the sun at his back.

"The sun is losing strength," I said to Sabas, "a sign that a new season is approaching."

Sabas took his finger from the wall and contemplated the tip, white with lime. He walked to the door and before leaving said to me:

"If Nemesio comes back, tell him how mad I am at him. He abandoned his post. He offered up my crackers to your appetite. I'm taking my clothes. It seems we'll be after that man for all eternity, Miguel."

No sooner had Sabas closed the door than I began to scrounge crumbs from the bed. I didn't do it greedily. Nor from hunger. I collected them one by one as if I were picking them up through flowing water from the bed of a river. The very small crumbs escaped me and were carried off by the silent current. I don't know how long I was fishing, but when I stopped and turned my eyes back outside, I saw that the afternoon was turning brown and the ground was the color of ash. Shadows were rapidly curdling on the horizon. I stuck my head out into the street air, and then, from some part of the sky, the smell of moon reached me. I didn't like it one bit: with the town illuminated, the search for the guitar would continue and perhaps, at last, they'd find him. They were people to be feared, the men of the house. Bitter-blooded. The moon was swelling in the sky like a seed. I couldn't see it but I could feel it. Lights lit up on the plain. The only source of light in our house was a kerosene lamp. But the lamp never left the kitchen. The madmen had attached it forever to the tabletop. In the dimness, I found the chair and sat down. With effort, one could pick out the shape of the guitar on the wall: it could have been any kind of stain on the whitewash — water, time. I also thought that perhaps Sabas, with his sluggish index finger, had erased the outline of the shape. So I got out of the chair and went over to the wall: nothing: the shape was no more distinct up close.

The moon woke me. It was looking at me through the window, suspended from the lintel. I put my hand between its brilliant face and mine. In the shade of my hand I examined the sky. A couple of stars and a brightness as if it were dawn. I got up. I took my clothes, folded under the pillow, and began to get dressed. The hard light of the moon on the floor reflected onto the walls and onto the shape of the guitar, now totally visible. I was not going to stay in the house. I would also get the rest of my clothes from our common closet. Dressed, I smoothed back my hair and walked toward the wall with the guitar. My heart was leaping in my chest. The moonlight was making my legs cold through my pants, but my thighs, in darkness, were warm. Before I got there, I opened my right hand, palm forward. The moon had begun descending through the sky and was sinking deeper into the shadows of the room. I put the palm of my hand in the center of the shape of the guitar. The wall there had the consistency of flesh. It didn't strike me as absurd. It was as if I had been waiting to encounter something like that. I know Sabas thought of doing the same as I was doing now, but he hadn't dared. I took my hand from the wall. My heart was beating softly, placated at once. I turned back toward the window: I couldn't see a single star. The moon had eaten them. And it wouldn't be long before it sank. So, thinking I wouldn't have much light left to go searching for the man myself, I hurried out of the room to get my clothes from the closet in the adjacent room. The hallway was illuminated as if by its own light, significantly more subtle and penetrating than the light of the moon, which made it beautiful beyond measure. I wanted to touch its white-washed walls, beat its air with my hands. And then I heard the guitar. I thought it was in my room. The guitar was crying through its dark eye like a woman in distress. I headed back. The man had returned, had mocked the men of the house, had succeeded in tuning the guitar. . . . I walked with my heart leaping again in my chest. . . . But I didn't find anyone in the room. And the guitar had stopped playing. The desolation overwhelmed me. I felt my afflictions returning. I lay down on the bed, which floated in the moonlight, its brass headboard and legs looking like gold.

I closed my eyes.

The moon would soon be swinging to the other side of the sky.

They would never find the man. And I was going to sleep forever; forever in this womanless town.

Translated by Mark Schafer

Temptress
of the Torch-Pines

Gloria Velázquez

Gloria Velázquez (Tepatitlán, Jalisco, 1947) has co-authored the works Lenguaje y Comunicación *(1980) and* México y La Paz *(1987). Her novel,* El Mitín, El Financiero *(1991), includes a chapter on the residence of writers Katherine Anne Porter and D. H. Lawrence in Ajijic, Jalisco.*

Outside, the scraping of mallow-plants thrust in old pails, the deliberate chirp of crickets, and an invisible new moon . . .

—I've hardly ever touched you, Choco. I've done my compatriots a favor in your case, but they're about to learn the party's over.

—And why so, Don Seve?

Two lit spheres surrounded by gray cat enter the room, jump toward the empty seat . . .

—Because they're ingrates. They come asking favors, and just when I need them most they betray me: they took my wife's side. They say it was my fault, that I'd completely thrown her over because of coming here to you.

—And who are these people who betrayed you?

Severiano takes the question and the pitcher of *atole*.

192

—Who do you think? My bloodbrothers and next of kin. Give me a break! As if I were to blame for her running off with somebody else. Who can make head or tail of that?

—*You didn't give her sons.*

—No, I didn't give her sons. Am I supposed to produce them out of thin air? She never wanted to sleep with me. No other way left but by the Holy Ghost . . . . Don't you have any more blue-corn tortillas? Give me another.

The two burners of the stove, lit.

—I like you because you know how to keep your mouth shut. You knew everything, didn't you? For women like you, there are no secrets. I'm sure Basilisa came around to yell at you. If you'd only told me, I'd have left her that very day. You're a woman's woman. You kept your mouth shut. That hurt her more. She doesn't know it, but I've hardly ever touched you, Choco. *Her lips are pouty. I've got an idea you're the one who let the cat out of the bag.*

Over the stone fence a runnel of light, the sparkle of night, the din of the small world . . .

—Basilisa was waiting for a reason to leave. *This poor son of a bitch thinks his wife left on my account. With all his good-for-nothing ways, he ought to be wondering why she didn't light out sooner.*

—I've always treated you with respect, unlike my pal Fulgencio; the only reason he comes around is to paw at your legs. And how can he help himself? They're still so nice and firm. I've never forced you to comb out my hair either. They just envy me. It cuts them to the quick that you care for me. And I've always cared for you. I never got around to building you a house back then, and I hid you in this ramshackle stable so people wouldn't gossip. *No way am I going to set you up in a house alongside the church.*

—How you go on, Don Seve!

On the table, a black mortar full of tomato chili pepper, a hand-pestle stuck to the boards, a wicker basket for the tortillas and a painted wooden tray full of bean pods.

193

—Did we ever lie down together among the cornstalks?

—No, Don Seve.

Damn it all. Then who was that with?

—Let's make a date; it's high season.

—For corn?

—And for love.

—You have a lot of whims these days. Here are the tortillas.

The cat draws close to the aroma of the stew. It rubs up against the woman's ankles.

—I've sacrificed myself so much for Basilisa, as you know better than anybody. I hardly ever come here. Am I right, you already knew, she ran off with somebody else. It doesn't hurt me, on the contrary, I drank all the mescal I found in the house, just for the hell of it. Because it's you I love; I never loved my wife. *More like Basilisa never loved me, she got married so she wouldn't be an old maid, so she wouldn't walk around with her ears burning.*

—A long time ago, you did love her.

—Not anymore. She ran off with somebody else. You're the real saint, Choco, I'm going to build you a big house. The two of us together will put it up, bit by bit. We'll have to get together the adobes and the roof tiles; you'll have any animal you damn well please. Come here, sit down in my lap.

Me among the oxen; am I a saint? Tomorrow he'll get over his drunk and I'll fall from heaven to hell. —And where are you going to build me a house, Don Seve? Basilisa's brothers own the land.

—The Hermosillos don't own all of it; from here down to the plain and up to the top of the hillside, you can put a house up anywhere your eye falls. I'm going to be your man; you can count on me for your needs. Tell me where to level off the ground, because you're going to be mine,

Choco, whoever wants honey let him draw it from his honeycomb. You want your house?

She stoops down to give the cat some food, with all the patience in the world. *Good God! She's still thinking it over. These northern whores sure give themselves airs. Now watch her turn me down.*

—Leave the cat alone!

—You think I could pass up your house? Here, Don Seve. Some nice beans will take the fire out of those chilis.

—I'm not complaining about the food. Nobody around makes meat and beans like you do. *Maybe I ought to build her a house in town. She waits on me hand and foot, hardly talks, and is clean about everything.*

In the room's doorway a flickering of weak light, the flight of mosquitoes crossing through the shadows, the smoke of a lit candle-globe. . .

—Look, what a monster of a tortilla. I don't think I've ever served you up one this size. Wait a minute, stop grabbing my legs. Keep your hands off. I'm not finished frying the tortilla yet. It almost looks like a hunk of sky right after dawn breaks. Look. The blue-corn tortillas are just for you. Wait a minute. *This old man has really screwed her over good. That's what he comes for when he comes. He sticks his hands everywhere and leaves me like a chili on a hot grill. If he only had what it takes—but all he does is get me stirred up.*

—I know, I know, Choco. You leave all the good stuff for me. But you still haven't answered my question straight. Do you want me to build you a house? God knows I should. I'm not doing you a favor, big-bottom, you've earned it. Don't lose faith. If you could only see the remorse I feel in my soul when I just think about how I've thrown you among so many dirty little sinners. I made myself a pimp on your account; and on your account I'm going to make myself a man. Even though I'm up in years I can start over again. Or am I right, Choco?

—All those dirty little sinners, as you call them, have taken good care of me.

—Forgive me! Don't you see it was me who stuck you back in this bog? The least I can do is build you a house. *What didn't I put over on her when I first brought her here; she was barely twenty years old, she was a little thing who'd gone to pieces. She doesn't want to come sit with me. She doesn't believe me. Taking a good hard look at her, I think I could live with her. But no. I'll string her along for a year, just so when Basilisa finds out it will really get under her skin. Basilisa thinks I'm a good-for-nothing man. I'm fine for a forty-year-old whore, and more. She'll see. She'll realize what a man she lost.*

The heat of the stove and the voices, the scraping of chair legs and footsteps. From the fire-glow to the table; from the table to the fireglow . . .

—You've always been a man. A man's a man, no matter what his age. *Poor blockhead, he feels like he's thirty.* Basilisa doesn't know what she left behind. *And I knew everything.* A mixed-blood woman came to gossip to me about the lawsuit. *That's why I put more chili in his meat.* Keep your courage up! *If he only knew that his brothers-in-law have already forgiven Basilisa. Such an old miser. Who could stay with a man like that! All those bags of beans, corn, coffee, everything I have they haul out to me; Severiano, on the other hand, wants everything free; just because he lets me live in his stable he feels he has the same rights as his brothers-in-law.* They envy you, that's why tongues started to wag. What Basilisa did is a betrayal. *I'm surprised she put up with you this long.* Don't worry yourself, the woman always ends up on the losing end. *When she lets herself.* I can imagine her already screeching she's sorry. *Right now the poor soul is probably happy as a lark and according to what Altagracia told me, he's the one who raised a stink. He told Basilisa he was tired of her, she was too proud, that he didn't owe her anything because I was the one he came to when he needed to ease his mind.* The viper-tongues are saying that you and I were humping like animals in the corral, and that's not true, as you yourself said: between us there's been hardly anything but respect.

—That's why I want to build you a house.

—They also say we spend our time doing nasty things in front of people. Another tortilla? *The old boy has it right, I don't say much, but when I do talk, I talk a blue streak. I got so timid because one time they ran me out for having a loose tongue and I was left in the street just the way the good Lord brought me into the world, the same way this guy came to know me.*

196

Now that I'm thinking about a little house for myself, I feel pretty tired and I want to be the madam.

—Don't give me any more, come here, sit down.

—Look, Don Seve. I'm still good-looking, don't you think? *He doesn't have any idea that every day I plaster my face with honey. And I never eat supper, so I won't get a potbelly. And on top of that, every day I pray to Holiest Providence not to abandon me.* Yes, Don Seve, here I come, don't grab, wait a minute, let me finish. That's why I want a house. You're too kind. Basilisa doesn't know what she gave up.

Good God! She's starting to believe she deserves a house because she's good-looking. No, if I build her a house it will be to get Basilisa's goat, so that she'll know I still can.

—You look like you're thirty, you're well-preserved.

Spirals of smoke from a burnt tortilla; the cat's body stretched toward the night . . .

—See! Now the tortilla's burned.

—Sit down right here! *Take advantage of my being drunk because in my right mind there's no way I'd go through with it.* Let's continue this talk about the house.

—First I'm going to put on some coffee. *I don't want him falling asleep. It's going to be a long night.* Would you like another meat taco? *All my life I've hoped so hard for a little house, just like the one I knew in Tijuana, long before Severiano took me away from that mule-driver in Mexicali. I never had to have these talks with him. I was very happy in those days. We were five sweet young girls living there, but already streetwise. Like they say, the five fingers of the hand weren't enough to keep count anymore. That's where I turned fifteen. The madam's name was Imelda, may she rest in peace. She ran me out because some mangy slut told her I was trying to hog all the clientele. She sat there polishing her filthy nails. It was her fault they ran me out. But I'm to blame for what happened after that. The upshot was I said to Doña Imelda: "If you run me out, your house will fall down on top of you." She ran me out, and the next day the government bulldozers came to demolish the quarter; that's why I don't talk much. I don't even like to think anymore. Just last Sunday I was imagining Don Severiano without a wife, drunk, sitting here in the very state he's in.* Would you like some more *atole*, or do you want to wait for coffee? Go ahead, drink it up, to take the fire out of the chili. *The name of that house in Tijuana was Temptress of the Torch-Pines. They didn't used to call it that. One day the man came along to christen it. He said us sweet young girls resembled torch-pines, because we were skinny, we looked alike, and we knew how to burn.*

—What are you laughing about, Chocolate?

—I'm imagining my house. Then I'll tell you just how I want it. *The man said to Doña Imelda, here, I made a sign for your house, "Temptress of the Torch-Pines." The name brought us luck. It gave us all a luster; little by little we became women. Oh, what a house! At first we only had a few clients but as soon as that name stuck the place filled up every day. I'd come down to dance to northern music; there was a little runt who played the accordion. We were good friends. Sometimes he and I would go inside and dance to the music, no way could we do anything else. He started playing a song for me that ends "Where do the dead go?" Who knows where they go. . . .*

—Do you know where the dead go, Don Seve?

—The questions you ask, Choco. So you do want a house? *Poor thing, she's never expected so much out of life before. She's happy. It never entered her head that someone might build her a house. I'm definitely going to build it. I feel comfortable with her. She knows what tastes good.*

—Here's your coffee, black. I'm almost done. I haven't eaten a thing. I spent the whole day clearing away weeds, it rained a lot. Yes, Don Seve, I'd like to have a cute little house. *Without windows, but with skylights above that can be opened during the day to let the air in.* I want it to have walls finished with wood. *And a shiny mosaic floor; also a long hallway, and at the end, four baths with showers and hot water twenty-four hours a day.* A cute little house, with five or six paintings of the sea and leaping fish. *In the front, a salon with room for ten tables.* And don't worry about the girls, I've got my eye on a few here in town.

—What girls? You can have one to help you with the chores, so you can spend your time on me, serving me, having my meals ready.

—Do your remember the daughters of the widower Epitacio? The poor girls are starving to death. They come here to eat almost every day.

She's so carried away I'm starting to look like a sultan to her.

—So do you want to come with me? Do you want to be my woman?

—How do you like the name? *Temptress of the Torch-Pines.* Do you like the sound of it? Get up a head of steam, Don Seve, I'm ready, I'm going to treat you like I do Don Santos. Look, Don Severiano, you're not getting any younger. You can't take your land to the grave with you. Think about it!

—Think about what? I've been feeling you out all afternoon. I want to build you a house, of my own free will, and not for a year, but for the rest of your life, Chocolate.

—Then build me one the way I want it. *He'd better have deep pockets. It will make you young again.*

At ten in the evening, when everybody's asleep, we can open for business. Those who can't sit on their sins can come to amuse themselves. We'll service the unhappy souls, we'll give them a good workout, wake them up; let them sing, let them dance, let them have some conversation. Only a little liquor, so they won't get drunk, a few shots, and then we'll torch the pines, like Doña Imelda used to say.

—It will be a respectable house. No scandals. A beauty, how about it, old man? Would you like more coffee? I'll scoot the pot up next to the table. I came here with you because I let myself believe I'd have my own house one day. Since that night we arrived, I set my sights on that hilltop, the one by the pasture. I've always imagined my house on top of it. *I heard the music of the swimming fish and saw everyone happy. I was behind the counter tending bar and my girls were content, tending to the clients at every table. They sat in their men's laps, like this, rubbed the men's bellies, like this, stroked their graying hair, kissed one ear, then other, and the nape of the neck; like this. Then they caressed a hand here and there; they played handsies, hooked arms . . .* The house would be lit with candles. Since you first brought me here I've been dreaming about that house. Oh, Don Seve!

—You don't love me, Chocolate. You're making fun of me.

—The other day I asked you who that mustache belongs to. You just laughed; and you still haven't answered me.

—It's yours, big-bottom. You want your house?

— Yes, Don Seve. It's the only thing I want in life and I want it to be called "Temptress of the Torch-Pines."

The heat of the straw mattress and the sleeping mat; the toasty room, the light of the candlestick; the chill of the crickets.

Translated by Johnny Payne

Two Poems

Víctor Manuel Mendiola

Víctor Manuel Mendiola (Mexico City, 1954) studied economics at the Universidad Nacional Autónoma de México. He is the codirector of the publishing house Ediciones El Tucán de Virginia. He has published Poemas *(1980);* Sonetos a las cosas *(1982);* Triga *(1983); and* Nubes *(1987), from which the following poems are taken.*

The Room

Dogs are barking
and something inside you—
in the farthest room of the house of you,
in the deaf shadow of a silence
where you watch yourself alone
closing the windows
and listening to
the lost, bewildered dogs
in this cold country that is time,
in this camp of the hours exposed to all weathers—
goes off with the dogs and howls.

Like the Ocean

The dead man asks
for some response.
The living watch and say nothing.
The dead man grows troubled,
he talks about his world of shadows,
he talks about everything that is silenced
and that bothers him.
He explains, he argues
the theology of the sun that disappeared,
the sun that is burnt soot-black.
He goes to the slate,
he writes the word "death"
in many styles
and he whispers in the ear
of the living.
The ear grows larger and larger
till it surrounds the dead man.
Then the living
hear the sound of the sea.

The Memory of Silver

Carlos Montemayor

Carlos Montemayor (Parral, Chicuahua, 1947) has published two dozen volumes of poetry, fiction, essays and translations. He has been a professor at the Universidad Nacional Autónoma de México since 1974. His first work of short stories, Las llaves de Urgell *(1971), won the Villaurrutia prize, and since that beginning his work has won many additional prizes. Montemayor has written prologues for editions of more than fifteen authors and has published essays on such writers as Virgil, Quevedo and Pound. He has translated the poetry of ancient Greek and Latin, as well as Portuguese and Brazilian writers.*

My father had the habit of smoking at night
while sitting outside the house.
The summer heat was flooding the world.
All of the stars gathered above us
as if none could be lost.
I used to look at the mountain where the mine was
and in the distance I could hear the sound of the mills,
the subterranean rumbling of metals, men and rusty water.
I thought that silver was white, bright like rain falling at night,
or like reflections on the river or quiet pools of water beside
    the cliffs;
I still believed that it lit up the mine like a great waterfall.
I didn't know that it was black,
that it was a stifling summer
like an asphyxiating or deadly foam,
and that men were falling like new nights

down a starless windless shaft,
without a father smoking at their side.

Translated by Russell M. Cluff and L. Howard Quackenbush

Adolfo Riestra, *Bather* (1989, bronze)

Dogs

Roberto Vallarino

Essayist and poet Roberto Vallarino (Mexico City, 1955) is the author of Invención del otoño *(1979),* Textos paralelos *(1982),* Exilio interior *(1982) and other books. He also edited the anthology* Primer encuentro de poetas y narradores jóvenes de la frontera norte *(1986).*

All night
the dogs barked.

In the morning
people found the body.

It was a barefoot boy
who had stopped crying.

Yesterday
the dogs began to bark again.

Marcela and the King Together at Last on the Boardwalk

Luis Humberto Crosthwaite

Luis Humberto Crosthwaite (Tijuana, 1962) has established himself as a true border writer. Born in Tijuana, Crosthwaite brings cultural references from both Mexico and the U.S. into his work. He has published two volumes of short stories, including Marcela y El Rey al fin juntos *(1988), from which the present selection is taken. In 1991, Crosthwaite received a scholarship from the Fondo Nacional para la Cultura y las Artes, during which he finished his novel,* La luna siempre será un amor difícil.*

Part One: Marcela

She once had a cat, her only companion, but now she was alone again. The years, like the cat, had gone out the window, carrying the furniture and the carpet with them.

The clock strikes.

She gets up, bathes, dresses. She catches the first bus to town and arrives at work before all her co-workers. She takes her place at the same desk, the same typewriter, the same tasks.

Eight hours later, she goes out and takes a walk for the same stretch of time.

Same as always.

No one greets her.

No one says to her, "Excuse me."

Rock never got as far as her.

That's the truth.

She never got as far as rock.

No one invites her for coffee in the afternoons or asks her out to dance or dinner or to filch tomatoes from a gringo's ranch on the other side of the border.

Her life has become one, two, three . . . (she gets up, bathes, gets dressed . . .). She didn't understand that variations exist:
one three two   two three one

Marcela is forty years old and little by little (goodbye Marcela) the wind carries her out to sea.

She feels that the soap operas are a consolation when one of the protagonists is named Marcela and lives happily with her husband.

There was a time when Marcela understood people.

It was one of her stages: she walked through the crowded streets and entertained herself listening to the voices, listen did you know that
my brother stole my cousin's wife
the Yankees are in Central America, those bastards
I can't get off this stinking drunk, cheers!
what's-his-name's been in jail three weeks

What do you think.

She understood everything.

It was the most constructive period of her life—as she told it. Being understanding was ideal and educational but she didn't take long in putting an end to it. The indifference of the passing crowd made them stop mattering to her. No one said "Pardon me" to her and she decided not to say it to anyone.

She was fine that way.

Owing to these circumstances (Marcela always in a bad mood), her only companion opted for the happy, reproductive life of alley cats.

Amen: to despise people is also good, once in a while.

Another stage, she would say a little later, to the King.

The last one before the beach, before she might have abandoned downtown where the people are colorless, and might have remained seated near the ruins of the boardwalk.

She discovered that many of the people walking around there looked like her. She got used to watching them. Each one with his own style, and at the same time, identical to the next.

Like Marcela.

Heck.

It was on one of those days that she saw the King for the first time.

Part Two: The King

On the border it is common to find beings like Elvis. Bums who, frequently drunk, hang around the parks, sleep on the benches or lie down near the liquor stalls waiting to be carried away by the police or forgetfulness.

whichever comes first

Like it was with Morrison, Joplin, Hendrix.

The figure of Elvis, fat and covered with silver, diamonds on his belt and fingers, appeared suddenly asking for directions back to his Las Vegas penthouse.

Poor guy: he didn't know it was all over.

The End, Morrison once said.

Elvis approached a beach bum. He said to him:

"I've been so lonely

"I've been so lonely I could die" – but the guy kept walking across Revolución Street.

Without answering.

Later Elvis saw a traffic cop. He screamed at him:

"Oh let me be (oh let me be) your teddy bear."

The policeman was not moved. In jail, the sad gringo was relieved of the diamonds that adorned his wardrobe (they took them as payment for the fine) and later he was thrown out on the street with a few pennies' change.

Elvis was a man in his forties who didn't bother with work. He tried to get some, but it's difficult in the big border towns. There were only a few places that still had live music: among them, one, Mike's, had just hired a rock singer. A real boring chick.

Sorry.

The rest weren't interested.

"You look too much like the King."

His attempts to explain were useless.

He had the bright idea of singing on city buses, but was kicked off the first one he climbed up onto. The passengers preferred kids singing *norteñas*, songs from up North, and no longer cared much for fat guys with hairy ears singing rock and roll. Those who knew. What's more, his bad luck made him choose the Kilometer Eleven-Los Pinos route, where the people are even more packed in than usual.

Maybe on other routes. Who knows.

Owing to his disappointment, he stopped taking care of himself and got sickeningly skinny, his clothes turned to rags and in this way (someone said he had no alternative) he began bothering the young women who in those days strolled down the boardwalk.

That didn't work out, either.

You and I know the King was born to sing.

And nothing else.

Back then, you could park your VW and see a lot of guys like Elvis on the beach, guys known for their disagreeable odor and appearance, for their long beards and filthy, tangled hair. Talking to themselves, maybe, or screaming that they are the King, each one a different king.

How many times has this writer, seated under an enormous beach umbrella, sipping coconut milk, speculated on which of them was the real King?

A few years ago.

Now the boardwalk doesn't exist.

What happened was a storm that left the streets bitten into like a huge tuna-fish sandwich, the restaurants and picnic spots torn to bits, worm-eaten victims of time and not of the high tides with their waves and salt.

The corners without traffic lights.

The blocks without corners.

Now there are no people.

No one likes the sad spectacle of the boardwalk.

A few bathers once in a while.

And Elvis walking alone, writing his name in the sand and watching it disappear in the foam and seaweed.

ELVIS

Sometimes he walked far enough north to reach the border.

The border is a fairly big sign that says: "HEY, YOU. DANGER! YOU ARE ENTERING THE UNITED STATES OF AMERICA, THE WORLD'S MOST POWERFUL COUNTRY. DON'T DO IT!"

There were heroic days when the King dared to cross it, but when he got a few meters past, guards with pistols approached him.

Elvis no longer gave explanations, he felt too alone. He wrote in the sand, "Love me *tender*, love me *sweet*" and returned heavy-hearted.

One time Elvis entered the sea and spent a long time in the waters of the Pacific. The waves rose and fell like a Carlos Santana riff, cry of the land, heavenly smile. When he got out, he looked even more unpleasant but his odor was like a fishing port, sweet to this writer, bothersome to others.

A woman spent her time contemplating him with neither sadness nor happiness. They were the only ones on the beach. The sun came a few millimeters closer.

"I am the King. My name is Elvis."

Strangely enough, she seemed to understand.

Part Three: The Border

Moved, the King spoke with Marcela about Buddy Holly, Priscilla, the rhythmic motion that could exist in all hips (he didn't say "pelvis"); he spoke about drug addiction, about how to win at "Twenty-One" in some Las Vegas casinos, and about the border, halted in the north for some time.

"That's it," he said to her, showing her the sign.

Marcela told him about her work, her old, ungrateful cat, the extra hours and taxes. She also gave him an intensive course in shorthand, using the sand for a blackboard.

Immediately they fell in love.

Marcela didn't mind that Elvis was divorced.

They walked northward, talking, until they reached the billboard ("HEY YOU," et cetera). Marcela said that close up the words weren't as large as they seemed from far away.

And so it was that, having nothing to do, she decided to cross over the famous boundary called "The Border," known in other places as the line of little crosses drawn on all the maps, which we are taught to respect in grade school.

The King did the same.

Both began their trips toward the beach, without any particular direction in mind.

A bit later the guards showed up.

Part Four: The Last Straw

Marcela and Elvis together at last.

The others, the fools, yelled "STOP."

The helicopters arrived with their best searchlights to point them out. Elvis felt like he was on stage.

As they continued walking, here came the reporters and TV, and in the distance the sign grew smaller and smaller till it disappeared.

The guards began to shoot.

Are bullets good for anything?

Marcela and Elvis kept on walking. She understood rock for the first time. He sang his old hits under the intense light of the helicopters. There was in all this something much better than in Las Vegas.

The stupid people never understood that for Marcela and the King neither they nor their pistols even existed, that like the border they were only little crosses on a map burnt a long time ago.

Translated by Amy Schildhouse

Germán Venegas, *The Master Devil* (1983, ink on paper)

The Never-Ending Story

Alvaro Uribe

Alvaro Uribe (Mexico City, 1950) is Cultural Attaché for the Mexican embassy in Paris. Fluent in French, Uribe spent a number of years as an editor for the bilingual literary magazine Altaforte, *published in France from 1978–84. Uribe was also a member of the literary workshop organized by the Instituto Nacional de Bellas Artes and directed by Guatemalan writer Augusto Monterroso. His publications include* Topos *(1980),* El cuento de nunca acabar *(1981),* La audiencia de los pájaros *(1986) and* La linterna de los muertos *(1988).*

It's very easy for you to ask me to tell you something about the people around here, but it won't be possible. This could seem like a story about people, about personal things, about good luck and bad luck, but it really isn't. There are no longer any stories just about people.

So one day Xavier, the son of Doña Santos—the widow who married again, to Lieutenant Barroso—left his house at night, his pockets empty, ready for anything. A little earlier that same day, something bad had happened to Chucho, the storekeeper's son. It was business as usual, as he put it: that is, divvying up the cash he and his friends get from the sales of the cars they steal. His share was one hundred pesos, and when he was almost home he put his hand in his pocket and realized nothing was there. He looked through all his pockets and retraced his steps back and forth three times, but no luck. He needed that dough (Felipe, the one who works in Chucho's papa's store, told me so) because he had lost a bet and to pay it off the easiest way had been to borrow the money from the cash register and return it that same night, before his father Don Porfirio did his accounts. Since Chucho couldn't recover the bill, he gripped his knife and went out into the night to see if some Christian would make his task easy. But I was telling you about Xavier. He had left his house and was walking without any particular direction in mind when he saw the wind

213

pushing something on the ground. He bent down and almost couldn't believe his eyes: a hundred-peso bill was slithering in front of his feet by itself, without anyone else having seen it. Xavier was merrily on his way to the bar when he heard footsteps behind him and thought he saw an enormous figure coming close to him.

He felt something crash against his head and then a very sharp pain in his arm. Early in the morning he awoke in the hospital, having been knocked on the back of his neck and knifed in his left arm. When he asked if they had found a bill in his pants, they told him no. He knew only one person the size of the shadow that had attacked him: Chucho, and he made this known to his stepfather, Lieutenant Barroso. The night before, Chucho had returned home early, with sweat on his face and his hands trembling. Felipe told me he went with him to open the cash register and saw how he put a hundred-peso bill on top of the other four or five that were there. In the morning some policemen came and without further inquiry took him down to the station, to speak to Lieutenant Barroso. The lieutenant didn't know whether to believe his stepson or not, but he was interested in improving family relations, so he ordered them to rough Chucho up a bit and then lock him up. Meanwhile Don Porfirio was so ashamed that he was beside himself. Wise in the ways of the law, he took out several hundred-peso bills from his cash register and went down to the station. There he swore on his dead mother that Chucho would never do this again, he would make sure of it, and he convinced Lieutenant Barroso—with his oath and two hundred pesos—that there was no need to make a big legal fuss about the whole thing. That night the lieutenant went home and was so happy to see Xavier on his feet again that he gave him one of the bills Don Porfirio had given him. Out of pure joy Xavier went and used it all up at Zurita's bar. The next day Zurita stocked up on food at Don Porfirio's store and paid him with a hundred-peso bill that ended up in the cash register. After giving Chucho two smacks on either cheek, Don Porfirio put the bill in his hand and made him promise to give it to Xavier, since that money was really his, and God help Chucho if he didn't return it. So that the hundred pesos ended up again in Xavier's hands and who knows what he did with them, or rather, what they did with him. That's why I was saying that stories are no longer just about people. Because then we realize that, as a pal of mine says, we're just puppets of fate, and fate is just a puppet of money, and maybe money is a puppet of something else, and so on and so forth, till you come out God knows where.

Translated by Suzanne Jill Levine

The Emancipation of the Lunatics

Oscar de la Borbolla

Oscar de la Borbolla (born in Mexico City, 1949) teaches at the Universidad Nacional Autónoma de México (UNAM), where he did his undergraduate and graduate work in philosophy. Borbolla received his doctorate in philosophy from the Universidad Compultense in Madrid. He is the author of a collection of short stories, Vivir a diario (1982); a collection of poetry, Los sótanos de Babel (1985); and another collection of short stories, Las esquinas del azar (1987), which won the Cuento Plural prize in 1987.

Had journalism withheld bold type and sensationalist tone for an occasion that truly warranted them, we could debut them today with ample justification: we wouldn't be defenseless against the most important news of the century and faced with a benumbed public opinion incapable of being surprised. Because in truth and in fact, the resolution passed recently at the heart of the UN represents, without a doubt, the most important decision that has been recorded since this international body was formed. It heralds the beginning of an era more luminous, more democratic and more just. Today, at last, the State of Madness has been recognized as a free and sovereign State, deserving of membership in the community of nations. The longest and most misunderstood of human struggles has culminated in the recognition, by absolute majority, of the emancipation of the lunatics.

The history of this emergent people, whose racial features have always been unmistakable in Mongoloids, in fact dates back, it is known, to the dawn of civilization. No people, social class, or ethnic group has the painful memory of such uninterrupted abuse as that suffered by lunatics.

215

Deprived of their freedom, subdued by straitjackets, lightning-struck by electroshock, poisoned with tranquilizers, isolated and beaten, lunatics have persisted; they could not be exterminated nor could their heroic social maladjustment be defeated. Indomitable in the face of punishment, they have defended their right to think another world, to dream another way, to establish diverse, casual alliances. Schizophrenics, paranoiacs, hysterics invincible after centuries and millennia of repression now win recognition of their distinct state.

With the UN resolution, the badly named "mental illnesses" are legitimized as being merely different, like values, idiosyncrasies, and nationalistic sentiments. The supposed "mental disturbance," the so-called "nervous breakdown" or the longest-lived belief that turned lunatics into "beings possessed by the devil" are revealed in all their reactionary crudity, with all their brutal baggage of dominant ideology. The incorruptible march of humanity toward total liberation, the press of man toward an ideal democracy in which we are all equal, pantocracy—all seem to have reached one of their highest rungs.

Triumph, however, was not easy: the International Front for the Liberation of Everyone (IFLE) had to rise above irreparable losses in order to deal the blows with which it successfully subdued the opposition. In the final moments, Freudians and Skinnerians managed to put aside their internal differences, presenting their true single face, and this global stratagem threatened the efforts of millions of lunatics fighting individually on the couch or in wild riots in the insane asylums. Only the tenacity of the compulsives, the mistrust and the reasoning capacity of the paranoiacs, the war secret guarded to the death by the catatonics, the creativity and fantasy of the schizoids and their phobic potential along with their uncontainable neurasthenia made possible the outcome we now know: the majority of countries in the UN conceded the moral defeat of their neurologists, psychiatrists, psychoanalysts and psychologists, as well as philosophers, anthropologists, sociologists and even engineers who had served as advisors and co-authors of oppression.

The new State has received for its territory the parcels of land on which stood the now abolished hospitals, rehabilitation centers, therapists' offices and clinics. Lunatics can now be seen pushing the space those locales once occupied through the streets of every nation to throw it into the sea and thus build the great artificial island that will be the definitive place for every lunatic to live his lunacy in freedom.

In the simple yet frenetic ceremony that capped the signing of the aforementioned resolution, and amidst the strident cheers and unrelenting cries, the IFLE let its immediate plans be known: to declare autism as its official language and to advocate for the nationalization of a large percentage of world culture created by lunatics; the works of Nietzsche, Van Gogh, Hölderlin, Strindberg, Swedenborg, Althusser, Ravel, Artaud, Nerval, Coleridge and many others will be reclaimed.

With our most uchronic enthusiasm, we salute the birth of the State of Lunacy, whose independence must legitimize the hopes of other minorities and majorities still subdued.

Translated by Mark Schafer

Discoveries

Eduardo Langagne

Eduardo Langagne (Mexico City, 1952) studied dentistry, music and film. He was the first Mexican to win the Casa de las Americas prize (1980). Recently, he won the Premio Nacional de Literatura Gilberto Owen (1991). Among his published works are Los abuelos tercos *(1982),* Pegaso herido *(1985),* Navegar es preciso *(1987), and a book of translations of Bulgarian poetry.*

columbus did not discover this woman
nor do her eyes resemble caravels
vespucci never mapped her hair
no lookout ever shouted land-ho at sight of her—
although gulls do fly
      near
           her body
and on her continent the sun rises every day—
this woman was not discovered by columbus
nevertheless she was in the west
she was an unknown place
and to find her
it was necessary to spend a long time traveling
with a blue solitude in one's head

The Natural Thing To Do

María Luisa Puga

María Luisa Puga (Mexico City, 1944) is a novelist and essayist. Among her published works are Cuando el aire es azul *(1990),* Pánico o peligro *(1984),* Accidentes *(1981),* Intentos *(1987) and* Itinerario de palabras *(1987), on which she collaborated with Mónica Mansour, and from which* The Hidden Language *(see p. 317) is taken.*

Woody Allen has done a lot of harm to society. So many people have identified with him. Men and women. And now a lot of them are running around loose out there. They're terrible and difficult to detect. In the beginning, at least, it's almost impossible.

It's my fault, of course—who told me to get involved in something that doesn't concern me? Although he got me into it, that's true. He put me in the middle, and then, amazingly, like it was the most natural thing to do, he began to speak in the plural.

And so, suddenly, I inherited a complete family in which I was the only one who played no part.

I'm talking about him and his mother (who'd come from another country to spend her vacation with her son; to get to know her grandson). It had been five years since they'd seen each other. The grandson was two years old. And he had a mother, of course. But the father and mother had been separated for a year. The boy's mother had a new boyfriend (who in turn had a son and was also separated, et cetera—what a nuisance, couples).

Is it necessary to mention I'm divorced?

Anyway, one day I met the little boy. I say that because the first one I noticed was the boy: so small and agile, with smiling eyes and lots of unintelligible but very expressive jabbering.

I was just learning to drive, although that day I didn't have my car, because it was downtown that all this took place, and I didn't know my way out of Coyoacán.

I hadn't paid much attention to him, before, to tell the truth. I must confess it was because he was shorter than I am. A prejudice, I know. And when I saw him I imagined him married to a feminist who spends Saturdays in therapy or something—with round glasses; a sociologist. That he must have brought the boy with him to the publishing house, on a Saturday morning. . . and that he was happy, a very modern father and all that, seemed logical to me.

We were going to have a meeting to launch a literary book series. Suddenly he said I don't know what about some book and rushed up to the next floor, returning a few seconds later with the book in his hand. His hair mussed, his eyes sparkling. Short and stocky. And the little boy coming and going in miniature. So alike. I felt good.

Later we got a lift to Coyoacán.

In the back seat, on his lap, the boy slept. He was talking, hugging the boy, caressing his ear. His hand. The boy's face against his chest. Something liquid coursed through my body. I like him, I thought. He'd already told me he was separated and that he had the boy on weekends. He'd take him to the Parnassus bookstore, in Coyoacán, his favorite place. During the week the boy was with his mother.

When we got to Coyoacán the boy woke up in the midst of an awful stench.

"Do you have diapers with you?"

I should have realized then: the fussing with everything, the bag from which all kinds of objects emerged, the loud scattered monologue, and his trying to be cheerful.

But I didn't realize.

The pants had to be washed, and while he ironed them in my bedroom, I played with the boy in the living room. Drawing, chatting: Algbdrgal! Nundrlglvaal! And he, while ironing, was looking over my books, my things, my house. He would poke his head into the living room and ask about everything. He kept ironing.

Then: Where are you going to have lunch?

I should have realized.

My inexpert driving produced jerks and swerves that filled the boy with glee, me with laughter, and as for him I suppose he liked me. Could we go to the movies sometime? Well, O.K., sometime.

220

A week later he called. Ah, but today I can't. Better to have coffee on Saturday at Parnassus.

How suddenly strange is the world, with a little boy. It becomes interesting. It gets sharper and stands out. It loses its utilitarian aspect. I'd forget everything and suddenly I'd remember: him. . . do I like him? I didn't really know. Once he put his hand on my shoulder. Yes. Another time he talked to me for a long time looking into my eyes. No. And the boy in between, so tiny and resolute in his smallness. Funny, eloquent.

But in the afternoon I was like: See you. I have to. I was just going.

Weeks of this till one day I invited him to somebody's party.

One expression of his I didn't like: a deliberately sweet smile; deliberately affectionate. Perhaps nervous. Definitely tense. But why a smile? I ask.

He would arrange for someone to stay with the boy. He shared the apartment with a friend who at the time was out of town.

I wasn't imagining anything. I didn't want to. I agreed to take a taxi to his house around nine: I still didn't dare to drive at night.

Alone, at home, I was doubtful. I fell asleep. At ten the phone rang. I fell asleep, I said. A quick little laugh, very psychoanalytical, on his part. Will you invite me to breakfast tomorrow? I asked him. I don't know, I have to see. . . . I was going with some friends. I'll have to phone them. . . . O.K., I'll stop by early in any case.

I dreamed about him all night. He'd come closer, he'd get lost, I'd lose him, he'd pass by me. I was getting anxious. I saw a huge house covered with a single blue carpet, which also covered floors, beds, tables, little platforms, stairways. All this was full of people arguing animatedly, vehemently, with a lot of gestures. Did I mention he was Argentine?

I woke up very early, and never before having left Coyoacán in my car, I went, really nervous, down Gabriel Mancera.

Naturally I got lost, and I felt even more rushed. And he didn't have a phone. The address, the numbers of the building and the apartment had buzzed all night long through my dream.

When he opened the door, the sun entered my whole body; in a nearly naked room he and the boy were roaming around with such a lost, vulnerable look that I hugged him as if we had been kept apart for years by a war.

And I spent the day there, getting to know them. Slowly learning to love them. Surprised.

I began to drive better and at any hour. He'd ask me to take him here or there, like it was the most natural thing to do. To pick up the boy, to drop him off at night. He never realized how afraid I was. Sitting beside me, he'd chat about anything, with that tone of nostalgia, of detachment from the present, that people use to evoke childhood. He thought he also had to show me where to turn. We'd go out all the time and my hands would sweat. I felt like the city was stalking me, like it was violent and waiting for an opportunity to jump on me.

During the week we'd stay at my house. My apartment is tiny, and with two persons it fills up completely. We'd walk around, disconcerted. We didn't know where to put ourselves. I'd try to cook and he'd kiss me on the neck. He'd put his arms around me while I was setting the table. Until we'd go to bed, and then time would soften, it would unify, and our low voices would slip through it smoothly.

And it was inevitable that our respective lives were springing back up in their own reality. The time that I dedicate to writing. The time he dedicates to making enough money to pay for his son. In order to live. The disturbances from the difference in rhythms. The disagreements. The first arguments. Because immediately, the insecurity. The fear of getting hurt. You're ready to be loved; but to be ready to love, to *love*, I mean, you insist on a lot of guarantees.

I'm talking about those moments when, in a new relationship, the other person turns out to be so profoundly other. Unknown. You almost feel relieved: he has nothing to do with me.

It was the little boy who kept drawing us together. The little boy and, I think, the car. That going out in a Volkswagen that I was learning to drive, with him as a guide—since the truth is that I suffer from a kind of topographic cretinism.

But stories about couples are so tedious, so repetitive. You always have the impression that the circumstances are going to shed some revealing, definitive light. And so the urgency to say: It's just that, look, I . . .

Just at this point, his mother arrived. A little woman bearing a tremendous anguish. A furtive, penetrating blue gaze, that knew how to personify exhausting burdens, but also, all of a sudden, unexpected happiness. Nakedly childish.

She would stay with the boy's mother, since more than anything she had come for this: to get to know her grandson.

Hmm, I thought, here we go. And I didn't even think it, to tell the truth. I felt it briefly because there wasn't much time. It was such a new situation, and it was advancing so quickly on so many fronts: one Saturday morning, before his mother had arrived, he asked me to meet the mother of the little boy. What for? And he said something that he'd later repeat often, always leaving me without an argument: they're a reality. They exist (she and the boy). But that day, on top of everything, her boyfriend was there.

The little boy was smiling, elusive. He didn't get close to anybody. His mother was preparing his diaper bag, and all of us were like we were hanging around without knowing what to say. Very friendly. Very meticulous in our respective descriptions of the weather.

I came back to attention once we were all in the car. Where to? Me, chauffeur. Brand-new mother; girlfriend: where are we going? Wherever he wants, for the boy.

For this reason, once his mother arrived (not the night that she arrived, when he, in a perfectly natural way, had already arranged that we'd all go—in my car—to pick her up; I was the first to back out; then the others), I had to meet her and, again, everybody there, without knowing what to say, plus his mother, who looked at us all longingly.

But all in all she made of us what she wanted. A little soup? Nobody wanted a little soup. We would have liked a drink, but no, a little soup. Leave? Not a chance. A little soup.

That night I knew that I didn't like the situation. I knew that I felt very alone in that relationship. I don't know why I stuck around. A sickness, I think.

And him?

He had a lot to think about: his mother. The way in which she got along or not with the boy's mother. The boyfriend had the good sense to go on a trip. Not me. I let him convince me that it was absolutely essential to be at his birthday. His mother was going to make a special dinner.

I don't have a mother. Literally, I mean, although maybe in another sense, too. I don't have a mother and I don't know what you do with them. What you say to them. Besides, I thought that the important relationship would have to be with the mother of the little boy. For that reason I was there, but not completely. Not even close. And he came and went from one house to another; from one situation to another, getting all disheveled, full of remarks and complaints. About the necessities, all of them peremptory, of the situation. "A major crossroads," he said it was.

Imagine that.

One day he told me that he was very insecure. That what's more he dropped everything; that he tripped over everything. Just like Woody Allen, he said.

The last straw was one time when we had agreed to meet in a café. I arrive, and the whole family's there. The only one missing was the little boy's mother's boyfriend (who was on a trip, as I said). The whole family. On an outing, then. And him, disheveled, overseeing everything. The center. The boy, from one lap to another.

By then I was feeling completely out of place—interested, yes, although uncomfortable because apparently I had nothing to do there (there, where all the roles were being played to perfection), but as if I were chained to them by a curiosity which, I insist, was sick.

The conversation, it's true, flowed with an extraordinary amiability. The attention we all paid to each other, how fabulous. Except for him, naturally, as he hurried eagerly from one place to another without sitting down for a minute. Prowling around us. Stretching the net in which he had us trapped. Could it be on purpose? Frankly, I don't know. It didn't seem like it. But his poor mother was suffering. Sometimes she'd look at him as if begging for help, clarification, something. When she didn't find it, she'd turn to the little boy, and she did it brusquely, with a grandmotherly severity that would leave us all speechless, upset, because the little boy wasn't doing anything. He was the one who was doing the best. Why didn't she leave him in peace?

It's that she was a mother par excellence. A mother, one of those mothers who has to be the only one, and her son had placed her in a rather vague situation.

So, friendly, social, distant conversation was the only recourse, and how we all bored each other.

That day turned out very badly, although cordially, and after courteous goodbye kisses, we were all going home to our own houses. Then I saw him move away, crushed, while his mother was helping the mother of the little boy and he wasn't finding anyone to turn to. To complain to.

He had to know—didn't he?—that our relationship was going nowhere. Or maybe it was: he was going to consolidate the grand disorganization in which he lived. All I had to do was stand firm in the midst of everything. Firm and serious—for when he had to turn the boy over to me because he needed his hands free.

The little boy and I had fun. We disconnected ourselves from the others. Those grown-ups who were tiring themselves out trying to exist harmoniously, naturally. With his unrestrained language and his little body, he'd climb up on my lap and we'd play at talking about a circus that we'd seen recently.

Yes, it's true, during the week we were getting together, he and I, and we didn't think too much about the fact that, more and more often, we didn't have much to say to each other. Especially me, since he always had plans to take the boy to this place or that, or his mother shopping, or why don't we go to the movies.

And at night love, the love that would have to sustain so much; that would have to have arisen from something more than this "crossroads situation," although his mother had already left after putting *me* in charge of taking care of her son, and the boy's mother in charge of the boy.

I expressed my doubts that things were going well, and he was surprised. At first he'd told me: I'm going to treat this relationship with the meticulousness of a craftsman.

It's that we wanted to be very level and straightforward. A relationship of equals. It would be ideal, right? The boy's mother with her boyfriend, and the two of us. Why not? The most natural thing to do. The boy had learned to call both of us Mama.

He was also surprised when I told him that I didn't feel that I really knew him. I knew the boy's father and also the ex-husband of the boy's mother. And, just slightly, the son of the tiny woman with the little blue eyes. I had learned how to drive, that's true, but I didn't feel like we were going anywhere.

And when a few days later I called him and told him I was pulling out, he replied: You're terrible, that's no way to talk about it.

Translated by Judith de Mesa

Forget Uruapan, *Hermano*

Dante Medina

Dante Medina was born in 1954 in the small village of Jilotlán de los Dolores, Jalisco. He has published several studies on literature; short stories, including Léerére (1986) and Niñoserias (1989); two novels; a book of travels; and many poems. He currently teaches literature at the Universidad de Guadalajara, where he is the director of the Center for Literary Studies.

I have not succeeded in verifying his true name. Or hers. When I asked the policeman who had gone to prevent the supposed, and publicly advertised, suicide, he said those things often happen, that he'd recommended to him that he have a drink and then forget about her, and why should he have put in his report the name of a depressed young man, who this same police officer advised to forget the woman who had left him, and whom he had reprimanded expressly in order to get him to forget her. The policeman forgot her before the young man did. Or never knew her name.

Since I myself failed to ask the policeman his name, and there was no written record in City Hall, I have no way of beginning the investigation all over again. Even now I ask myself: was it worth the trouble to spend so many days in Uruapan, to go all the way there from L.A., question the likely witnesses, just for the purpose of finding out two names, his name and hers?

"Uruapan has a lot of attractions," they told him.

The National Park, the Cupatitzio River, the Tzararacua, the avocados, the young women. Hadn't he ever been in Uruapan? It seems he said yes, he'd passed through, at least, or he'd spent a vacation there, a long time ago.

226

I took·a plane to Guadalajara, and from there a bus to Uruapan. I stayed in the Hotel Victoria. I pretended to be interested in getting to know the city, although some people say I knew it already. I let them say whatever they wanted, just so I could get information. I didn't remember his name, or hers, so that's what I informed the officer of, who had also failed to retain such facts.

"It was a long time ago, right?"

"Yes," I told him, without either of us being clear on how long.

"It was a long time ago—like how long?" I answered him, with the hope that the officer would say how many years ago.

"Well, you know. . ." he said, and the only thing I saw was that the officer was a very old man.

In L.A. nobody knows anything about this, but in Uruapan everybody does. Or seemed to know. What threw me off is that there wasn't a single informant who didn't conclude his account with some excuse: "That's more or less how I remember it, but who knows," "Things seemed to happen more or less like that," "Well, it was never really clear to me," "That's what people say," et cetera.

Because—yes—he was one of those guys who likes to ask himself how they get the lead into pencils.

The thing about her leaving him nobody doubted: it's the heart of the gossip, a kind of blues of being left. That she and he were in love, that they "seemed to be in love," is another given, for those who tell the story with the greatest enthusiasm. Now that I mention it: everyone I went to was happy to tell me the story, and no one was surprised when I'd say, timidly, that everyone else was telling me a different version.

"Ah, well, then who knows?" they'd say, and leave it at that.

"When she went away, she left him a letter, explaining," I was told by the women who ran *Vanities*, one of the newspapers. "I know, because he came in here, really shattered, asking me to publish it with a note by him in which he asked her to come back and forgive him. He used to publish things now and then in our paper. But I refused to put her letter and his note in our weekly, because I was afraid of scandal."

"What kind of scandal?"

"Well, people were saying that she'd left him because of his problems . . . let's say . . . of a psychological nature. And beyond that, in that note that he wanted to appear in our paper, he asked her to meet him at Devil's Knee, at midnight on a Friday the thirteenth. You understand I have my duty as the head of this paper to protect our readers. . . ."

227

"And what do you know about him?

"I never saw him again. This thing with the girl really hurt him."

"And the name—him or her?"

"I never knew."

"Do you still have the letter she left him, that he brought around asking you to publish with that note of his?"

"The letter yes, the note no. The note—he told me he was going to photocopy it and plaster it on every wall in town. But I don't believe he did, although who knows, with all the work I had here I wasn't going out much."

"May I see the letter?"

"No."

"What kind of things did he write for your paper?"

"Detective stories, every time with a different pseudonym."

A woman of some years told me, in the Café El Patio, what she considered was the authentic version. Apparently, he was already living with her, or they were engaged, or involved with one another; whatever, they were a couple. That was when people learned about him—downtown, a handsome marriageable boy; and out on the edge of town, a married man with a wife not so young as he, a man of whom in time it was learned how much younger he looked than he was.

She never forgave him being already married, and in any case she wanted to keep him for herself. Coolly she asked her father for a pistol—or her uncle: memory fails—who wasn't surprised, given how odd she was. She went to Zumpimito, knocked coldly at the door, and said, "I've come for the man who your life's getting in the way of," and she fired. Tense but composed, she went to find him at Los Portales and told him, "I left her where she fell, go to her so she can say goodbye to you."

He managed to get her to the hospital. She didn't die.

Two days later, she passed herself off as a relative of the wounded woman, and confronted her in her sickbed, scaring her to death. She said, "When you get out of here if you don't leave your husband I'll come back and kill you." She promised she would, she'd leave Uruapan, she'd go north, to relatives in California, in San Francisco or L.A., she'd go, and not to kill her, for pity's sake, she'd leave the man.

There was no need. That very day she died of fright.

He asked her where she had been. She said visiting a woman friend who was ill.

They went off to live together, or they got married, this the older woman did not know because she had finished her coffee and without caffeine she couldn't remember, and she ordered another coffee so as not to remember anything more and finish the conversation.

No doubt some of the suffering that he owed her, after her revenge, was why she left him.

As far as credibility is concerned, there is some agreement that this woman has an excellent memory, although she tends to confuse some facts with others. "It may be that in this case it was like that, but maybe not; everything depends on what she told you."

He also left a note, explaining, although it seems to have been written later. It was sold by the wait-captain at El Tarasco. He swore that he'd received it wrapped in a large-denomination bill at a big fifteenth-birthday party at El Pie de la Sierra, from a young man who was pleading with him to find the woman who had left him and he'd give him this little piece of paper. One thing he couldn't tell him: the girl-friend's name.

The bartender kept it with the evil hope of being able to blackmail this young man who was sending such desperate messages. Useless: instead of a signature there was only an illegible scrawl. He saved it as a juvenile trophy of the ridiculousness of drunks in love. Now he could sell, for dollars, this piece of paper that was worth so little to him he scarcely remembered it. He had trouble finding it, folded up with newspaper clippings from the police blotter and rosaries and votive offerings of his mother's, who now with age considered this piece of paper her own property, one of her personal fetishes.

Even after the sale of the note, the bartender remembered how his mother had grumbled and cursed, and treated him like a thief, a traitor, an insensitive lout. Why should it bother him that a woman left a man, something that happens every day? His ancient mother said back to him, "Only once in life does a woman leave a man, on one day." And she began to cry, this woman, his mother, who till that day the waiter, wait-captain, bartender, hadn't seen cry since childhood, even counting the time when he was getting on his poor mother so much that he was going around acting gay.

The note that he sold, at a very high price, said only:
Who the hell are you, for the love of God.

There are those who believe that this could all be fiction, part of some unfinished novel, or a story that is still being written. No one has denied his inclination for writing: quantities of love poetry and love letters and love messages show clearly that he was accustomed to loving by means of words. Someone seems to recall that he won a local newspaper contest for the best poem to a mother.

Or that the note—the only evidence of a reply to the woman who left him, since after she left there is no trace of him—could be not the lost fragment of a literary text still to be written, but something made up by the bartender, eager to sell information, or the theft, by this same person, of a scrap of his own mother's past.

From the information and accounts of other informants (among whom are the man at the stand on the corner of Manuel Ocaranza and El Portal who sells spicy potato chips, and the potato-juice vendor at the intersection of Madero and Cupatitzio) he fell back on friends, men and women, with whom he'd spent time in the cafés. Yes, a waiter at El Patio told him, she had several women friends, and some men friends, not as many. . . . "They might remember him, since he—the waiter—remembers, although we waiters, you understand, we remember faces well, and clothes, and even shoes and people's haircuts, but we don't often learn anyone's name." What he would know to tell him, "What I do know to tell you is that he didn't dress like around here, he didn't wear shoes like around here, and I think he was living in a hotel, the Hotel Victoria, because one of my wife's relatives, unless I'm mistaken, did his clothes for him, yes . . . that was probably him. Because, like I said, he didn't dress like around here. Or like somebody from Morelia, or Apatzingán, not even from Mexico City or Guadalajara. He dressed like people from farther away."

"His men and women friends still come here, some of them married now, others single, in the afternoon, for a cup of coffee or some ice cream. The men end up with beer and watch the boxing on TV, some nights."

He waited. Then the waiter introduced him to the women friends, who behaved as if he only wanted to flirt with them, a well-known trick just to start up a friendship so as to get to a commitment to go together and who knows and with the help of God even something more. Yes, they all remember him, but inexplicably they did not remember his name. The blond wants to gain the advantage and suggests nicknames: "Noname," "Sweethearts," "Chocolate" . . . and a little brunette who's no prude and doesn't want to be left behind, either, thinks she remembers that he hit on her, with the nickname "Outsider," and she remembers him well—or sort of well: "He was about your height, but without a mustache, with longer hair and a softer voice; he was always talking suggestively and he'd rub you a little under the table with his leg. At least with me, he always asked, 'If we go together, will you swear that you'll never leave me?' And to tell the truth, handsome as he was, I was afraid of his past. Nobody here knew much about where he was from, and not a thing about his parents. And if I'm still not married it's not because I'm ugly but because I'm hard to please."

The other young women at the table also remembered some of his nicknames: "Tomcat," "McDonald," "You-bring-her." He wanted to make sure that it was the same person who had all these nicknames, that they weren't confusing him. "You know," they said, "probably not — although who knows — of course he did!" because these nicknames could have belonged to other men, with similar problems, if you only knew, "In Uruapan there are so many good-looking girls who leave the men they love."

I'm on my way back to L.A. I've just taken off from Guadalajara. I'm returning with the hope that my companion, my wife, my beloved mate, will not be the same as in Uruapan. Let her refuse to give me her name for other reasons. Let her never up and leave me for no reason. For the moment, as a minimum defense, I'm going to continue to refuse to give her, me too, my name.

Translated by Reginald Gibbons

Mónica Castillo, *Incorporeal* (1990, oil on canvas)

The Dawn

Carlos Montemayor

For a biographical note on Carlos Montemayor please see page 203.

In memory of Víctor Aldrete,
who liked to remember stories like this

"That's all Ramiro can say? That he'll be waiting for us at his house at one in the morning? In ten minutes? Naturally, I'm sure he told you, 'Go wake up that damn fool Víctor and bring him to me to kill his friend.' Right?"

Eustaquio did not attempt an answer. Víctor could refuse to go with them. But it had to interest him more to intervene, to delay the encounter.

"And you think Samuel Gámez is going to be easy to find? How can we be so sure he's there? Tell me that. Four years ago they thought the same."

The other men had remained outside Víctor Velásquez's house. Eustaquio began to worry, to feel a sense of urgency. When Víctor got up from his chair, Alfredo took a deep breath and stretched his legs as if he had just walked a long way. Their eyes followed Víctor's silhouette across the courtyard of the house. Alfredo had confronted Samuel Gámez four years before. Exactly four, in March of 1932. Now Gámez had come back, giving in to the need for the same land, the same men. Eustaquio did not want to wonder what he would have done in his place. Nor did it matter. For Ramiro and Alfredo, it meant one more chance to hunt him down, to kill him. For Eustaquio it was a job, a day's work like

233

many others; natural, necessary, and as dispassionate as the river sweeping its waters along or the daybreaks spilling their light onto the earth. The only thing he lacked was certain knowledge of who would fall this time.

He went to the door, opened it, and paused on the steps. They were all still there, mounted on their horses. Raúl looked over at him indolently from among them, not particularly curious about Víctor's decision, just waiting for the answer.

"He's coming," Eustaquio said. "We'll have to wait for him a few minutes." Raúl nodded as if Eustaquio had delivered a long speech, as if he had offered a minutely detailed explanation of what he thought of the situation. He turned towards the others and gave a faint, triumphant smile, friendly.

Eustaquio felt the night growing colder. Even if it didn't rain or snow, autumn might soon give way to winter. Only the whickering of the horses could be heard in the street, the occasional stamp of a hoof. He wanted to drink something hot, a cup of coffee, slowly. He groped for another cigarette in the pocket of his leather jacket. In flashes, he remembered the anxiety that used to grip him when, as a teenager, he would go hunting in the sierra with his father and uncles. When the rifles, the shotguns, the cartridges, the provisions for the trip filled the whole space of the house and yard with a smell that was more alive, more decidedly human. But it was different now. Maybe because of Ramiro's determination, or the fear Alfredo was struggling to transform into assurance. He heard easy, warm laughter from Santiago and another man who had lit cigarettes. The men's voices reached him like an affectionate reunion, in a sonorous heat of earth and joy, as if the night had a fever that they were sitting up with, watching over. Someone among them had to die. Or perhaps none of them. Not even Samuel Gámez. The night seemed safe; there were no signs of battle. Every man who knows how to kill learns to hear the earth's warnings. Now he heard nothing. Nothing forewarned in the air, in the night that had grown colder, in the sky where the moon swelled intensely, as if to illuminate only the calm, the peace, the sleep of all things.

Víctor came out along the side of the street. Eustaquio had sensed him before the squeak of the grating's hinges, before the steady, secure sound of the distant horse had reached him. Without turning around, he called Alfredo. The horses stirred a little, nervous, tossing their necks. He watched as Víctor approached them, rifle fastened to his saddle, cartridge clip at his belt, the revolver, with its wooden handle, hanging at his side. Gonzalo handed Eustaquio the reins. Eustaquio ran his right

234

hand over the animal's neck, caressing it before mounting. When he looked at his watch it was a quarter past one. They were an hour late. It could take three hours or longer to get to the ranch where they were to find Samuel Gámez, still enough time for them to place themselves in the most strategic positions.

They moved along the side of Alvarado Alley toward the river. Near the poplars the water wasn't as deep; its quiet flow barely rose above the horses' hoofs. They went up Lerdo Street toward Las Quintas. In the men's silence, Eustaquio sensed not fatigue but an obscure cloud of emotion emanating from each one of them. He gave a sidelong glance at Alfredo, who rode along smoking, unwavering in his feelings. Only three of the men didn't know Samuel Gámez, but Eustaquio himself was one of the three. He could not understand why they were pursuing this man so urgently. Nor could he understand why Gámez would come back to the same place, why he would face this danger. "We can't use men who don't know him," Ramiro had said. "With hatred you can smell anyone out. They'll sense him from miles away. Don't doubt it." "But with my men we'll have enough," Eustaquio had insisted. "With Santiago and Raúl, it will be enough. We are ready to do whatever you say, right now." "We need more than authority," Ramiro had replied. "We have to teach everyone that you can't kill, steal cattle, stir up the Indians, all of it, without being punished. There's a lesson that has to be taught." But Eustaquio repeated that something wasn't quite right, that the other men weren't necessary, insisting: "They only know how to kill in the streets, in groups. They don't know how to hunt a man down. They don't know how to wait. If Gámez knows those moves as well as I do, he'll know how to meet us, because he came back of his own free will."

Ramiro was already outside his house, waiting. A farmhand was holding the reins of his horse, which was very agitated, shying toward the wall of the house.

"Decided to come along, Víctor?" he said, looking the group over. "I'm glad to see that you're with us. These two are yours?" he asked Eustaquio, who nodded. "All right, gentlemen," he said, "we're heading for the Velásquez ranch. Víctor's cousins' ranch. We have to be there before sunrise."

"You can't all go in," Víctor, who had moved ahead of the group, warned them. "It's heavily guarded, enough to resist an attack by three times as many men as we are. It's my family's property, not open country. We're going for Samuel, but I'll go in alone and if he's there I'll convince him to come with us. All of you will stay behind at the entrance, as my escort. But I'm warning you, Samuel won't come out alone. And the man who fires, the man who wants to kill him, won't live to see him dead, won't have time to celebrate his death. Is that agreed, Ramiro?"

Eustaquio realized that the night was beginning to take on a certain meaning, an order that emerged from the tension they were all feeling, from an imperceptible movement of hands on reins, from the gazes focused on Ramiro. A cloud of strength, of awareness, began to cover them, to palpitate in the hands pressed against saddles and horses, in the first signs of life, of meaning, of night. He saw that Víctor understood the silent answer of bodies and eyes, the intention contained in these men's passion. He felt a twinge of sympathy for him, for his strength.

"All right. You heard him, gentlemen," Ramiro said. "All of you know what has to be done. Each of you knows his part. From here on in, there won't be any changes."

He tugged the reins to the left and the horse wheeled, nervous, chewing the bit. They struck out across the fields at a gallop. The earth's noise covered the men, louder than the pounding of hoofs. Eustaquio thought gratefully, intensely, of how many years it had been since he had ridden out into the night, feeling the wind's freedom, the silence of the world that is invulnerable to the thoughts of others, to the agitation that seems to grow in the horse's body, in the taut vigor of its neck, in its slow, pungent sweat. In the saddle, every horseman begins to feel the depth of his body and of his delight in the open field, the night, the wind, in the silence through which the voice of all things speaks—even if at the end what awaits is a hunted man, even if what awaits a man is death itself, that religious fall onto immeasurable, harmonious, warm, noise of the earth. From time to time he looked at all of them. And he tried to decipher the emotion that Alfredo couldn't seem to contain and that made him fidget, spur his horse, and tense his face as if he were biting a delicate and intensely sensitive nerve to which thousands of thoughts and desires were attached. There was unmistakably a hope toward which he was stretching his life, his anxiety, his urgency. Near Villa Escobedo they could see a few campfires lost in the distance. The smell of the streams, when they crossed them, rose along with the water, soaking animals, riders, the leather of saddles and boots. The night had grown colder, but all of them were sweating, enveloped in a warm mist of fatigue. Close to San Rafael, on the mountain that overlooks it before descending into the valley, lay the reservoir's immense, serene mirror. Joined to the wide expanse of hills and mountains, beneath the luminous moon which was beginning to sink across the sky, the gleaming

236

color of the reservoir's water extended, stretched out like a tired body, like the immense wings of peaceful, immutable birds surrounded by the plateau, on the side of the mountain, inundating the horsemen and the dust coating them with smells, humidity, a more intense life.

When they stopped to rest, the horses were tired and breathing heavily. The men walked up and down to get the stiffness out of their legs. Raúl took two bottles of brandy from his saddlebags and handed them to the men. When they finished drinking they passed the rest to Eustaquio, who was sitting against an ash tree, trying to listen to Ramiro and Víctor who were talking a little further on; he could hear the force of their voices, and that Ramiro was on the defensive. That meant that Víctor was right, or else that he was the stronger. A few steps away from them, joined to them by a common interest, Eustaquio thought he heard something more. He didn't want to turn immediately; he tried to sense the nature of the cloud of urgency that had drawn near. It was a feeling of fear, not of vengeance; not of bravery, nor of hate. Then it happened, when the body stepped forward with force. "It's a gun," he managed to think vertiginously, while his hand, even quicker, was already aiming at Alfredo, who was astonished to find himself confronting a weapon that seemed to have risen from the darkness, from the grass, from the tree's roots, from a remote and dangerous warning of abysses, of void, in which Santiago, too, Eustaquio's man, was whispering to him firmly, but with something in his voice like a child's innocent surprise that was utterly foreign to the moment.

"Put it away, Alfredo. Calm down."

Then the same thin, whispering voice drew Alfredo away from there, as if his body had requested it, as if it had only been waiting for a sign to flee. Smoothly, turning almost imperceptibly toward the ash tree, Eustaquio holstered his gun without getting up off the ground. Then he picked up the bottle of brandy and went toward Ramiro and Víctor.

"It's four in the morning," he said when they sensed him approaching. "I think that in ten minutes more we'll be ready to go on. If that's all right with the two of you."

He handed them the bottle. The night was colder next to the river. The smell of the running water, the sound of the crickets, an occasional whinny, made him feel that they were enclosed, that they had entered a roofed place, not exposed to the weather. Before asking anything, Eustaquio thought about Alfredo's tension, about the speed with which he himself had acted, not to calm him, but to threaten him, to aim at him, to make him feel that he, Eustaquio, was in command, not him. That it was for Eustaquio to draw his gun, not for others. But deep inside he was surprised to see himself defending Víctor, not Ramiro. And just then, as he approached them, he had asked, calmly and clearly, when *the two of you* say so. This was a new movement. He remembered that a goose will take refuge deep in the marshes, and the way it moves the waters can be felt as if it were projecting its presence from its hiding place. When a deer hides, when an animal moves through the underbrush, its movements can be perceived from a distance, beyond, in all the places in the forest, in the thickets. And they are signs that this life is here, that the world is moving, that living destiny is opening up in front of the prey. It is the secret language through which life communicates itself before the final encounter. And in the silence of things—the branches, the wind—in the stillness, the danger of the air, the prey, too, senses, comprehends the footprints, the trail of what is pursuing it. The signs are for both. And both take heed, raise their heads at these warnings and the world they create. "He's waiting for us, too," Eustaquio said to himself. "He knows that someone like us is coming. That he's going to find someone like us next to him. He must know it. And Ramiro doesn't understand that, but he does," Eustaquio said to himself, preparing his question, looking at the two men's silhouettes, smelling Víctor's odor. Because fear is a sign, it is the movement produced by death, the presence of the animal that moves behind the bushes, that hides, and that can die, too. He would have one of his men look after Ramiro and the other, Alfredo. The others could act, or die, or understand. It didn't matter. But he had to look after Víctor, he had to watch, to be on the lookout for the least movement of what must die, of what could kill.

Ramiro took two swallows of brandy. Víctor took a long pull and handed the bottle to Eustaquio. He raised it to his mouth but didn't drink; he let the brandy wash over the skin of his lips, warming, burning his tongue, his gums. Then he spat. And only then did he ask—in an assured tone, alert to catch any stirrings in the underbrush, because an idea was beginning to make itself clearer within him, to show him once again the complex yet simple action of those who hunt, of the fear that also hounds those who hunt—

"What did Samuel Gámez do?"

"He killed, Eustaquio," Ramiro said in a tone meant to put an end to the conversation. "That's what he did. Kill."

Víctor was surprised. He turned toward Eustaquio as if he didn't know him, as if he had just realized for the first time that he was there with them.

"Nothing," Víctor answered. "He defended himself against four men who tried to kill him. He defended himself against four assassins, Eusta-

238

quio." Ramiro did not appear to have heard Víctor's words, or to have registered the force of his voice. "That's why none of these men must attack," Víctor insisted. "If they do, I'll be the first to fire. Understand, Eustaquio?"

With calm precision, Eustaquio's sense of the danger was developing. Not because Víctor openly opposed Ramiro Chávez's instructions, but because it wasn't enough to find a man or to arrive with a warrant for his arrest. It was no longer enough, now, to be the figure of authority. Nor was it enough to say that Samuel Gámez was a criminal, a fugitive. Víctor was necessary, in order to come face to face with him. Gámez would not come out alone. They would not find him unarmed, either. But then surely he wouldn't have come back to the same place. Maybe he wasn't just an outlaw. Maybe it was true that a large group of miners was behind him, as Víctor said. Eustaquio felt, again, that it made no sense to go there like that. Calm and patient, Víctor was waiting for an answer. He seemed to have said everything. His large, steady eyes with their greenish light were waiting without urgency or malice. He separated his lips, to draw in a breath or to say something more.

"Understand, Eustaquio?" he said again, finally. "This has to be made very clear to your men, because it's up to them to hold the others back. They're afraid. Afraid to kill. Afraid of being killed."

Eustaquio listened to him with a certain pleasure. From a distance, he sensed the movement of the men, the smell of the earth, the cool of the poplars and the ash trees. Everything seemed harmonious, peaceful: the sound of the water in the river, the whickering of the horses, the voices. The bottle was still in his hands; the glass was warm by now. He was beginning to have a complete, exact idea of Ramiro Chávez's dangerous game. In some obscure way it rose up through the earth, through the sound of the river, through his body, the certainty of death, that more than one of them would die. Afterwards, the others could attest to Gámez's faithlessness, to his attack on Víctor: they could swear that it had been necessary to kill him. All of them had been told. They had to kill him. But the important thing now, the thing which explained that the night was real, that the chase was certain, was that deep in the underbrush that surrounded them and that was becoming more visible, Víctor *understood* what they wanted to do. Ramiro had confidence in the men who were accompanying him. It couldn't be any other way with Eustaquio, Santiago or Raúl, who had proved themselves to him over long years in the sierra. But the other men, even though they had the same passion to kill Gámez, were of no use to him. Not like that. Not in a tranquil, patient search.

"I understand that we're going to arrest a man," Eustaquio finally answered. "That's all. And we have to arrest him. Not go back empty-handed. Tell me if I've understood correctly."

Eustaquio held in his breath, slowed the rhythm of his respiration and opened wide all of his body's senses to hear the movement in the underbrush, to listen to Víctor's voice and to grasp deep within it, in its slow, clear words, the sign he was looking for. It was as if he were moving toward the edge of a cliff, an abyss in whose shadowy depths the destinies of all the men gathered there, all their remaining moments, could emerge and in the heat and chill of that void, as animated as the transparent night, enlivened with crickets, toads, sounds, stars, the past hours, the trail they were leaving behind them could at last be understood. He listened to the slow, measured movement of Víctor's body, as if the ground were soft and he were treading it to assert himself, to find a secure, solid spot where he could remain standing for hours, pondering innumerable thoughts. The impulse was calm, fearless. An impulse that Eustaquio had seen hundreds of times over the course of many years. But Ramiro had another movement, a kind of anxiety trying to control itself in a deeper and more silent respiration, trying not to pass into the legs, the head, the mouth. The river's movement was natural, quiet, like the passing of the wind, like Eustaquio's gaze on the man's face or on the tree silhouettes on the opposite bank, the concentrated darkness amassed in the riverbank, in the dawn.

"I'll explain it to you better, Eustaquio," Víctor said deliberately, as if only the two of them were there, as if no one else were listening and they were discussing a secret that had been kept for many years, cherished for many years among families, across deep, limpid nights. There was a real interest in being heard, in making his words, too, a real expression of everything that he portended. Ramiro seemed to move, but it was only his desire to listen, to lose not a single one of the words spoken by the voice making its way between them like the river through the earth, pushing hours and distance aside. "I'll explain it to you better," Víctor said. "Life is very delicate. It's very simple, Eustaquio. It breaks like a piece of glass. You know that. You've seen it. Death seems impossible, life is strong, nothing shakes it. But you know how easily it can be done. And you also know, and I want you to understand, that behind life is a fortress like rock or like the walls of a dam, and that is the strength of a hunted man who's defending his life. Not a frightened man, like the ones with us. No. The hunters want a life in exchange for nothing, but the hunted man wants *his* life in exchange for others. Understand, Eustaquio? You and your men mustn't forget this. And look out for the

240

others. Because they don't know. They want to kill—only that. And all they can do is die—only that."

Eustaquio was beginning to feel something like euphoria. Triumph showed in his face. No one can hunt men, kill them, if he doesn't know how to decipher them. The stag, the puma, the goose must be understood. Their lairs, their answers must be understood. And he had already deciphered it, had grasped it several hours before. His answer, the voice, the body's weight beneath the phrases, in the chest, in the blood that was forming the words, was long-awaited, certain. This man understood; this man, therefore, had also deciphered him, Eustaquio. There were two of them now, who had drawn close to each other. Two of them in the underbrush, divining the hidden lives, merged in a single night, a single search. And Ramiro still didn't understand. Nor Alfredo; in him there was a terror, an obscure anguish, lightless and unconscious. In some way, Eustaquio wanted to reciprocate, to let Víctor know what there was certainly no need to say. But he had to do it, it had to be made clear between the two of them. For a moment he stopped watching Ramiro, the horses trying to shake off their bridles, the men who were still conversing a little way off. No, he needed to be more careful. Someone was listening to his footsteps; his footsteps, too, were rustling in the underbrush, giving off a scent, leaving a trail. He lifted the bottle of brandy to his mouth and took a swig. The hot, sweet liquid burned his mouth, his tongue; it entered his body knowing everything that had to be done, as if it were reuniting two friends, two acquaintances. He handed the bottle to Víctor, before asking. Víctor's eyes continued to meet his as he took the bottle, not hiding what had now been made clear, that his resolution was beyond all doubt, beyond all argument.

"Do you know Gámez?" Eustaquio asked, finally, when Víctor gave the bottle of brandy back.

"That's how it is," Víctor answered laconically, as if there were nothing to say, as if to affirm a thousand times that they were friends, that he knew everything, that he understood everything, that it was enough for two men to make things clear. "You'll know him soon enough, Eustaquio."

"I know," he replied, feeling that he lacked an understanding of their positions in respect to each other—who was the double hunter, who the prey. He had to make an effort to admit it to himself, to spread before his own eyes what the next few hours would be. It might already be later than four-thirty. He began to feel a certain giddiness of the moment, a certain animal awakening in the dawn. The murmur of the river, the less intense noise of the crickets, the earth, the reddish moon already close by and growing on the horizon, about to set. That was how his body seemed to him, his thoughts, a certain collapse of ideas, of stillness. He needed to know if Víctor was his enemy or not. If the only two men who fully understood were on the same side or not. If their lives did or did not need to be protected against the others. If he could believe in that during the little time that remained. Unexpectedly, as if he had sensed for the first time that he had been left exposed, alone in this open space that he wanted to understand, that he needed to clarify, he heard Víctor's voice, his intention clearer now, his tone relaxed, but with all the lucidity that Eustaquio needed in those minutes before they continued toward the Velásquez ranch:

"Do you have a friend, Eustaquio?" And before Eustaquio had understood, before he had perceived in the man's gaze the clarity that was permeating his body, his skin, his firm conviction of danger, he heard, "Because otherwise you couldn't understand it. I promise you."

Then Eustaquio smiled. He raised his head toward the ash trees spreading over them and saw the dark, dense fabric of the night, the stars, more luminous now, falling toward the horizon. The wind blew, delicately cool. He turned to look at the man, at his eyes. Víctor, too, seemed to smile. Then Eustaquio looked at the ground. He saw the three pairs of boots, the grace, the quiet, whispering earth of that night. He slid his right foot over the grass, feeling the whisper beneath his boot, the pulsation of life. The river's quiet waters flowing by them, the distant voices of the men and the sound of the horses were the counterpart to the underbrush of life in which the two of them had glimpsed each other, in which they had recognized each other. Ramiro Chávez began to move; it was time to go on. Eustaquio turned toward the east. The sky was slowly beginning to change, as if a light cloud of very fine powder were starting to rise through it, tarnishing the stars, suffocating their brilliance. Day was breaking. A powder of light was beginning to ascend towards the depths of the world and would reach them in less than an hour with the truth they were waiting for, pursuing. This man was his enemy. He had to stop him in time, before his own face could be revealed, before his own life could be captured. Instinctively he turned to look for Santiago and Raúl. A light sleepiness of sunrise, of fatigue, was beginning to fall over all of them as if the immaculate night, suddenly cold beneath the ash trees, next to the river, were heavy, and they were carrying it on their shoulders because their ribs and arms were aching.

"Let's go!" Ramiro shouted, advancing toward the rest of the men.

His voice came from very far, as if from the void, from complete nothingness, the abundant nothingness that lengthens nights of wait-ing, nights of mourning. Eustaquio finally saw Samuel Gámez as a danger, not a perplexing motivation. It no longer interested him to know what type of man he was. The moon had set. He looked at his watch: it was twenty minutes to five. The sun would rise in less than an hour. In less than an hour their day's work would be completed. Before mounting his horse, he called Santiago.

"I'm going to watch Víctor," he said in a low voice, holding the reins. "You take care of the others. Especially Alfredo. He could make a mistake. Have Raúl watch Ramiro."

He raised his eyes: something was on him. For the first time he felt that something was on him, hanging over his head, over his life. He turned his face to the left: Víctor, mounted on his horse, pulling the reins back firmly as the horse tried to go forward, was watching him steadily. Santiago followed Eustaquio's glance and found, in the dark-ness, near the shadow of the ash trees, between the forms of Octavio and Ramiro, Víctor's gaze. They couldn't see the eyes. They could feel the gaze, the weight of his presence. It took Eustaquio a few seconds to realize that they were waiting for him. He mounted and made his way through the group.

"More than fifty minutes to go," Ramiro said.

The wind changed direction. It was blowing at their backs now, from the north, through a light cloud of brilliant, ultrafine powder, luminous where the darkness of that October night was opening to reveal the purple-red seed penetrating the air and staining animals, hands, cloth-ing, men's eyes, with its color. The earth's sound was different; a sound of insects, animals, clouds stretching immense across the skies, as if for an infinite instant the reddening dawn was expanding with all of life, with all the sweetness that the world only delivers then, at sunrise, on horseback, to the lives that are crossing it, to the intense bodies that are crossing its own life, its own echo of blood. Eustaquio felt the aromatic air entering his body more abundantly, like a force that could explode it, absorbing the intense sunrise that was opening and stripping everything away.

As they came over the hill the fields where cattle grazed spread out beneath them. In the distance they saw the shadow of the ranch build-ings. The light that would rise through the sky's violet darkness, like a wall giving away, seemed to be resting against the earth. It was the black, purple light of an enormous branching vein that was making its way through their lives, through walls and hills. Near the wells, toward the marshes where the trees where concentrated, he still couldn't quite see

243

the movement of the cattle. Eustaquio felt the wind growing stronger, cleaner, already warm, bringing a low murmur of day. And he detected another smell: that of the excitement, the agitation that was rising through all of them. A horse let out a long neigh, rearing up on its hind legs. Víctor kept his, which moved several steps to one side, under firm control. As if some fear, some timidity were holding them back, they moved slowly down along the fences at a walk. Víctor leaned down to open the gate. Ramiro followed; then came Eustaquio. In a matter of minutes the air had become less dark. The color of the sunrise was slowly falling on their shoulders, on the horses, on the earth. But beneath the murmur of daybreak in the thickets, the sound of the birds and grasshoppers which was everywhere like a fine powder of life, he kept his attention on the silence, a silence that seemed to float like a cloud of waiting. Several dogs began to bark in the ranch houses. Eustaquio could make out the sheds, the open doorways of the storehouses, the walls of the houses behind them, still dark. The silence surprised him. He didn't like the silence. He turned toward Alfredo, then toward the other men. He began to feel a sharp point of heat in his chest, in the pit of his stomach; sharp heat in his throat that yielded only to the heavy breath expelled by his bitter mouth. He knew perfectly well that it was fear. But he was used to living with it, to using its strength, to restraining himself in the face of its strength. It was for that they had come. For that, he would keep his attention on these moments, this stillness.

"Here, no further," he told Ramiro Chávez, almost whispering.

The horses stopped moving. They were sweating, their flanks heaving. The men could smell the animals' sweat, the pungent odor mingled in their clothing with the smell of earth, of cattle, of human dwelling places. Eustaquio mentally calculated how far they were from the doors of the storehouses. No rifle could reach them at this distance. A hill covered with oak and walnut trees sloped down to the right of the houses. From there, someone would be better situated than in the houses themselves. To the left, the countryside was flat; no one could hide there. The minute asphyxiation of fear came back to his throat. He raised his head and looked at the sky: the purple and blue fissures of dawn were widening. The hill they had just crossed was rising up darkly, barely illuminated by a powder of incipient light; Eustaquio ordered two men to go back there and stay on the lookout for any movement whatsoever, when the sun rose. He sent Santiago, Alfredo and another man to one side of the storehouses. The others stayed with Raúl, guarding Ramiro and Víctor's path. The dogs had stopped barking for a few seconds. Now they were barking again. Eustaquio could almost feel the steps, the presence of the men who had calmed the dogs down. One of the animals went towards the second storehouse. It paused a few steps from the door, barked and went back to join the other dogs. Eustaquio felt a sense of urgency. Then, when he saw that all the men were in their places, a sudden calm fell over him. He unstrapped his rifle from the saddle and laid it across his left arm, as if he were on foot, firmly planted on the earth. He placed himself on Víctor's right and they moved forward laterally, so as to be first to come within visual range of the back walls of the houses. Already he could see the windows, the barking dogs, more clearly. The silence was pure. It was a limpid, unmistakable sign, like the footprint of a stag or a puma. When they couldn't see anyone in the rear of the houses, they halted their lateral advance. With a nod, he indicated that they should now go forward toward the first house. Eustaquio changed the position of his rifle, and pressed it against his right leg, parallel to the horse's body. He saw that Ramiro was doing the same. Suddenly he felt the wind again and remembered that he had forgotten, that he had paid no attention to the slight human smell, rank and salty, that was beginning to fill the air, the morning: garbage.

"That's far enough," Eustaquio ordered. "Now you go on alone," he explained to Víctor. "We'll cover you. We're within range of any rifle." Before Víctor had stopped completely or turned toward them, he added, without emphasis, "You'd better not go in the house; wait for him outside. Don't try to get off your horse, Víctor, because I won't let you go in. I could even kill you."

Ramiro Chávez wanted to intervene, but Eustaquio told him to be quiet. At that moment it was impossible to explain to him that he might have to die before they did. Víctor pulled the reins back and turned to look at Ramiro:

"He can't come alone. I told you that, Ramiro. Don't be surprised. Hold your men back, because they're not going to be caught off-guard."

"No," said Eustaquio. "They're not. We know. Now go."

As Víctor's horse began to move off, they could from time to time hear the chattering of crows and pigeons in the trees to their right. Eustaquio glimpsed the shadow of a crow leaving and returning to one of the walnut trees. He kept his gaze on the tree an instant more, waiting for the flight of another bird. Several small pigeons flew quickly out across the sky which by then was beginning to redden and fill up with light, as if the birds had found a pond and were surreptitiously testing the water's temperature. Víctor moved forward at a walk. When he was ten meters away, Eustaquio raised his rifle and, serene, unsurprised by the steadiness of his pulse, the assurance in his body, he placed it on his shoulder, aiming. At the least detonation, from anywhere among these buildings, he would fire. He thought that perhaps he, too, would die that morning, and the tiny anguish, unhurried, familiarly, sensibly, with a certain mingling of love, rose from the pit of his stomach. But he was aware of the tension Ramiro Chávez felt beside him, the nervous movement of the horses. He could hear the dogs barking and see the light that was inundating them, restoring the outline of things, the earth, the stones. He could be afraid, his eyes could follow that body as it moved off and at the same time he could feel the steadiness of his own body as it aimed, his unwavering pulse, waiting. Without looking away, without ceasing to aim at the center of what, at that distance, was no longer a man, was already a thing without smell, without feeling, he became aware of that.

"Did you see the door?" Ramiro Chávez exclaimed. "Did you see that door, Eustaquio? It's him. It's Gámez. He's here. I know it's him."

"Yes," Eustaquio thought. But to move the rifle toward that shadow was to die for nothing. It was to risk firing at an illusion, a ghost that he still couldn't hear. From that distance, with the light of dawn falling abundantly around them, opening up like the beating of immense, liberated wings in space, in the sky, the light opening to everything, to all beings, to all the vigorous, new sound of the earth, the birds, the colors, the lives, everything had to happen: Gámez's approach or his flight, the sweet flowing of the day, of the wind, the possible loss of his gaze at the center of that back, the cawing of the crows and the pigeons flying through the air without understanding any of it. Beneath the day's sonorous awakening, beneath the luminous current of the minutes already open and warm, the living body fiercely grasps the silence that watches from other eyes like his own, from another pulse like his own, from an identical waiting. Eustaquio spoke to Ramiro slowly, without turning his head:

"Ramiro," he said, "Leave. Now."

Ramiro looked at him in astonishment without understanding the change in him:

"Are you crazy?"

"They're going to kill you. Leave, now."

Many interminable seconds went by. Deep in his rifle's sight two silhouettes joined, then stayed still, producing a greater silence in Eustaquio's ears, in his tension. Ramiro was hesitating to withdraw; he was gripped by fear, maybe it was too late for him to go. Eustaquio must not move his eyes toward the other figure. He had to make do with the vision the light was giving him. But he knew intimately, deeply, that he was observed, that someone was aiming at him while he was aiming at that body, far down, in the houses where the other man had appeared. He heard Ramiro begin to withdraw. In the distance, he could see that the man was tall, blond, perhaps the same age as he was, thirty-five, it didn't matter. He was armed; he recognized the rifle's glint. And the morning's strenuous light poured down, noisily open, clean, already warm, and everything seemed to gleam and to contain the light. All at once he smelled the wind, remembering that he had forgotten the wind again. And now he smelled something faraway, like something he had known a long time ago. And he was moved by the morning's heat, he felt an unaccustomed joy in his fatigue, a humble happiness in life, in Víctor's body which, deep in his rifle's sight, descended from the horse, smoothly, about to fall onto the grass forever like a caress, like a bird's wing beating deep in fear itself, deep in the lost night of his long wait; he steadied his finger on the trigger and felt that his rifle was the most indisputable, the most restless part of the world; now that he, too, might die, now that the distant silence slowly, unrecognizably exploded in the detonation of all mornings, the voiceless, fluttering light rising from the deepest well in the world, despairing, unrestrainable, flashing forever, finding him forever.

Translated by Esther Allen

The Cenote* at Zac-quí

Elsa Cross

Elsa Cross (Mexico City, 1946) obtained her doctorate in philosophy at the Universidad Nacional Autónoma de México and studied Eastern philosophy in India and in the United States. She has taught the history of theater and literary drama at the Arte Teatral school of the Instituto Nacional de Bellas Artes. Her published works include Canto Malabar (1987) and El diván de Antar, which won the Aguascalientes poetry prize in 1989; the critical study Le realidad transfigurada en torno a las ideas del joven Nietzsche (1985); and a translation of Saint-John Perse's work entitled Canto por un equinoccio (1987).

Water with a green skin.
Slime climbs up the rock.
Trees hugging the walls
let their roots hang down.
Water resonates inside the rock.
Its coolness envelops me.

An open vault covers the pool.
Hundreds of swallows dance;
their cries reach the water,
scarcely brushing the surface, like their wings.

I rip the moss-green cloak
toward the transparent water of the bottomless pool,
toward voices heard within, farther and farther down.

---

*cenote: a deep rock pool or natural well sacred to the ancient Mayan people

Such blue water,
such a clear cry in its depths.
Open to currents
the rock pool blushes when August begins
and someone dies in its waters.

In August
the god, discovered in his hiding place,
heard his besieged people's prayers.
The god of water and storm,
his response was the lightning bolt —
ripping the roof off the grotto above the pool.
Women and children sank,
Mayan and Spanish warriors sank.
The water god carried off in his arms
both strangers and his own.

Every August
startled fishes,
red waters,
broken sandstones,
rain —
          he kisses his sister of the depths:
water bluer and bluer,
the god's mouth.

For you the voices of drowned children sing,
for you the warriors shout,
for you they lose,
for you they triumph.
Into your throat the spears are thrust.
For you the women's sleep
unravels on the looms
                    — spindles made of bone —
and the echo of their voices
                         comes in waves.
The murmurs change your water's hue.

Oh hooknosed god, you're a better friend below.
You play with the children you devoured.
Their little voices swim like fishes,

turn,
sing,
come up to the surface to sigh.

Translated by Cynthia Steele

Javier de la Garza, *Weeping and Sighing* (1991, oil on canvas)

Brine

Carlos Chimal

Carlos Chimal (Mexico City, 1954) is a science writer at the Center of Research and Advanced Studies in Mexico City. He has also published the tale, Escaramuza *(1987), and a book of short stories entitled* Cinco de águila *(1990). He is at work on a novel for young readers about the sixteenth century in Mexico, and a futuristic novel about the Western Hemisphere.*

to Isabel Fernández and François Gresteau

A she-cat slipped through the dry, scorching night. She had just described a pirouette, and was re-entering her neighborhood impregnated with celestial perfume. Without an echo to take note of her, she glanced at the divine glory in the slumbering west and proceeded to examine her paws, beginning with the forepaws, which she gently licked, then moving her muzzle back to her haunches, which she cleaned as well, stretching her warm, wiry, tranquil forelegs to their full length. She sleeked down everything she had washed and continued on to her chest. Then she scrutinized herself for fleas, rubbed against a post, and left in search of food and entertainment before anything could try to block her way.

A man passed in front of her, moving in the opposite direction with abrupt steps. He couldn't seem to get underway, and his disconnected, unexpected pauses would have drawn the gazes of passersby. But the street was deserted: quicker than anyone else to achieve her aims, the she-cat, too, had disappeared from the scene. Passing under the second lamppost, the one the animal had elected to rub against in proof that her electric fur and the sparkle of her eyes were as powerful as any

251

human light, the fellow unveiled his sleep-adder face, piercing and suspicious of God. Then and there, as he had done so many times in the past several hours, he raised his eyes to the sky and lowered the corners of his mouth, surrendering all his bearded perniciousness to the Cherub Cat, son of the Angel Tiger.

The she-cat reappeared on another corner. She observed the movement inside an establishment at the other end of the block, and gracefully directed her steps toward it; over and over, she savored the contact of her cushioned plantars with the stone smoothed by the passage of horses, carriages and automobiles. At the entrance were the words *Brine Bar* in red letters (she saw them as dark green) against a yellow background (that she would hardly have been able to see anyway). Inside she-cats were being served; at the tables she-cats talked, laughed and drank, solitary she-cats read a newspaper or a book, she-cats wrote on delicate blue paper in elegant notebooks. She joined one of the groups, which celebrated her arrival.

"Just in time!" said a beautiful Burmese, all shades of white, with face, paws and ears the color of coffee and round, pale blue eyes that cast their sharp gaze on the new arrival. "Miacis is going to tell us an old story, with animals."

Miacis was a lovely feline of vast proportions; her powerful dentition evoked the saber-tooth (though only across time), but her fine bluish fur gave her a certain resemblance to a marten. After slowly and deliberately licking her much-coveted silken rays, she turned her amber eyes toward the group that had gathered to listen to her today.

"I hate to disappoint Bastia, but I'd rather talk to you about two women . . . "

"Women?" Bastia interrupted.

"Yes."

"But we came here to learn about our own!" the Burmese said, her meow growing louder and louder, "not to hear stories about humans!"

"They're women," one she-cat intervened.

"What does it matter!" said another. "They've despised us and they've worshipped us, but we don't need humanity."

Miacis was unperturbed. She waited for the hubbub to die down and went on:

"As I was saying, in the early afternoon I slipped into the Velodrome in search of a refreshing glass . . . "

"I insist!" Bastia howled. But before the protest could become generalized again, Creature, the last one to arrive, let out a meow of warning.

"Leave her alone!" and then adding, with a disconcertingly vertiginous change of tone, "We didn't come here to rip each other up over humans, they're not worth it; but if Miacis has something to say about women, it must be important to her, and we are going to listen to her."

Miacis smiled for a second and began speaking again.

" 'A gin and tonic,' I told the bartender, who growled as he served me and sulked when he got his tip. Then when I turned around to look the place over I saw Bobcat at a table, an old love of mine. Good old Bobcat. Really an unbearable tom, but he's got a nice mustache on him."

All of them except Bastia meowed and laughed gleefully.

"I walked along the counter and he recognized me right away. 'Miacis, darling, it's me, your precious pussycat!' and he pounced on me, trying to bite me where only he knows how to. But the years do take their toll. As he tried to jump from a table to the counter, he slipped and fell on his poor back. He always was a little ridiculous and he made me feel sorry for him lying there like that. I went to him, licked his chest and changed the expression on his face. He couldn't stop begging my pardon, and took me to meet his new owners. They were a couple of blond women, 'The fat one with the very round face and the brownish hair that's almost shaved off is named Julia; the other one, with chestnut hair, green eyes and one continuous eyebrow is Konstanze, look at the smooth, fleshy slope of her shoulders,' Bobcat told me in his usual authoritarian way. He didn't have to tell me what they looked like, I was looking at them!"

As boisterous meows sounded here and there, Peekaboo suddenly showed up. Her arrival gave the group another opportunity to exercise its lungs. Once again, Miacis continued.

"The two of them were sitting across from two guys, calmly telling them their story. Bobcat and I joined the group, stretched out, closed our eyes and gave ear:

" 'We met him here,' Julia said. 'He'd been living in a hotel in the Plaza Real and he was down to his last dime. There was an altercation with the manager, and since his Spanish was terrible we had to help him make himself understood. Konstanze speaks fluent Swedish, so he was very grateful to us. So grateful that the minutes were passing and we couldn't get rid of him. We started to get worried.

" 'As the days went by it looked as if he had regressed into infancy; he was like a little dog that's lost its master. We made the fortunate mistake of inviting him for a drink.'

" 'Hey!' one of the guys said, catching the paradox."

"Men are so obvious! And they want to be our boyfriends!" three

Angoras shouted in unison. Miacis waited patiently, then picked up the story:

" 'Yes,' Julia continued, a frank smile passing over her heavy cheeks. 'At first we thought we were going to regret it, but due to his alcoholic intoxication he quickly fell back into a state of drunkenness. During a moment of lucidity, he told us about one of his first experiences, in Rio de Janeiro. After a night on the town with some Norwegians, he wakes up to shouts and loud noises out in the street. He looks out, and the first thing he sees is a policeman who assumes firing position and unloads his machine gun into the man trying to escape. The policeman went to the body and counted the holes, twelve in all. Later, as the small crowd watched, a jeep picked up the cadaver and drove off.'

" 'Millions have seen that,' Bobcat said, half-asleep.

" 'No doubt,' Julia answered as if she had heard him, 'but the fact is that after arriving in Spain he decided to join the Foreign Legion. First in Las Palmas and then in the Spanish Sahara. Some Finns belonging to forces that had been stationed there some time before advised him to be trained as a guerilla: you travel by car, there are no long marches, the pay is better and you can carry a pistol. "What were you doing in that place?" we asked him. "I don't know," he answered. "I had never been a soldier, never even wounded anyone. Maybe it was for the money, the adventure." '

" 'Or to top it all off,' Bobcat added in my ear.

" 'He learned how to parachute,' Julia continued, 'how to fight in hand-to-hand combat, throw grenades, use mortars and a variety of firearms and explosives. "We were very busy during the daytime," he told us, "and at night we slept like hogs. You feel secure with your buddies around you, protected.

" ' "All the legionnaires were in the same situation. Abandoned in the red desert, far from any civilization, over our heads the most beautiful starry sky in the world, drinking like royal Vikings . . . I thought about the school in Stockholm, the discipline of the house, my responsibilities to my family and society."

" 'He gave us a long look and spat on the floor.'

" 'But that wasn't really war,' one of the guys said.

" 'No, not yet. The Saharans wanted to expel the Spaniards from their territory but they were too peaceable; the Moroccans showed their teeth but never shot to kill. It was a long wait. One night, while he and a Finn were melting chocolate over a candle, adding water and cognac, they heard shots on the upper level of the fort. They raced toward the noise and surprised a psychopathic Spaniard who had gotten drunk and fired his machine gun at his own buddies. As they try to restrain him, an officer gets a bullet in the knee and a Dutchman another one in the belly. For the second time, death.'

" 'So then he tries to run away again,' Bobcat meditated.

"Konstanze and Julia nodded. The afternoon had faded but not the heat, so they ordered another round of beer and gin and tonics.

" 'He had a plan: he signed up as a volunteer to guard the fort at Christmas and while the troop was celebrating he left his weapon behind and fled for the Moroccan border, about a hundred kilometers away. During the day he buried himself in the sand like they taught him, with only his nose pointing towards the sky. Finally he arrived in Morocco. He was taken prisoner and spent three months in a real hellhole of a dungeon. "I didn't get discouraged. For the first time in my life I had lived, maybe even with greater intensity than in my childhood when I ran into the woods and searched desperately for a hideout, my own imaginary world. The only light was my mind navigating the incredible seas of the imagination."

" 'Thanks to the Swedish consul, he was finally able to scrub off the dirt that encrusted him and throw his Foreign Legion uniform away.

" 'He soon finds himself back where it all started, in Stockholm. "What was I going to do there?" he said to us, as if it weren't something he were really living. "The only thing I had learned was how to kill!" Civilian life was unbearable. The courts had prohibited him from seeing his daughter; his father-in-law had threatened him, which meant that he would have to bash his head in if he ever so much as crossed his path. His parents had taken his chair away from the family table. People insulted him; he didn't have a friend left in the city.'

" 'He never tried music?' one of the guys said slyly. 'The violin, for example? Music soothes the savage beast.'

" 'That depends,' Bobcat meowed, peeling back his eyelids. 'You use nylon strings, don't you?'

" 'He had a taste for reading,' Konstanze interrupted. 'Of course, nothing like we thought, but in jail, after a bank robbery that gave him some money for a while and surrounded him with police informers, he started to write. The day before he got out of jail, he wrote: "The day of freedom has arrived and all I have is my future. I think I can still kill her." '

" 'Kill who?' Bobcat interjected, startled. 'His mother?'

" 'His wife,' Konstanze answered.

" 'Society remained the same, nevertheless. Too little work, too many demands. Love ran out from between his fingers; he met a girl he identified with, but decided on a second marriage with someone who had credit cards and a name. He was no longer young (when we met him he was in his forties), so the Swedish government gave him a tiny pension to make sure he would put up and shut up. "But I had a calling, I was a soldier, and in the Middle East we were in big demand. In an area of only slightly more than a thousand square kilometers, Falangists, Druses, Leftist Lebanese, Syrians, Libyans, the United Nations, agents from the U.S., the Soviet Union, France and England were all competing with each other to see who could make the biggest hole in the ground." '

" 'And so our hero arrived in the paradise of mercenaries,' Bobcat said. 'And then?'

" 'He joined the Falangists,' Konstanze continued after a sidelong glance at Bobcat. 'Christian troops in hell. "We were always loaded on amphetamines and benzadrine when we fought . . . The Arabs too . . . It was just a TV show." When he was with the two of us he tried to hide it, but inside he knew very well what was going on. It was a modern war, ferocious and economical, scientifically planned with an eye to the future. Orders were to shoot at the heels of the juveniles, to make sure that they wouldn't grow up to become soldiers. With adults, you were supposed to shoot at the stomach or the knees.'

" 'Why?' one of the guys asked.

" 'Medical care is expensive,' Bobcat answered without batting an eye. 'But it doesn't cost a thing to bury a corpse.'

" 'Then,' Konstanze went on, 'he got stabbed in the belly in a Beirut street. He was picked up by U.S. troops and sent back to Sweden. He returned to Lebanon because the pay was good: he deposited part of it in an account for his daughter, who must be an adult by now.'

" 'He still refused to hate,' one of the guys said sarcastically.

" 'Hatred is resolved through vengeance. They had orders not to shoot at the United Nations troops, so they only harassed them with threatening bullets that grazed by and made them dance, raw adolescents surrounded by tough old foxes, veterans of Vietnam, Cambodia, El Salvador, Africa, Asia . . . you fight a couple of hours and then you go back to camp and do drugs.'

" 'You still think you're going to find him?' one of the guys asked.

" 'Yes,' Konstanze answered, with all the assurance of a mother."

A large, robust Chartreaux with copper-colored eyes set up a profoundly melancholy meowing whose sounds became as articulated as those of a human baby. But a gray-furred British Blue, her eyes tinted with orange, let out minute, delicate, grating wails. Bastia thanked

256

Miacis with exclusive courtesy while Creature gazed at the storyteller in perfect admiration.

"It's Peekaboo's turn," said Bastia.

Peekaboo, black with symmetrical white stripes running the length of her svelte, elongated body, was bizarre, irrational as a foot in the mouth. They said that her wild disdain had originated in an unfortunate encounter with a viper that had bitten her, causing dramatic hours of convulsions, vomiting and paralysis until her former owner, a mountaineer, had made her ingest an effective remedy. She turned her remote and enigmatic gaze on the assembly of female felines and began her tale:

"At the San Jaime crossroads, a powerful voice which was neither that of automobile horns nor that of friction caused by the growing dampness of the milieu, could be heard in the chimerical edges of time. An old Rex, skinny and light, her curly fur fine and silky, her back arched and her limbs long and straight, stopped at the intersection of Princesa and Platería. She looked towards one or another of the segments opening on the other side of the avenue, and then raised her eyes to one of the windows, where two weasel shapes were moving behind the balcony, one of them that of Commissioner Sebastopol, the other of Inspector Pujoll who, the brim of his soft hat casting a shadow over his mug, was waiting for the commissioner's tantrum to end.

" 'Fuck this shit! When can I get started?'

" 'Listen, Sebas, I've got this poor animal for you ready to swear he's a member of the ETA, the GRAPO and a hundred other things.'*

" 'What are you saying?'

" 'Nothin', it's just that the Catalan Blue Division stopped me. What the hell they waitin' for to get that goddam Warsaw Pact over with?'

" 'C'mon, Sebas, leave it. The cat's not gonna die.'

"The phone rang.

" 'Huh? Yes, Colonel . . . Right away . . . Yes, at your Lordship's house.'

"Without another word to Pujoll, the commissioner left and went straight to an elegant suburb. There he was received and given instructions. Then he returned to headquarters.

" 'Pujoll!'

" 'Hold it, Sebas, the goddamn cat's already a corpse.'

" 'Who cares! We've got to mount a real operation!'

" 'Too bad. He would've been good evidence . . .'

---

*ETA: Basque separatist organization; GRAPO: extreme-left Spanish political organization

" 'Forget that, Pujoll. All of you, take heart! Spinach, saddle up Patent Leather!'

"Heedless of the dense, oppressive weather, the rider and his mount cut across Barcelona's wide firmament to head with resolute elegance for the distant Basque province. Everyone who caught sight of them exclaimed:

" 'There goes Sebastopol! Whatever he wants he gets!'

" 'It's because he's got connections in Madrid.'

" 'That's not all of it: bravery counts for something, too!'

"Later, Sebastopol guided Patent Leather down into a cold, forested place in the Basque mountains and dismounted. Warily, he approached a cabin, pushed open the squeaky door, and went in. He gazed at those present and smiled in satisfaction. The weasel's right arm, Aldo the Corsican, was there; he controlled the neat sporting houses on the Costa Azul, and, only a couple of months before, had scandalized the newspapers by making bitter threats against a Devon Rex who had published a pamphlet denouncing the criminal atmosphere of those casinos. There, too, was the French raven Jean Pierre Perret, a former parachutist accused of causing a fire in a shoe factory, for which at that very moment he was doing time in the Valencia jail. Most importantly, the crow Mohammed Khiar, alias Mehemet, was there, an Algerian mercenary who, for his fearlessness, was one of Sebastopol's favorites: he used to stroll around Bordeaux and Bayonne with his hood on and a machine gun in his hand, hunting fatcat. He had lived in Valencia, passing himself off as an Arab sheik's son studying in Barcelona, breaking hearts in his metallic-gray Ferrari. Mehemet was valuable for his connections in the Bordeaux underworld and his bitter animosity toward all things feline.

" 'O.K., boys, let's get to work.'

"While Perret drove a green Renault toward the border locale of Bayonne, Sebastopol was already dreaming about the Laureate, the medal that hung on the chests of those who had performed the greatest services for the nation.

"A few minutes after seven P.M., the car stopped in the rue de La Fontaine and Mehemet got out, wearing a blue "kangaroo" and a highnecked sweater that covered part of his face. Aldo followed him, wearing a red raincoat and jeans, and they headed for the bar in the Hotel Hendayais. They entered the establishment, full of local felines and a few Basque refugees, and made a full sweep with their automatic rifles. They ran back to the car without even trying to intimidate the few witnesses who happened to be around, got in and in less than a minute

258

they had covered the kilometer and a half separating the bar from the border with Irún. The border guard's checkpoints were in front of them. Perret hesitated for a second.

" 'Judas priest!' Sebastopol screamed. 'Go!'

" 'Have you got the money?' Perret said.

" 'What the hell do you think? YES!'

"So Perret floored it, jumped the French border guard's checkpoints, leveled a metal barricade and collided with a post firmly anchored in Spanish soil.

"Instinctively, the Guardia Civil surrounded the vehicle, pistols and machine guns unholstered.

" 'Holy shit!' said Sebastopol, between Mehemet's legs and Aldo's arms. He got out with his hands in the air.

" 'Take us to the Superior Police Corps at once!'

"At that moment, elements of the French border patrol appeared, demanding that the individuals who had just jumped the checkpoint moments after perpetrating a terrorist act be handed over to them. There were pushes and threats among the three official groups over the jurisdiction of the detainees. Sebastopol showed his teeth and said:

" 'I demand that the territorial rights of Spain be respected. Call whoever it is in Central Command that's in charge of the fight against terrorism!'

" 'Shaddup, you sum'bitch!' one of the guards answered, and used the butt of his rifle to send Sebastopol sprawling in the dust. Nevertheless, just to fuck the French over, the officer in charge of the Guardia Civil detachment, which had indisputable primacy since they had been first to arrive on the scene (and, above all, because there were more of them), agreed to make the phone call. But, holiday or not, it wasn't easy to locate the person in charge of that command.

"Mehemet went over to Loperena and said in a low voice:

" 'Turn off the border lights.'

"Sebastopol quickly understood that he wanted to keep the French gendarmes from identifying them. This was granted them, as well, which allowed them to reassume their jackal shape.

"Finally, well after ten P.M., the bureaucrats in the Irún Police Headquarters got through to the chief of Central Command, who gave them instructions to transport the detainees to Madrid immediately without any kind of identification. Before leaving, Sebastopol excused himself:

" 'Sorry not to accompany you, gentlemen, but Patent Leather is waiting for me. It's been a real pleasure working with you. Adieu!'

"Perret, enraged, tried to jump on him, but was roughly restrained.

" 'Our money!'

" 'Of course, next time you pass through Barcelona!'

"A few days later, Perret fell victim to a deadly trap against the ETA that he had set up in San Sebastian. Aldo never left the Valencia prison again. Only Mehemet was in any condition to receive, in a luxurious Barcelona hotel, six million pesetas for 'services to the state.'"

"And the old Rex?" a Burmese asked, disconcerted. The others looked at her pityingly, as if to say, "Don't you know who's talking?"

Peekaboo gazed at her in all calmness. She answered:

"Two days later she went down to a café in Montcada Street that, as usual, was jammed. Rex and her date found a couple of empty seats next to an old, sinewy Korat tom with wide ears and a tapering muzzle that he was moving with pleasure. A black Bombay she-cat came over to them.

" 'We have hake today. Would you care to try it?' she said.

" 'Yes, and a carafe of white,' the date answered.

" 'So you knew this place already,' Rex said.

" 'Uh-huh.'

" 'Food's good, isn't it?'

" 'And cheap.'

" 'And there are some good-looking critters around,' he added, feeling for the curvaceous shapes of the Rex, who meowed with gratification.

"The old Korat tom, who'd been watching them since they got there, intervened:

" 'She's a fierce little pussycat, so don't try to mess around with her, she doesn't let the sharks get too close," he said, referring to the Bombay but keeping his eyes on the Rex.

" 'None of that, Grandpa,' said the date. 'When you're burning up inside, sooner or later you're going to beg for water.'

" 'Hah," the old tom answered, and went on tearing up a piece of bread onto a plate of chorizo and beans. He continued, "She's the way cats used to be . . . Listen, I'm telling you, the day this city was in the hands of its true owners, the workers, she-cats like her were walking shoulder to shoulder with us . . . '

" 'Who?' Augustine asked.

" 'The FAT,* young man, the feline people's only friend . . . And with these'—he drew out a long knife—'and a few bombs we defended those she-cats and they defended us.'

---

*FAT: Federación Anarquista del Trabajo (Anarchist Labor Federation)

"Looking at the naked blade of the weapon, Rex was mesmerized. The Bombay she-cat came back with their food, then with the carafe of wine, and told them, 'Bon appetit.' When she noticed the knife on the table, she scolded the old Korat.

" 'Put that away, nobody wants that!'

" 'Forgive me, sweet Irma. I was just telling these young people about how we defended the city from fascism.'

" 'O.K., O.K., that's enough.'

" 'Listen sweetheart,' the old tom went on, in a mellower tone, 'there's no way you could bring me another serving . . . ?'

"The young she-cat looked at him in mild irritation, shook her head, and took his plate.

" 'You've got nothing to pay for it with, Grandpa!'

"Rex had barely emerged from her state of enchantment, and, like the American, she was avidly stuffing her face. She sipped the wine and offered some to the old tom.

" 'Come on, Grandpa. Let's drink to liberty.'

" 'Cheers and anarchy!' he said, raising the glass imperceptibly.

"When they left the place, an electric storm was raging outside, with torrential rains and cascades of water breaking in between the mountainous valleys; Rex's mood was changed by a dense, invisible surge that gave her gooseflesh. She set out for Headquarters, climbed up to the roof, and broke in as far as the hallway leading to Sebastopol's office; she lost another night along the way combatting around a hundred rats. Then she slipped to within a stone's throw of the two weasels.

" 'Hi, Pujoll! Everything in order?'

" 'Everything perfect, Commissioner, sir . . . !'

"Sebastopol checked to make sure Pujoll had carried out his orders to the letter. Meanwhile, Rex studied their necks.

" 'Good! Let's keep up the good work, Pujoll.'

" 'O.K., Chief! Another important mission to carry out, I suppose?'

" 'That's right, Pujoll . . . Let's go!'

A Mercedes-Benz transport truck, silhouetted against Montjuich, unscathed, awaited Sebastopol's heavy boots.

" 'You may return to your post!' he would have said to Pujoll, brandishing his whip. Pujoll, standing at attention, would have laughed and laughed.

" 'At your command, Commissioner. I hope you enjoy yourself with Patent Leather . . . He's a terrific mount. He'll take you anywhere. Even the wingèd horse born from the Medusa's blood would have paled with envy to see Patent Leather ridden by such a spirited horseman!'

"Pujoll would have uttered these inanities and even worse ones, for example, 'Rising toward the snowy whiteness of the sky in a picture of singular beauty and elegance, Sebastopol . . . ' Yes, and then perhaps he would have gotten lost on the Avenida del Generalísimo, if it hadn't been for a well-placed blow from the Rex's delicate, sharp blade that detached the heads from their bodies."

There was no pause before the clamor erupted. It looked as if they were going to destroy the dining room, the kitchen and all the flower-pots in the city. The unscathed Tonkinese opened their muzzles like no one else; the Abyssinians, with their menacing green eyes, cheered from their throats. Bastia had to cut off the uproar. It was Creature's turn. Without further preamble, she began:

"His was one more among the dozens of rucksacks that the vacationers were carrying. Joseph, a light but robust Javanese, born in Mexico, with long hair the color of oats, was just one more, among the fanatic rabbits (fanatics for soccer, the train, traveling, summer), the soldiers with a few days' leave, the families emigrating between uneasy territories with borders that were, nevertheless, precise. The World Championships were a blessing, since Mary enjoyed days of rest and better humor. To Joseph's ears, Mary's meowing over the parallel lines of steel sounded magnificent, like a new music in the air. The ancient and arcane stigma of love, as fast or faster than the locomotive and its convoy, overcame the cities' battle to expand. Mary and Joseph, worried, looked out toward the horizon that was the prelude to the Basque provinces.

"Mary was all kisses and caresses among the soot and sharp chips of steel spewing from the factory's gigantic mouth. Seeing the crowd of cats file out and disappear into the city, Joseph held fast to the svelte figure of his beautiful Javanese with her long, silky coat, blond with creamy blue spots. Mary was a tight squeeze and few prayers. There was no time to lose. Wreathed in smiles, Mary was a well of running water. Facing the high ovens of Portugalete, they decided to take the road going north. Joseph looked at everything as if for the first time. The fishing was better in Santander, and in Picos de Europa they saw how the Nuberu rowed by in his cloud, in search of a fertile field on which to unload his cargo of rainwater. The Nuberu, a being between a god and a genie, very tall and very ugly, clothed his body in skins and always wore an enormous old wide-brimmed hat. Mary and Joseph were witnesses to his colossal strength when he sent a squall flying all the way to Asturias. As they entered Galicia, the earth flowered with Galicians while the Moors gravitated underground. Rendered invisible by a magic spell, Joseph and Mary played at discovering them in the streets, invoking them in a thousand different ways. Like the mule driver in Castros de Trelle, on the outskirts of Orense, they offered wine to the Moors who lived under the earth that they had honeycombed with numerous galleries and two doors. Mary stood in the door that faced east, while Joseph was in the one facing west.

"The mule driver's wife had told them that her husband received many gold coins. Mary and Joseph admired the golden illusion that repeats itself day after day in late afternoon, under whose mantle they had to hold each other and say: 'A *San Andrés de Teixido vai de morto o que non vai de vivo.*' ('He who does not go to San Andrés de Teixido alive will go there when dead.')

"When they arrived in La Coruña, Mary climbed to the top of the tower of Hercules and Joseph could imagine the first rays of sunlight that unveiled Geryon's lair and Zeus's own bastard son as he chopped up the rapist. Mary came down. He pressed himself against her and buried his forehead in her lap. Suddenly an old man, looking at an engraving of some fellow, exclaimed, '*Fixese, xa non tenen isas cadeiras ni isos peitos tan fermosos . . . agora sonche moi fracas . . .* ' ('Look at this, they don't have those beautiful hips and breasts anymore . . . nowadays they're skinnier . . . ')

"In the blink of an eye the scene had changed, and it was no longer La Coruña but Vigo, with its impudent boys—'from a whore and a Portuguese was born the first Viguese'—and its girls decked out in sharkskin. La Coruña's hustle and bustle and Santiago's petrified meditation were behind them. Now it was Vigo, Celtic Town, the ephemeral discotheques, the fashion designers, the photographers, and Semen Up in The One-Armed Man; tonight, Mary, Joseph and all the others would have to move, spin and drink, as if the cathedral of Santiago de Compostela's Pórtico de la Gloria were about to collapse. They had to move, because the sacred cows are still sacred, because no matter how early you rise it won't make the dawn more modern. And at daybreak, as the purified earth of the Viguese alchemists received the revivified seed, Joseph and Mary found room in the Kremlin.

"During the day, the gates of the People's University were open. There in the electronic classroom was a middle-aged Atlantic cat, Bibiano Hillock, who taught his students how to use synthesizers and a variety of different mixers. The author of 'A Danza do Aluminio,' music for bagpipes, flutes and shawm, instructed dozens of cats in the new musical technology which they would put into practice night after night in this gray, rainy land.

"But Mary was as transparent as time is fleeting. Joseph knew then that some would be the last flower of a dying plant, while others would be the first blossom of a perennial bloom. Joseph and Mary, with the red weather showing them the way back, were humming 'The Bagpipers Will Come' while a few patient cats built more *zanfonas, charrascos,* bagpipes and the organistrum, so that Galician music would not die out forever. As the hours passed, a sinusoidal silence took hold of the residents little by little; they were irritated because outsiders, vagabonds of the World Championships, were trying to explain their own things to them. Mary and Joseph found themselves on the border. The land of Camoens was just beyond, and Mary's whole body was no longer reflecting light. Cautious, distant, she was acquiring the disconsolateness of the Moorish woman who, on receiving from Joseph a bundle inside of which was a huge, four-cornered loaf of lovely wheat bread, complained that one of the corners was missing, nibbled by the beloved messenger himself or, even worse, by some stranger. And the loaf which, when it was uncovered, had to transform itself into a steed, now suffered from the lack of one of its forelegs.

"So it was that one cold morning in June Mary led the magnificent, mutilated horse to the outskirts of Vigo, took out a revolver, and killed it. Later, unwilling to wait five hundred more years in this sadness, she approached the highway and apprenticed herself in the art of holding up her thumb.

"Alone again, Mary went back, not to Bilbao this time but to Barcelona. She had eaten wheat and she had drunk wine, and she felt her profane body slipping through the Santa María barrio. Soon she had an opportunity to cross through the gateway of an old building and rest on the roof. She scanned the interior patio and saw a window that was wide open. She jumped for it.

"No one heard her go in. With her head held high she glided toward the living room. On a table were the remains of a modest salad of lettuce and olive oil and a little of the thin beer called Xibeca which every hairless female felt obliged to buy. That or a wine aged with something more than haste. She took the rest of the lettuce. Then she looked toward the street and decided she'd like a catnap. She stopped on the outer ledge of the balcony and perched there. Suddenly she felt like she was burning. She touched the latch and understood that it had been an illusion, a kind of terrible thermal shock that extended into the deep meridian of the piece of planet earth she carried inside herself. She looked out the windows and watched the regular motion of the horse show in the old Borne market. Beautiful, long-legged horses were led by at a walk, in silence, in a sober caravan of furrows and solid heads, throats, powerful chests and alternating forelegs; as they turned toward the passageway, the contingent of groups absorbed a final and strange form of animal eroticism. In contrast, intervening between her and the last spectacle was one of the horses' showiest characteristics: the existence of a single elongated toe and not five. If it had developed that way, a horse with five toes would have needed much heavier bones in its legs. As it is, the single toe reduces the weight of the foot and thus the energy necessary for the gallop, because the transversal section of such a bone has to be sufficient to support the tensions of compression and torsion to which the gallop subjects it. As Mary well knew, a single long bone has greater resistence to flexion than five bones with a transversal section of equivalent total area would have. She knew it from 'induced' experience since she had many times felt the sensation that remained in her former master after he had dismounted. She also knew it from books, that accursed mane which exaggerated, which distorted. She imagined caryatids churring, hunted down like partridges. The vast weight of a library on her shoulders. Caryatids filing past for the Khan's pleasure, describing the vacillating, hapless and comical walk of the Chinese duck, thanks to the thousands of manes (from art to computers, from private property to squalid collectivity) that stir each time the sole of a foot presses against the barren earth . . . "

Creature cut herself off and stopped speaking. All of them had withdrawn into themselves. Bastia quickly resorted to music. She knew that any kind of melancholy or mysticism could only lead to lassitude among the orators, so she made a quick jump over to the jukebox and chose a happy, danceable tune with a good beat. The effect wasn't long in coming. The she-cats made wheels, rounds, fandangos with their paws and muzzles, with their quick gazes and their sharp tails, and on the stones that prefigure the city's thoroughfares, a man began to recognize the profound emptiness of his soul as his breath, one exhalation after another, let out a gentle, peaceful breeze.

Translated by Esther Allen

Javier de la Garza, [Untitled] (1986, acrylic on canvas)

The Lizard

Mónica Lavín

Mónica Lavín (Mexico City, 1955) studied biology at the Universidad Autónoma Metropolitana and has dedicated herself to ecological research and ecological workshops and writing for children. Her first book, Cuentos de desencuentro y otros, was published in 1986. She has collaborated on several publications concerning cultural affairs and currently writes for El Universal. The present selection is taken from her latest book, entitled Nicolasa y los encajes (1991).

I was a redhead, before. I'm not complaining about my hair, or the heavy makeup that I have to disguise my face with, or this little room with a radio and one window with cheap curtains. What I hate is not seeing them; all I have to do is think about them and I feel it like a driving cold knife in me.

My room was so pretty. The one that, when I turned fifteen, my mom had decorated pink, with a mirror-dressing table with lots of little bottles to perfume the occasion. For a month I bragged to my girlfriends at school and my cousins and a few boys who came up to my bedroom just for a moment. The little lamps on the bureaus had pleated rose-pattern shades. The bureaus had white curled feet, and in the drawer with the gold pull was my diary with its little lock, my letters from Lorena and my photos of Robert Redford and Jorge Rivero. I also got hold of one of those forbidden magazines with naked women that made me feel nervous and start to perspire just from seeing them. I had a record player just for me, and my secrets that spun with the invisible grooves. I painted my fingernails several times a day, sitting on the rug with my stack of records lying all around me all out of order.

My dad used to spoil me a lot. He said I was just like his sister Chata, who had died very young. One time he even bought me a piano, because I wanted to learn how to play. The teacher came to the house for three months and the one who learned was my dad, for at night and after a few drinks, I don't know what of, he used to remember and play very slowly, with a lot of sadness, some Augustín Lara songs.

In any case my little dad forgot that I was his favorite when Mauricio went to him to complain about me. He had the same critical expression on his face as my husband, and said I was his dead daughter. This really hit me, it knocked me to the floor and I begged him to let me talk to him alone. But Mauricio made fun of me while he was poking me in the legs with the toes of his shoes. Dad didn't look at me, but his hand was shaking, and I held it tight; he allowed me this last gesture.

I would have liked to confide in him before that, when I used to spend the day watching TV and eating crackers, as if that way I was driving away my fear that Mauricio would come home late again. Because he almost always did, and I would be asleep and everything and once or twice he woke me up to make dinner for him and his friends. I objected one time and he hit me in the face, and he said if he brought home the money it was my duty to do what he told me. I would be very anxious when I made breakfast for the children and sent them off. He would stretch slowly and yell at me to satisfy his morning desires, which for me had become real torture, a painful thing to do, because my vagina was too dry. I would play with the children in the afternoon, and then I could forget about his acne face and his hairy white belly. It almost seems to me then that not everything was a duty.

"Mauricio—what a ridiculous name," Andrés had laughed. Then he smelled my neck and full of passion he covered my body with kisses. At night I would promise myself I wouldn't see him again, but by noon I was ringing his doorbell. Andrés was a student and would always be at home with his mattress on the floor and cushions arranged along the wall. I would fall down on the bed so eagerly and get undressed so slowly that it seemed like he had been holding back everything for this frenzy. We would spend an hour naked making love, looking at TV, me wrapped around his slender body while he kept studying the book in his hand. He used to say that without me at his side he wouldn't be able to concentrate. And even though I knew I was too fat and worn out, I began to feel younger and like I had something that was worth putting up with Mauricio for.

I met him in the supermarket around the corner from the school. He helped me very kindly with the bags and invited me to have a cup of coffee at his place. Saying yes didn't seem either bad or good to me. I was so bored that I went thinking that something might happen. While we were walking I noticed his strong neck, his relaxed hands, his noble eyes. I began to want him. I don't know what must have passed through his virgin head, but when we got to his house we put the bags on a table and immediately, without coffee or wavering, he kissed me. This was what fifteen-year-old dreams of love were made of.

Every day after this meeting I had to buy something at the supermarket. Only, one day we fell asleep. It had been a cold, quiet morning, and we were lying sheltered under the covers of Andrés's bed when it turned four in the afternoon. When I got home Mauricio and the children were waiting for me in the living room. I said I'd been assaulted, I pretended to be agitated—which I was—and weepy. And they put me in a car and drove me far away and took the rings and earrings I had hidden in my shoes. Mauricio wouldn't believe me. That night he didn't go out and he stared at me while I was putting on my nightgown. I felt that the caresses of Andrés were showing on my body. He came closer. Why do you have your brassiere on inside out? I blushed. He pushed me onto the bed and left. He came back three days later, completely broken, filthy, said he had gone with Roxanne his little girlfriend who was a prostitute, and so what. And threatened to take the children away from me.

I stopped seeing Andrés, who was calling me, desperate, in the afternoons, and Mauricio got really ugly. He made me make love till I was exhausted, three times a day, by force and with a kind of morbid pleasure in it, and with a rage that I accepted as my punishment. One day he turned affectionate and almost nice. He gave me a drink and then insisted that I tell him what the other man was like and if I liked him in bed. I looked at him without saying anything, and the tears burst out of me in a silent torrent.

The next morning I wanted to see Andrés. I made sure Mauricio was at work and I escaped by bus. I knocked at his door and crazy with happiness he hugged me while I cried like a baby. We loved each other for an hour and I left promising myself not to go back. But I did, I said it was only for a little while and that was enough for the door to fly open and Mauricio and some other guy to come in. I felt ridiculous covered with the white sheet among Andrés's physics books and with his body shaking, and in a low voice he asked them not to do anything to me. Mauricio hit him in the nose and he was bleeding and they took me to the police station almost without any clothes on.

He took the children away from me and with them, the illusion and the fantasy that Andrés had been giving back to me. They told the children I was crazy. I imagine that little by little they came to believe it, especially when my mother brought them to visit me and they found me with strange makeup on and anxious—in such a poor room and my hair half black, half red—and they didn't know how to approach me or what to talk about, and I didn't know whether to hug them or give them candy.

One day my mother came alone and said that they didn't want to come anymore, they were afraid of me. After that, nobody came, not even Andrés, who loved me so much, not even the reflection of my pink room, just the distant melody that my father used to play on the piano. Then I started climbing out the window of my room and stretching out on the narrow window ledge where I could barely fit, and warming myself in the afternoon sun. One day I heard children's voices and I saw one pointing to me: "There's the lizard."

Translated by Reginald Gibbons

Two Poems

Aurelio Asiain

Aurelio Asiain (Mexico City, 1960) is a poet, critic and essayist. He has been a literary editor for Vuelta *magazine since 1983 and has published a book of poetry entitled* República de viento *(1990).*

After Everything

You're right: without a doubt
this was the ocean and it rocked us
between one shore and another, it shifted
the sheets, it marked with spume
the cries of farewell or arrival,
it tossed dead fish onto the decks.

You're right. But in the port
waiting for us was the hunger of the rats.

Life

Really, who would dare to be quiet
so as to listen to himself?

Far, far below the fever
of dream images
clamoring voices
what remains
is a pure stubbornness of blind
fibers.
            Not asking for anything,
an absurdly faithful heart, against the night.

The House at 5 Allende Street

Héctor Carreto

Héctor Carreto (Mexico City, 1953) studied film at the Casa del Lago and Spanish literature at the Universidad National Autónoma de México. He has organized several literary workshops and has published Naturaleza muerta *(1979), which won the Efraín Huerta prize, and* La Espada de San Jorge *(1982), which won the Carlos Pellicer prize in 1983.*

They've knocked down a colonial house at the center of the
    universe,
half a block from Tacuba Street, half a block from Donceles.

But this house returns at night
to be inhabited:
it still likes to hear my creaking
on the spiral staircase,
or the reverse:
it makes me listen to a dialogue of the ghosts,
in an unknown tongue.

Other times, I find myself at the center of the courtyard.
I look up:
the sun has stopped moving, at dusk.
A damp and ochre hour:
the color of the skin of the house.
Its breathing is the water spiraling over the bathtub drain.
There, in the bathroom, I can't see the bottom;

they say there's an iron staircase
that does not go all the way up to the top.
Upstairs, in the kitchen, the same:
the stairs don't go all the way down to the bottom.
It's the hour when the gods of the house appear:
my grandparents, whispering—I feel it—about some
     money-making business or other.
As if they'd stepped out of a photo album
I see them from a distance, blurry, almost motionless,
especially their sharp talons,
their thick lips.

Sepia glows in everything at this hour.
Night is a black angel that keeps coming down.
On the roof, however, there is a slow dripping.
In the pupils of the rain I am broken.
Here is where I lived the first instants of my life:
winter, 1953.

Now they're building a Banco de Comercio.
But I am still standing at the foot of the steep staircase
that leads to the sealed room
I've never seen.

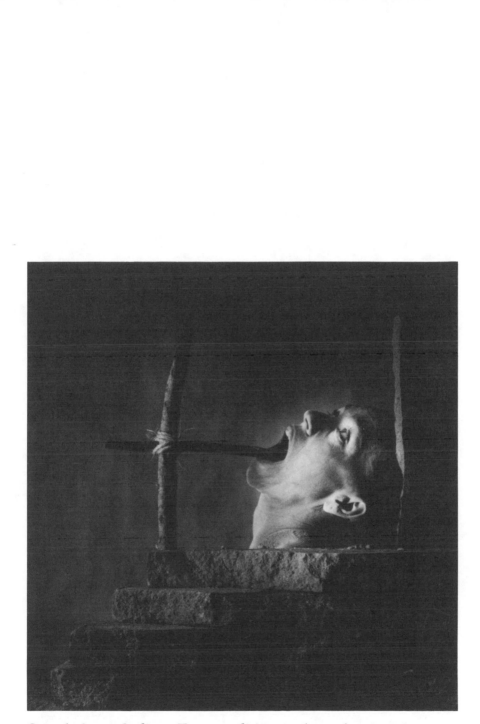

Gerardo Suter, *Codices: Tzompantli* (1991, silver gelatin print)

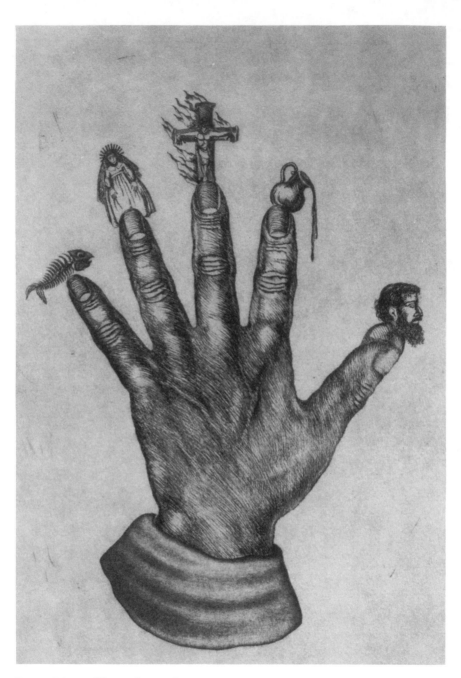

Lucía Maya, *Heart Lines I* (1991, engraving)

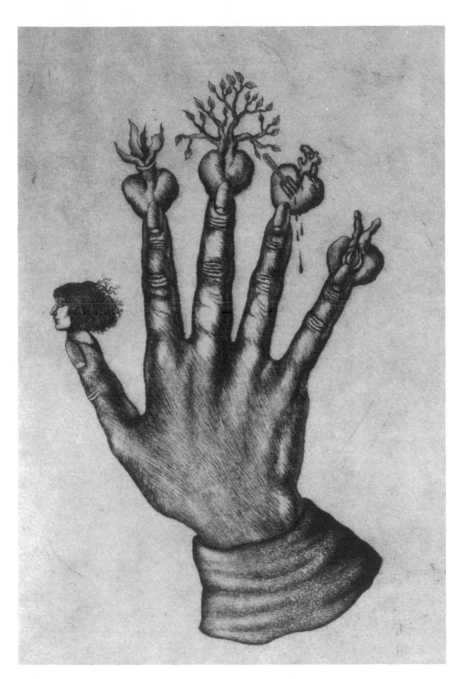

Lucía Maya, *Heart Lines II* (1991, engraving)

From "How Robert Schumann was Defeated by Demons"

Francisco Hernández

Francisco Hernández (San Andrés Tuxtla, Veracruz, 1946) received the Aguascalientes poetry award in 1982. Among his many published works are Mar de fondo *(1982),* Oscura coincidencia *(1986) and* De cómo Robert Shumann fue vencido por los demonios *(1988), from which the following excerpt is taken.*

A strange restlessness arose
in the forest when you were born.
Satanic creatures poured the quicksilver
of Pisces into a clearing
and the combustion of galloping
unicorns shook
the vertigo of darkness into dissonance.
"This child has to be some kind of saint,"
your father said when he looked at your hands.
"He'll be my bright light," said your mother,
her eyes bandaged.
The table grew living sprigs
and tears shone on the walls.
The chapel bells rang
without anyone touching them—even the wind.

Owls overthrown by crows
orchestrated your cradle song
and the night took you into her arms
like a newborn bolt of lightning.

Two Poems

Antonio Deltoro

Antonio Deltoro (Mexico City, 1947) studied economics at the Universidad Nacional Autónoma de México. He currently works on the magazine Iztapalapa *and is the author of two books of poetry,* Algarabía inorgánica *(1979) and* Donde conversan los amigos *(1982). He also took part in publishing a collective book of poetry entitled* Hacia dónde es aquí? *(1984).*

Thursday

Thursday dawns at the same hour as every other day and
    much more openly.
It's so generous to me that it enters my hand as warm and
    exact as a ball of sponge.
Discreetly, like things that look like nothing, on the outside, it
    dawns cloudy, sometimes,
as if Wednesday hadn't announced it with sharp cries.
It's so serious, undoubtedly, that it's a surprise, traveling calmly
    through Friday nights.
You eat it in slices like a tangerine and in the afternoon it
    tastes like an apple.
Thursday's present in every Thursday—even today, which is
    Tuesday, it's present.
You can walk on Thursdays the way Jesus did on the water of
    Lake Tiberias
and without ever stepping on Monday or Sunday, straight to
    Thursday.

Thursday mornings are filled with sidewalks, streets,
     newspapers,
there are people who live them on Wednesdays and people who
     live them on Fridays,
I live them Thursday like an incredibly long, intense journey or
     like a dream that doesn't want to end.
It's not even twelve and I've already met women who have
     made me feel great,
the ball has bounced off the wall, an old man has filled me
     with age.
On Thursdays time stops, poetry and friends appear,
it's a day of strong legs and serene glance when many lives go
     on by night.
I let go of the steering wheel and I'm going to fly, it's Thursday
     in the time of the world,
it's Thursday on this cliff over the narrow beach,
today it's Thursday this morning, it's Thursday on Thursday's
     lips.
Along the viaduct white walls guide the car through the night,
all time is Thursday between one bridge and another on the
     way home.
The tree of Thursday is broad, like time on Thursdays,
birds fill its high branches, and cleave the air:
Thursday sky is an far-flung archipelago of islands.
To climb the first branches of this tree is to look close up at
     distance, to get up on astonishment and ride it,
to know that if one Thursday is a tiger, another can be a
     volcano, and look like one.
In the morning, when the schoolyard opens, filled with games,
when you finally go to history class,
when the afternoons make you skip class, and the chemistry
     notes
forgotten in the classroom are left behind among the studious
     boys and diligent girls,
it's a rehearsal from afar of the departure you'll make someday
     by night.
Also on Thursdays, people kill themselves, but it's not the same
     as on Monday on Saturday,
Thursday suicides are serene, irrevocable suicides,
that sink forever into the waters of Thursday.

Sunken Landscapes

I introduce myself with expert skill, the image of uprightness
    and charm,
I smile and say hello, I am moved.
I'm like everybody else—someone domesticated by entire
    generations:
the teaspoon lying on the checkered tablecloth.
I'm not an eagle or a tiger or a coral snake,
although sometimes I leave my human form.
I've sought myself among beetles and chickens, men and
    stones,
on the border between the street and the weeds,
between a glass bottle and sand,
between a city rat and a country one.
I don't know what order I belong to, I only know that I am
    fierce and wild.
In search of the sky I look at the pavement
and I hear, from under the sidewalk,
the impotent increase of the grass, the water lost
down dark channels, and voices gnawed by rats,
tremors that will lift sunken landscapes up again.
At night, to the steady pendulum of insomnia,
I go with the dogs on their chimerical journey toward the wolf,
and with them I find myself between the moon and men.

The Navigable Night

Juan Villoro

Juan Villoro (Mexico City, 1956) was a member of the Guatemalan writer Augusto Monterroso's literary workshop. From 1977 to 1981, Villoro produced a rock radio program called "El lado oscuro de la luna." He currently edits for music magazines. In the early 1980's, Villoro served as cultural attaché for the Mexican embassy in Berlin. He is the author of Palmeras de la brisa rápida, un viaje a Yucatán (1989), a children's book entitled Los golosinas secretas (1985) and a recent novel entitled El disparo de argón (1991). He has translated books by Georg Christoph Lichtenberg, Graham Greene, Truman Capote, Arthur Schnitzler, Hugo von Hofmannsthal and Gregor von Rezzori.

Over Monte Albán you could see soft, purple, swollen storm clouds. The two couples paused on top of the tallest pyramid to look up at the sky, just like cattle before a stampede.

"Look, a turtle," said Yoli, pointing out a violet cloud.

"Maybe it's going to storm," said Adriana.

"No, they're dry clouds," said Samuel.

Incredibly dry. Dry turtle. Dry Tortuga, Héctor thought, like that island opposite the Gulf of Mexico. Dry Tortuga, sounds like the name of a cocktail. He smiled to himself without saying anything.

Adriana went up to the edge of the precipice. Beneath Monte Albán lies the valley, stretched out like a tablecloth. Adriana stuck a finger in her mouth, feeling content, gazing at the brick-red dirt running up to the crowded houses. She laughed, just because she was feeling good, because the four of them were there in the Zapotec city, seeing the ruins. She thought about the Conquest, about the Spaniards who came here centuries ago wearing tights and baggy breeches.

Monte Albán was an immense cemetery. Adriana remembered a song

283

about drunks who frequent graveyards as she watched Héctor take a shot of mezcal, but she decided not to get mad about it, not now. She went over to Héctor, stroked his hair, and stood there beside him with her arm around his waist.

The last visitors disappeared down the road to the exit; the tourists were going to the graveyard, too. Adriana laughed again; she had a bubbly laugh that sounded like she was gargling.

Samuel observed the sky, feeling like a sailor, an English captain at his command post, because everyone knows that real captains are from England, and anyway, Samuel's parents were from there. He remembered his trip along the British coast, the ocean pounding under the mist, the imaginary sea voyages, the shipwrecks left dangling from a coatrack.

Samuel warned that it would get dark soon and they wouldn't have time to climb down from the pyramid. Héctor, Adriana and Yoli believed him, because it was impossible for Samuel to be wrong about something practical, and they were barely halfway down when they found themselves in the dark and had to guess where the steps were. Then they could feel the grass which is beginning to eat away at the stones and which stretches down toward the exit.

They walked toward the parking lot. The Renault-4 would be waiting for them farther down, on the highway that descends to Oaxaca; it hadn't had the strength to reach the entrance to the ruins. Héctor thought about the road to Oaxaca, about the rattling car lurching along the highway, hitting all the potholes, and about Samuel riding the stick shift like D'Artagnan, as if he were dueling someone inside the engine. The gears shift down like a fencing foil and the car follows, jumping along and making a noise like machine-gun fire. Héctor closes his eyes. What roads. In the United States they must be as smooth as landing strips, lined with gas stations and yellow taxis.

Samuel looked at Héctor in the rearview mirror, laughing. "Just imagine all the cantinas there'll be in Oaxaca," said Samuel.

"Come to think of it, I've got about half a bottle of whiskey with me," said Héctor.

"Jesus," said Yoli, smoothing her short blond hair, "all you guys think about is getting drunk. You can at least wait till we get there."

Samuel glances at her out of the corner of his eye; he saw her light beige sweater, her pale lipstick. She looks really good in pastel colors, Samuel thought. He strokes her hand while he is shifting gears, and the car moves down the road, swaying from side to side like an iguana.

Yoli turns on the cassette player, Joan Manuel Serrat is singing something, and Adriana and Yoli look at each other for a moment. Neither one of them likes it when the two men start drinking; they don't do it very often, but when they do, goddamn. But they're really cool anyway, thought Yoli.

Héctor takes a shot of whiskey and passes the bottle to Samuel.

"Here you go, Englishman," Héctor says.

"An Englishman from Bondojito," Yoli says.

Samuel glances in the rearview mirror at Adriana, who looks serious, then he turns toward Yoli, who slides over to whisper in his ear:

"It can't be true that you're from Bondojito. You're a nobleman, a blue blood, isn't that right? Wasn't your daddy a king in England? The Ugly King of Mardi Gras, at least?"

Samuel takes a sip of whiskey, Yoli bites his finger to see if he has blue blood, and he thinks it's a shame he has to drive all the way to Oaxaca now that Serrat is singing something about the sea and you can see Yoli's blue eyes, deep blue, you think about going to sea, that you've always wanted to do something with your hands, to hoist a sail, cast off, you can sense Yoli a few inches away, her eyes; we have to paint hell blue, Serrat says; you can see the sailboats anchored along the coasts of England, your own failure; but who's a sailor in Mexico?, you stroke Yoli's hair, she really knows how to dress, pastel colors suit her perfectly, and the car disappears, bouncing along toward Oaxaca.

In the Monte Albán night, Adriana remembered the road up the mountain. She had behaved badly toward Héctor. On top of the pyramid, a few minutes ago, it hadn't bothered her that he drank; but on the highway Adriana had had to take a swig from the whiskey bottle, making a funny face, as if she had eaten gunpowder.

Yoli had laughed lightheartedly, as usual, taking things in stride, because she was afraid to speak in earnest, with Daddy's language, the language of monuments, laughing because life is a joke and what matters is knowing how to tell it.

Adriana had looked at Héctor as if she were about to cry, seeming to ask him why so much self-de-struc-tion, with the word chopped up by her tears.

"What's the difference, Adriana, each of us digs his grave as he sees fit," said Héctor.

"Shut up!" Adriana shouted.

"Enough already, Héctor, lay off," said Samuel.

"But it isn't like that, Adriana, we're just fooling around; anyway, we're not even alcoholics. Why make a big deal out of it?" said Héctor.

And he turned toward Adriana, who seemed fragile. He felt depressed but couldn't stop baiting her. She must like it too or else she wouldn't go with him. Héctor saw Adriana's face without any makeup, her black hair.

"Sorry, man."

Adriana feels guilty when she remembers it now, as they are walking toward the Monte Albán parking lot.

By now you couldn't see at all, and Samuel had to use his lighter like a little beacon lost in the darkness.

Héctor passed the mezcal to Samuel. Yoli didn't let him drink.

Héctor could feel the mezcal sliding down his esophagus, remembering when he was in a cantina, down there in Oaxaca, and he suddenly saw a really tall guy come in talking like a child. Later he and Héctor were drinking at the same table.

"Where ya from? You talk kind of funny," said Héctor.

"Australia, but my voice is like this because of the balloons. It'll go away in a minute."

"Hey, kangaroo! I'm Héctor," he said, shaking his hand.

The rest of them had gone to the fair and he was sitting there finding out that the Australian was six foot ten and talked that way because he had swallowed helium gas, which freezes your vocal cords and makes you talk like a child for a while.

Up on the Ferris wheel, Adriana could feel the presence of the city. The cantinas were sprinkled everywhere, as if someone had dropped them from a cloud. God was playing jacks with the devil, He lost, and the jacks fell down, turning into bars. Héctor was probably inside one of them; later they would go pick him up, along with a really tall fellow. Adriana would feel the hot vomit on her shirt, thinking he was an idiot, how could she put up with him, she must really love him a lot.

Meanwhile, Héctor is sitting in the cantina, interested in everything the Australian has to say. He is thinking, there at the table, as if there really were a voice of the conscience, that you aren't going to die, that mezcal wasn't a step toward the grave, in a little while the three of them would come by for you, you're a burden on them, on the English captain who is your best buddy, you made them go off without you because you really dug being alone, you remember Adriana's sad look, really cool, but you know that dogs also have a sad look about them. You can hear the music coming from the arcades on the main plaza: trumpet, marimba and drums: Zapotec jazz, incredible. In the mezcal you can see a transparent hell while you're thinking: no, hell is what we carry inside us everyday, inside our shoes, this isn't the worst part, if you have to change anything it would be somewhere else, you have to make a watchmaker's revolution, modifying tiny things, yes, you have to become your own master, but in the way you tie your shoes. Goddamn, you're too much of an intellectual; that's why you're better off watching the Australian, the landscape before the flood, before everything gets drowned in the mezcal that is going down to your stomach like an anchor. You listen to the music; it is Indian jazz. Of course, Mexico is the world capital of Indianness. You want to hug the Australian but you don't have the strength anymore; you let your hand, then your face, fall down on the table; the music bounces off the wood; you can hear it better, you close your eyes until you feel Adriana's cold hands; you vomit on her and the world doesn't really matter very much anymore; everything spins around like the rides at the fair.

The night was too dark, a black glove that held them captive. They walked toward the exit, very slowly, as if they were inside a cave. When they reached the ball court they stopped; it must have been nearby but they couldn't see any light; how strange. Adriana pressed against Héctor; it was pretty cold.

"Look at the ball game," said Yoli.

"Who's playing next Sunday?" said Samuel.

" 'Racing,' from Monte Albán, against 'Sporting,' from Chichén Itzá," said Héctor.

They stood there a while trying to make out the ball game. Yoli had talked like she could see it clearly, but they could barely make it out.

Héctor thought about Adriana; she had changed there at Monte Albán. He kissed her; why is it that women always have moist lips? How cool.

"Don't let them take the initiative," said Yoli, kissing Samuel, who felt the sweet taste of lipstick, the scent of soap, of bubblebaths with plastic ducks in the tub.

It was the darkness but also the lips that approached you, setting out on the voyage in the middle of the night, transporting you far away so everything would turn into autumn. So your mouth was sowed with wheat, the hair on your arms stood on end from the rain of fine sand and the world turned into an orange, into a hard candy in the form of a lifesaver, into a wooden chair, into the sawdust on the floor, and it was your tongue, your language that moved forward on a bicycle, a nervous cyclist, swallowed up by a night as black as shoe polish.

They started walking again. Adriana, at Héctor's side, regretted what had happened the other day down in Oaxaca. She remembered the hotel and Héctor stretched out on the bed after his drinking binge. Samuel and Adriana told him he was inconsiderate for drinking so much. Samuel said he realized that he himself drank too, but not like that, that he should be more thoughtful toward poor Adriana. Héctor listened to them without saying a word. He felt a little better; a hangover is just a little angel who hovers around you until you belt him one and he goes tumbling out over the balcony. Yes, if he really tried, Héctor could get up and leave Samuel and Adriana there crying alone.

When Héctor left, Samuel and Adriana felt relieved; he could damn well go wherever he felt like. But he was away for a long time and Yoli went out to buy some things and, while she was at it, to see if she could find him. Adriana went to take a bath; she came out a little while later looking hopeful, because Héctor should be back by then. But, staring at her wrapped in a towel, Samuel told her that neither of them had returned yet. A few drops rolled down her thighs to her bare feet. Adriana's eyes filled with tears and then it was like a kaleidoscope exploding and the little pieces of glass slid down Adriana's cheeks and you embraced her, realizing that he was an idiot, but when it came right down to it, so were you, because you were holding your best friend's girl, naked under a towel. You caressed her damp hair and told her he'd be here anytime now.

"Matter of fact, I'll go get him," said Samuel, seeing Adriana's expression; he might have given her a kiss, but he controlled himself and, outside, he felt the Oaxaca sunshine hit him in the eyes.

When they reached the exit to Monte Albán, Adriana was thinking that she shouldn't have hugged Samuel; that was how she had started drifting away from Héctor.

They shouted something, but it was a game of jai alai; the words bounced back from the abyss. Walking around like this was too dangerous.

"Let's not fall," said Adriana.

It took slipping on the rocks as they moved forward to make them realize that they were insects in a gardener's boot.

"You can't see anything at all; we'll never get out," said Adriana, who really felt at peace there, reconciled with Héctor. Anyway, if they were having a good time, what did it matter if they stayed there till dawn?

They started walking again; all four of them felt that harmony which the stars in the Milky Way must have, stretched out over their heads with its classic image of spilled milk.

Samuel put his arm around Yoli's waist, walking toward the grass again, toward the navigable space. He remembered his English parents, with their dry pink skin. Without realizing it he started talking about it, about his father's beating him with a belt, the rigidity, the discipline, and then not being able to set sail forever, to cross the North Sea filled with ice drifts, Florida with dolphins romping around the bow of the ship like his hand romping around Yoli's nose.

They decided they weren't going to be able to get out; they'd better wait till tomorrow. Héctor felt Adriana beside him and remembered that, before they climbed up to Monte Albán, she had acted really different; it was as if something had happened. It hadn't worried him that she had seemed distant over the past few days, but now that she was nibbling on his ear, he had to give some thought to the change in Adriana. Héctor didn't believe in magic, so he had to rule out the possibility that the potbellied devil statues of the Zapotecs had changed her when they had desecrated the Indians' cemetery. No, he didn't believe in divine punishment, so he decided to go backwards, a flashback in the movies, the way memory is supposed to work.

Héctor had been sitting in the plaza looking like a complete fool, until Samuel came up and told him that Adriana was worried.

"Let's go to the hotel, old man."

Héctor had walked along knowing it was his fault but that, when he got to the hotel, he wasn't going to apologize to Adriana. He smiled at the thought that he was a masochist, that it was going to hurt him as much as Adriana, but he didn't want to get back together.

Later Samuel and Héctor saw the bluish walls of the hotel room. Héctor wasn't fooling anyone; murderous little swords darted out of his eyes. This is where Héctor's memories clouded over; he knew there was an argument, that he wouldn't let Adriana hold his hand, and the whole thing started turning into a fight.

Héctor was convinced that Adriana understood him. That's why it didn't matter what he said; the point was for her to go ahead and get mad and leave the room as soon as possible. Samuel jumped up and told Héctor to leave Adriana alone; he was talking to you as your best friend, your brother.

"You're right, Sam, why don't you go get her?"

Yoli stood there joking around as if she weren't taking the whole thing seriously. A good friend, Yoli, but Héctor could never fall in love with her.

Héctor thought about Samuel, about the role of consoler that he had just entrusted to him. Yes, Samuel was a handkerchief where everyone could cry to their heart's content.

In the patio Samuel goes up to Adriana and knows that the inevitable must be played out, the Gospel according to chaos, the storm. Adriana is crying and you tell her to calm down a little, to go for a walk with you.

You feel like you're walking out into a country full of dust and stray dogs. You take her hand, and over your head is floating a dark stain—remorse—because you're taking your best friend's girl away from him. Adriana loves Héctor but she doesn't care anymore whether she suffers with or without him; and her tears feel cold as Samuel's lips draw close. They both know there must be something about this in the Bible; they would have to clip that section and slip it under all the doors so people would know that they weren't the first, but when all is said and done that doesn't save them from anything and the stain keeps on floating there in the air, getting bigger and bigger.

Héctor remembered it all at Monte Albán, up to the point when Samuel went to get Adriana; something must have happened then. But he is suddenly aware of being on the grass; he stretches out and so does Adriana. Samuel and Yoli also lie down. They kiss, and dainty fragile streetcars glide over their bodies.

Afterward Héctor tells them about the Australian, that he was a giant but he swallowed helium gas out of balloons so he could talk like a child. A fellow with enormous boots. And Héctor remembered the hotel room again. Adriana asking Samuel to make a knot in her blouse, Yoli convincing herself that nothing had changed, using jokes to gloss over what Héctor had already seen—he had practically forced Adriana to do it. Everything fell apart then; they decided to go back to Mexico City, but first they had to visit Monte Albán. At least they were still good tourists.

So they climb into the car that doesn't reach the top, all four of them speaking with great tact; nothing had happened. Samuel and his exact estimates—a hundred more yards and we'll be there—the four of them walking toward the entrance to the ruins. Adriana laughs, listens to Héctor, thinks he is nice, that going with Samuel is like a substitute for the friendship between them, that all it did to Héctor was replace him.

Adriana felt content. She saw Héctor and, as a farewell gesture, hugged him, and they walked into Monte Albán together.

Samuel lit the cigarette lighter again; they looked at each other in silence.

"I've never seen so much darkness before," said Samuel.

"Yeah, it's as if we were in the belly of a whale," said Héctor, feeling Adriana's hands around his neck, warm as a pancake.

He could see Samuel through the flame of the lighter; he looked like he was about to cry. Poor Sam, with no boat, not even a canoe like the ones at Xochimilco. Héctor stands up and lands a gentle blow on Samuel, as if to say it doesn't matter, fella, Adriana's yours; because he knows that that night has been only a respite, that when the sun comes up they'll go down to Oaxaca to continue the battle that he's already lost. If he runs into Samuel and Adriana in Mexico City, he'll cross the street. No, it isn't that easy, and Héctor thinks about the night that hasn't ended yet; it is a long time till dawn, till tomorrow, brother. Lightly he pokes Samuel again so he can keep feeling the respite, Adriana's hands moving slowly over his neck like a sailboat disappearing into the darkness, loaded down with bread, with honey, with arrows and amphoras of wine.

Translated by Cynthia Steele

Dulce María Nuñez, *Mason with Jaguar* (1988, oil on wood)

291

The Time I Got Drunk

Bárbara Jacobs

Bárbara Jacobs (Mexico City, 1947) is a writer and translator. Before beginning her studies at the Universidad Autónoma de Mexico, Jacobs spent time studying in Montreal. Her first book, Doce cuentos en contra, appeared in 1982. She has also published a collection of essays entitled Escrito en el tiempo (1985) and a novel, Las hojas muertas (1987), which won the Villaurrutia prize in 1987. Her latest novel, Las siete fugas de Saab, alias El Rizos, is due to be published shortly in Mexico and Spain. Jacobs lives in Mexico City with her husband, Augusto Monterroso, the well-known Guatemalan writer.

La Güera has sworn she's my friend and when we see each other she gives me a big hug and tells me, "I'm so happy to see you" and everything but I'm not so sure. It's true that she has shared some important secrets with me, like what to put on your eyelashes at night so they'll grow longer and won't fall out and will look like an Arab woman's; and it's also true that she's let me listen when she talks to her boyfriend on the phone, so I'll learn what to say to mine when I have one, but I'm not sure. You see, I've also caught her in some lies, and that's what makes me wonder. Is she really my friend?

For instance, the other day her hair looked so pretty that I asked her: "What did you do to your hair?"

"Nothing," she answered, and she threw her head back and sent her blond hair flying; it got even shinier and wavier, like what happens to the hair of the models who advertise shampoo on TV. "So it's true," I thought when I saw La Güera's hair—see? I didn't believe TV; I thought they used tricks. That a shampoo could never, ever work such magic.

"Whatta you mean, nothing, Güera? Come on, don't be like that."

"Well, I did wash it, but I didn't *do* anything to it."

292

Then I found out she had spent all morning at the beauty parlor; that they had given her a whole lot of treatments and then dried her hair with infraviolet rays or something like that.

That's when I started wondering whether La Güera was really my friend. Why had she hidden the business about the beauty salon from me?

I played dumb, because that night she had invited me to a party and I needed her. See, I don't know how to put on makeup or get dressed up for things like that. Anyway, I don't have the right *kind* of clothes, and she had to loan me some. It was my first party.

It was horrible, except for one little part. A really handsome boy whose name is Claude, because his parents are French, came up to me and said:

"Do you want to dance?"

I was sitting on one of those little rented chairs with the name of some soft drink on the back. I told him no, that I didn't know how, which was true. Seriously. And he was about to walk away, probably to look for some other girl who was also by herself, when La Güera appeared. Right away she realized what had happened, because she leaned over and whispered in my ear:

"Don't be a fool."

And she straightened up and then Claude said to her:

"My name's Claude. My parents are French. Do you want to dance?"

La Güera accepted and they went off to dance and she doesn't know how. Claude is the one who is her boyfriend now and he calls her on the telephone about three or four times a day. La Güera lets me listen on the extension in her mom's room. In there almost everything is covered with real soft brown velvet, and the bed is on a sort of platform, also velvet-covered.

La Güera and I aren't just friends. We're also cousins. Her dad and my mom are brother and sister, and we live close to each other. So close that, in order to get to her house, all I have to do is cross the yard. Then I look for the key under a rock; only La Güera and I know which one it is. The bad part is that sometimes the key is covered with sow bugs and then I throw it down and feel grossed out for a while.

I'm almost always afraid to go back to my house alone, so La Güera keeps me company, but only as far as the door. She never goes inside my house, even though I spend all day Saturday and Sunday, and practically every afternoon during the week, in hers. I like her dad better than mine. When I'm all alone I wonder why I couldn't have been his daughter. Our fathers are so different! And mine is an ogre. Everyone knows it.

The other day I even got drunk, all because of my dad. Well, and my mom too. Because of what's going on between them and I see it. My brothers and even my sister have grown up and moved out, so they're lucky they don't have to see any of it. When they come over they make sure first that Dad isn't home, and Mommy acts like they're her only children and she never gets to see them. When that happens she doesn't treat me so well. All she says to me is:

"Susana, go get the crackers," or the tea, or whatever, with her singing voice.

Sometimes my sister asks me how it's going, but I don't think she really wants to know, because when I'm just about to tell her she glances at her watch, jumps up and says:

"I have to go!" because her husband is about to come home and if he doesn't find her there he'll kill her, she says.

"No you don't," I tell her, but I say it in a low voice. I don't think she even hears me, or else she doesn't understand me, because she doesn't smile or say anything.

The day I got drunk was horrible.

My dad was locked in his room and it was about two in the afternoon. My dad spends practically all his time in that room and doesn't let anybody else go in there. I'm the only one he'll let inside, but only when he's gone. I make his bed and run the vacuum cleaner and dust off his papers, but not very well: if I read anything I shouldn't, he'd catch me by just looking me in the face. I avoid his eyes and that gives me away. He'd dig his nails into me, I'm not sure where. He sleeps by himself. He goes out for about two or three hours a day, but I don't know where he goes or anything, now that he hardly works. He just tells me "Good morning" or, when he comes home, "Hi," if he sees me around.

As for my mom, he doesn't speak to her or look at her or anything and, if they run into each other on the stairs, they both pretend they didn't see each other. They pretend to cough and look the other way. Or if my mom looks down, my dad looks up at the ceiling. The worst part is when they run into each other at the turn in the stairs, where the steps get tiny on one side, like on the pyramids. It's horrible. Because then my dad, without *saying* a word, lets my mom know he has the right of way, and my mom—and this is when I hate her—makes like she wasn't even planning to go upstairs, if she was going up, and she backs down to the bottom. And so she *yields* the right of way to my dad. I'd like it if she didn't do it, but she does.

Anyway, that day my dad was locked in his room and he called me. He opened the door and started to shout at me. When he calls me like that I feel horrible, like someone's going to go by on the street and hear it and think things are really bad at my house. At first he started calling me in a more or less normal voice, but then he started yelling louder and louder. He was calling my name:

"Susana, Susana," and I hurried as much as I could in the bathroom, which is where I was, and went to his room.

Then he told me, with the door barely cracked open, to go downstairs and tell my mom that he said he never wanted to *see* her noodle soup again, and if he so much as saw it again he would throw it in her face.

"Yes, Dad," I answered, because for about the last five years I've been carrying messages back and forth between my dad and mom.

Before, my sister used to, just like she used to make my dad's bed and clean his room. But when she started going to the university, my dad started hating her and burning her books. Then she started to sort of defend herself and hid all the books she bought in her car. She had a red Volkswagen, all beat up, and she kept it in La Güera's garage, as a matter of fact. That is, in La Güera's parents' garage. And she pretended she didn't have a car or books or anything.

So when my dad gave me the message for my mom, I went downstairs and delivered it. My mom was in the kitchen fixing dinner, because we don't have a maid. My mom and my grandmother do everything (except my dad's room, which I do). My grandmother is very, very old and, even though she's *really* good-natured, sometimes you can tell it's hard for her to do things. When she doesn't think anyone's listening, she complains. She and my mom get up as early as they can every day, around five, even if it's still dark, or cold, or Sunday or a holiday. My grandmother loves to say, "The early bird gets the worm," and it seems like she's saying it for my sake, because I'm lazy.

The first thing my mom does when she gets up is drink tea that's so bitter, it even *smells* bitter. Then she and my grandmother start doing things. By the time I leave for school, they've already done nearly everything and I can't imagine what they have left to do, but when I come home the house is—I don't know—as nice as it could be. I wouldn't say it's as cool as La Güera's house, because at my house everything is sort of old, sort of used up. For example, the carpet. It's really stained because of my brothers' children. They're babies so they do everything on top of the living-room carpet, right in front of everyone.

Once I overheard Mom saying on the telephone to La Güera's mother that all she cared about was that I come home to a *nice* house, so I would want to spend time there. I felt horrible, because the truth is that I don't like to spend time there. It smells like bitter tea and the carpet is disgusting.

But what bugs me the most and even makes me cry is hearing my dad slam the door at night when he locks himself in his room and then my mom slam the door behind her and my grandmother. My mom doesn't slam her door as hard, but it makes me just as sad.

When I get home from school all I want to do is lock myself in *my* room. If they call me to supper, a lot of times I holler that I'm not hungry. I also don't like spending the afternoon with my mother and grandmother. What they do is watch one TV program after another; sometimes they even start falling asleep, or the picture gets fuzzy and they don't even notice. It's horrible. Well, my mom also spends a lot of time talking on the phone, and drinking lots of tea, and eating lots of crackers, but always with the television on. That's what afternoons are like at my house, and that's why I cross the yard and go looking for La Güera, so she'll teach me how to be like her.

Just like Claude, who saw me first, but stayed with her once he'd seen her; the same thing happens with everyone. With our girlfriends at school, with their mothers: everyone sort of falls in love with her. Me, for one, because she's so pretty. It's funny; I'm a blond too but no one calls me "La Güera"; I wonder why.

Anyway, as I was saying, I went downstairs to give my mom the message.

"Mommy," I said, "Daddy says he never wants to *see* noodle soup again."

I didn't dare tell her the part about his throwing it in her face if he *saw* it again. Not so much because I was scared as because I felt sorry for her. It's just that my mother's face is covered with what's left after you've had a bad case of smallpox, and before she used to put on all kinds of face creams, *French* ones and everything, to get rid of the pock marks, or to fill them in, I'm not sure, but the thing is, it didn't work. And her face stayed that way, all pockmarked.

When I gave her my dad's message she was cleaning a chicken by candlelight, and my grandmother was washing the dishes wearing some red rubber gloves.

When I told them about the soup, they were speechless. There was such a silence that I was speechless too. I thought maybe I had announced I was *going* to tell them something and they were waiting for me to say it, something dangerous.

So I repeated the message and they turned and looked at each other, obviously scared. Then, still not saying a word, they stood there staring at the Bunsen burners, because we don't have a stove. And, more specifically, they stared at *one* of the pots on the Bunsen burners. They looked at it and started exclaiming things, then finally asked each other:

"And what are we going to do now?"

My grandmother was waving the red rubber gloves around and I shivered, like I used to when I was little. I had an urge to tell them not to do anything, but then I remembered the part of the message that I hadn't delivered.

I went out. That isn't exactly true; I went to the bathroom, which is where I was when my father had shouted for me to go to his room immediately. I haven't mentioned that there's a plant next to the window which opens up at night and closes in the daytime, or that when my father shouted my name the leaves shook. Anyway, I locked myself in the bathroom and stood in front of the mirror and took off my blouse. It was still the blouse from my school uniform, because unless I go over to La Güera's house, I don't change my clothes; I leave my uniform on until it's time to put on my nightgown.

I turned around a little and looked at my back in the bathroom mirror. It looks horrible, full of pimples. Horrible. Really. I don't know what to do but pop them, even though when my mom catches me doing it she gets furious and asks me if I want to look like her or what. But I know her face was from something else and it doesn't scare me. As a matter of fact, it makes me feel braver, and one day I even told her:

"Leave me alone."

But the day of the noodle soup I stayed locked in there in front of the mirror longer than usual, thinking hard and looking at my back, but the longer I looked at it, the more disgusted I got.

I remember thinking a lot about La Güera, that I'd like to see her back to find out once and for all if she really doesn't have any pimples. I've already told you that, even though she's my friend, I sometimes doubt her and think she's hiding things from me. For example, she has never put on a dress that's low-cut in back; she always wears the kind that's lowcut in front (maybe because what she has got in front is really pretty, who knows, but her parents let her). Also, she has never gotten undressed in front of me, and when she comes out of the shower she holds a bathrobe under her chin while she's getting dressed, so I won't see her. On the other hand, when she invited me to that party I told you about, La Güera made me take my clothes off in front of her, so I could try on the dress she loaned me. I was embarrassed but I did what she said and didn't even partly cover myself up with a bathrobe. Anyway, that day she even made me take a shower. She tossed me a sponge and a bar of soap over the shower curtain and said enthusiastically, "You're lucky, they're new," so I would feel really privileged or something. But I didn't get excited or anything. I think she gave them to me just so I wouldn't use hers, because I'm sure she thinks I'm disgusting.

As I was saying, something made me stay in the bathroom, something seemed to be telling me:

"Susana, you'd better not leave."

But all at once I heard a door slam. And it was like a sign or an order. It was a command that my body started obeying as if it had a will of its own. I hurried and got dressed again and, all nervous, I went downstairs.

The order took over inside me:

"Look or else I'll kill you," it told me.

So I went.

When I reached the last step, the screams I heard almost made me freeze, but the voice inside me pushed me on, walking, running, flying, to the kitchen, where the screams were coming from.

At my house, in order to reach the kitchen you have to go through the breakfast room, which is where we eat breakfast, dinner and supper, because the dining room doesn't have a table or lamp or curtains or anything: it's an empty room where we're going to put furniture some-day, so we can invite all our friends over and be really happy, or anyway that's what my dad and mom both used to tell me when I was little.

So I went through the breakfast room first. That's where my father's place was set. He eats all by himself, before the three of us do. We don't sit down until he's eaten and locked himself in his room. I noticed his napkin was unfolded, as if he had started eating and had gotten up and was about to come back now. There were the salt and pepper shakers, the bread, all the sauces my dad always wants on the table, even though he doesn't use them or anything. And there was his glass of wine, too.

The screams coming from the kitchen weren't words, just screams: "Ah, ay," and that sort of thing. You could also hear the kind of sounds that come out when you're clenching your teeth and trying not to scream. And finally, a sort of moan or squeak or something.

In the kitchen, I saw my father standing with his back to me. He had his arms down and hanging from his right hand, I think, there was a deep bowl with a few drops of something or other running out of it. Standing in front of him I could see my mom, her face covered with noodles. She was crying, and her chest heaved up and down just like a toad. And somewhere in the general vicinity, next to the sink, was my grandmother, with her mouth hanging open. And when I looked closer I could see that she was standing with her legs apart, too. In between her black, laced shoes, like half-boots, there was a puddle just like the ones my brothers' kids make on the living-room carpet.

When I realized what had happened, I started to cry. My dad turned halfway around and said:

"Susana, button your blouse."

I had left the bathroom in such a hurry that I actually hadn't buttoned it or anything.

That afternoon I got to La Güera's house even earlier than usual. Her parents were still sitting at the table, but since La Güera had already gone to her room, I barely said hello to my aunt and uncle and went looking for my cousin right away. I heard my aunt and uncle asking me what was wrong, but I didn't answer them. In fact, I *ran* to La Güera's room.

She was getting dressed to go to the theater with Claude; then they were going to supper afterwards. She smelled really good, like wheat and dew and early-morning mist, I thought. I asked her what perfume it was and, when she told me the name, I burst into tears again.

I cried and cried, and while she finished getting ready and everything, she tossed me a box of Kleenex and said:

"After you calm down you'll tell me all about it, Susana."

I'm not so sure. What could I tell her?

Anyway, once I had finally calmed down a little, my cousin told me she had to go, that Claude was about to come by for her.

"But we'll talk tomorrow," she said, and left.

As I watched her walk away, it occurred to me that the next day I wouldn't have anything important to tell her.

That's when—because of all these things and some others I don't understand—I got drunk.

Translated by Cynthia Steele

Toward the Horizon

Jesús Morales Bermúdez

Jesús Morales Bermúdez (Mexico City, 1956) studied philosophy and social anthropology; these studies, as well as his experience working with the Choles Indians from Northern Chiapas, have contributed greatly to his indigenous themes. He is the author of many essays and works of fiction, including: Para entender la realidad donde estamos (1978), Los cuentos de la tierra (1986) *and* El memorial del tiempo o Vía de las conversaciones (1986), *which won the Bellas Artes de Literatura Testimonio prize in 1987.*

After a while another little boy came into our home. I remember those days because there was plenty of corn growing in the mountains; my brother Benito got lucky and got a deer, and between the two of them, Catalina and Catalina's mother fixed a huge pot of *ciguamut*.* The relatives got together. We really ate and drank. Don Diego and my brother-in-law Agustín played for us, one the violin and the other the guitar. Don Diego's old father was already dead and his grandson was taking over his trade. And his grandson and I were friends. We used to raise hell together, and one time we even got away from death. But if death wasn't powerful enough to take us, it did come to feed on my son's little body. My son was fat, nice and fat, and I never understood how he got sick. I bought a radio and liked to listen to it real early in the morning or when I got home from work. That day we were getting ready for a fiesta. We were at home. My son in his bed, just two months old, a baby, and fat. We were listening to the radio for a minute, then we went

---

*Ciguamut is a stew made of venison (which may be replaced by goat, chicken or beef), potatoes, carrots, and cilantro, which is eaten throughout southeastern Mexico [author's note].

300

over to look at the baby and we found him dead. This was during the celebration of All Saints' Day. It was when we decorate the altar for the dead. In the middle of mourning my son's death, I went to decorate my altar and arrange the offering on it. My wife, in tears, was making the tortillas, boiling the meat to place on the altar, as food for the saints. I put a New Testament, which I had just bought in Spanish, there, even though I didn't know anything about God or preaching or anything. I didn't even know how to read. I just bought it because I liked it.

In the only room in our house—there was no kitchen and everything was sort of crowded together—I lay down for a little while. I felt sad and I wanted to think it over, my little boy's death. I put my hand over my heart. I listened to how my wife's crying rose, she was in so much pain, as much as she would have liked to be strong. Deep in my heart I felt compassion for that woman. She's really devoted to me, to the kids; she puts herself out fixing meals, making all the arrangements when we're getting ready to move on. I can't complain about my wife. I made no mistake when it was my time to choose. And as strong as she is, she runs the household really well; she takes care of the clothes, sees that there's always oil in the lamp, and light bulbs. Her health is strong. She has legs like big strong oaks. It's the first time I've ever seen her fall like a wounded bird, at the tragedy of such a short life.

Hoping to console my wife, I dared to ask her if it could be true that souls come up to eat the food on the altars. If it wasn't, what was the use of my altar, my candles, the little things in my offering, my wife's home cooking? I was struggling with that doubt and was anxious for some sort of response, especially so my wife would feel better, but instead she cried even more. Lying there like I was, talking softly with my wife, it happened to me in a flash; as I held my hand over my heart, my spirit left my body. My spirit slipped out through my fingers; my fingertips were like a conduit, and when my breath had left me, my foot jerked and I was dead. I could feel, really feel, death, and from some hazy dimension a long ways from reality, I looked back at my body, my lifeless body lying on a *tapexco*.*

At the instant you die, you contemplate your body: it's just a piece of something, with no value, no movement or substance. The spirit, though, marches on happily, happily through mountain streams bathed in light, in great sweeps of radiance like the beds of great rivers. That's what happened to me that time, when, after a short journey, my spirit

---

tapexco (*tapesco*): a homemade bed frame common in rural Mexico, made of branches, twigs or reeds tied together

was standing before two roads. My spirit encountered a wide road and a narrow road, a cross standing between the two roads, the cross of those who throw drinking parties or those who have two wives. Next to the cross there were some soldiers, getting devilish delight out of using their rifle butts to hit everyone who came by, and constantly setting a bad example. My spirit's eyes rested there. That's when I saw the procession of souls. First I saw the ones who are spirits of dead people: fathers, mothers, brothers, sisters; souls someone is expecting to enjoy the offerings: offerings covered with oranges, meat or *posol*,* or tortillas, or whatever is put on the altar. And just like how when you live in the world, you go to the cornfield and bring back your sack loaded down, so the spirits of the souls went along carrying their little sacks. I really saw it. I don't know what strange power allowed me this knowledge and I saw the knowledge. And I saw the other souls, of dead people that no one's expecting. These souls walk along with their hands folded, crying and crying, waiting for some compassionate person to offer them something. These souls eat very little. There's no fruit-filled altar waiting for them, nothing, and they march along hungry, suffering, maybe until the next year. That's what I saw; there's the cross; there are the soldiers, a seven-headed snake**; and there are the soldiers hitting people right and left, and I barely managed to escape between the two roads and get away from death. But it isn't true that I got away. I should say, that's what I tried to do. I saw myself walking along, like a soul on the Day of the Dead. And I only walked about a thousand meters, beyond the dimension of consistency and air. I walked a thousand meters and immediately I stumbled on a sort of church, a big one, about five hundred meters long. I had seen it once before, in a horrible dream: one gloomy evening at sunset, coming home exhausted from the long trip I made to find out about the organization and its benefits – tears of powerlessness, of weariness on the last hill, the road was so steep – and on the way to El Ceibal I went through Zapata, through Majastic, Naranjos. And traveling along exhausted, hungry by now, without any *posol* or tortillas in my

---

posol: a drink common in southern Mexico and Central America, made from roasted, ground maize and water

**The seven-headed snake is a symbol of the underworld in Mayan mythology. According to these myths, a person must ride a black dog to seven places, each containing a fragment of its life. The seven heads, then, represent the dispersal of life, which can only be overcome when the snake is reduced to its normal state (with one head) and is made useful to people. It is used in the underworld to hang hammocks from or as a beast of burden [author's note].

bag, with my foot aching and fear in my heart because I was going through a town with a reputation for being hostile, for having strayed from its ancient religion, I pushed myself on in order to get out of there as quickly as possible. And on the farthest hill of Naranjos, the most beautiful town in our region, I ran into a group of men chatting in a church doorway.

"Who goes there?" they asked me. "A person or a thing?"

"A harbinger of the future," I answered.

And:

"Halt," they told me. "Come see the ones who stare out of their niches without seeing."

My heart was filled with fateful curiosity. I wanted to hasten my footsteps, to run, but the will power holding me was even stronger, a growing fire urging me to see the colonnade of that church. I looked up at the front of the church and contemplated its facade on different stories: each of them was lined with niches, in half arches held up by slender columns. Emptied of the images they were designed for, their first beauty was changing form, as if it were dissolving into mist. The different stories and the niches looked like the grimace of an enormous skull coming close and withdrawing, with its booming face: a trembling inside my bones. I tried to shoo the image away, because my flesh could stand the fear no longer, and when I turned around to look at the men in front of the church, they turned into mummies, into grinning skulls, reaching toward me with their jeers, their hands, nearly grabbing my neck, my life, in the midst of their mockery and my fright.

Certain I was about to die, but still holding firmly onto the green pastures of life, once again I ran for my life, terrified, to get away from a vision, from fear, and my footsteps went into the chapel and ran into complete darkness, the mummies behind me reaching out their hands toward my neck, with lots more, infinitely more skulls mocking me from their countless niches, their desire for pleasure coming to rest on my body. I realized it was impossible to escape and, in an act of serenity, I stretched my body out on the earth, with my center at the very center of that church. Then the abyss, and I don't know how I returned to reality inside the walls of my village.

That's what happened during my dream and that's what I was faced with when I left the place with the roads. This time there were no men at the door; instead, a radiantly beautiful woman.

"Good morning, Miss," I said . . .

"Good morning, Sir. What is your wish?"

"It's my wish to go in and see the celestial Lord, the owner of this house."

"Come in, then; unbar the three doors."

One by one I took down the bars, massive doors made of *chicozapote*,* lighter than air. Still, when I was on the other side, closing the double doors, an old man blocked my way, asking me:

"Who gave you permission to come to this region of winged shadows?"

"No one," I told him, "no one has given or denied me authorization. Desire led me here, and here I am. Are you by any chance looking for a way to dissolve me . . . or the vision?"

"Lord of Protection . . . " he said to me, and I looked upward and stopped paying attention. I looked up at the ceiling of the house, but the house, which had no roof, opened up to the infinite, balmy, deep blue sky, the very sky built by the Son of Mountain. For one light-filled instant I perceived the coming together of my grandfather and my father. The heiress of the Holy Moon, Saint Lizandra** of the long hair and lovely eyes, was delivered to me as a reward for my suffering. And I wanted to see my father, to see if he still had his shriveled-up leg. And I wanted to see my grandfather, and know the brilliance of his wisdom, but maybe because of my scant knowledge, neither figure accompanied me. On the other hand, the lovely, radiant, serene, long-lashed moon shone silver against blue steel, peaceful for my sake, pouring out her arms and legs as if to spill the rain. I reached out my arms to catch her, but tirelessly she evaporated, giving way to another presence: that of the celestial Father, along with Jesus Christ, crucified, and the Virgin Mary. There the three of them stood; there was nothing else. Then Jesus lowered his hand from where it's nailed on the cross:

"Son, it isn't your time yet," he told me. "It isn't your time. You should all keep doing the things you do. That's good. Look for everything wherever you go. Adorn your altars. Gather together the oranges, pumpkins, sugarcane, flowers, candles, incense, *aguardiente****. Today isn't your time. Go back, go tell the grandparents about this. The time of your arrival is yet to come."

---

chicozapote: a variety of the tropical fruit tree *zapote*, known in English as sapodilla plum or sapota

**Santa Lizandra is a Mesoamerican version of the Moon Goddess, a queen or princess of the villages associated with the harvest, festivals and magic [author's note].

***aguardiente: a home-brewed liquor consumed in rural Mexico

And water fell on my head. Time returned again, and my spirit entered my body once more, but I couldn't feel it entering. I didn't feel myself returning. When I came to I was lying in my bed, defenseless. Sitting up with my head in my hands, I started crying inconsolably.

"Did you see what happened?" I asked my wife.

"I just saw your foot jerk, like you were already dying," she said.

"That's true, all at once I was dead," I told Catalina. "I found myself dead, in the other dimension. I'll tell you what I saw, but I'm so glad I found my life again. I can't tell you how sad it made me feel, because I wouldn't get to see your face again, our daughters' faces."

Translated by Cynthia Steele

Nicaragua

Héctor Manjarrez

Héctor Manjarrez (Mexico City, 1945) was a Guggenheim Fellow in 1972–73. He has published two books of poetry, including Canciones para los que se han separado *(1985); two books of short stories, including* No todos los hombres son románticos *(1983), which won the Villaurrutia prize, and from which "Nicaragua" is taken; and two novels. Manjarrez has translated works by Artaud and Charles Olson and has published essays on Jack Kerouac, Witold Gombrowicz, Katharine Mansfield, Milan Kundera, Henry Green, Juan Rulfo and others.*

for J, D, R and F

> *I once said to someone — in English — that the shape of a certain branch was typical of the branch of an elm, which my companion denied. Then we came past some ashes, and I said "There, you see, here are the branches I was speaking about." To which he replied "But that's an ash" — and I said "I always meant ash when I said elm."*
> — Ludwig Wittgenstein (*On Certainty*)

X took a look around him. . . . The line for Aeronica wasn't too long, but it was very slow. Almost all the Nicaraguan travelers had big detergent boxes with them, full of heavy objects. Mexico really did seem developed compared to most Latin-American countries, with their frequently puny economies and usually small cities. X could only guess what was in those boxes. Household utensils and spare parts, maybe. X didn't know what was available and what was scarce in Nicaragua, where he was going for the first time. He noticed that the Aeronica staff wasn't checking the baggage very carefully.

A few days earlier, a bomb had exploded at the Augusto C. Sandino

Airport—on the eve of the arrival of López Portillo, the president of Mexico. Mexico's foreign policy was useful to Nicaragua, the PRI and people like X. If his own out-of-favor, bourgeois president was going down to Managua to defend the Sandinistas, why shouldn't X go and see for himself what a revolution was like? He was waiting in line to go. A few meters away, on an orange plastic chair, an obvious government agent sat making a note of who was traveling to Nicaragua. In Managua, X would hear a story about the security detail accompanying the Mexican delegation: those goons had offered the cute little Sandinista cops money for their Uzis, Galils and AKs, told them they could name their price; can you just imagine those kids—so taken with their role as models and friendly champions of revolutionary order—trying to convince the Mexican goons that their weapons had no price? And the Mexican delegation's whiskey had flowed freely at that COPPAL meeting,* also according to X's sources. But except for Cuba, no other country had helped Nicaragua as much as Mexico—everyone told you that. Traveling with a Mexican passport had not yet become an embarrassment.

Like everyone else, X wondered how much longer Mexico could go on the way it was. It was more than obvious that the end of an era was at hand; the new one had yet to reveal its essence. . . . The popular forces had been crushed, the left had collapsed and the State was discredited. The peso had just suffered a one-hundred-percent devaluation: X's trip was already a luxury; it would take him months to pay off his loans; and meanwhile, the peso would be worth less and less and the powers that be would notify the world that Mexico couldn't pay its debts, and soon, the country would be short of capital and the nationalization of the banking industry would be decreed. . . . Just how the state of the economy would change the way people lived remained to be seen.

The system, the repugnant and redeemable Mexican system, was full of leaks but still afloat. You could go to Nicaragua or Cuba fearlessly, with few precautions, thanks to the small but significant gains realized via the development of civil society, for those citizens educated enough to understand the term "civil society." Most Mexicans still put up with poverty and oppression without the organization or violence it would take to put the State on guard. . . . The most successful state in Latin America. The middle class and its American Dream. The Mexican dream. The country's institutional inertia: "Yours will be the last liber-

*COPPAL: Conferencia Permanente de Partidos Políticos de America Latina (Permanent Conference of Latin American Political Parties)

ated territory in Latin America." Other days—infinitely and incomprehensibly harder—lay ahead, were already at hand, had yet to come.

Someday they would change the rules for that country called Mexico which X had known for almost four decades. . . . X's generation had been fortunate. Their entry into professional life had coincided with the years when the institutional crisis—as yet only political—predisposed the system more favorably toward the middle sectors. And in 1968, hadn't that generation even considered itself a major force? Given the economic crisis, they couldn't assume that as forty- and fifty-year-olds they would necessarily enjoy security and material comforts; but they were neither young enough nor old enough to be the first ones fired from their jobs. No, his generation could hardly be considered unlucky. . . . They had their classical-music records; they had enjoyed the mambo in its heyday, and the cha-cha-cha, and rock and roll—even the bolero revival—along with the Cuban revolution and the sexual revolution. They had had their time to dream and come to terms with reality relatively free of pressures. X couldn't complain. He could go to Nicaragua, get to know that country and, while he was at it, put something of a personal crisis into perspective.

As long as you weren't poor, Mexico was a reasonably developed place. . . . Fortunately, not too much so. Also an example of inequality and hybridism (anything can be learned), culturally rich, ethnically very diverse, climatically prodigious. . . . Urbane, nationalistic. . . . And the crisis, compared with those of other countries, still allowed for a certain indifference. Mexico had all kinds of comforts, both ancient and modern. And wasn't the capital—that urban catastrophe unmatched in human history—a truly unique place? A sort of twentieth-century capital. X could love his country, and Mexico would require no excessively arduous proof of his affection.

His country might stir him to indifference or exasperation, but it inspired in him neither hatred, nor bitterness, nor that patriotic passion to which Latin Americans are sometimes so addicted. X could afford that. He could feel a critical devotion toward his country and an almost good-natured contempt for its ruling class. . . . To each his own. What he detested about Mexico and Mexicans sparked not resentment, but irritation and irony; and he liked living there. Someone like X, pal, was incapable of unremitting wrath toward Mexico, however justified that might have been.

The authorities engaged in selective repression. There was no tyranny. As long as it wasn't exercised, there was freedom. At other times and places, X really had hated his country with a passion, but now he refused to understand the passionate relationships of exiles to their native lands. If only you had seen Chile in those days, if you had been to Buenos Aires. . . . If only you had known Mexico in those years, felt how hopeful we were, seen the trade unions and communes and publications and couples and triangles we formed, shared our experiences and our aspirations. . . . I suppose to you those are privileges, abominable luxuries, and insignificant to boot; very insignificant, in fact.

But maybe the country would escape southern-cone-ization.* There was no denying that Mexico was an unusual place. Very unusual. Possibly the most unusual of all. . . . We're not like you, brother. We have our blatant defects all right, but also our hidden virtues, one of which happens to be knowing our defects inside and out. And we'll survive. . . . Mexican nationalism isn't what it used to be: it isn't as strident, abusive or melodramatic as it was—at least, not always; nor as metaphysical; it's more discreet now, more self-assured. Yes, this hateful, infuriating, oppressive country is unusual.

The Chileans were taken in by their own myth. . . . The Chileans didn't think Pinochet would lead a coup, or that the dictatorship would last so long and do away with the Chile they knew. Or that when the old Chile died, so would the friends that made it such a nice place to be. So clearly the Chileans are unusual too. . . . X knew that sooner or later history would dictate a new set of rules for Mexico. But history still hadn't severed the secret ties—some of them touching, others shameful (all of them profound)—that bound Mexicans to one another. History still hadn't covered the country with blood, only splashed it. It was still possible to believe, or presume, or hope, that "the real Mexico" would save the country from the very same monstrosities and cruelties and humiliations and ridiculous arrogance inherent in "the real Mexico," and from slaughter and destruction as well. . . .

What would the preconditions be—and how humiliating, oppressive, overwhelming, criminal—for loving or simply living in Mexico? What would happen once mediocrity lost its still faintly gilded edges? X feared that some things peculiar to Mexico and Mexicans would be lost—which is not to say that he found those things admirable or even appealing. What to do with that conservative core of his? X wasn't anxious—the least bit anxious—to take on the pain of forced exile. Or the horrors of war. He didn't want to lose what he had: his books and records, familiar places, love affairs, friends, children, habits. But some day that old Mexican stoicism would run out. Some day Mexico might be part of the

---

*southern cone: Argentina, Chile and Uruguay

atrocious history of Latin America. X knew only too well what that meant; and he knew he wasn't ready to face it.

For now, having chosen to leave, all he had to face were his private hells and personal tortures. That was uncomfortable, but. . . The people he loved most were still alive—even those who might well have been dead. Not all of them were Mexicans, but they all lived in Mexico. . . . On that score he need have no second thoughts about leaving. He would see them again, even if car accidents did account for more deaths than guerilla warfare. He would tour the revolution, and then he would be back. He would go to Nicaragua as both skeptic and believer, in his characteristically intellectual way. X was up on the history of his century. He had little use for revolutions. He put great stock in revolutions. That's just the way X was. An X kind of a guy, in the year X and country X.

As he studied the Nicas in the line, he didn't know what to make of them. They seemed provincial—like Mexicans from Nayarit, perhaps, or from Jalisco. . . . They didn't have the mestizo look about them of central Mexico, the south or the southeast. Not that this made them any more cosmopolitan: there was something both offensive and very endearing about their collectively underdeveloped demeanor. So far, revolutions had been a matter for *sudevelopés*—people like these who seemed only halfway formed. . . . Moreover, X still needed to experience the full breadth and depth of Mesoamerica (with a dose of Caribbean thrown in for good measure). That corn-based culture had only gotten to him once, as he came down from Coahuila to San Luis Potosí: it had horrified him then, and he had cursed it for saddling the center of his country with so much submissiveness and pretense. . . . Platitudes, dark expressionless faces, fatalistic outlooks, hypocrisy, deprivation. None of that ever seemed to change. . . .

But in the new Nicaragua, Mesoamerica would move him in a different way. X would discover that Mesoamerica, politically nonexistent, stretched all the way from Mexico to Costa Rica, as well as into X himself. He would understand why the Nicas, Salvadorans, Guatemalans and Hondurans all considered themselves Central American, and why he found Central Americans so endearing. I'll say no more about that feeling of X's, because I don't want to sound ridiculous. The Nicas have a great flair for language that in X's mouth would seem really phony, and Salvadorans can talk about war with a tenderness X would display only hesitantly while making love. . . . As for Guatemalans. . . Suddenly finding himself in Nicaragua, right smack in the political heart of Central America, in the foothills of Mesoamerica, was quite a shock to X. It left him totally dumbfounded.

Underdeveloped and provincial as it was, Nicaragua seemed like a very distant Mexico, even older than his grandparents: outdated, primitive, unworldly. But Nicaragua might also be the future. The smell of corn, convoluted ways of thinking, a peculiar sort of humor, terrible drunken binges, incredible male chauvinism, quickness to take offense; but also a people in arms, the authors of that incredible insurrection, a people that now could read and write, a people so eager to talk and share their enthusiasm and their attempts to build a new life. . . . What kind of a place was that? A place that made sense, where people you had never seen before, people you sometimes talked to for all of two minutes, could change your life. Peasants who were (no longer so) ignorant. Political sectors no longer so grotesquely sure they had a corner on truth. Children rushing over to grab the militiaman's old M1 rifle, so you could take their picture looking proud.

The revolution was barely three years old. Almost everything was still to be done. In Nicaragua everything was a revolutionary act and as such, a source of emotion. Addressing a stranger as "brother," teaching people to read and write, fixing a water pump, servicing a truck with no tools, discussing the day's events. Everything took on meaning in that tiny country, so poor, so persecuted, so terribly underdeveloped. It was simply another world. You had to be there to understand it. From the outside it made no sense for X to get a lump in his throat over something as trivial as the training of young militiamen, or an even more prosaic and less heroic billboard announcing that some article never produced before the revolution was now available at a rate of X units per day. . . . Once you got there, you had to be very uncaring not to be deeply moved every day and ready to help with anything you could, in any way, at any time. And to tell certain friends that it was possible after all to have both a head and a heart. . . .

Mexico was different. Much bigger, much richer, much more diverse. It seemed intolerable that in such a huge and wealthy country, there could be so much material and cultural poverty. During his stay in Nicaragua, X never stopped thinking about Mexico. The people this and the vanguard that; different ethnic groups this and the PRI* that; corn this and the economy that; and populism and freedom of expression and consumption and nationalism — as he saw it, everything had to be reex-

---

*PRI: Institutional Revolutionary Party. The sole party of Mexico's political system

amined. Nicaragua was one of the most important places in the world; solutions of vital interest to everyone, even people who would never benefit from them, were being debated and tested there. In that nightmare known as Managua, X couldn't sleep, not because of the unbearable heat but because he was thinking and questioning constantly; and he was moved as he had only been at Palenque, Chartres and Hagia Sophia—holy places, where life and death had meaning, even if you weren't in love. In—of all places—Managua, arguably one of the ugliest, dreariest cities on the face of the earth.

D had told him: "This is our revolution, brother. The Cuban revolution belongs to So-and-so and What's-his-name"—referring to mutual friends of over fifty years—"Nicaragua is ours." D wasn't Nicaraguan, but he had fought on the Southern Front. J (a man) and R (a woman) would tell him: "I work up to fourteen hours a day, then I have military training to boot. At bedtime, I hit the sack like a ton of bricks, brother. I'm doing all I can, but what the revolution does for me is more." X believed them: he was in Nicaragua and he had known them for years. Neither they nor F were Nicaraguan, and F would say that all he was missing was a woman to share it with. The revolution is good for your soul, but it's no paradise; it's no substitute for other needs and desires, and you can suffer a lot when it's in trouble. X's internationalist friends were pretty lonely as a rule. They had broken ties with their own countries, or their countries of exile, and the satisfactions Nicaragua offered were purely revolutionary. . . . But as a certain little girl would say: "The great part about the Nicas is that things just hit them. . .right out of the blue." All you had to do was read their accounts of the insurrection.

But X still had forty days to go before he went back to Mexico, to tell people all this and hear them say that he had "lost his critical sense" in Nicaragua. Was that all? He had over a month to go before he would return from there and try to explain, to people he had been close to at crucial times in his life, that Nicaragua was Latin America's greatest hope and that no, the Sandinista Front wasn't like the Mexican PRI or the Soviet CP—that what the Nicas were doing was something new and different. . . . Some would find him naive and dogmatic, foolishly optimistic, absurdly enthusiastic.

As I say, that's what happened when he got back to Mexico City, with its five or six times more inhabitants and money and civilization and history than were to be found in all of Nicaragua. Some people there already knew how much would be at stake if the revolution were overcome or defeated. They were fairly numerous, and with them X could relive the fervor he had found in Nicaragua, unhounded by reproachful looks from other friends whose greatest aspiration was never to be taken in by anyone. He would never share his criticisms of the Nicaraguan revolution with those friends; that would only convince them that he was virtually a fanatic. He didn't want to be thought naive, much less give the impression that he considered himself "more revolutionary" than they were. They hadn't been to Nicaragua and that was that.

He still had those forty days to go—exactly—as he stood there in the airport watching the Nicas and wondering what class they belonged to, what their hopes were, what they believed in, where they were getting five hundred dollars for their tickets and what they were carting around with them in those cardboard boxes. Soon he would have occasion to see that class differences under Somoza weren't anywhere near as great as they were in Mexico; and that poverty in Nicaragua was tolerable, unlike that of millions of Mexicans. And that what the Nicas referred to as their *haute bourgeoisie* reminded him of many middle-class Mexicans. . . . And that Nicaragua was less indigenous and less Mesoamerican than Mexico.

What X didn't know was that he was on the verge of an unforgettable love affair. As he stood there in line, all he could think of was how incredibly little he knew about Central America. It still surprised him, for example, to hear Central Americans address each other tenderly as *vos.* . . . But X would mend his ways. . . . That love affair would be a big help. It would cause him to search, explore, look and listen avidly. He had no idea, in the airport, that he was about to fall in love with a country and its revolution. Given his critical sense, X's love for Nicaragua wasn't blind, but it was wholehearted. Never simplistic, his affinities and aversions reached new and purer depths. Highest on his list of aversions was his hatred of gringo imperialism and those grisly stooges who murdered with their mugs full of words like *Fatherland, Freedom, Religion*—which, when uttered by the Sandinistas, took on unaccustomed dignity for X. . . . How incredible that despite the constant harassment, the campaigns of lies, the attacks from Honduras and sometimes from Costa Rica, the Sandinista revolution should still be so full of humor and tenderness. That tiny, destitute country, so devastated by the earthquake, the war of liberation, and then by floods, had been targeted for destruction by the most powerful country in the world. . . . His hatred was livid, sharp and sound.

Even with a knife in its teeth, Nicaragua knew how to smile. That was extraordinary. A people that needed peace and a better life was being hounded, ostracized, beleaguered, slandered, shot at. If Nicaragua was invaded . . . The Nicas knew, by now, how to fight and what to fight for. An ordinary invasion made no sense. Better a few fistfuls of dollars, so that a bunch of clowns from neighboring countries would carry on about democracy and freedom and fear of communism and love of God—the idea being to drive Nicaragua to a coup and force the Nicas to strike one blow, just one, in exchange for all the blows they were taking. . . . And those miserable brutes from Somoza's National Guard, the ones who tossed children into the air and skewered them on their bayonets, those perfect examples of underdeveloped barbarity (different, but no worse, than that of Auschwitz and My Lai), were getting provisions from the gringo army and mortars and Galils and FALs and M1s and RPG4s and walkie-talkies—all airlifted into Nica territory. And what if the European social democrats decided to go along with the gringos and cut off aid to the Sandinistas; and if its own institutional crisis led Mexico to distance itself from the Sandinista Front; and if Venezuela got tired of having its strategy ignored in the rest of the region; and if all the hounding and weariness and exasperation spawned fatigue and disillusionment in those sectors least in need of major changes, or among Nicaraguans still prevented from enjoying them by their alliance with sectors of the bourgeoisie?

Tomás Borge told his torturer that his revenge would be to see to it that the torturer's children and those of his henchmen learned to read and write. . . . How generous, gentle, brave and full of humor the Sandinista revolution was. But not its enemies. Not the fleshy, pompous Monsignors, draped in purple, with their faces like obese rats', and their beady eyes, and their mouths full of people, freedom and God. Not the bourgeois S.O.B.s, whose conversations in the bar and barber shop of the Intercontinental, and at La Marseillaise, X would eavesdrop on: *darrrleeng, Sandinista totaleetarianeesm ees drreaadful* (because that's exactly the way those poor devils talked, like caricatures concocted by the most disaffected leftist mentality). . . .

And what was the revolution doing? The revolution could do so little for that poor, devastated, tiny country, "where greatness is limited to lakes, and to leaders who are short in stature; for in Nicaragua even the volcanos lie low. And the other great thing about Nicaragua is its earthquakes, the main one being its people." After Somoza killed fifty thousand Nicaraguans, after the bombing and destruction of Estelí, after the legendary struggles of Matagalpa and Masaya, those beautiful names that circled the globe, what could the revolution do?

What the revolution could do in its early years was very little. It couldn't bring socialism to Nicaragua. It could bring the promise of a revolution unlike any other; and mass participation; and other successes and failures; and an armed population; and the recovery of—or search for—a national identity; and a certain redistribution of income; and reading and writing; and agrarian reform; and dignity; and an alliance with interested members of the bourgeoisie. . . . Really very little. But even that had to be stopped! It was too good a beginning. The creativity, generosity and humor of the Sandinista revolution had to be stifled. The people had to be intimidated, so their revolutionary struggle would be not creative, unpressured, enthusiastic, lucid, but defensive—even paranoid, if possible. . . . Nicaragua couldn't be allowed to set an example. It was time to teach her a lesson. Revolutionaries and peoples couldn't be allowed to claim that they could change things, unlikely as that might seem, but only, if things went well, that they had managed to survive. That was why they were hounding a poor, tiny, sparsely populated territory that so few people had heard of until 1979: so that the Sandinista revolution wouldn't go its own way; so that Nicaraguans would find making their own history very hard; so that everything would go on costing blood and tears and sacrifice; so that an entire people would never rise up again. . . . It was one thing to look down your nose at gringo tourists in the airport, or Mexican tourists on their way to Disneyland; it was quite another to want a gun to defend Nicaragua, to want with all your heart to be of service, or to understand the need for a slogan as simple as *Patria Libre o Morir.**

(J would tell him: "Revolutions are not for romantics. To make a revolution you have to be very tough, and sometimes that small part of you called a soul feels very much alone. I miss Mexico when I think of my friends, and how comfortably spoiled you can get to feeling there. But on the other hand, I don't want to leave Central America." That was what J would say, being no less romantic than D, F or R.)

Translated by Louise B. Popkin

---

*"A Free Homeland or Death"

Georgina Quintana, [Untitled] (1984, ink and pencil on paper)

From *The Hidden Language*

María Luisa Puga

For a biographical note on María Luisa Puga please see page 219.

With a few exceptions, Mexican writers have a tiny readership; we live in a very limited world considering the vastness and diversity of the country, and our literature is often just as confined.

Until recently, the Mexican novel evolved primarily in Mexico City, for Mexico City, which is precisely where you find the small number of readers of Mexican literature. It's still true that, in order to publish a book, to distribute it, one has to go to Mexico City, and, in large measure, in order to write it, too, since traditionally it's in Mexico City that the nation's cultural life is concentrated.

What's more, writers themselves have established, as a literary theme, a rejection of the national reality, and it's not unusual to come across impeccable, well-structured novels that have nothing to do with it. Not that literature should invariably relate to reality, society or daily life—literature relates to everything, and anything can be literature, but what can't be done without is pertinence.

It would be helpful not to forget that culture isn't just some delicate, fragile and extremely expensive ornament, and that it would have to be the outcome of our passing through time and of the way that the evolution of social consciousness can shatter atavisms and prejudices. By the same token we should remember that the literary world reached the point of closing itself off into an intimidating, hermetic circle. This served as an escape from ugly, insensitive and uncontrollable surroundings. Therefore, for the unchosen, that is to say, for the great majority of the people, literature has always been something for which they have no time, money or interest.

I am convinced, nevertheless, that in Mexico, the habit of reading is very prevalent. Look at the pressruns of the comic books, *fotonovelas*, fashion magazines, and the sensationalist fiction of the yellow press. Stroll down any street in any city at any time of day and you will find people at bus stops, in the subway, at construction sites, in tortilla lines with their eyes fixed upon a text, which, illustrated or not, attracts their attention.

The publishing houses and cultural institutions despair of devising a way to elevate people from this cheap, commercial literature to a more profound and educational one. So they launch popular collections, book sales in supermarkets, all kinds of promotions. But the problem isn't a lack of interest nor even education. A well-written text is perfectly appreciated even in the remotest regions of the country. It is now time to define what a well-written text is to the reader.

There is the literary reader, who searches for literature in the best sense of the word: originality, great expressive capacity and structure. He's a well-informed reader who frequents literature with a critical attitude, and who himself probably aspires to write. The hardened reader is something else: tenacious and curious, he looks for literary quality, but not as a prerequisite, because what interests him is exercising his imagination. But there is also the spontaneous reader, the ordinary individual who has integrated reading into his schedule as an additional activity in his life. A normal activity—like going to the movies or watching television. This is how most people read, and they read books to the extent that books are seen as a propitious part of normal life, not as an activity that is considered virtuous and superior to the rest of daily life.

This is the same reader who reads the comics and the cheap gossip magazines, because these are the materials to which he has access in a natural way, not necessarily because they happen to be the easiest to digest.

Within the educational and intellectual sectors of the country, they say without much demur that people don't read. They don't know how to read. They are not accustomed to reading. They become literate but still don't read. Television hypnotizes them.

However, you can watch television even in the regions furthest from Mexico City, but the libraries even in the larger cities contain nothing but dusty old books.

The truth is that in Mexico we all complain about each other: about

318

some because they don't read anything but comics, about others because they don't read anything but literature. Those who work in the field of literacy complain that the people they teach then forget what they've learned, and the latter complain that they forget how to read because there's nothing *to* read. And if you criticize them for learning to read just to become addicted to comics, they have the right to respond: that's all we can find.

In order to reach the reader, the Mexican writer must overcome all of these obstacles. It's clear that those who write in a country like Mexico belong to the class of those who have power. They are the ones who can choose a career and dedicate their entire lives to it, even if they can't live off of it. But they are irredentist middle-classers, and most of them have Mexico-Citified themselves. Nevertheless, they have understood that their class is not something that belongs to them; above all it isn't a culture; it isn't an end-result but part of a process which one should get to know, absorb and be able to leave behind.

To journey, then, outside Mexico City and lecture on literature provides for a unique learning experience.

ONE: The powerful sun beat down

The Secretariat of Public Education (SEP) coordinated everything as part of a larger "cultural promotion" program. Mexico is divided into various circuits, and I received the second and the fourth: Tijuana and Ensenada, and Ciudad Obregón and Guayamas. Also the villages surrounding each town.

Leaving Mexico City for an unfamiliar city in the provinces usually ends up producing a strong impression. A Mexican city that one doesn't know. And at first sight, an unfamiliar town usually seems unfriendly and ugly. It seems to be a deserted place inhabited now by force. A feverish invention of who-knows-what interests. It seems sad and squalid, as if left untouched by the hand of God. What can one know of the illusions that the children and adolescents have grown up with in these streets that have all the typically Mexican street names: Morelos Avenue, Madero, Hidalgo, Benito Juárez . . . What can one know about their lively corners or their more disturbing areas? About their savor? About their light? All you see is a big town that infuses one with total lethargy. That makes one yearn for the relentless bustle of Mexico City, which despite its chaos always offers the possibility of an image we can consider our own. I mean . . . a timid *chilango** only pokes his nose out once in a great while.

I was supposed to give thirty-four talks on Latin-American literature (34!). And what about Latin-American literature? The points I wanted to touch on were: appropriation of one's own language, how we're taught to read, what we read, how language colonizes, identity through language. I didn't know there would be so many talks until the last minute. Two daily. In preparatory schools, technical schools, cultural institutions. . . . [. . .]

But to see Cuidad Obregón and reflect on my talks was one single reaction. I don't know what I imagined. I don't know how I'd been imagining the north all this time. Very industrialized, very rich. Imposing in a certain way. Scorching hot and rough. Above all very reactionary. I don't know what kind of images I associate with the word "reactionary." Perhaps the same ones that I associate with the word "communist." But to see the city and sense that there was something rather absurd about my talks was a single thing. [. . .]

The powerful sun was beating down, and so the streets were deserted. Not a soul would pass by before 3:30 or 4:00. At the primary school where I was scheduled to talk, they had no idea I was coming. There was no one who could tell me anything. The only telephone number that could clear up the situation was busy, or more likely out of order.

SEP, I thought. So far from SEP. [. . .]

At the second school they were waiting for me, they had heard of SEP, and they had the fliers, a room for the talk, except the literature students weren't there and it had to be first-semester students, what can you do, in the end they're all part of the same school.

The teachers were inquisitive, enthusiastic, young, probing: hey you, what's happening? People who dedicate their lives, time and effort to the task of teaching. It gives them dignity. "And here," said one woman, "the problem isn't that the students don't have the things they'd have in Mexico City, the problem here is the same as in Mexico City: television, false images, the lack of a sense of ourselves. They have nothing to get hold of."

In such a hot climate or hot region, everything happens in the open air, in short-sleeve shirts, it's an exposed existence. The school consisted of a group of scattered little houses that brought together both young men and women, huddled here and there, playing chess, curled up reading, whispering, calling out to each other, all of which seemed a

---

chilango: slang for a native of Mexico City

happy scene in the late afternoon, when at last you feel a bit of cooler air. Because of the space, because of the way in which the different groups were huddled about, involved in their activities, because of the way in which the teachers arranged for the talk, the time went smoothly and amicably.

TWO: May they not think about store windows

[. . .] I left Ciudad Obregón at ten in the morning to give a talk in Vícam, which means "spearhead" in Yaqui. It wasn't a "CBTIS" this time, but a "CBTA." That is to say, a technical high school with students studying agricultural technology. The other acronym (CBTIS) stands for something so subtle that I still don't completely understand it. But I have decided not to collect information. I want to feel like I'm learning, familiarizing myself. Of course my itinerary is only an approximation of reality. The telephone numbers and names included in it don't correspond to what actually exists. The principal changed jobs, or the location's no longer the same . . . and most often, there's no telephone. Not to mention the schedule I carry around or the lack of any geographical reason in my program. I must continue adapting myself as I go, as I begin to understand and gain confidence. But already I know very well that moment of arriving at a very rural-government-looking building, asking where the principal's office is, introducing myself and discovering that the people there are very open, very eager, very anxious to accept any help from SEP. *Any* help.

Vícam is a town that has fought to maintain its cultural identity. It's arid and high-up. It's right beside the highway, and it has the same infrastructure as any larger town. And it's a town that hardly anyone notices. You really feel a will to exist, but on condition of being what you are: Yaqui. There's a bank, three schools: primary, secondary and prep. Businesses, a taxi stand, little restaurants and country dwellings spread out. The people of Sonora, whether mestizo or white, complain: "These Indians and the Maya are spoiled by the government. They give them everything and look at them, they live like animals, they don't want to civilize themselves." This is true. They haven't alienated themselves. They're not Sonoran. They're Yaqui and Maya . . . they're Indians and their homes aren't towns born by chance, but rather cultures that intend to survive.

The boys come from all over at the agricultural school where I gave my talk. They travel by bus to get to school, sometimes without having breakfast. They get out at 3:30 or 4:00 in the afternoon and, without having eaten anything but a small morsel and a Coke (that's what there is), they return to their homes at night.

I came to speak to them about literature.

Skinny little boys, nervous; wide-eyed little girls with quick reactions. Young people wanting to learn. It seems strange to say this: they want to learn, they look for ways to learn, and even mistreat themselves to learn. They use their youth to learn.

I wanted to chat with them. For example, I asked one boy: You in the green shirt, how about this? And they all crowd around with a horrifying timidity. They whisper intensely to their neighbors or simply bow their heads or shade their faces. Talking, going out, presenting themselves, no. Not out of fear but out of modesty. They make up the school and as a school they are bold, merry and noisy. But as individuals they negate themselves. It's too violent. Also, one of the teachers told me, "Remember, they're Yaquis, they're translating from your Spanish." They seem to be slow, but in fact they're putting forth a double effort.

As I was speaking to them I thought: I hope they're not thinking about the store windows in Mexico City, the well-paved streets (of the Mexico City I live in), all the reflections of so many advertisements. I hope they don't hear all the confusing sounds that a city-dweller brings along. I wanted my words to resonate with newness in the grass, in the air, within the space that was filled with such fresh youth. . . . I tried to tell them that reading literature is not an academic chore, but an activity as agreeable as running or breathing or eating. I tried to make them understand that reading doesn't rob them of free time, not if they find a book that interests them, that appeals to them, and that speaks directly to each one of them.

I think this was the first time I ever thought about the Mexico City school kids, and I said to myself: If those kids had this space . . . if these kids had everything Mexico City offers.

I don't know how many there were. We were in the library at the Vícam agricultural school, where the typical books were on display, you know: Sor Juana, Alfonso Reyes, Octavio Paz, Carlos Fuentes . . . thanks to them we're international, but we haven't managed to get our people to read. We've managed to get them not to read. That's for sure. But internationally. The kids in Vícam don't need this. They had had literature classes, yes. Some of them remembered reading *La Celestina* (*The Matchmaker*) and *El Cantar del mío Cid* (*The Song of the Cid*). My God, how tedious. Poor things, I thought, nothing has changed. No wonder we hate to read. If we'd been given some literary training with those texts, but no.

322

They took control of our language, filling it with expressions that aren't ours, that don't speak to us.

Why read when you can talk about everything you dream of, every-thing you desire? So I asked them what book they would like to see written. What story would they like to hear. What. Little by little, with a lot of grinning and poking and intense commentary among themselves, they clumsily disclosed their likes. So then I discussed the work of young writers. The stories their books tell. What they are searching for.

And those timid, almost absent kids, when they get motivated to speak, have a fascinating clarity and accuracy that's amazing. They know exactly what they want and what they are looking for. What they won't accept. What they discard for lack of interest. Their intuition about life is so strong that not one tedious detail distracts them.

In this windowless room, with the noise of an air conditioner, I was impressed with all I had seen, with my new understanding of how closed Mexico City is in relation to the rest of the country.

A young woman in Ciudad Obregón said to me, "Poor Sonora, so close to its neighbors, so ignored by Mexico City." And this is because the culture of our nation emanated from Mexico City, and there is nothing more alien to our nation than the idea Mexico City has about the nation.

THREE: They were a people

Sluggishness, apathy, neglect. Indifference, suspicion. Egotism. People are very misinformed, but more than anything else, they're mistreated by the system. In Mexico City we humble ourselves daily. Everything gets to us: from the noise and environmental filth, to fear, disgust, the dislike we feel toward others, toward the streets, toward the outside.

I spent the whole day in Guayamas talking to students and teachers from three different schools. The bright glances, smooth skin, graceful bodies were very familiar. Their expressions were steady but inattentive; I came across the same thing on all three occasions. The three adminis-trative offices were the same, reeking of bureaucracy, of killing time no matter how, but suggesting also some effort to make things meaningful. The playgrounds filled with sunlight and excited shouts and races, the boys and girls, were the same as well. And in the background was Guayamas, a very important port town, according to a radio advertise-ment attempting to stimulate the feeling of belonging the same way I was trying to stimulate reading. Of Latin-American texts. [. . .]

They were a people. One people with very specific rules. What was happening in baseball? How did Guayamas do? What unified them—say, a businessmen and a journalist—depended on the outcome of the game . . . and it occurred to me that that's what it meant to be a country. This is culture: this custom of coming in and ordering a cup of coffee, which, despite the plastic, the lack of esthetic beauty, offers a ritual, an invisible but specific cultural link. I thought: these Sonoran guys, despite everything, are an ethnic group, a language, an understanding of the world. And I thought: it's the school that sows confusion, fragmentation. How disrespectful, no? I was there thanks to the Secretary of Public Education. But I thought: It's the school that alienates people, because it doesn't arise from their own needs. It is born in some centralized place that conceives of education as a process which ideally puts makeup on us; it "civilizes" us, but not so that we will gain knowledge of a way of being that is our own—knowledge of ourselves, of what we truly long for. Rather, the school injects us with other people's desires. It teaches us to wish for things we don't really want. It doesn't help us to find ourselves. And I thought: It's because the school doesn't arise from people's needs, but from an idea, taken up somewhere else, of what education should be.

To see the children in those schools I visited, with their good health, their youth, their motivation to learn, and then to see the effects of the school on them, alarmed me. A few save themselves, but most do not. Those who save themselves do so not because they're exceptional but merely by chance. By a chain of coincidences. But in a country like ours- or maybe one should say in any country—education should create critical, steadfast, solid individuals.

I know, for example, that we all need to write. All of us, at one time or another, should translate our perceptions of things into written language. All of us, in a word, have the right to feel that the language is ours. And this should be a basic part of an educational program: the appropriation of language.

FOUR: It's time for someone to help them unfold

[. . .] Clearly, many students must study in order to do what they want. Others, the great majority, figure that what they're doing is living their lives; their time. And school is one of those unavoidable places, and one of the many activities, against which you must defend yourself. Like so many others that the adolescent discovers while discovering the world.

The students attend, but they're not present. It's time for someone to help them unfold, to interest them. They are Mexican boys and girls whose lives take shape in much the same way as ours have. It's important to go and find the keys to this, and it's not easy. Each talk teaches me something. I'm experimenting with different approaches.

FIVE: Individual language

There are two things that are never sufficiently addressed: the lack of reading habits and institutionalized bureaucracy. We would be better off connecting the two. I don't know yet. Let's see: in primary school they didn't teach us. They didn't teach us that the language was ours, nor that in our language this, that and the other were done. They did show us how to deepen our voices in order to speak of our Native Land, of our Heroes, of our country's History. Our Heroic National Hymn – the lyrics of which we grew to understand only years later, because when we used to sing it every Monday during the salute to the flag, we used to imitate sounds that seemed to be words, but were never able to grasp their direct meaning. We made ourselves into a nation within the incomprehensibility of words. Just like today, when I talk to fourteen- and fifteen-year-olds about literature classes, about Spanish, about reading and writing or whatever you want to call the academic system, and I see frustration in their eyes. But this is so even in Acapulco or in Ciudad Obregón, with that sun, with that midday drowsiness and the ancient Spanish language that falls on you like a suffocating avalanche. So much enunciating of everything exactly right, and what did it all have to with you at that moment? Language turned out to be something alien, and a colossal bore. When what you wanted was to live, to feel something. On the other hand, you would have been dazzled if they had buried us under more comprehensible, ordinary words. Words in which we could perceive an echo of our own lives. Because a child after all does have his own life, his own perception of the world. The desire for a future. A tremendous desire to fight and make it real.

But primary school turned out to be a huge bucket of cold water – not to show you what reality is like, as adults believe, but that checked your desire for knowledge, for the discovery that is natural to every human being.

Therefore what is "ours," what would need to be national, the thread that would need to stitch us into a design which over time would constitute us as a nation, is turned into a tedious, monotonous speech, full of obligatory capital letters that you have to submissively leave standing. And why not a nationality made out of a grouping of individuals? If instead of teaching us history the way they do, or Spanish (language/literature) the way they do, they could have shown us what was happening, what people were writing, what people were really doing, wouldn't we understand much better what we're becoming? But then, of course, we might become more demanding with regard to what we're told by the system that organizes us as a society. Maybe then we wouldn't accept the rhetoric that crushes us day after day, like those Spanish literature classes. We would probably become more critical, more vigilant regarding clarity, and regarding the consequences of so many speeches and promises. We would probably be more autonomous; and less submissive.

The problem is that in not teaching us the usage and comprehension of language beginning in primary school, they took away the most important weapon a citizen can possess: his own language. Language for making use of intuitive perception; for arguing against and combating manipulation; for expressing dissent or for encouraging the participation that could pluralize the dominant language.

Isn't this one of the characteristics of the Third World? It has been deprived of language. Nations invented by nations that came to be because they had language. Before we were nations we were cultures, cultures with a perfectly clear language. A language transmitted from generation to generation with a respectful attitude, a concern for continuity, for perpetuation. Probably cultures that did not practice the social equality we now defend, and for that reason cultural formations to which it would be pointless to return. But from which we can indeed use certain things. We were a unity. And now we are not. And we are not, I believe, because of the system that continues to feed us on alien ideas.

It is absurd, it is unreal, it is humiliating that anyone pretends to create Mexicanness with radio commercials; using imitation kermess music in public squares and parks. What is Mexican—nationality (not nationalism, which is the cheapest, easiest feeling to arouse), cultural identity, I suppose—is created only with true rootedness.

SIX: The plan and the reality

[. . .] We also don't talk enough about bureaucracy, which in underdeveloped countries (as well as developed countries, although to a lesser extent) does criminal damage. In this country, it would seem that bureaucracy is a greater enemy of the citizen than is the corruption of the system. It is a presence invisible but thick, and it succeeds in stifling movement. Bureaucracy is criminal in the way it hinders a vision of the nation as a whole. Criminal, the way in which it lies heavily on the urgency of organization that is now needed.

I mean criminal, but without any moralistic intention. At this point, to take pleasure in moralizing would also be criminal. Because what we have too much of already is resounding speeches and inflated tones of voice, and then there are the ideologues. In other words, what we have too much of is language that hides reality. And no one is able to control this chaos.

Our crisis begins with education. [. . .] First with primary education, as I've said, because if we do not give the child a comprehensible language, but rather one that is alien and tedious, then education makes the child hide his need to express himself and keep it inside himself. What he learns, then, for going out into the world, is the language that is spoken "out there," a language which insofar as he uses it well, will permit him to "integrate himself" into that society where, from this moment on, his connection to it is false. Neither is language emanating from the individual, nor do we see ourselves reflected in the language that surrounds us. [. . .]

SEVEN: Modesty and words

Today's talk was different, more centered, more serious. The school wasn't any different than the others in terms of structure and the number of attending students, but it was a Normal School, with future teachers to whom one could talk about what does and doesn't happen in primary school. I had a very good impression of the principal. A person who thinks and fights for his educational work, who knows the world is divided into those that have money and those that don't, and that the latter group must be well-prepared if they want to do something for their people. He says, "I don't know if it's on purpose or not, but I notice that the public schools seem to have a lot of political hassles. It's these students who every so often are prevented from forming solid groups, because of the time they lose in the politics. It's as if someone wanted to prevent them from finishing their education. Perhaps this is true because well-prepared new groups would pose a danger to the system. In private schools, no one interrupts the program of study." Another thing that you notice is that even with some positive reinforcement at the middle levels and more opportunities to study, even in the smaller cities, the time available in the various study programs for artistic appreciation or for the humanities has been reduced.

He's the first principal I speak with face to face. I've only greeted the others in passing. He seems to be truly immersed in his work and understands the daily problems of school. It's also in this school that I have felt the most curiosity from the teachers about the problems I'm laying out, and where there are more efforts to stimulate reading. What's more, I felt the students' attention, their seeking, their weighing of the information they are receiving. I liked the clarity with which they spoke to me about other texts that live in their imaginations. As I said, the texts these young adults most often read are texts from the U.S. that have been translated, like: "How to be Successful in Business," or "Diary of a Drug Addict," "Diary of an Alcoholic . . . " One student used to carry around a journal, and when she read these other diaries, she didn't dare continue her own. She didn't have any "heavy" problem, and didn't feel she had any right to write about herself.

I talk to them about writing as a necessity for every person. Like a space, a possession to which we all have the right. About language as an instrument that belongs to us, that is the only one that gives us some power against surrounding reality. Writing and reading are like a conquest of a way of being, but not, I repeat, because everyone is going to be a writer. To be able to express oneself clearly, to be able to answer rhetorical or manipulative logorrhea with a pondered argument, is the germ of our freedom. I talk to them about Latin-American literature as a search for cultural identity, like the individual's search for a place to put himself in the social fabric — what role he will play in that social fabric, how he's going to nurture it himself: with what critique and what participation. [. . .]

On occasion, an overwhelming sense of dejection comes over me and I seem to be talking in vain. It's not because I feel the talks aren't worth the effort. Something always happens, I discover something. I suppose that I also leave something behind, but it's as if I'm speaking in the middle of a storm or a train station. Things are said and heard, leaving perhaps an indelible impression on their consciousness, but if there's no continuity or echo, however distant, however unattainable in the external world, over time they will be buried by what they do hear constantly. And what is constantly heard here is the power of money on the one hand and the United States on the other, although the latter is glimpsed as if through a hole on the wall: the gringo television on Cablevision, which doesn't depict daily life in the United States, but is a gringo production aimed at colonizing the gringos themselves, more than anyone else. . . . I'm talking about gringo soap opera.

The other thing they see is Americanized Mexican television, which will mold Mexicans into something they are not. And finally, there's cultural television, also Mexican, which seems to suffer the same effect, I think, as my talks and encounters, at times: they're ephemeral and disappear into dust clouds since there is nothing in the surrounding reality, especially no resources which could reinforce what is said or communicated. In this way, culture is somewhat of a remote luxury in these parts, and who knows who created it and who cares about it. It's brought to us every once in a while.

I try to communicate to these students that they are culture, their presence, our lives. Not the big show from Mexico City that costs money for a ticket, or that's free because you're a student. Culture, I tell them, is educating yourself, it's discovering, so that when you venture off later into the world you can make something of it all. [. . .]

We talked, the principal of today's school and I, about how what's important is not that the promotion of culture coming from Mexico City should speed up, should consolidate, but that it should go plant seeds so that each place will produce cultural activities of its own that give it meaning that is more profound, more creative with regard to daily life. Not to create a more "cultivated" people, who are so well versed in the questions that make up the typical table talk at a café, but to gain a greater autonomy, a greater sense of certainty in their way of being.

EIGHT: Voluntary reading

[. . .] My biggest challenge is to draw the students out. Make them try to express themselves. Infuse them with confidence, not about knowing "something," being prepared or being loyal to the school, but about being able to say what they want to say.

It turns out that, of course, the ones who talk are the "leaders," whether because of social class or diligence of study. However, suddenly one of the quiet students will talk, one of the least articulate, and what moves him to do so is not confidence, but the irrepressible desire to make what's important to him his own.

What I try to do in my talks is rouse them so that each one discovers his language. Not necessarily so that they'll love Latin-American literature, or even reading, although I really insist that the act of reading belongs to every individual, and that if our society gives it little attention, it is still a pleasure to which we all have a right. I emphasize at every opportunity that in the act of reading there is a freedom that isn't present in other activities.

What I want to stress is language as a right to being. Not to learn it in order to speak "beautifully" in the style of lawyers with their farragoes of rhetoric, who become real acrobats of meaninglessness. But language as a tool to animate our social customs, our history, our goings-on.

Yet I see myself talking in front of these students, these 120 faces, and suddenly I remember: there is not a single Latin-American author in the bookstores; they are all gringo authors in translation; there isn't a single cultural activity in the towns or villages. In some places, there are one or two libraries, but you enter and they're the saddest little holes in the world. Every once in a while you come across a pile of books on a display table next to some "cultural bureaucrat" who already chose the books that interest him while the rest of the books serve as messy untamed decor.

In other words, there is no "cultural" presence, and cultural not in the sense of ornamentation, but in terms of coherence, of societal expression. Culture as the outcome of the life of a society. This is the nature of English, French and American literature. Consider William Faulkner's work (which as literary form has so influenced our writers, but not in terms of content) as part of society's struggle, through its writers, to speak, to search, to act. Thus society struggles against and questions itself. [. . .]

NINE: The border

Tijuana is noise; one incomprehensible nuisance piled on top of another, with the help of microphones. Men who appear on street corners, brandishing their index fingers in pedestrians' faces while shouting: Taxi! Taxi, *sir!* Aggressive signs with huge red letters inviting you to a party, to the "curious shop," to drink. Nostalgia and pain are drowned out by the *redova**, by mariachi and rock. Prostitution, lost sadness and solitude. Calculating, scornful, indifferent, blue stares; and dark, hopeful ones, maniacal, stupefied by vice.

---

*redova: a wooden percussion instrument

But it's also a town attempting to structure itself with dignity in the presence of "the border," in view of "the other side." In the face of the other.

The modern section is clean, efficiently signposted, and has wide, fast, well-built roads. Tijuana is a group of mountaintops, whimsically populated. One million permanent inhabitants, one million floating, whom the rest of the country, because of unequal resources, have pushed there, toward the cheap American door. The bargain basement for the Americans themselves. People from all over our republic, and not just the republic, flock here with enormous hope of entering the neighboring country. This great hope is nourished by two things: in some cases, the individual's betrayal of his country; in others, the country's betrayal of the individual. Those from above and those from below, the privileged and the ruined, stand together at the door of that great department store, that factory of insufficient and expensive dreams which is our neighbor.

"And the PRI" said a Tijuana woman, "deluges us with Mexican propaganda so that we'll quit being border people, and they tell us—in a tone of good sense that is mostly a warning—to be Mexican." Infuriated as she says it. In pain.

Nevertheless, the city still preserves traces of what was once Mexican in direct opposition to what is American: the old part of Tijuana; the responsible attitude of the Tijuanese regarding the right to be both a border *and* Mexico, without it being necessary for anyone to rub their noses in commercials about being Mexican, just because according to the PRI they're going to form a nation. As if the PRI wanted to build the country in the same way you construct a novel: based on language. This would be possible, yes, if language emanated from the individuals who constitute society, but not if who's talking is the system. After all, despite the looting of this country, we are still Mexican and we haven't forgotten this so much as to need reminding by the political machine. Now it turns out that we haven't known how to value what's ours? That we haven't been loyal enough to the country? That we've let ourselves be seduced too easily by our neighbors from the North?

Oh, please.

Them saying we're not moral.

But who are they talking about? The floating population that mixes with the permanent inhabitants of Tijuana?

Why do people read more gringo best-sellers than Latin-American authors? Because of colonization? Or is it because of the lack of resources? (These useless, wacky books are often times even cheaper. But more than anything else, they are on the shelves. The others are not.)

I insist: the appropriation of language, confidence in our own language—so as to achieve the greater autonomy of a society made up of individuals who in this way could resist the tedious lectures under which the politicians are constantly burying them in order to distract them from the increasing deterioration not only of their quality of life, but also of their very expectations of life.

People don't cross over to the other side because of the effects of colonization, but out of hunger, plain and simple. Meanwhile, in primary, secondary and preparatory schools, they "train" the adolescent or youth to speak "correctly." Like little animals who are going to be broken into the latest technology, where cultural imperialism does dominate. "O.K.," said the leader of a workshop in reading and writing, "in the first semesters students learn how to distinguish between kinetic, phonetic and iconic languages. . ." What?! I was shocked, what is that? [. . .]

We are afraid to speak; we are much more afraid to write, I tell the masses of teenagers I've faced over the past fifteen days, because school has taught us that language is solemn, that it's for the learned, who wear ties and clear their throats when they're about to speak. But in all of the students I have sensed a desire to create, to express themselves, to say something and to refute it, and they *don't* have the tools.

I try to give them Latin-American literature so they'll find the way. A literature that belongs to them, that corresponds to them, that could help them. And I realize that my main obstacle is SEP. Not only do their curricula fail to include Latin-American literature in even the most minimal way, but also the bureaucracy is such that, I've said it before, everything else is more important than learning.

And this type of contradiction is more and more palpable: they spend loads of money on cultural services, of which I'm an example, instead of providing the schools with proper libraries, since there's no point expecting (at least not yet) that booksellers will behave as promoters of culture.

If the schools (primarily the middle and higher levels) in each locality are not converted into springs of culture—their own, self-appropriated culture—the whole interior of the country will forever remain a passive spectator of a culture emanating from Mexico City, which as we all know is a parasite on the rest of the country. It's as if the country were the wealthy patron of Mexico City, so it could produce culture. But the culture that Mexico City produces is of no interest to the rest of the country; it's too urban, too focused on itself. And for this reason I now understand why people would sometimes rather read the story of a Texas cowboy, who from having nothing makes himself into a rich tycoon, than the stammering chronicles of a "Mexican storyteller," better labeled "Mexico City storyteller."

Our country continues to be Mexico City, but the possibility of "the Mexican," of an authentically rich and creative language, a language capable of generating a great novelist who would participate in the Latin-American tone, lies in the country as a whole.

I say to the students: Culture is you. What do you think, you, in the green shirt with the striped sleeves and front pocket, it's you I'm asking, and don't give me that . . . *Who, me?*

They all watched him. He said:

"Me?"

And this is the issue: nobody believes that what happens has anything to do with them. Nobody wants to speak. Nobody wants to mentally organize what they would really like to say. And this is because we are afraid of language, because nobody taught us that the language was ours, that we make up culture.

TEN: The other side

San Diego, as one would imagine, is completely indifferent to what is happening in Tijuana. We all know what is happening in Tijuana: there's a mixture of people of every different origin and circumstance who want to go to San Diego, and there's also a whole world of gringo tourists dying to return to San Diego with their unbelievable bargains.

You can't feel Tijuana's anxiety in San Diego. As a matter of fact, there's no time to feel any anxiety in San Diego. You have to go fifty-five miles an hour on the highway, follow all the traffic signs without missing the right exit or the highway could take you as far as Los Angeles.

The city rises toward the sky amid a prodigal nature that doesn't mind taking uneven steps: the greenery proliferates everywhere, embracing the concrete, peaking between houses. The only thing that competes with nature in San Diego is the signage. With its diversity of shapes and colors, its extremely loud typography, you seem to be entering a circus of various voices all calling at you, and achieving a spiraling infernal racket which you have to take in, or else, as I say, you run the risk of landing in Los Angeles.

Later on, once inside the city, it's surprising how smallish it is, how vulnerable the people are, walking around in their sneakers and with their customary upward gaze at the skyscrapers. They don't make a sound, gliding cautiously on the pavement, probably hoping not to upset Uncle Sam, who doesn't for a moment cease to watch over them: "enter here," "leave right lane open," "continue," "EXIT ONLY" (this appears against a yellow background indicating some kind of warning), don't do this, don't say that, don't think. Behave according to instructions, behave yourself, behave yourself, you better behave or else . . .

Oh, but so much has already been said about the mechanization of the United States, about the cold and simpleminded people, their sluggishness, their ingenuity, their lack of sensitivity. I go into a bar and the level of noise I encounter makes me feel like a solitary mouth open in an interminable hysterical frightened howl. Strident laughter, stiff hugs, people moving about constantly without any reason, but above all without much result; flitting about from table to table, they always end up sitting alone somewhere, panic-stricken in their disturbing restlessness.

How they've grown, how they've fattened up, the Americans. A great number are borderline-deformed. It's so sad and depressing when you look at the faces of these giant bodies, because the gringos have lost their legendary, healthy glow and seem to be containers of large doses of unhappiness.

But everything's in order, everything's clean and organized. Here life rolls smoothly, so that except for the occasional group of latinos or blacks who on the street corners produce a little hubbub, the rest of the world gives no reason even to be noticed. It doesn't fit. Life's rhythm hasn't left any space for it.

There's a notorious concern for nature in San Diego. There's a wonderful zoo where animal life is confined, but luxuriously so. Let's just say that the zoo is the animal-Hilton, and those who work there genuinely hold the profound conviction that sooner or later all animals aspire to end up there. Certainly the chickens and the doves circle freely among people, and after a while, one tends to pity them because they didn't qualify for a more prestigious spot. They remind me of the workers, of the people waiting in Tijuana.

Life is stable in San Diego; they say there are definite goals: health, freedom. And you see young people running athletically, who will later get fat; you see elderly people who already got fat, and then, because of their heart conditions, got skinny, and now run around in silent panic; you see the career mentality of middle-aged women who relieve their loneliness by profusely inhaling pure air.

And what consideration they have for invalids. Invalids have become just like production defects in the United States, yet the Christian spirit

334

prevails and instead of considering them useless, it pities them and relegates them to a special place. I wonder if the man I saw today in the zoo (apparently injured in Vietnam), blessed with an excellent, motorized wheelchair, in the midst of the movement of the people, out in the morning sun contemplating the monkeys, thought it was all worth it or not.

It seems that people have no idea, they just believe. And maybe there's no alternative. Even more so when there isn't a clue about how to find one. They have only a language, that is all, and it starts in the cradle. But it's not theirs, either. For if the Mexican high schoolers remain outside language because no one genuinely cares to make it his own, the Americans, before learning how to live, before knowing themselves, already belonged to a particular language: the American dream. The big-power strategy. It's the same as the Revolution in our case. Fortunately, ours is less efficient than the American system.

Tijuana is definitely far away from here, alien because in imposing its presence as the gateway to this great country, it can only be the enemy. The same as any group of people, any society, representing a style of organization different from this one.

Yes, much has been said about the United States, the great majority of which was brought to light by the Americans themselves. There's nothing left to say. San Diego is amazing, in the same way that a most gracious little woman of the moneyed classes appears to be so charming, but this isn't about whether Tijuana is more beautiful than San Diego; what matters is that between the mariachis who play all night long on the streets of Tijuana, in front of the popular cantinas just on the other side of the Nelson Hotel, and the fatsos who traipse around in the streets of San Diego, there's not much difference. Despite everything, the United States understood that in order to have power it had to colonize its own people. Mexico, on the other hand, believed that the *idea* of democracy was enough. Never mind its people.

Translated by Annette Cowart and Reginald Gibbons

335

An Historical Adventure: Notes on Chicano Literature

Martha Robles

Martha Robles (Guadalajara, 1948) is primarily an essayist, but also a fiction writer and poet. With degrees in sociology and Hispanic literature from the Universidad Nacional Autónoma de México, Robles has taught courses ranging from the history of education in Mexico to literature and society in places such as Mexico, Holland and the United States. Currently she does research for the Philology Institute at the UNAM. Among her works are Educación y sociedad en la historia de México *(1977),* Memorias de la libertad *(1979),* Inscripción de su Presencia *(1985) and* Escritoras en la cultura nacional *(1986).*

When Mexicans begin to delve into the political and social particularities of our emigrants to the United States, we discover the most resonant effect of the struggle of that Mexican-North American minority: their literary expression. Alienated from the memory of their magical universe, hopeful of its importance, alive in its imaginative fecundity, ready to confront their new reality amidst the contradictions of North American capitalism, their writing expresses a cultural mixture that it would be impossible not to recognize. The Chicano world comes to us through hybrid words, evocative of a Mexico conjured up in the face of ghost towns, with anglo echoes that qualify and name another reality: that of ethnic, economic and social rejection.

As for literature, that of the Chicanos belongs, for the most part, to the

336

peasant world.* Its texture is confused, sometimes magic, simple in its structure, complex in the mixture of meanings of a neolanguage in which we note the realms proper to Latin-American history: that of colonialism, from the point of view of the disinherited; that of capitalism, as it reflects the voice of those who struggle to overcome the adversity suffered in their homeland; that of the emigrant who evokes a past shrouded in mist and who has not yet determined the character of his own identity; that of the person who is not fully in the nation where he resides, who lacks a country, in the sense of a place to belong to, and who founds his sense of belonging on hope. His daily concerns: working the land, the rigors of farming, the exhaustion of the sun, racial discrimination, family cohesion, the rape of women, and a frontier *machismo* in response to the insecurity of life. This writing has not sprung up in Mexico because the distance between the rural peasants and the university culture cannot be bridged. Despite social hostility in the United States, that distance has been minimized in an industrial society that has made it possible for the children of a group made up mainly of rural peasants to *be* university professors and writers. The relationship between their immediate past and the first fruits of that success have produced a singular literature, which is not an additional chapter of Mexican literature, nor an appendix to North American literature, but the very own writing of a minority that has decided to live in a land that was once part of their own country, but is now a different nation which, despite all this, and in no small part despite itself, is gradually assimilating them. This is bilingual writing which has not yet made its choice between the two languages and which, inasmuch as language creates the work of art, will define itself in terms of one or the other. The bilingual aspect is necessarily transitory. Chicano literature, in this case, confirms the social reality of that minority: Mexican in its origins, its traditions, its myths, and North American in the decision to live in the United States. This is not the writing of exiles, but of a community forging its own historic identity.

For Rolando Hinojosa, it is a literature comparable, in its characteristics, to that of the North American Jews. There could be some similarities; however, we note an essential difference: Chicano literature is not that of a people dispersed throughout the world, but that of families, rural peasants for the most part, who have crossed a border to live on the land of their ancestors without having, like the Jews, the book as their nation. The comparison would be complete if, in some country bordering Israel,

---

*Here, "peasant world" is used to translate "the world of the *campesinos*." Wherever this translation reads "rural peasant," Robles is using the word *campesino*.

the Jews had crossed that border to live, work and forge a destiny distinct from that of their country. Chicano writing is, in this regard, singular in being the first expression of a group of emigrants without any precise identity, without nationalistic aspirations and on their way to probable assimilation into North America.

We are witnessing a drama of collective identity. The mythification of daily life dominates their narrative. A Mexico that is not Mexico surrounds the nostalgic existence of in-between characters, of imprecise beings in whom, despite their vagueness, we can recognize personalities that range from the "pachuco" to the "ladino," from the "peladito" to the hoodlum of the slums; that is, they try to make themselves Mexican through the postures of universal misery, of the very violence of uprooting and the macho attitudes whose crude expression can only be traced to the influence of Mexican barbarity. Chicano works are characterized, in another sense, by a strong presence of that which we could call "the third country," which is neither the United States nor Mexico, but an intermediate cultural borderland, a bridge of nostalgia and a road of particularities that are, perhaps, managing to consolidate themselves into a new twentieth-century culture: one in which a return to supposed origins arises under the sign of the economic domination of the capitalist dream.

The possibility of miracles and of supernatural protection is the live wire of the profane vision of their empirical Christianity, which presents itself as a socially cohesive element. Nondogmatic religiosity is conducted along that wire as it makes God a presence incorporated in daily life and a consolation in an implacable environment of sin and salvation; of nightmare and a dream of the possible. Despite this magical-religious thinking, Chicanos identify more with a remote pre-Hispanic origin than with contemporary Mexican culture. To know who they are, as a people, is fundamental in order to describe precisely their struggle and their conquest of civil rights in a Protestant society grounded in the positivist principles of the modern era.

Some Chicano writers affirm that they are not striving to assimilate themselves, nor to be assimilated, into North American society; that their identity is a form of recognition of their true roots, so that they may be respected as a minority that is, and will be, part of the United States. Considering the history of other minorities in that country, the outcome of that decision is difficult and unpredictable. It should be added, in this respect, that their efforts have the indirect support of Mexico's geographic proximity; such efforts may also be a spiritual resistance to the living conditions that have been imposed on them. Or a form of criticism that tries to purify a likely future assimilation.

For us [in Mexico], it is difficult to understand their purpose because we have not been a people of emigrants. We are facing an unknown historical experience. Chicano writing will express this historic adventure: to be neither Mexicans nor North Americans, but a people who, like the hyphen that joins two surnames, belong to a new existence: the Mexican-North Americans.

On the one hand, Chicano literature expresses that unknown realm in constant formation, and on the other hand it help re-create it. In the history of literature such cases are infrequent, but they do seem amazing and meaningful to us. Chicano writings are predominantly popular, and do not yet have the polished style of a work of art. They are not, nevertheless, minor works. In them we perceive that literature acts as a process leading to the definitive work that expresses the consciousness of a new people or a new cultural voice. [. . .]

The importance of the work of Chicano writers belongs to that heritage that charges writing with the formation of the spirit of a new people, in this case neither Mexican nor North American but different and, nevertheless, linked to the country of its origin and the nation of its historical adventure.

Translated by Judith de Mesa

Nahúm B. Zenil, *Confusion II* (1991, mixed media on paper)

Tea Blues

David Huerta

David Huerta (Mexico City, 1949) presently serves as cultural attaché for the Mexican Embassy in the Dominican Republic. He has edited widely for such publications as Gaceta del FCE *and* La Mesa Llena. *He was also editor and publisher of the* Enciclopedia de México *as well as director of the book series of* Biblioteca del Estudiante Universitario. *Huerta has published several volumes of poems, including* El espejo del cuerpo *(1980) and* Incurable *(1987); a book of essays entitled* Las intimidades colectivas *(1982); and several anthologies.*

The silent tea
has filled up
with razors.

The blue sky
filters through
the golden drops

and multiplies
on the stack
of sharp edges.

Sheets of perfumed
water
and sheets

of sweet steel
under the fire
of the silent
         sky.

Four Poems

Verónica Volkow

Verónica Volkow (Mexico City, 1955) studied literature at the Universidad Nacional Autónoma de México and at Columbia University in New York. Her works include Litoral de tinta (1979) and El inicio (1983), both books of poetry; two works of translation, Antología de Elizabeth Bishop (1987) and Antología de Michael Hamburger (1989); and a book of prose entitled Diario de Africa (1988).

From *The Beginning*

1

Hunger is the first eye of the body
the first eye in the night of the body
the eye through which the flesh first sees flesh

and a darkness of blood opens inside

> the eye
through which my feet   my teeth
> my fingers see you

> the eye
through which I look at you   just like centuries ago
in the night of touch

> that night
so close to the night of the fish

of the tiger
of the serpent
so close to the first night of life

we are the beast
again when we close our eyes
and our bodies grasp each other like jaws
attached to the taste of forms

Translated by Iona Wishaw

9

Deep darkness
that strips the skies
and with its fingers reaches the stars
deep darkness
in which the simplicity of fire
burns in the distance
faraway   worlds open
                        their secret faucets
and forms are the bed
of primeval sources
water sings the light of your throat
and the course of the river in the silence

                        mine of distant fires
night reaches your depth, too
bodies
into their secret mineral are transformed
bodies are desire
with the clarity of water
in the darkness of the mouth
or with the simplicity of a sudden star in the hand
from distance?
with touch?
from nothing?

                  what
did men carve the first fire from?

Translated by Iona Wishaw

Popocatépetl

Here among the rocks the tragedy begins
here in the dripping ulcerating ice,
in the jagged cliff,
in the blind weight of stone.
Here   so much being,
so much of being nothing for nobody,
so much softness of moss in among the weeds
and of snow on the sleeping inclines,
so much softness of the wind across the sand,
of the wind among the thistles and clouds.
Wind that occurs in this place like an anonymous fate
as naked as the spectral
passage of the water—
solitary wind that erodes the crags,
wind everywhere,
even in the pores of the smallest stones:
wind that is the apparition
of the face of time.

Quito*

The undulation of new mountains, the slowest waves,
crests suspended over troughs of stone,
sky reflected in the weight of dust.
City over this awkward unconcluding ocean,
endless flood on which houses are built
and life's gaming boards are set up
with bodies and coins to be won and lost.
Someone knocks at a door
or awaits a man who never arrives,
someone murders his brother
or betrays the friend he loves most,
someone is weeping in a story he does not understand;
and from father to son and from son to son
the sorrow feels new when it begins
but in the eyes of a god it may be
more monotonous than wind over ocean.

---

*Quito: capital of Ecuador, in the Andes

Naturalization Papers

Myriam Moscona

Myriam Moscona (Mexico City, 1955) was born into a Bulgarian-Jewish family that had emigrated to Mexico. A journalist as well as a poet, she has written and produced the radio program of the Instituto Nacional de Bellas Artes for several years. She has adapted works of Juan Rulfo for radio. In 1983 she published the collection, Ultimo Jardín *(1983).*

We daughters of foreign women
were born with minute compasses.
In nobler days
we visited Parisian museums.
We went into the Louvre in search of the Gioconda.
We too grew up amid adversity
and smiled predictable smiles.
If the war blew us out of the Old World,
a gust of wind condemns us to double vision.
We'll remain for perpetuity.
Torn between staying and leaving,
we'd like to give birth to storms,
so our blood will fall on terra firma
till our roots are lost in history.

Translated by Cynthia Steele

A Life

Raúl Bañuelos

Raúl Bañuelos (Guadalajara, 1954) studied literature at the University of Guadalajara, where he now is at work on research at the Centro de Estudios Literarios. He has published five books of poems, including Puertas en la mañana (1983) *and* Cantar de forastero (1988). *His work has won awards and has been reprinted in several anthologies.*

A fish told me some long, awful things about the river.
It told me that the river stones are so hard
because of the water beating against them.
And that it's the rain that hurts and overjoys it
more than any other thing whatsoever.

A fish told me some broad, awful things about the sea.
It told me that its waters are more hurt and overjoyed
    by the river
than by any other thing whatsoever.
And that its bitterness comes from the rainwater beating down on it.

A fish told me some long, broad and awful things
    about man.
It told me that his hardness comes from the bitterness
    beating on him.
And that it is life that hurts and overjoys him
more than any other thing whatsoever.

A life told me some long, broad and awful things about man.
It told me that his bitterness comes
from not being either the sea or a river or rain
and from being a man, like any other thing whatsoever.

Georgina Quintana, [Untitled] (1985, ink and collage on paper)

The Canary House

Ricardo Elizondo

Ricardo Elizondo (Monterrey, 1950) has published a book of short stories entitled Relatos de mar, desierto y muerte *(1980), which contains the following piece; and a novel,* 70 veces 7 *(1987).*

When a high wind howls through town, setting the streetlamps to bobbing with its furious gusts, her madness seems worse than ever; she really goes crazy then. She wanders up and down banging on doors, her desperate cries filling the air, but only when the wind blows. The rest of the time she roams about with that jug slung around her neck, muttering to herself, and not meeting anyone's eyes . . .

Sebastian arrived in town when he was two years old. No one knew where he had come from, and as the woman who brought him was chronically ill-humored, no one ever asked about him either. After much speculation and lots of rumors, no one really cared anymore; they simply dubbed him Zoila's stepson.

The truth was that the motherless Sebastian was entrusted to Zoila the spinster by the boy's grandfather, who in his younger days had been her suitor. Zoila agreed to take him, not because she felt at all sorry for the orphan, but because he reminded her of her old flame. When she got him home, she didn't know what to do with him; so she handed him over to her servant, who for all practical purposes became his stepmother. And did she ever! Violent, volatile, sex-starved and surly, she never exhibited the slightest trace of motherliness. The boy spent his early years in back rooms with the servants, near the fig trees, playing with dogs and scraps of wood and learning where chickens, cats and baby birds came from. Truly accountable to no one, after a few more years Sebastian was jumping the back fence. Heading first for the plaza and then for the gullies down by the river, by the time he was twelve he was hanging out at pool halls and saloons, where he would go to watch and earn a few pennies running errands; for Sebastian was good-natured and good at taking orders—a cheerful boy on the outside, and on the inside a forlorn child in need of affection. Being clever as well, as he stuck close by the big ice tub brimming with beers or the green table where he arranged the shiny balls, he soon learned to deal with people and, above all, to think for himself. And though it surely wouldn't do him any good, each night between eight and ten he dropped by Zoila's house, just so she'd know he existed, in the trite but fervent hope that she'd call him over, or better yet, need him someday. Envious of Don Joel's house and family, Sebastian would watch in torment as parents and children came and went. Each noon he paced back and forth outside the kitchen and dining room, where Don Joel sat facing the window; but the pharmacist never noticed the boy—so happy was he to be eating with his children while his wife, quietly tending her flock, scurried diligently from table to hearth. There was no comparing that house to Zoila's: all her birds and shrubs meant nothing, if there was no love there; the spinster paid no attention to him at all, and as for the attention he got from his nursemaid, he was better off without it. Nothing he might do would ever change that; the woman who took him in was perfectly happy simply to see that he was fed and that once a year he got two pairs of pants, two shirts and two pairs of sandals. With so little fertile ground in the house where he grew up, Sebastian's soul was bursting with unsown affection. The night was so lonely in those back rooms, that he found himself sleeping less and less and spending more and more time in the streets. One night he fell asleep at the pool hall and it wasn't that bad; after all, there he was really alone, so he could expect nothing of anybody. From then on, he never spent another night at Zoila's house, but deep down he kept on searching and hoping. Full of longing, but as wary as a battered dog, he dreamed of a house where the sound of his name would echo sweetly, where his hands and feet and strong, healthy body would be put to good use by caring people. And he found it.

Sometimes in her madness, the wretched woman wears flowers; weaving them into her tangled hair and tucking them into her torn, dirty bosom, she dances gleefully—a sad, disjointed dance, a nursery rhyme abandoned in some remote corner of her memory. . . . On the far side of town—the opposite side from the graveyard—was where the painted women spent their nights showing off their smiles and their legs. One day, a customer from the pool hall sent Sebastian after the black whip he had forgotten at the establishment run by Lupe "Big Tits" Pechos the night before. Rickety old houses along a winding alley. There couldn't have been more than fifteen in all, large sheds made of dried-out wood, some pink, others green, all with dirt floors. The fanciest one had a windup phonograph and on the wall, pictures of naked girls with pudgy, milky-white bodies. Sebas came in and asked a woman eating noodles— on the table in front of her, a platter of fried meat and a big bottle of red soda pop—if he could see Señora Guadalupe Pechos. As broad as a barn that woman was, with droopy eyes spilling over her plump cheeks and a much too tiny mouth. She looked him over carefully in the dimly lit shed; never before had anyone said "Señora Guadalupe" with so much respect. She saw the boy's feet in their old sandals, his faded shirt where yellow roosters once had crowed, his big eyes and his kind heart. She asked him his name, where he lived and what he did and she didn't eat anymore because she gave the soda pop to him and the meat too, all by itself, without tortillas, so you'll be big and strong. She got up for a bag of candy and that was when he saw her huge breasts like ripe melons. When Sebastian, holding back, took a single piece of candy from the bag she offered him, she filled his hands full; here, take the whip and come back soon. That he did; he was back in barely an hour and Guadalupe showed him around the brothel, naturally, as if she were showing off the rooms of a boarding house to a very old friend. Sebastian learned everything by heart: where she kept the paper and the cakes of soap, how many bottles of liquor she left out on display but never more than the ones that were out there now; how she kept the rest of the drinks and the packs of cigarettes under lock and key, along with the money to buy off the authorities and pay for the music, in case no one else offers to do that. Without so much as a second thought, after just one after-noon Sebastian was an integral part of Lupe Pechos's establishment. He never asked how much he would earn or what his responsibilities would be, but simply grabbed the broom, went down to the plaza to see if the ice had arrived, brought it back, set up the drinks, lit the gaslights and, looking serious and dependable, stood there behind the bar, trying to read his boss's mind and happy to feel so important; because from time to time, Guadalupe would call him over and just between the two of them, forgetting about what the women were up to, she would comment on this or that, sort of asking for his opinion, and she even gave him the big pocket watch so he could keep track of how long the rooms were in use. Poor Sebastian had to learn everything by heart because while he could read a little, he couldn't write at all. Guadalupe took care of that the next day when she set him to copying out the letters of the alphabet. After a few weeks she was dictating to him from old magazines, bottle labels and even the novena of the Saint of Bitter Lives. He also learned simple arithmetic and his multiplication tables up to twenty.

That crazy woman wanders aimlessly from house to house, and the other women in the neighborhood give her food. Chunks of bread, a boiled potato, oranges, figs: she takes them all; she'll eat anything, as long as it's cold. But if something hot touches her lips, she howls with pain. Tearful, she writhes in anguish, her hands over her face, spewing forth hailstorms of unintelligible sounds that burst from her throat, worn out from so much shouting and weeping. . . .

After two more years, by the time he was fifteen, Sebastian had spent many sleepless nights keeping track of the drinks he served each customer—bedraggled shepherds and peasants in their Sunday best, from Saturday afternoon on. The pungent smell of ammonia and the bitter dawns of spraddle-legged women dried up his feelings, cutting him off from everything but Guadalupe's eyes, for he truly loved her. To him she was always *Señora*, and he never laid a hand on her. The old madam knew—with so many years of streetlamps, stab wounds and flesh-scented mattresses behind her—that even the longest rope in the world couldn't tie the boy to the business that was her life. Sebastian had all the makings of a family man, with children and a wife with clean braids to cook and sew for him. Just how he had found his way into her heart she never knew and never would. What she did know, as she lay there in her tiny room each morning, only half awake, in the pink light filtering through the whore's quilt hung over the window, was that her food tasted sweeter since he had come. No sooner did she open her eyes than she would think of Sebastian, first of all, before anyone else, and that made her happy; then, shuffling about and jiggling her gelatinous jumble of cheap jewelry and flesh, she would rush out to make him breakfast, because I'm the one who cooks for Sebas, no hussy with rotten teeth and a taste for other mouths is going to feed him. The two of them lived happily together—Sebastian getting no salary but learning and feeling at home, and Lupe calmer now, feeling fruitful as she entered old age. On one of those Saturday afternoons—Lupe would always remember it, even after the tragedy, in the far-off town where she lived, crippled and full of gout—an especially changeable one, hot in the sun, but freezing in the shade, business was booming and the brothel was packed with customers because at Sebas's suggestion (he had gotten the idea down at the saloon), they had begun to serve cheap, spicy snacks that doubled the sale of drinks. As Guadalupe ambled happily from table to table entertaining the men with her bawdy jokes, someone from one of the groups asked if they could raffle off a yearling, right now, as soon as the tickets are sold; you can have any number you want for free, if you'll just let me do it. Sebastian picked the number: I like twenty-six, if your ticket wins you can keep the calf and I'll give you what it's worth in cash, maybe you'll end up raising cattle. The next morning, they called Ramiro the butcher over to Lupe's place: give me a price for the black heifer in the patio, will you; my Sebas here won her, she's all his. As soon as Ramiro named a figure, Guadalupe headed straight for her room and came back with nine gold coins for Sebastian, I'll owe you the rest. Now I'll buy that heifer from you, said Ramiro, but she's not for sale, that cow is mine and her name will be Gloria. That was when Guadalupe felt Sebastian slipping away; his die was cast, and as she watched him stroke the cow out in the patio, she checked out her cards to prove it. Six of clubs, a business deal. Ten of diamonds, lots of money. Queen of hearts, a woman of his own. Ten of hearts, lots of children. And two other cards she refused to read, because their sharp edges cut her right to the soul.

The madwoman can't stand a roof over her head; she spends her nights out in the fields. In very cold weather, she nestles in with the lambs. The shepherds don't stop her; after all, she's doing no harm. She never goes near the fire, but moves off in the distance like a sorrowful shade. Then, late at night, she sings to the moon and stars with the mad voice of a lunatic, rousing the dogs with her broken song. . . .

With one of the coins Lupe gave him, Sebastian bought fodder, the best he could find; he watched Gloria grow stronger day by day on the plentiful food and water he gave her. One morning he found her sniffing at the air and rubbing her teats against the sacks of fodder as she tried to mount them. She's looking for a mate, Guadalupe told him. Down at the saloon, Sebastian found out where the best bull was; and taking Gloria there, he paid another coin so the huge animal in the corral could mount his heifer.

Gloria bore a calf and gave lots and lots of milk, all of which he sold; with the income, he rented a plot of land to build them a corral.

Sebastian still lived with Lupe and though their arrangement appeared unchanged, both of them knew their days together were numbered. Gloria's calf grew up and both cows were bred; again, both bore female calves. Five years after he won Gloria, Sebastian had two dairy cows, two others pregnant for the first time, and all four about to calve. In the sixth year he castrated two young bulls, sold a third and rented a plot to grow crops on. He had five cows and a good piece of land. As he had to tend his crops, little by little he stopped going to Guadalupe's. The day she realized that Sebastian hadn't slept there in two months Guadalupe accepted the inevitable; but, deep down inside, the boy's good luck was a source of sadness.

The first thing he planted was sorghum. Beautiful beyond description was the sight of the first pale green sprouts against the slate black of the earth. When the fodder grass reached to above his knees, Sebastian stood in the middle of his sweet-smelling malachite field, puffed up with pride, the tingling of his skin spreading deep into his bones. Then, with unbridled curiosity, he watched as the emerald-green stalks bent under the weight of their clusters, rich with grain, great with gratitude. At harvest time, he chose the finest spike of all, the most beautiful, as big as his torso and golden brown like the thigh of a desirable woman. He took it over to Lupe's and quietly, without a word, handed it to her in the middle of the shabby dance hall. Guadalupe's nipples curled up into her throat as she hugged him tearfully, gushing with emotion.

During the hot season, the hapless woman spends her days at the dry riverbed, looking for puddles to soak in. The sight of children at play brings back painful memories, and she weeps privately, in silence. Riveted wherever her memories overtake her, she can spend hours turned in on herself like viscera, then like a stomach cooking up mysterious brews spew forth energy that has her banging on doors and windows, eyes bulging, scrawny, skin-and-bone arms flapping desperately. . . .

Sebastian changed; now his adolescent fuzz was a thick mustache. The odd-looking creature that had showed up at Guadalupe's house — with his bony hands and feet and his long arms and nose, he looked like an overgrown mosquito — turned muscular and manly. Well-proportioned, with a genuine smile and a forthright gaze, he won people over easily. A hard worker and a good businessman, he soon had a following and a reputation. After two more years on his farmlands, he moved into the only boardinghouse in town. There he rented the best room, with a private bath, three meals a day, and laundry included. Adventurous

355

when it came to investments, he rode his money hard, buying, selling, and taking risks. Before long he was lending money, and success sang loud and sweet in his ear. To Sebastian, everyone was a candidate for credit, as long as they offered guarantees—and sometimes even without. His money came back, if not in cash, in kind. Mule drivers who gambled gave him mules, fabrics and combs of tortoise-shell and ivory. He got goats, and heifers, and foul-smelling lots of tanned hides. He rented two large rooms a block from the plaza to use as an office. And Sebas, Zoila's stepson, was called Don Sebastian. With twenty-eight years in his generous hand, well-liked and respected in town, pretty girls could not help looking at him openly. But Sebastian remained a loner and a bachelor.

More than anything else, Sebastian was drawn to cattle-raising. He liked watching the animals graze at midafternoon, and listening to them bellow at night. At first, his choice of studs was a matter of guessing, sheer intuition; at worst, a bad guess might lead to the slaughterhouse. Soon he realized that what he needed was a good breeding bull—the local ones were all right, but not the best—and he began to put away money, with an eye to owning the most magnificent stud for miles around. It took him months to save enough; and by that time, practically all he had were five carefully chosen cows—Gloria among them—and the hefty sum his bull would cost. Leaving things just as they were and telling no one about his plans, one morning he headed north. As he rode from town to town, he kept his intentions to himself; for he could get all the answers he needed without asking questions. Arriving at the local saloon and claiming to be poor, he would ask for the cheapest thing available; by the end of two hours, he knew all there was to know about the saloonkeeper and the town, and by dusk he had decided if it was worth his while to stay over. That was how he heard about the fair in Santo Santiago, where all the gambling and betting goes on. He knew from experience that farmers rarely gambled, whereas cattlemen like himself, carefree and adventurous by nature, took great pleasure in fondling a deck of cards and rolling the dice. So he changed direction and headed for Santo Santiago, convinced that he would find his breeding bull there. He never dreamed he would also find the Queen of Hearts that Lupe's cards had foreseen for him.

Her calmest times come during the rainy season. The townspeople noticed that on those days, with the gummy, gray streets full of mud and water and a steady drizzle saddening the sky, she would be reachable in her madness, if not sane. Dawn would find her sitting on some doorstep, gazing into the distance like a sorrowful dove. Three or four kind women would clean her up, cut her hair and nails, inspect her tough, weathered skin, dress her in rough, sturdy fabrics. Always far from the fire, never with hot water; always out in the open, never in sight of children . . .

Old Zachariah was the owner of the "Santo Santiago" even before he was born. His mother and an aunt had opened the rickety old shop when one was left a pregnant widow and the other a deadbeat without a job. Hoping to make enough to live on and look after the son and nephew who was on the way, the two women pawned their medals and chains, rings and earrings. In the big room facing the street, with a few boards stretched over two barrels for a counter, they strung up pork sausages stuffed and seasoned by the mother-to-be, who was very good in the kitchen, and set out large sweet-smelling platters of freshly baked bread, covered with clean napkins. Both of them would get up before dawn; and while the aunt opened the store, the mother, stoking the fire, prepared jugs of cinnamon-flavored *atole* and large earthenware jars of sweet *tamales*. By midmorning, you could see all the way to the bottom of those jugs and jars; and by then, the mother had put the kettle up to boil with the chunks of meat which at noon, crispy and hot, would disappear quickly from the counter. The shop gained ground as Zachariah romped and thrived among sacks of corn and beans. The mother and the aunt grew old and died, and Zachariah married a sickly woman who bore him a sickly daughter as well. By then the store was well-established; it produced enough to cover expenses, but due to some shortcoming on the part of its owner—lack of brains or of backbone—it never would be a gold mine. Zachariah's sickly wife died and, at fifteen, his daughter had the aches and pains of a seventy-year-old; however, that didn't stop her from falling in love when she was twenty-eight. The character in question had her drooling the day he first kissed her and crying and in a jam when he disappeared three months later, leaving her with bouts of nausea and fainting spells to remember him by, and a round belly to fill out her skirt. Zachariah wisely accepted his daughter's pregnancy without a fuss. The baby was a girl and they called her Natalia. Quiet even as a child, she took after the shop's foundresses. As Zacariah's granddaughter grew older, his daughter's complaints multiplied: coughs, pangs, dizzy spells, poor appetite, rheumatism, palpitations and all the rest. One fine day she stopped complaining, and a week later she died. Since Natalia had always felt more like a night nurse than a daughter—make me a cup of purslane tea; my God, I'm dying; heat up those compresses, the pain hasn't let up; you're damned lucky you're not

357

sick; don't make those faces at me or your hand will shrivel up; rub me down with alcohol, with vinegar, with rosemary-and-clove water; bring me the chamber pot; make me a mustard plaster—to tell the honest truth, she was more relieved than saddened by her mother's death. Zachariah grieved, but being a closemouthed old codger, he just stayed behind the counter while his granddaughter took over the shop.

Natalia had deep-set, sad eyes and round, ample hips. She wore her jet black hair in a knot on top of her head and she never smiled, living in or through the decline of her family with apparent indifference. After his daughter died, the old man traveled the same route as had all his blood relatives at one time or another. Since the famous foundresses had done so almost simultaneously, they had died without knowing what hit them, bewildered and beside themselves with foolishness. They say the aunt turned into a simpering coquette in her old age, painting her face with white lead powder and the reddest of vermilions until she looked like an oversized Kewpie doll, and fashioning long, brittle, multicolored necklaces with dyed pasta from the kitchen—none of which would have been objectionable, only towards the end of her days, in her senile second childhood, she strung them with threads of saliva and beads of snot. As for her mother's long decline, only Natalia, who cared for her, knew it well. As a child, she thought she had a diamond inside her head, sparkling like the eyes of the evil man who was her father: I'd like to send it to him, her mother would tell her; one of these days I'll get it out of you with the axe, but don't worry, then I'll glue your bones back together with egg white. Nights were torture for the terrified little girl, who learned to sleep with only one eye closed so she could watch over her own head with the other. From then on, her sleep was as light as a tiny baby's sigh. Knowing what she did about her mother's nuttiness, Natalia wasn't worried to see her stop talking, because—as her mother put it—when my voice comes up from the tip of my big toe, it makes everything else hurt worse as it goes by. When she died a few days later, her mouth was all twisted from trying to keep it closed. Now the old man had made friends with three cockroaches; two are hardworking and dependable—he would say—and as for the third, we'd better stay on his good side because we don't want him for an enemy. Each morning as soon as it was light, Zachariah would drag himself over to say good morning to the three insects. He would scold Natalia for not saying a big hello to his friends before she opened the store: you've got a mouth like a mule driver's and you get up with a chip on your shoulder, it isn't the boys' fault if you can't find a man, yesterday they said you're just like a scratching hen, that's why they're afraid of you, but I feel sorry for you if you eat them, I'll bust your hide with the bar from the door, you have no heart, I know you by now and the only reason you haven't stomped on them already is that I never let you out of my sight. That was why Natalia never smiled. One afternoon, a man came in asking for cigars; Natalia, her back to the counter, was arranging some bath soap and scented hair tonic on a shelf. His voice hit her like a thunderbolt. When she looked at him, a knife of frozen fire cut her from her core all the way down to her feet. She couldn't take her eyes off him; her mouth filled with water, then with sand, then with water again; her lip was trembling as her clumsy hands fumbled for the cigars. He looked her over slowly, never blinking—her hands, her breasts, the hollow of her neck; when he looked into her eyes, Natalia filled the dark shop with a dazzling brilliance, her face brimming with a huge unprecedented smile, as great as her excitement, as radiant as the glitter of glass. Sebastian stood there in a daze; with his heart in his throat and the skin on his arms and belly on fire, he had an incredible urge to rub his nose along Natalia's entire body and bury it in her flesh, to smell her until he was sated, to smear her young female body with the saliva and kisses of his desire, to feel her thick, black head of hair nesting between his neck and his shoulder. Mad with lust and longing, with the impassioned tone of a trumpet he asked her name.

That night Natalia went to meet him, they walked down to the plaza together, and as he pampered her with ice creams and sweetmeats, they talked a little about the future and a lot about the past. On the way home, he took her by the shoulders, hugged her roundly, and gave her a kiss she still remembers.

A week later Natalia was as happy as a lark and Sebastian had forgotten all about the bull. He stayed in Santo Santiago for three whole months, while she, suddenly showing her mettle, in just four weeks sold the store, along with the rest of her possessions, the house she lived in and the orchard, and took her grandfather to the doctor to see if he was up to traveling. Natalia and Sebastian got married early one morning, with no ceremony or celebration. They bought the bull; and in a big wagon, with only the barest necessities, the old man propped among pillows and plush, and the bull—tamed with a little permanganate—riding in back, they headed home.

The woman is a living reminder of her misfortune. No one could possibly forget. Children were taught to love and respect her, not to taunt her when she danced, to understand the grief that struck her on a windy night, with neither rhyme nor reason, like a terrible bolt of lightning out of the blue, smashing her soul to pieces inside her breast, her body plagued by its destiny of broken glass, ears pierced by nails of fire, dark swarms of gnats chewed up and vomiting . . .

Sebastian liked all things golden; the heart of a poppy was golden, and so were the first rays of the morning sun. His first gift to Natalia was a cloth just that color: she looked radiant all dressed in light; his little marigold he called her, burying his lips in the nape of her neck. They went to live at the boardinghouse. Natalia gave him all her money, and needless to say, Sebastian continued to prosper. Like a wellspring of constant, clear water, the fruits of his labor yielded land and livestock, and he collected the rest in pools until there was enough to buy a house. That's what he was up to the night old Zachariah died, after three whole weeks spent singing "Pinto beans and purple flowers; that's how lovers pass the hours." Dinner was over, and Sebastian was tracing the floor plan of his house with his finger on his wife's thigh: the roof is no good and there's no grating on the windows, but it's a stone house with a high wall around it and five rooms all in a row, the first with two doors—to the street and the patio—and the rest with just windows; I'll have the grates made right away, of iron, with sills so you can put out your plants and hooks for the lanterns; the first room, the one with the doors, has a fireplace and a big stone ledge where you can keep your pots and pans, and right here on the wall there's a storage shelf, do you like it? She was about to say yes when a nasal cry from the old man told them the pinto beans he had cooking in his head were burning. Natalia pulled on her dress and ran out barefoot, and Sebastian caught up with her, shirtless, still buttoning his pants. They found Zachariah doubled up on the floor, clawing at his chest. Sebastian picked him up and laid him on the bed, then—still barefoot and shirtless—ran off to get the doctor. By the time he got back, the old man was limp and almost cold; Natalia crossed his hands over his breast and closed his eyes. They used some of the money for the house to buy a plot in the graveyard. The whole town turned out for the wake, at Sebastian's office, two blocks from the plaza. Guadalupe Pechos didn't open her place for business that night; instead, all draped in black, she went over to the boardinghouse. Natalia shed a few tears on her friend's round bosom; then she put on her veil and the two of them went to sit with the body.

They were friends from the day they met; Guadalupe had all the makings of a mother, and as soon as she heard that Sebas had returned with a wife, she got two tiny gold earrings and a big medal out of her secret place, put on a light brown dress of dotted swiss, and filled a basket with fine bread; then, parasol in hand and looking like a sultan's wife, she presented herself at the boardinghouse. Sebastian introduced her to Natalia with a broad smile and again it happened: Guadalupe, the madame so well-versed in life's cruelties, gathered Natalia to her ample bosom; and Natalia, knowing at once that she was loved for who she was, felt her feet come to rest for the first time on the safe, solid ground of that mature, loving woman's soul. She simply fell for Lupe, and that was that, because she could talk to her about everything: about her countless—and by now, erstwhile—fears, about her insane childhood, about how lonely life was in a house full of invalids, about her love for Sebastian, and, with total candor, about the pleasure she found in his bed and his caresses. Guadalupe, secretly advising Sebas, taught Natalia to indulge her appetite spontaneously, without shame. Their joy as a couple was all-encompassing and complete.

For two weeks after the tragedy, they kept her bound to her bed with folded sheets. Her torn mouth, raw tongue and swollen lips made it impossible for her to eat. Six times a day, they fed her through her nose—warm broth, boiled with poppy fruits to calm her furious, snake-like contortions. Day and night, they burned mint leaves, lettuce and marijuana in her room: perhaps breathing the narcotic vapors would dull her anguish. For two weeks that woman struggled amid smoke and restraints, consumed by a boundless suffering not of the flesh, chipping away at her sanity. By destroying herself she destroyed her memory, her contact with the present; for her reality was more agonizing and repulsive than a nest of scorpions. Then one day she fell silent, beaten down and obstructed, unsound in body and soul. . . .

Sebastian bought the house, added beams and a thatched roof to make it cooler, put solid grating on the windows, and sturdy wooden shutters of fragrant mountain pine; last of all, he painted it a golden yellow. So pure was the color and so brilliant in tone, that the house stood out among the others even at high noon, when the blinding glare merged gold, sand and sun into one great glittering vibration. Twice a year they repainted it, always the same color. People called it the Canary House, golden like cactus flowers, and spring mushrooms, and luminous clouds on a late summer afternoon.

Natalia bore six children, one after the other. Six little flowers, six treasures, six shouts echoing through the patios. When she had trouble giving birth to the sixth, Sebastian showed up at Lupe's place very late and in tears. Calling it quits for the night, all the midwiving whores met in council: you, run down to the Green Donkey and get Skinny Minnie, fast; and you, go tell Cross-eyed Kitty I need her. Faster than you could say "Jack Rabbit," Guadalupe gathered all the old hands at women's problems right there outside the shabby brothel. Minnie showed up tying on a shawl, Kitty with her characteristically crooked walk; from the establishment across the street they got Carmen the Clunk and Cot Legs. Marching all together in six-eight time under Lupe's command, they covered the twenty blocks to the Canary House. One by one, you've each got five minutes to see what's wrong with her; Carmen, you start. The doctor went off to fume in a corner, his hair on end: it's coming shoulders first, either I open her up or it dies. Carmen the Clunk took a look at Natalia, measured her, was about to touch her when get your hands off her, they're filthy, a basin of alcohol next to the bed; Minnie, you're on good terms with Don Joel, go ask him to open the pharmacy. She didn't have to, because Don Joel, here I am, whatever you want; the women from the neighborhood too, Doña Guadalupe, just let us know what we can do; everybody out, to the barricades, to the streets; you'll see, this pack of mules will pull Natalia out of the mud. And pull her out they did. Heaven only knows how they turned the baby around. The fact is that when the doctor heard it scream from his post in the kitchen, all he could say was my compliments, ladies, my compliments. What they couldn't do was relieve Natalia of her pains, she had no high fevers or bleeding, just a bloated, uncomfortable feeling. Guadalupe forbade Sebastian to touch her: it will be very hard, son, but you'll have to stay away; don't pay attention when she calls you or looks at you out of the corner of her eye; hold your nose, so you won't smell her; don't forget that if you get her pregnant, she may die on us.

They divided their marriage bed in two. So he wouldn't give in to temptation, Sebastian began sleeping in the last room to the back, surrounded by kids. For the first few months, Natalia stayed in the double bed in the third room; then she noticed that aches and pains aside, some nights what kept her awake was thinking so much about her husband. To guard against the weakness of the flesh, Guadalupe gave her potions that cooled her blood and brought down her fevers; then she sent her to sleep on the kitchen floor, alongside the door to the patio. The baby had its third birthday and the ban continued. Tired of sleeping alone, Natalia would beg one or another of her children to keep her company; but as soon as they thought their mother was asleep, they escaped to the last room, where all the fun was. There they had wrestling matches and sang, and Sebastian would make up stories, mimic animal noises, make bets with them; and then they would drop off to sleep amid shouts and laughter, with their loving father nearby. The truth is that Natalia didn't insist too much either; she was at work by the crack of dawn—giving Sebastian breakfast by the light of the oil lamp—and Guadalupe's potions had calmed her down: half a glass at dusk, before the sun goes down, then take a cold bath. By two hours after nightfall she'd feel her eyes start to close, put the children to bed, bolt the front door, open a shutter in the door to the patio, spread a mattress on the floor, blow out the lamps and candles, brush her hair and watching the night through the tiny, open window, doze right off, and sleep like a log.

Guadalupe, the tough, tireless madam, cracked under the weight of the disaster. When a man on horseback brought her the news, she was alone at her place, counting up the day's receipts and figuring her girls' commissions. The early-morning silence was thick enough to cut with a machete. Women wailing in the street; a dense, agonizing sadness among the groups of men; that odor clinging like vines to the adobe walls and over it all, the teeth-rattling, bone-chilling outcry, ghastly and anguished, of the raging young woman, her hands tied, held down by other arms and hands—arms and hands joined to faces weeping with impotence, contorted with grief and rebelliousness, soul and substance of despair. Guadalupe remembered her cards, the two she had refused to read because their edges foreshadowed the fatal outcome. And the stout madam, so tinselly and tarnished, just fell apart. With her life gone to pieces, a muddy morass darkened her brow. Why wonder, why know anything at all; she cursed that Saturday when Sebastian won Gloria, cursed her nine gold coins, swore at herself, at her whoring flesh and bones, unrepentant, unfit to live; and with her last ounce of strength, she gathered Natalia's crazed body into her arms. Shivering and over-flowing with grief, she organized the funeral. Lupe Pechos's establishment never opened for business again. . . .

It happened on a spring night, a dry spring that followed a dry winter. Strong winds whistled their lullaby day and night, howling through sleep and waking, hissing down chimneys like a quail's call. They never knew for certain what caused it—just bemoaned it forever after. Hearing screams and cries in her sleep, Natalia refused to wake up; but of course, for those were the screams of her children settling in her ears. She slept until the gruesome gold pierced her eyelids and the stifling smoke burned on her tongue, then awoke with a start, terrified at what had seemed like a dream: her whole house lit up in gold, gone up in flames the color of her husband's symbol. Feverish tongues of fire blazed from the beams, the white walls crackling brimstone blue. That was when they broke down the door and dragged her outside. She turned her head and heard the tolling of the bell, signaling some disaster, echoing furiously through streets and houses, begging urgently for help. Men and women running with jugs and pails and blankets and shovels. Hysterical impotence of desperate men whipping beasts pulling wagons with barrels of water. All together now, the Canary House is on fire; together, we need all the help we can get. The sizzling wind blew gusts of scathing laughter. Groups of children filled endless buckets at the well; women dirtied their best blankets with earth and water and anguished sweat; gangs of men ran back and forth never thinking about fatigue, heavy loads of water, picks and shovels trying to tear off the sturdy grates, and some of them, wrapped in the mud-caked blankets, dashed into the fire to rescue whatever they could. My children, cried Natalia, as the hot, whistling wind raised her petticoats. My children, she cried and cried, as her marigold house spun out its pure tone and golden froth in the fluttering feathers of countless incendiary flames. The wind roared insatiably; all the jugs of water and tossed earth were useless, and Sebastian's gold colored the night. Wrapped in quilts of trailing mud, Natalia clung to the grating outside the last room, raucously invoked the saints and God the Father, cried out to all her children, full of wrath asked Providence for mercy, begged forgiveness for her sins, clawed at her face and on the verge of madness, bit the charred rifle of her seven-year-old son. Four men held her down and tears came to her eyes; and screams and tears, grief and anguish all at once. A few seconds later the roof caved in, the beams broke free and in the rooms all that remained was the sputter and squeak of wood and the pestilence of scorching death. . . .

Translated by Louise B. Popkin

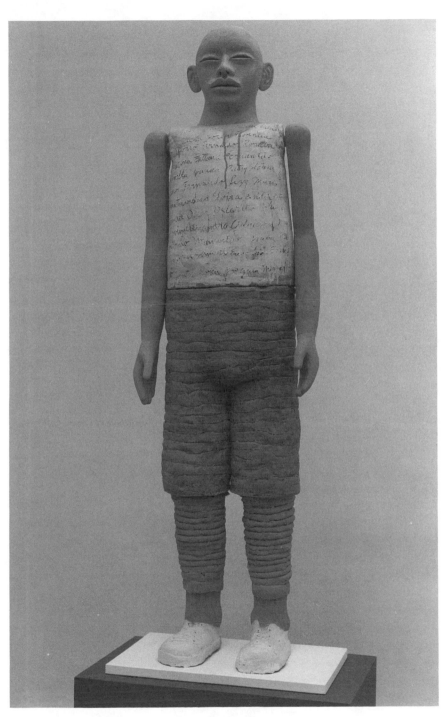

Adolfo Riestra, *The Immortals* (1984, fired clay)

Art and Monsters

Bernarda Solís

Bernarda Solís (Mexico City, 1950), has served as the chief editor for artistic education at Coordinación General de Educación Artística del INBA. Presently she is the general manager at Editorial Domés. Her books of short stories include El mismo camino *(1983);* Sin permiso *(1984);* Con un bull para la cruda *(1986), which won the national prize for short stories; and* Mi vida privada es del dominio público *(1988), which contains "Art and Monsters."*

Had she sworn never to do the same thing again and to distance herself from everything and everyone having to do with the word *Politec*,* under no circumstances would she have found a single pretext after hearing, "I'll wait for you here at eleven."

She didn't think it would be a visit like the one at Vlady's studio where all the paintings had reds and blacks that looked as if they had been hurled down from as high up as the roof; but without knowing exactly why, she was reminded by this house on Chihuahua Street of Leobardo's studio, and Leobardo reminded her of the presence of death, always lying in ambush; and perhaps this is when she would reject the idea of entering, and yet she found herself hearing the same, muffled sounds of the doorknocker lost in the depths within.

Who knows how long she had felt that urge to forget, within the privacy of her own thoughts, the memory of Leobardo, of death. He had asked her at a cocktail party for an exhibition opening if she'd pose nude for a painting but it wasn't until after several refusals that Leobardo

---

*politec: slang for the Instituto Politécnico Nacional, the technical university of Mexico City

agreed to do a portrait of her face. She held that difficult position for hours while he, sketching on canvas, told her about the latest avant-garde trends in painting, about his hellish lifestyle in Paris and about his peculiar relationship with a certain Cleotilde, who had just committed suicide in her apartment on the Seine as an aftermath to certain issues related to ontological problems, according to him; ecological, she thought—for, like a homage to Marat, Cleotilde was found in the tub bathed in a sea of blood, with her hand extended, and instead of a suicide note they found an essay on the floor concerning the pollution of the earth's waters.

There were two turns of the lock and she saw Leal's image outlined by the frame. His eyes watched her from above. In the entrance hall, she observed the dozens of canvases, one behind the other, and an antique hatrack, so old its mirror had lost the ability to reflect.

She gave her name and was led to a room full of piled-up furniture, a trunk in the center and a stone fireplace with hanging sculptures of hands in various positions that had lost their original alabaster hue. On the walls, innumerable paintings; another living room covered in dust; the feeling of death; the memory of Leobardo; the impending why's without answers.

"Careful, watch out for the hole," and he pointed to the trough covered by the carpet.

They climbed up a staircase that made noise and shed dust with every step and as they ascended she remembered that after a few weeks during which Leobardo wouldn't allow her to see the progress of his work, in the end he showed her the portrait. It was a tropical forest, a jungle, in which one could just make out an eye amidst the foliage, hers supposedly, and her surprised reaction caused Leobardo to explain to her that when the body isn't rendered in the nude, the face, which is the expression of the soul, remains hidden. And with this she had agreed to pose in the nude.

"Come over here," he told her, and sidestepping paintings and brushes and canvases, he invited her to take a seat.

His figure appeared delicate, clad in dark clothes and vest. He stroked his beard and pulled out an album from his papers.

"Choose some photographs for the book while I put on some water for coffee."

She leafed through the album and stood up to observe a portrait that was still fresh, on one of the easels. The expression on this face distracted her from the sensation produced by the filth accumulated on the tops of metal cans of paint, the dust spinning snake-like on the carpet, the disarray of flasks and caps on the floor, the pieces of unused charcoal that seemed to have been around for twenty years, and distracted her also from his footsteps, the creaking of the wooden stairs, and only when she sensed him close to her did she succeed in saying:

"I like it very much."

Enthusiastically, he pointed out the modernist influence, the importance of Matisse; he pulled out another painting from the bottom of the bathtub explaining its expressionist nature; and he made her go down to the entrance hall where she had seen the trunk and he showed her more drawings, a silverpoint etching, a sketch for a mural. Then after some other works piled on the table in the dining room, which was ancient with years of dust and disuse, they returned upstairs again; she tried to avoid the hole but inevitably she stepped in it; and without asking any permission she began poking her way around the furniture, on top of chairs, and underneath them; she opened up a book on *art nouveau* and, superimposed on top of a photograph with vignettes of the times, there was a love poem written in a very fine hand, and he led her to the history of his family, the thirty-six years difference in age between his mother and father, the great grandmother who supported Uncle Luis's lifestyle of a dandy by making Baby Jesus dolls, with clothes hemmed in gold thread, that she kept under bell jars where they lay as if forgotten here and there.

"How awful," he said, "you have been stained with cobalt blue. At least it's the most expensive hue of the palette."

She followed his gaze which focused not only on the stains, but persisted intently up and down, from her breasts down to her legs, just like Leobardo's look when he saw her nude, when he tried to force open her thighs, so he could sketch her in a posture of indifference, until, after months of living together, she finally consented the last time. She thought of him, his expression still full of paint when she came in from the street, and how the two of them ended up in bed like animated characters right out of a Gauguin painting.

He took the burlap, soaked it with gasoline and started cleaning his paintbrush.

"You are so beautiful that not even you will be able to prevent me from doing your portrait," he said, his hand pretending to land accidently on her thighs.

She looked into his eyes, remembering Leobardo's language, wanting to leave running, to forget the photo of the mural which Rivera ordered washed down, to forget the sketches done to a rhythmic beat, Leal's essay *Art and Monsters*, she thought that it would be better to leave at that moment, that insanity and health were as united as life and death; she looked at her watch and thought about time passing, which Leobardo had talked about, evoking Proust; she looked at her watch again in anticipation of leaving for an appointment she couldn't miss and just as she was about to say she would be leaving, he got up, he looked at her again in such a way that she closed her cape with both hands; she was getting her purse.

"The coffee should be ready," he said, then he went downstairs.

Again, she felt resigned, her cape fell open, she crossed her legs, he appeared behind the banisters and looked through the slit of her skirt.

"You know, there's something perverse about you," he said. "I don't know, perhaps like some character from the time of *The Directory*, maybe from the Marquis de Sade."

She didn't know how to respond, covering herself again; still, she couldn't leave. Leobardo had used similar words to describe her. "If you could be someone besides yourself, you'd definitely be Juliette, never Justine," he told her while making sketches for the work called *The Driving Descent of Aphrodite*, and then he began to work uncontrollably on the canvas, furiously merging reds with greens on the palette while listening to *The Entry of the Gods into Valhalla* with the volume cranked all the way up and reciting at the same time entire passages from *Thus Spake Zarathustra* in German, until when the brass section and the entire orchestra reached its loudest pitch, he covered her in massive strokes of purple and orange tones, and shoved her up against the canvas over which she ended up falling, leaving a pattern of spots that resembled a continuous movement of arms and breasts and hips.

"I hope it will please you," Leal said, setting the tray on the table, staring at her knees.

He took out a sheet of paper which he put on the floor, a pen and inkwell, stood up in profile across from her, his eyes traveled around her body, he closed his left eye, turned in order to see her from another angle, while she let her coffee cool, wanted to leave, remained motionless holding her breath, conjuring up afternoons filled with Leobardo's caresses, his fingernails stained with permanent ink.

"Might I draw you in the nude?"

Those had been Leobardo's first words; they were also his last when she waited for him in bed after a long session of caresses and passion, his mark fixed on her body in the form of petals and pistils and trains of ivy wrapped around her waist, falling from her neck down to her pubis, and then she went to look for him, and screaming a *why* that resounded inside the bathroom, she found his feet hanging down and his tongue sticking out, very far, in a way she had never seen in anyone.

She wanted to say no, no nude nor a single minute more in this studio, but her fingers, as if independent of her, obeying more his thoughts, began to unbutton her blouse, her clothes fell to the floor, her body an earth tone, she sat completely still like a little wax Baby Jesus doll with no bell jar, he adjusted her, marked her with his ink prints on her shoulders, spread her thighs, and she, with her eyes closed, sat listening to the scratchings of his pen on paper, the sound of his footsteps on the stave, the water dripping from the faucet, and then silence, she remembered the resounding of her *why*'s when she found Leobardo; not wanting to open her eyes she remained in the pose hoping her body would fill up with twenty more years of dust.

Translated by Annette Cowart

Red Slippers

Luis Zapata

Luis Zapata (Chilpancingo, Guerrero, 1951), the author of the best-selling novel, El vampiro de la Colonia Roma *(1979), currently makes his home in the suburban city of Cuernavaca. His work includes fiction, plays and translations. Other works by Zapata are* Hasta en las mejores familias *(1975),* Confidencias *(1983),* En jirones *(1985),* Melodrama *(1987) and* La hermana secreta de Angélica María *(1989).*

—Why didn't you say hi?

—Because I'm not a whore. I don't know him, I've never even seen him.

—But this could have been a good opportunity to get to know him. You could have started talking with him, asked him what he did, where he was going then. . . . I don't know, chat with him, it's the thing to do.

—And afterwards? What scares me is afterwards.

—Afterwards, he would have asked: "And you, what are you up to?" And you would have answered: "Just out for a walk" or whatever would have occurred to you.

—Yeah, how easy.

—And then he would have begun to try to make a pass at you, would have invited you to have a drink or go to his apartment, or take a drive in his car, or I don't know, it varies.

—And then what?

—Well, after he invited you, you'd have told him that you were working. Like this, look: "It's just that . . . you know . . . I'm working," like that, you see, with this tone: "It's just that . . . you know . . . I'm working." Then you'd agree on what and for how much.

—But it's already real late, they're about to close.

—C'mon, don't be such a pussy. Now's the best time.

The only thing we wanted was to dance. Dance. Let ourselves be moved by the music, by the feeling the music gave us. Without knowing where it would lead. Lose all previous points of contact, all possible references, and let our limbs take on a life all their own. Without thinking. Hardly realizing what was happening, which was best because nothing ever happened anyway.

—Now wink at him.

—What? Wink at him?

—Yeah.

—He'll laugh at me.

—Don't worry.

—And if he's not out cruising?

—C'mon, of course he's cruising. All you've got to do is to see how he's standing. And his handbag.

—But maybe he's not. Or maybe he's here for something else, to meet up with someone.

—What an ass you are. Only these kind of guys come here. To get together with someone it's better to go somewhere else.

—But I'm not going to wink. It doesn't come naturally. Think of something else.

—Keep looking at him.

—How?

—Like this, real intense. Don't drop your eyes until he looks this way.

—He's looking this way. Now what do I do?

Since we were little boys. We liked to put on plays. We almost always invented them: The Black Widow, The Prince Who Couldn't Touch the Ground, The Seven Magic Coins. Maybe because theater was what we came across first, or because it was, in a certain way, something close to dance. Maybe we saw a play performed by some theater company from the capital and it impressed us and we decided that was something we could study. Or maybe just for fun. Afterwards, someone must have brought in a dance group and we realized that theater was just a way station on the road we wanted to take. We started dancing. We started listening to records and inventing steps and putting them together. We danced all the time we were together. Danced until our legs hurt. When we weren't together, too. We talked on the phone, and we danced like that, with the phone tucked under our ears. Each step had its own number, from the ones we created for our dances to the ones we saw afterwards and assumed were classics. Then, we'd just put the record on at the same time and by phone we'd determine the steps we had to do: the number seven, the ten, the forty-three, the twenty, the fifteen — fifteen almost always worked as a climax. Eight, fourteen, usually we'd finish with thirty-seven, which was extremely complex and spectacular.

—Smile at him.
—Like this?
—Yeah, like that. What are you waiting for? You have to take the initiative.
—I can't smile just like that. Tell me something funny.
—Oh, don't be so provincial, what's he going to think? These guys like worldly types. Light a cigarette.
—But I don't feel like smoking.
—Doesn't matter. Light it and smoke it as stuck-up as possible. They like snobs too.
—Like this?
—That's better. You see, it doesn't take much work to be a sophisticated lady.
—He's already gone. Now what do we do?
—Wait for another.

When our families realized what was going on — of course it was impossible to keep it a secret since we danced all day — they began to accuse us of being faggots, they told us that only women do that kind of thing, and not all kinds of women, either, only the shameless ones. We didn't pay them any mind and we kept dancing, although we were a little more cautious doing it in front of them. Our parents tried to find other outlets for our energy. They suggested we play basketball (we were already fourteen or fifteen years old), join a sports club or play with the boys in our neighborhood, or at worst paint or write to keep from making them look ridiculous in front of everyone.

—Look, that one. That one definitely pays for it.
—Why do you say that?
—You can tell by his clothes. Look how he's dressed.
—How? He seems quite normal, like any other guy.
—That's right, like any other guy, but with money.
—I'm nervous.
—Don't be a baby.
—I'm going to chew my fingernails off.

—Light another cigarette.
—My hands are shaking.
—O.K., give it to me, I'll light it for you. . . . Here.
—Thanks. What time is it?
—Twelve-fifteen. Why?
—No reason.
—He's coming this way.
—What do I do?
—Smile at him. More. Keep looking at him. . . give him a little sign to come closer.

Nonetheless—who knows why—we kept living there a while longer. Maybe because we had to finish our studies in order to pay them back, in some way, for all they had done for us for so many years, which actually wasn't much, since we'd begun working after junior high school. We had some real difficult times, especially when we discovered our sexuality—misdirected, according to our families. We fought. At times they yelled at us, at times we hit each other, other times they seemed to give in and realize there was nothing to be done. Our calling, meanwhile, hardened to the point of desperation.

—My name's Mario, he's Joaquín.
—(   )?
—Well. . . just hanging out.
—Out for a walk.
—(   )?
—No.
—We're from Saltillo.
—(   )?
—A month.
—And three days, to be exact.
—(   )?
—And you?
—(   )?
—What do you do?
—(   )
—In what?
—(   ). (   )?
—No. What, paintings and all that?
—(   ).
—Ah.

—Must be interesting, no?
—(   ). (   )?
—We dance.
—(   )?
—Yeah, both of us.
—(   )?
—Now?
—(   ).
—We're working.

At a certain moment we realized that we'd have no opportunity to do what interested us most, there—at this point, I suppose it's no longer necessary to say dance. Or else, at that moment our suspicions were confirmed. Besides the fact that there were few dance groups, we also wanted to study, acquire technique, hone our skills and experience, and we had no way of achieving that, there.

One day we also decided that we weren't going to take any more humiliation. We talked with our parents, we insulted them, they cried, they tried to hit us but we defended ourselves, and we left them a step away from a heart attack. We grabbed some clothes, sneakers, a few tights, and put them in a suitcase. We went to the station to buy our tickets and while we waited for the bus we began to make plans. We would arrive and the first thing we'd do would be to sign up for classes in some studio or academy. And to pay for the classes and our expenses we'd work in a group, or, at worst, in some nightclub. Mexico City would be the first step we'd have taken out of our mediocre existence.

—(   )?
—I don't know. It depends.
—What do you think would be fair?
—(   ).
—For both of us?
—(   ).
—No, that's not very much. What do you think?
—I don't know. You decide.
—(   ).
—Well, O.K. But you'll pay for cab fare back, right?

Translated by Kurt Hollander

Ode to Feeling Like It

Ricardo Castillo

Ricardo Castillo (Guadalajara, 1954) won the Carlos Pellicer prize for best published work of poetry in 1980. He toured the country with Jaime López to present Concierto en vivo. *He has also worked as a script writer for puppet theater. Castillo is the author of* El pobrecito señor X *(1980),* Concierto en vivo *(1981) and* Como agua al regresar *(1982).*

The greatest work of engineering is urination,
as far as drainage is concerned.
In addition, urination's a pleasure,
what more is there to say when you're pissing
in tribute to love and friends,
when you pour it hard down the world's throat
letting it know that we're brand-new, to put it bluntly.
All this is important
now that the world is spewing warnings —
a drunk's hiccups.
Because it's necessary to piss, out of pure love of life,
on silverware,
on sports-car seats,
on swimming pools with underwater lights
that are worth, for sure, 15 or 16 times more than their
        owners.
To piss till our throats hurt,
down to the last little drops of our blood.
To piss on all those who think life is a waltz,
to yell *viva la cumbia*, you people,

everybody wiggle your ass
till we shake all the mysterious stupid stuff completely out of
    ourselves.
And also *viva el Jarabe Zapateado**
because reality is at the back, to the right,
where you don't show up in a tux.
(Nobody ever cured himself of TB by pounding his own chest.)
From life's manger, I piss—
All I want is to be the greatest pisser in existence,
Oh mama, oh god, the greatest pisser in existence.

---

el Jarabe Zapateado: a Mexican folk dance

Free Time

Guillermo Samperio

For a biographical note on Guillermo Samperio please see page 54.

Every morning I buy a newspaper and every morning, as I read it, my fingers become smeared with ink. It has never bothered me to get them dirty, so long as I'm up to date on all the news. But this morning, as soon as I touched the paper, I felt extremely ill. I thought that it was just a matter of one of my frequent dizzy spells. I paid for the paper and returned home. My wife had gone shopping. I settled into my favorite chair, lit a cigarette, and began reading the first page. Immediately after learning that a jet had crashed, I started feeling sick again; I looked at my fingers and found them dirtier than usual. Overcome by a tremendous headache, I went to the bathroom, I washed my hands calmly and now, less shaken, I returned to my chair. When I reached for my cigarette, I discovered a black stain covering my fingers. Hurriedly, I returned to the bathroom and scrubbed my hands with a bristle pad and pumice stone; finally, I washed with bleach, but it was useless because the stain had grown and spread all the way to my elbows. Now, more worried than angry, I called the doctor and he said that it would be best to take an extended vacation or a long nap. Later, I called the newspaper office to lodge the most scathing complaint; the female voice that answered the phone merely insulted me and treated me like I was crazy. While I was talking on the phone, I realized it wasn't a stain at all, but rather an infinite number of tiny letters tightly packed together, like a swarming multitude of black ants. When I hung up, the little letters had reached my waist. Alarmed, I ran to the front door; but, before I could

378

open it, my legs gave out from under me and I fell to the floor with a crash. Flat on my back, I discovered that, besides the large number of ant-letters that now covered my entire body, there were also a few photographs. I lay there for several hours until I heard the door open. I had difficulty forming the thought, but finally I was convinced that I had been saved. My wife came in, picked me up from the floor, tucked me under her arm, settled into my favorite chair, thumbed through me nonchalantly, and began to read.

Translated by Russell M. Cluff and L. Howard Quackenbush

Monkey House

Efraín Bartolomé

Efraín Bartolomé (Ocosingo, Chiapas, 1950) studied psychology at the Universidad Nacional Autónoma de México (UNAM), where he also teaches at present. Bartolomé has won several prizes for his poetry. He is the author of Vivir en la ciudad *(1981),* Ciudad bajo el relámpago *(1983),* Música solar *(1985) and* Cuadernos contra el ángel *(1987).*

Why talk
about the guayacán tree that watches over weariness
or the cedar drum the logger is beating

Why name the surf
at the mouth of the River Lacanjá

Leafmirror   Lizard cradle
Spring of *macabiles* with astonished eyes*

Maybe this tongue will change into an orchid
This voice into partridge-song
This breath into puma-purring

My hand would have been a black tarantula writing
My happy breast a horde of a thousand monkeys
A jaguar's eye would unfailingly hit the image

        But nothing happens   Only the green silence

---

*macabiles: fish

So why talk

Let this love fall from the highest ceiba tree

Let it fly and cry and be sorry

Let this astonishment be stifled till it turns to dirt
Scent of the wild plum
Coypu
Leafpile

Two Poems

Coral Bracho

Coral Bracho (Mexico City, 1951) studied Hispanic literature at the Universidad Nacional Autónoma de México, spent time studying in England and France and was a scholar for the Instituto Nacional de Bellas Artes. She won the Aguascalientes prize in 1981. Her books of poetry include El ser que va a morir *(1982) and* Peces de piel fugaz *(1988).*

In This Warm Dark Mosque

I know of your body: the reefs,
the scattering flocks,
the restless, desirable light (on your burning thighs incited by
    the rain)
of your waves:
I know your thresholds as if leaving myself on the edge of this
    roomy, murmuring,
warm mosque: as if weaving myself (your gentle, dark smell)
    into the heat of its naves.
(Your sour, impenetrable orchards) I know of your fountains,
of the luminous, fecund expanse of their ripe and turbulent
    echoes,
of the patios of your shining sleep:

Leaving its nocturnal fire, its lascivious ivy, its veined marble:
the columns, the arches;
its fronds (in a gentle, furtive rapture).

Releasing oneself in the shadow—fragrant and profound—of its
    lively reeds,
of the glassy, gentle base of its columns:
Slackened, the light moves inside, impregnating itself (like a
    perfume clinging
to the lime of marble) to this inhabitable seething; upon your
    thighs its eagerness spills:
in its niches, in its smoking and resinous rooms,
sliding. Wine, fish, mantle, seedbed:
this smell. (In your belly the light opens a thick foliage that
    extends the coasts, that returns in its waters)

Traveling over
(with anointed plants, warm, oily steps: skirts brush in the
    mist)
the filled, palpitating passages; the enclosures:

In the cells: the shady dew, the dense, visceral juice of your
    groin:

(In your eyes the sea is an abrupt twinkling held back by its
    crevice
—its tongue sways between these walls, between these doors)
    into the folds,
into the accessible buds;

                Yielding to the fragrance,
    to the blue, coppery vapors, the opaque brushing of the
    stone on your skin.

Water that cleaves, encircles, oozes—its rainbow-wet
edges—that joins its sniffing, thick
animal limpidity. Dunes, jungle, lights filtered by the sea.
    Incision of arabesques beneath the palms. Glass. The net
of high cryptic stained-glass windows. Foamy floor lamps.
    Touch with the forefinger
the blunt edge, the reliefs, the mud (in the wood the liqueurs
    coil, become dense,
slither down the honeycombed clusters, oozing);
the sucking metal of glasses, the plaster, in the granite

with lips (fresh, enameled lapses, amid the drunken voluptuous
    warmth);
the mosaics, the bile
of the inlays.

The mosque stretches between the desert and the sea.

In the patios:
The lilting splendor (sour murmur) of the orange trees;
    languor of the moss, the myrtles.

From twilight the wind grows, tints, tosses and turns, expanding
in the burning sand, sifting amid the drunken galleries, their
dampness. Oils churn and modulate the shadows in magnetic
mirrors. Metallic shine on the walls, under the fiery wedges.

(Water: ivy stretching and reflecting from its slow retention,
terse, diminished yearning)

—Tilting toward the voices,
toward the breathing hinges they cohabit with uncertainty—

Sinking into this fluffy calm, into this soft emulsion of essences, of
lewd earth; entwined, lost among these algae; discreet to its most
meticulous concavity, to the woodwrought hegiras, beneath this
hue, the coastal notion of your skin. Cells, white branches. Under
the waxed dome, burning (grapevines, ferns, thistles in the
tapestries; the whole night inserted beneath that crystal-clear
crackling) perfumes. Water perspiring in the cracks of the
extended shutters. (Brief, voluptuous footfalls.) Steps: cobalt blue.
Breathing amid the gushing grass, beneath this tile; dry traces,
worn down; tin in the corners of your lips, on your flanks; lichen
and saltpeter on the tips of your resinous fingers.
And between them.

Refracted in Your Life
Like an Enigma

Like a translucent mirror
the deep still pool opened among the shadows;
convex to this thirst
whence I drink, touching it as if it were
    a sphere in an inextricable enclosure,
beneath the liquid wake. A voice

—From amid the dance and evening ardor
a subtle song. Amid the green of amazement, of pleasure
  —What light, in the full heights, binds
in a clean clear way. —What the wind makes
quiver

and the fleece on the zenith among the Aeolian harp strings.
The crystalline eucalyptus. Sap
ciphering the calm
and the ways of the water

Whence I drink, as discerning as the reflection
of an impregnable contact: clear deep roots
in the vault of the luminous night.
Full deep chord transparent like a roar over the forests.
In the continuous hollow of the conch shell, against the leaden
    windowpane

—They toil

the slabs of ebony
before the bonfire reflecting
the circular
ochres of the edge; the trance—the amulet felt beneath those
    hot springs, that light—

Among the forests of birchwood,
like a flame.

(—The children trace their liquid howl in the bark of trees
like a vegetal phantom)

—The flames lick up the night, sip its fiery roots.
—Its fluid
roundness, its happening—Whence I drink, I grope

Translated by Suzanne Jill Levine

Adolfo Riestra, *Opera Singers* (1987–88, fired clay)

Two Prose Pieces and an Excerpt from *Magic*

Carmen Leñero

Carmen Leñero (Mexico City, 1959) completed her undergraduate and graduate studies in Hispanic language and literature at the Universidad Nacional Autónoma de México, where she is currently involved in research on semiology and theater for the Philology Institute. This selection is from Gajes (1988) and Birlibirloque (1987). Leñero has also published poetry; theatrical works, including Mas allá de la tierra and El silencio y la palabra; as well as her research on the spoken language in Mexico City (1990). As a scholar of the Consejo Nacional para la Cultura in 1990, Leñero worked on her forthcoming novel, Las piedras vivas. She has recently produced a soft-rock album entitled Casas en el aire, which contains her interpretations of songs by Mexican poets.

Kaleidoscope

Sweep away your love, singing in a jukebox voice. Your father who hits you if you come home late, if sin nests in your single woman's womb. Sew up your desire, which stalks you under the plumage of a thousand Ave Marías. The unwrinkled sheets; the husband in front of the TV, and the young ladies, early to catechism. They are the flowers of your eyes, passion of seminaries, virgins buried in the garden of your advice. Inhale the delirium, lying sleepless in the last corner of your innocence. Watching meandering words which, too often said, no longer say anything. Brandish your bewildered faith before the fantasy of chaos. Answer the phone promptly—polite, impersonal, just like they taught you. It's almost time for you to go down to the dining room, for them to raise your salary, for your boyfriend to finally ask for your hand in marriage. This afternoon for sure. And right afterwards, the blue nylons from the big showcase. There will be more than enough time to take your mother to the opthalmologist. The poor thing is dying from blindness, like them all. Then, blessed sleep. The pillow of clouds, certainly softer than his gray engineer's embrace after the wedding ceremony. Wash your soiled underwear in lots of suds, your enormous underwear impregnated with widowhood. No one looks at the flabbiness of your age. A creature of habit, you easily forget. Go shopping and buy up the scenery, for life still holds surprises for you, like the commercials say. Let the State take care of the children, and your husband, the investments. And you go off with whoever offers, to breathe in the sweet, forbidden air of any other city. . . . "Look at yourself in these eyes," Grandma used to say.

The Slippery Soul

I search for my soul behind the mirror's eye. I search for it in this sleepwalker's tread by day, and in the nocturnal slumber of voices. I distill the cries calling to the soul of a woman, caretaker of cemeteries, as she once was of sterile springs. At least, I search for its tracks. The places where it roamed. And blindly I retrace my steps.

I search for my soul in the body's potential classical profile, hidden beneath the tastelessness of flesh and the nude's battered curves. I search for the Greece of virile dreams in the angular bas-relief of the collarbone, and the blue gentleness of its seas in the shape of shoulders.

But inside all I hear is coagulated blood; bubbling clots of salt that sooner or later will burst; sticky humus snaking through clogged riverbeds. An old body hidden behind subterfuges of weary youth, insubstantial and heartless.

Wrinkles that don't line my face are now projecting their shadows on the walls, and I hear myself wandering over the house's stairways and flagstones as if I were watching myself from afar.

Alone at last, forever. Carrying my soul's corpse, still warm, over my stooped shoulders. Absorbed in the tracking down of tiny objects scattered on the ground. Raising my pupils to the cloudy skies. Wetting my heels in the asphalt puddles.

And we are nowhere, waiting for who knows what. Waiting for the sign or the conclusive proof of failure, sudden pleasure, the anonymous call of plunder.

The city's constant shaking comes between the sole of my foot and the earth, between my hair and the clear, silent firmament where the stars congeal.

I search for my soul hanging on the handrail in a department store. I search for it as I screw a light bulb into the lamp or press the button on a questionable elevator.

I search for destiny in your gestures as you're walking to me and your voice turns into a timid memory, and the glow of your eyes into a mere sign in a traffic jam.

I search for the voice, the syllable, the grunt: ferocious onomatopoeia that betrays the monster submerged in the pond.

I go from one station to another, stumbling along the green platforms of the quadrant. And nothing. No song evokes even the sudden disappearance of my soul. I tell myself that I need to drink some poisonous substance or something like that, to see if in the last drop the shipwrecked gaze of my soul will appear.

"Plick," sighs the switch on the night lamp. And in the darkness my open eyes follow the trajectory of a rickety truck that goes along, jumping over potholes, attacking speed bumps that ring like gourds, its fenders gnawing at the eroded edges of the sidewalk.

At the theater exit, the sluggish walk and bleary eyes of the yellowish spectators. The halfhearted invitation to dinner at Vips (an onerous consummation of the evening out). But a providential, miraculous cheeping of nocturnal birds survives the noise behind the gray creeper that runs the length of the parking lot; it disrespectfully competes with the roar of motors in first gear.

My patent leather high heels ring like metallic castanets over the uneven stone floor: tracka-tock, tracktrack-tock. A pacemaker whose rickety beat brings to mind flight, pursuit and rescue.

Out of the corner of my eye I look at the waxing moon, half hidden behind the very smoke cloud of its presence: a tilted white cheek, an interrupted smile. But no; it isn't the familiar smile of the soul I'm looking for.

And I sit there, ghostly, behind the wheel, driving along the half sole of a tottering highway. In my burgeoning double chin an unbearable flabbiness chirps. With the tip of my index finger I confirm the usual crevices at the base of my neck. I can feel the double wrinkle of my temples standing out like threads of boiling water. Run away? I knock three times on the door of purgatory—like in the stories. I push on the door and peer in. Maybe my soul could be found in that empty place, hanging from the branches of the void like a ripe apple on the verge of happily falling.

And I place my chest there in order to brake its fall. I lie faceup, my back feels the impersonal contact of the parquet floor. When you lie in gardens, on the other hand, you're not restricted by the limits of your body, and you drive away the sickly sensation of your own weight.

The water pipes make a metal gurgling, and gas whistles out of the stove's extinguished pilot lights.

I'm searching for the soul's soul. The least trace of its existence, at least, as I drink green water from the faucets.

Feeling my way, with my eyes closed, my hands run over the rough surface of the indigo carpet in the stone foyer. Lying on my stomach, I dissect its involuntary resistance. Over me float the static terrors of noon.

A winged motor, wasp's wings, is the sound my palm makes as it slides over the cold curves of the Formica furniture. And my sense of touch goes numb on the mineral slopes of a mythical mountain.

Rats scurrying through the neighborhood garbage cans are a flameless bonfire pretending to be filth with a crackling of cardboard, cellophane and aluminum foil.

The clouds grate against each other, behind the smog, when the hinges of a defeated eyelid move. Then acid rain falls; a rain that leaves its sticky inclemency on your cheek. Your hair stands on end, curls up, and you run for refuge to the poultry stand.

When the melancholic mermaid loses her way, out on the high seas of the Mexico City freeway, a sorrowful, evil tick-tock revives in people's consciences. And while they're waiting for the light to change, someone thinks about the fabulous aspiration of prolonging the intervals in that tick-tock, of making them elastic like chewing gum, like the snotty secretion of a time that's always got a cold. But the green light is too slow in coming; the intervals pile up on top of each other like schoolgirls at the half-open doors to recess. The wheel of the universe gets drowsy.

Who's calling me—"pssst, pssst"—from the thousand cardinal points marauding like a swarm of mosquitoes? Ay, ay, ay! It annoys me to feel someone tugging on the knotted strings attached to my arms and legs, to my copper phalanxes, to my crystal nails. The terror of asymmetry, of hair, of the gelatinous consistency of skin, penetrates me to the bone; ineluctably it stalks my female vanity, while the punctual rotation of the planet once again imitates the rhythm of the spheres, repeated seven times.

It's just that I have no one but myself to rummage around inside of. But my soul is nowhere to be found, either inside or out. Not in this house, nor on the eighth continent to be trodden by human feet, nor in the signs of a secret code, nor in the proverbial vapors of alcohol, nor in an embrace.

I hold my breath in order to make the delicious hollow in my stomach; I'm inventing the dampness of a very slight flood, which I sail over as my gaze is hypnotized by never having sufficiently pondered the contemplation of the ceiling.

Underneath me there is only the tickle of water; above me, the foggy density of a city I don't understand. Could my soul be wandering, lost, through one of its neighborhoods?

In the air I draw a city map containing avenues and highways of the future. A network of coordinates to trap the slippery soul.

I meticulously consult the telephone book. Friends' addresses, relatives' phone numbers, a list of medical specialists, of plumbers and presidents of institutions. What's missing from the directories is my own name. My soul must have carried it off in its luggage, that day when it scribbled on the back of a receipt those conventional little words that someone who's leaving us writes.

From *Magic*

The book has somehow to be adapted to the body, and at a venture one would say that women's books should be shorter, more concentrated, than those of men, and framed so that they do not need long hours of steady and uninterrupted work.
— Virginia Woolf, *A Room of One's Own*

It's true, we arrived too late for plenty. Too early for disaster. Like they say, let's sweep it away.

Enthusiastic chroniclers with quills frozen in midair.

* * *

In full possession of my mental powers, I renounce any powers that deny me the possibility of loving you, which is impossible coming from me, who in full possession of my mental powers am likely to reject you, who in full possession of your mental powers are likely to deny me the possibility of doing it, coming from us, from full dispossession of our undeniable powers.

* * *

Sad race, battered generation, a class of half-measures. We will be like gods at full height, feigning the dignity our grandparents had: soldiers and poets.

With a morbid jab in the womb, and total disillusion on the verge of insanity.

In an era of missiles, impotent in bed. Radiant with the oblivion in our humble hearts.

Nets of words won't stop our fall, we are the tightrope walkers of an empty circus.

Abortion after abortion we free our children from having to cry, later. We're a peaceful people, crazy and paradoxical.

* * *

Sir, miss, have you seen my husband pass by here? Of course, it is strange to run into "someone like that," a stray in the street. He said he was leaving to earn some dough, but he left the sweat of his brow at home. Another kind of sweat, too. That's no great matter, I've got good

393

cleaning tools. What's truly outrageous is that he forgot his most intimate keepsakes under the bed, and I'm afraid of bugs.

* * *

Something, "something" between us has broken—she says, distraught and in tears across from him. What was destroyed was a Chinese wall, a silk urn, a secret pact; a signal code, my sad heart and my bracelet; your mad love for me, the idea of shame, the blouse; the letters you wrote me, the telephone line, the silence.

And he, distressed to the point of nausea, mutters to her: "All that broke was a cup . . ."

* * *

When I was eight years old, I got the chicken pox. Away from comb and brush for three feverish weeks, my hair got tangled. My father carefully untangled it with his fingers, leaving threaded through it a permanent caress.

The next day, as I had expected, he sent me to the hairdresser's. And now, again with a fever, my thoughts are tangled, and I know very well that he could untangle them for me, but I hesitate at the memory of the next day.

* * *

Life comes and goes through my mouth. Kisses, ideas, moisture and sustenance through my mouth. Vomit and thirst through my mouth. And smiles, grimaces, lying and comforting. A call to silence; song.

* * *

I take my little habits seriously. Except for my pursuit of you, they're all harmless and discreet. For example, when I'm alone, I like to touch my breasts, because they have the habit of feeling warm. And to remember what happened to me as a girl, at the most inopportune moment. For example, after I have chased after you all afternoon, your hands have a habit of slipping up underneath my blouse, searching for that warmth of childhood memories.

* * *

394

And what if the recurring illusion of Me were an invisible bird flying over the abyss?

*   *   *

Woman, devote yourself to being beautiful. The impotent gladiator wants to take you to the ocean. There, flabbergasted, you will see a nuclear sunset over the beach. A broad flower rising, opening up like a spore for the sky to violate.
Sand clouds whirling under the cadaver. Do you see?
Devote yourself to being beautiful. And dance while the drum is sounding.

*   *   *

Papa, I love you. Psychoanalysis couldn't explain this love. Trendy sexist insults couldn't, nor the anthropological fear of incest. Mama couldn't. Come on now, carry me in your arms, read me those blood-curdling stories from the Old Testament, recite to me the vulgarities of Nervo, and cure me of these filial repulsions with your tenderest caresses.

*   *   *

In order to erect archival buildings they have knocked down the walls where lay the very last literary moaning.

*   *   *

The power of my desire has manifested itself. Now you want to legis-late. Institute a schedule for loving to love me. That's fine; that's terribly fine. I'm a reasonable woman: *mulier sapiens*. But keep in mind that I will be in the opposition until the power of your desire overcomes you and silently I legislate the statutes of distance.

*   *   *

Look you, you relentless hound of a conscience. Now that we are in crisis, I'm going to prepare you a juicy bribe in verse.

*   *   *

There's no time to be in love. Nobody gets paid to do it. We're just left with insomnia. There's no time for dismantling the afternoons and weaving together the mornings. Nor for an after-dinner smoking of your gestures. Love is alive only in the moments that we steal from someone else; that we steal ferociously from someone.

* * *

Maybe, Papa, turning back time, impregnating myself with your child-hood and squandering myself on the guilty, me enlightened by a girl's dream-like blindness, just like Samson, destroying the pillars of your house, hideout of the clan. Recovering you in my womb and asking: my little child, who hurt you like this?

* * *

"You only love yourself," you conclude, half empirically, half reproach-fully. I assure you, it hasn't been easy.

* * *

This one's for Papa; this one's for Mama; this one's for your brothers and sisters; this one's for Grandpa; this one's for god-the-father; this one's for the canary. . . . I keep following the same logic, but unfortunately they're no longer spoonfuls of soup.

Translated by Annette Cowart

Two Poems

Alberto Blanco

Alberto Blanco (Mexico City, 1951) has been prolific as a creator of poetry, translations, collages, rock and jazz music. A chemist by profession, he has also studied philosophy, and has a master's degree in Asian studies with a specialization in China. He has been a scholar for the Centro Mexicano de Escritores, the Instituto Nacional de Bellas Artes and the Fondo Nacional para la Cultura y las Artes. His books of poetry include Un año de bondad *(1987) and* Cromos *(1987), which won the Carlos Pellicer poetry award. He has also translated the poetry of* Emily Dickinson *(1982) and* Allen Ginsberg *(1986). In 1991, Blanco spent the year as a Fulbright scholar at the University of California at Irvine, where he completed the editing of his forthcoming book,* Antología de Poesía Norteamericana Contemporánea.

Paper Roads

High up
on the mountain
where the tireless pine tree grows

Up there
where the silence
turns to snow on the branches

There lives
a species of
crow that flies like a man.

Its wings
are the hope
of seeing the signs of the times.

Its cries,
white pages
on the black ground of dreaming.

Settling Accounts

The mind blows a bubble
with white clouds and everything else;
with my age (thirty), the sun
and a silent morning.

This is life, I say to myself,
real life, the only one,
the eternal promised life.

This car passing by
and the dogs barking . . .
The translucent curtain
and the droning of an airplane.

So this is life—
I say it again—
like someone who is becoming real.

Like someone who flows away in the current
and doesn't return to his body.
Like someone left alone
standing on his shadow.

Two Poems

Silvia Tomasa Rivera

Silvia Tomasa Rivera (El Higo, Veracruz, 1956) has published Duelo de espadas *(1984)*, Poemas al desconocido, poemas a la desconocida *(1984) and* Apuntes de abril *(1986)*.

I Saw You in the Park

I saw you in the park
feeding the pigeons;
we acted like strangers
talking about meaningless things.
A hot wind was blowing
and it lifted up your skirt;
your long legs ended up
breaking the ice.
I wanted to get closer
to the hollow of your arms,
but I don't want to think about
what's impossible.
Because I don't have time.

The memory of your legs is enough
to send me running wildly through the streets.

What I Wouldn't Give to Know

What I wouldn't give to know
                  what I'm doing here
on this threadbare sofa, masturbating,
              with an absent lover
who beats me—and whom I love.
Out in the street it's the same thing.
I pity men who call me
some word or other, thinking it's obscene;
they're like wounded birds crashing
into a window without glass.
I'm a woman out of sync with my time.
Just when I longed to be loved madly
by a longshoreman, or to roll around with a murderer
on a potato sack, I decide to put away my sex,
my breasts, my hair, in a crescent-shaped room,
and take my soul out to chase sparrows.

Translated by Cynthia Steele

Rocío Maldonaldo, *Sea Urchins II* (1986, ink on paper)

Storms of Torment

Carmen Boullosa

For a biographical note on Carmen Boullosa please see page 84.

First Storm

I want to tell about the downpour of dead cats.

It rained dead cats in the sunny patio of the sad house. They appeared, tossed hither and thither, enveloped in the terrifying halo of their cleanliness. They arrived there without a drop of blood, crushed, torn limb from limb, and darkly clean. Somberly clean.

They had just died. Those who touched them said that they were warm and supple, fresh flesh.

One day someone told me that a woman killed them to drink their new blood. That she cast the unburied corpses hither and thither, and, looking into my eyes insistently, she said: "always on the borders of the sad house."

I resisted the downpour of corpses, but when more than a dozen fell I saw myself drowning: I feared for my own blood and feared for myself: I was the only woman near the house and I thought that this insistent look wanted to put the blame on me, point to me as the woman who killed and shattered them as things, bursting and so filthy that I didn't leave enough blood in them to purify themselves.

I waited sitting on a bench in the patio to watch cats falling from some place and I saw her coming, enormous, ominous, carrying in her hands the dead animal, tiny in her enormous arms: that imposing woman was the storm.

403

Second Storm

Cinderella returns from the ball. She hurriedly puts on her shabby clothes, lies down beside the ashes of the hearth and pretends to sleep, hearing the sisters arrive. Her tears drop upon the ashes: mud does not form from those two materials, no figure can be drawn with them because they cannot capture any shape. One sister lightly kicks Cinderella's foot: an incomprehensibly disproportionate reverberation from the clash of the two feet, as if one of them weren't human. The blow does not harm her; when her sisters sleep, she is hurt by the dark, by loneliness, by being once more who she is. . . .

Third Storm

At each year's end, the kingdom's favorite painter does a portrait of the Queen. She keeps them in the East Room, where nobody, not even the sun, enters, because she does not want to expose her weakness for pictures: the artist's talent consists of coloring the same rosy face and eyes looking at the floor, dressed always in the same color, with her hands clasped and her hair gathered in a wine-red net, just as she was the first time he painted her.

This personage's figure, more difficult to see in the dim light, looks more and more masterfully executed as the years pass, while the Queen's face grows pale with the years that change the shape of her body and affect the texture of her skin. The painter carefully uses the tones that are more resistant to time: his pictures are not in any danger.

The storm began at the Queen's skirt, if storm can be translated as inexplicable disappearance.

The Queen's skirt was torn off the portraits. When she noticed it in the first one, she kept silent, waiting for it to be explained as an act of revenge, a magic trick that someone had devised to trap her. She even thought it might have been some timid lover who was seeking other arts to make her his. But she was forced to change her mind when all the skirts on all the other portraits followed, and after these the feet, one by one—not even in pairs—as if the lines that constituted the Queen were falling to pieces.

Who was doing this? The guards at each entrance to the room failed to find out. There was no window through which a thief could enter. It was inexplicable.

The painter confessed having dreamed of the absences in the paintings. The Queen, filled with fear, feeling threatened, ordered the painter to be put to death. After his death, she herself began to dream: her dreams showed on the Queen's living body what was stolen from the portraits, as she corroborated in panic the next morning. Thus she saw how she began missing her neck, eyes, face, ears, torso, hands . . . every night she attended her own dismemberment, dreaming each time only of the remaining parts, which had not yet entered the parade of disappearances.

When all that was left was her hair kept in the wine-red net, the Queen dreamed that her hair got loose and, out of some odd pleasure, angrily followed the path of kisses and embraces, of some strange passion whose joy the Queen had believed was confined to marriage. She saw the hair going farther and farther away and suddenly lost sight of it.

The next morning there was no Queen to verify that in the room of the paintings not a single fragment of those pictures was left and nobody could come up with the corpse so as to pay homage and bestow upon her the justice of entombed flesh.

In the East Room, which all were afraid to enter, on the stone floor a wine-red net tried to draw their attention.

Fourth Storm

She is born from a birth without any blood and violence other than herself: warm, pure water enclosed in the amorous form of a drop.

Her arrival into the world has something human about it: she is born into the cold and insolence. Any movement can disperse and destroy her original form.

She doesn't know her name.

She begins to roll along the enamored flesh, falling with ease, stopped here and there by little hairs, by slight rough spots in the skin and the jolts produced by the sobbing of the one who cries out of love.

She is, yes, a tear. She begins to understand it when she feels in her body the heat of crying and the unbearable cold of indifference. She tends to join with her identical sisters, but it's O.K., they all get along. Upon losing their form of drops dissolving in the loveless palm of the unloved hand of the one who cries, they understand that they are only the flag hoisted to accept defeat.

405

Fifth Storm

She flees. She flees. She flees, mercilessly, without herself. Because she can't stand her eyes with that wrong expression and her erring flesh. But the world in its place stands out. She flees, flees, but is not allowed to chance places. All the violence comprehended in this movement falls upon her. Singular and plural, overpowering, turning her into the enemy and the body of love: each eye of her lost face looks at a different point. She cannot show anybody the turmoil and the destruction, because, walled in, she who flees cannot escape; neither (she was walled in!) can anybody get near her.

Sixth Storm

I no longer hope for anything.

I am to be taken to the Beast's castle. In any case, it doesn't matter! The Beast's a beast and I will be the Beauty in his castle so that my blood there will not find death.

With my surrender I will invoke the death of my own.

The Beast will not kill me: he will recognize the smell of those who are related, he will know that I am not, like my father, flesh for his nourishment but rather flesh to dream and not to see the real, flesh for fantasy, flesh for the illusion of love. . . .

There I go! To the Beast's castle! To love . . . ! To the storm of torment!

Translated by Suzanne Jill Levine

406

A Season of Paradise

José Luis Rivas

José Luis Rivas (Ciudad de Tuxpan, Veracruz, 1950) is the author of ten books of poetry. His works include Tierra nativa *(1982), which won the Carlos Pellicer poetry award;* La transparencia del deseo *(1986), which won the Aguascalientes poetry prize;* El vuelo del vampiro *(1987); and a translation of Hugh Kenner's* The Pound Era *(1987). The Fondo de Cultura Económica will publish his collected poems, and* Vuelta *magazine will publish his forthcoming book, entitled* Luz de mar abierto.

> *And in the mighty mornings of the earth . . .*
> —Dylan Thomas

As free as anybody
            along the edge
of this undulating sheet of smooth blue glass
I wander the dark sand wherever my naked feet want to
    take me

The waves beat whips against the jetty
while the single sun
                covers my back
Gulls and *candiles**
             fly along the surface of the water
they rip it with their beaks
and from it take
             the freshest fish thrashing

**candiles:* tropical fish with eyes that glow in the dark

agonies
                    Cacophonous shrieking of parrots
radiant subversion in the kingdoms of heaven
on this morning with the face
                              of a god's sharp humor
and on its shining forehead
                              the benediction of a breeze
while beneath my forehead
            flame other mornings
                        powerful mornings of earth
with its arboreal power
                    and marine rage

As free as anybody
                in the morning of my thirty years
I sink my toes into the warm water
of the marsh that boils
                        and foams
when the langouste brood spiral
in their water-flight
                        where a moment ago
they splashed my nomad feet
                              and the sand where
shipwrecked jellyfish
            lie flaccid
star-tattooed conchs
kelp twisting around my ankles
                              sea snakes
periwinkles
            marine hallways
hermit crabs
sea-urchin watchmen
of the marsh and everything that the sea
brings treasurously in on tides from its vast dominion

A fistful of wind strikes my shoulders
thus the gods
                would push
anyone to whom it luckily fell
                        to witness the miracle

My kingfisher eyes plunge into the virgin water
Startled
            crabs
flee sideways over the green ocean carpet
and translucent
                        octopi hide in dirty caves
The wind whistles in the coastal palm groves this morning
when the sun
                to wake up
splashes itself in the water

All the expanse outspread
when the dew climbs an ivy ladder toward the sky
The light breaches golden chinks
in the thick-woven *limonaria* bushes while along the shore
simultaneously
                    a manta's sails
                                and feathered rigging unfurl
All the dazzling glare of the sky is copied
                            in the olive river-mirror
On mossy trunks
                crusty-skinned iguanas
                                    take the sun
while foxes scratch in the brambles
and hand-in-hand with the green profusion
one returns
                to the sea
along a practiced path
                    through palms

On the beach
            a royal crest
                            is grooming with its beak
the feathers that the wind
                    ruffles
                                        again

The starfish stranded
                at a tide-pool
                            frosted with sand
sparkles in the sun

and then tiny crabs
                    timidly peek out
of the sally-ports of their holes
and a new brood of turtles rushes in search of the water

Storm heralds
                    birds of the north
cross the sky
But life is a celebration
                    this morning
                              when the sun wakes
dreaming

Twenty years ago
                    I was a child
and I remember that the sun shone from sun to sun
it shone every day
and everywhere
        on the riverbank
        in the shade of the *guayo* trees
        under the palm-thatch roofs of houses
there were people who complained of the sun
Ay what sun
what sunny sun
                    this is
what sun we have every day
what dog-days sun
that makes the street-curs rabid
that darkens our skin
                              and bakes our bones what sun
that injects us with free vitamins
that rubs the lamp of lust
what sun that makes María go to bed with her boyfriend
on a mat
        under the *sapota* tree
and covered only
        with a soft poplin sheet
they spend the whole afternoon
                              nicely tangled together

Pretty soon
          the sweat is trickling between their legs
and a very penetrating scent
               like a luminosity envelops them
and then the one
          who's hiding behind the *caimito* tree to spy on them
stays there a moment
               shaking and ecstatic
and even though later he goes
               to cool himself off
               in front of the electric fan
or to lie face-down
               on the cool flagstones
he knows very well that this is catching
               and nothing's going to save him from it
and at all hours
          all he thinks about is going to bed
                         with María
to breathe her scent
               in the sheets she is scalding

Ay what sun
what scorching sun
Who could live without this sun? This sun
that warms frog ponds
and coconut milk
this sun that brings lizards out of their holes
this sun that splashes
pitchers of maguey juice over hot heads
and when it's far away
               turns into a magnifying glass

Ay what sun
what sultry sun
what sunniest sun
               this is
this everyday sun of ours
that shuffles the *lotería** deck with the sun-card in it
that feeds its cookstove fire

---

*lotería: game using a deck of cards with symbols, including the sun

411

with paper from the most venerable books
and ads for beer
Sun that creeps up the bed
                              where very close together
my little sister and I
                    half-sleeping
tossed and turned
                    all night
under the mosquito net

Ay what sun
that climbs the bed
                    crouches like a goblin
                              leaps
opens the window
                    and announces
                              a new day of sun

The Vetriccioli

Fabio Morábito

For a biographical note on Fabio Morábito please see page 92.

Our numbers grew year by year, certainly, but the old house in Bolívar Street managed to contain all of us without inconvenience or, rather, with a comfort that grew ever more subtle and intimate. Full of recesses and narrow passageways that suddenly widened for no reason, it seemed less a house than an amalgamation of many houses struggling to occupy the same spot.

Every corner was furnished with a desk, often no more than a simple plank to support the lectern and the inkwell. Other desks were built into the family's antique armoires, into windowsills and on lofts constructed to take advantage of the height of the ceilings and the slight protrusion of a passageway or a room. Even the least of the walls' concavities or depressions was not allowed to go to waste. There were desks jammed into cubbyholes so small a child would have had to struggle to fit into them, and in these niches as in all other parts of the house our work went on, by daylight or by lamplight, for ten to twelve hours each day. The bedrooms were on the upper floor, but it often happened that at day's end many Vetriccioli could be found sleeping at their tiny desks, pen still in hand.

When a new Vetriccioli was brought into the world, the elders, gathered in the cellar, chose the newborn's future workplace: the east wing, the lofts in the south end of the house (where once there had been a kitchen), the Arabian niches, or the central extension. After the baby celebrated its third birthday, it was given into the care of an uncle or an older cousin who taught it to become familiar with the lecterns, the drawers, the vertigo of lofts and dictionaries. By age six, the young Vetriccioli knew how to sit up straight, use blotting paper, sharpen pencils, make erasures without damaging the paper, and put a desk in order. He was taught to carry the manuscripts from one loft to another and to refill his cousins' and uncles' inkwells; at the end of the day he would hold up his ink-stained fingers proudly, and when he celebrated his seventh birthday he began to translate the first sentences and paragraphs which, in addition to training him, served to give the others an idea of what place in the family chain would best suit him in the future.

Indeed, every one of our translations passed from hand to hand to the point where it was appraised an infinite number of times, each new pair of hands contradicting the previous ones and then being contradicted by the next ones; one loft being contradicted by another loft, one armoire by another armoire, one wing of the house by the opposite wing. This could cause delays in turning things in to the publishing houses, but by passing through so many corrections and revisions the work, like a good chicken stock, became inpregnated with the style, the aura of the entire family, an aura which connoisseurs could recognize at first glance and which elicited the admiring exclamation:

"This is definitely a Vetriccioli!"

It was considered tasteful to cite our name along with that of the author, and people would say, "I've just bought a Molière-Vetriccioli," or "So-and-so gave me the last Vetriccioli: Heine's *Florentine Nights*." Or even, "I have a '42 Vetriccioli at home," without any mention of the author's name.

The Guarnieri, who lived three blocks from us in Turin Street, wanted to compete with us; their specialty, as they advertised it in the newspapers (they had the bad taste to advertise in the newspapers) was dead languages. But who can decree the death of a language? Though it may no longer be spoken or its era among men may have been brief, a language is forever embedded in the subconscious of the species and never ceases to re-emerge here and there. For that reason, it was often one of our youngsters barely able to hold a pen, ensconced high in a remote loft, who out of pure intuition delved back to the origin of a word in an ancient Caucasian language or in a Turkistan dialect that had been the despair of the family elders. To us, nothing was extinct, nothing had to be rescued from oblivion, there were only different strata in a continuous task. We saw the Guarnieri's division between living and dead languages as nothing more than a pretext for raising their prices. But what else could be expected from a family that worked in a three-

414

story office building without living together, competing among themselves, no doubt, and many of whom weren't really Guarnieri at all?

We didn't leave the house. A person needs some kind of firm conviction even to walk across a street, and as far as I know no Vetriccioli was
ever armed with anything that could even remotely be called a general
conviction or truth, outside of matters relating to our work; no Vetriccioli ever reproached anyone else's conduct either, except for the Guarnieri's opportunism. The ideas we ran across in the manuscripts that we
translated left us indifferent; we paid attention to the coherence of a
thought in order to translate it correctly, not to cultivate it or treasure it,
as the Guarnieri did. The pedantic conversations in Turin Street were
easy to imagine, full of disputes, immutable principles, flaring tempers,
and offended faces! How different from our dinnertime chats about
occurrences and deviations: what mattered was being together, hearing
ourselves conversing, and perceiving the secret inclinations and manias
of each one, the gentle clinking of souls. We had always known we were
no more than conveyor belts, and that thought thrilled us. We lived in
profile, half-responsible, half-alive. Our physique helped: both male and
female Vetriccioli were always slender, in contrast to the Guarnieri, who
were as adipose as their prose. The skinniest of them couldn't have made
his way through the niches and passageways of our house.

Not one of us had explored the whole house. In addition to its size and
its hundreds of recesses, the ardor we felt for our work hid it from us.
When one of us undertook a general reconnaissance he would quickly
grow bored, and wherever he finally abandoned the attempt he would
be assigned to a desk, whether halfway up or at ground level, where his
services were needed. These migrations, though infrequent, contributed
to the uniformity of our style by putting the different sectors of the
house, which over time had acquired their own peculiarities, into contact with each other. The Arabian niches were famous for abusing the
passive form, the period and the comma: work that was lively and
rhythmical when it arrived there would be solemn and circumspect
when it left. This was the so-called *Arabian cadence*, good for memoirs
and the epistolary genre, but inadequate for lighthearted or violent
episodes. The function of the great-great-grandfather and the other
ancients who lived in the cellar consisted largely of assigning each passage of a translation to the most appropriate sector of the house. For
lyrical outbursts, no one was better than the east wing. But the southern
lofts were unrivaled when it came to doubt, suspicion and inner torment. The author's slightest change of tone (a nostalgic digression, a
phrase veiled in resentment) would suffice to send the book traveling to

another part of the house, even if only for a few lines. And in each sector specialties flourished. A certain loft had achieved excellence in exclamations of repudiation, another in stammerings of wrath. Every day each manuscript would pass over dozens of desks and would be subjected to a morbid stylistic vigilance. And just as no Vetriccioli had ever explored the entire house, only a few had ever read a manuscript through from beginning to end. I mean that all our lives were spent among brief paragraphs and truncated phrases. This kept us from becoming emotional and losing control of the text, and sharpened our sensitivity to the value of each word, though it gradually made us insensitive to content and the linking of facts. Eventually this caused the eighth generation to lose completely its taste for dinnertime discourse. The elder generations' stories were no more than a senseless buzzing to them, and they quickly lay their heads on the long table to sleep; when they spoke they did so in sudden starts, emotionless, and then all at once they fell as silent as if they had never opened their mouths. They were the tallest and slenderest members of the family, whitish and spindly; they hardly ever mocked the Guarnieri, they hardly ever laughed at all; they didn't use dictionaries or grammars, and instead of asking for help when they hit a difficult passage, they pulled their feet and their stomachs in, closed their eyes, breathed deeply and found, as if in mute prayer, the word or the syntactic turn that would get them out of difficulty.

When they finally overthrew the rest of us, they did not unite; they amalgamated, since they had no confidence in each other, either. They were sick of the noise we made working, and their wrath exploded one winter morning. They went down to the cellar and their first action was to hang the elders. The daily routine of the desks had made us slow and they took all of us by surprise; many of us couldn't find the door to the street, others didn't understand what was happening until they were hanging from a rafter or a loft, kicking the air; the few of us who managed to escape never reassembled, and each one survived as best he could.

After that, the Guarnieri were more prosperous than ever. They added another story to their building on Turin Street and demanded to be given credit in books. This vulgar custom has spread. We never would have accepted seeing our name in print; all the difficulty and dignity of our work consisted in deeply convincing ourselves that we did not exist, in discovering that the author actually knew Spanish, that secretly he had expressed himself in Spanish and who knows what last-minute accident had obliged him to cloak his work in another language, the external layer of which we removed like bandages from a wound. How light and fluid each of the words became when we returned it to its original form! The Guarnieri fought to see their name printed in books and forgot that the secret of our vocation was slow and charitable rehabilitation. We were there to close the wounds, bring back health and restore things to their rightful places, nothing more.

When I walk down Bolívar Street now, scraping a stick along the garden wall, and pause another few minutes in front of the empty and decrepit mansion (*they*, as was to be expected, blind and deaf as they were, lost no time in annihilating each other after having annihilated everyone else, but I always made sure to collect the mail from the box and attend to it efficiently so as forestall any suspicion or curious question), I see all of them again: Great-grandfather Julio and Aunt Sampdoria, Uncle Cornelio, my brothers Pílade and Edgardo, all my cousins and uncles from the central extension, cursing, cackling and squinting in search of the right adjective, the most temperate turn of phrase. All the sectors wore themselves out in the same fever of perfectionism and though our number grew year by year, our house, fitting out a corner here and stretching itself a bit there, always kept a hidden fold or a virgin cranny for a new Vetriccioli. Of course we had to adapt to the new presences, make space for them, grow imperceptibly more slender, hold the arm closer to the body while writing, consult the dictionaries less so as to get in the way as little as possible, be more precise and temperate in our choice of words, try, in short, to burden the others only insofar as was absolutely necessary. And because of this each new Vetriccioli forcibly imposed a subtle reaccommodation, an almost imperceptible change in tone and style, just as the elders took irreplaceable words and cadences with them when they died. The one thing everyone shared was the fervor, the delivery of the manuscript and the consciousness that nothing was invented, that each of us was working on the others' work, was making corrections that would, in turn, be corrected, that originality did not exist and no trace of personality was appropriate, that all such traces had to be effaced, and that this was the essential difference between us and the Guarnieri, between their corpulence and our agility, between their multistory building and our old house in Bolívar Street where one could lose oneself among the thousands of recesses.

Translated by Esther Allen

417

Rocío Maldonado, *The Hand* (1990, ink on paper)

Notes on the Translators

Esther Allen's most recent translations are *Modernities and Other Writings* by Blaise Cendrars (Nebraska) and *Villaurrutia: Hieroglyphs of Desire* by Octavio Paz (Copper Canyon), both published this fall. She lives in New York City. ★ ★ ★ **Russell M. Cluff** and **L. Howard Quackenbush** translated *Schizotext and Other Poems* by the Chilean poet Gonzalo Rojas (Peter Lang, 1988), have completed the translation of *Finisterra and Other Poems* by Carlos Montemayor, and are currently preparing the translation of a collection of short stories by Guillermo Samperio. ★ ★ ★ **Annette Cowart** has lived and studied in Mexico. She worked as a special assistant to the editor on this issue of *TriQuarterly*. ★ ★ ★ **Judith de Mesa** has an M.A. from the Translation Program at the City University of New York. She is studying for a Ph.D. in English at the University of Miami. ★ ★ ★ **Kurt Hollander** is a writer, critic and translator. He divides his time between Mexico City, where he edits *Poliéster*, a contemporary-arts magazine, and New York City, where he edits *The Portable Lower East Side*.

Suzanne Jill Levine's most recent book is *The Subversive Scribe: Translating Latin American Fiction* (Graywolf, 1991). Her latest translations are of Adolfo Bioy Casares's *A Russian Doll and Other Stories* (New Directions, 1992) and, in collaboration with Eliot Weinberger, poet Cecilia Vicuña's *Unravelling Words and the Weaving of Water* (Graywolf, 1992). She is director of Latin American and Iberian Studies at the University of California, Santa Barbara. ★ ★ ★ **Johnny Payne** has published fiction in a number of literary journals, including *TriQuarterly*. His study of contemporary Latin-American and U.S. fiction will be published in 1993 by University of Texas Press. He teaches fiction writing and contemporary literature at Northwestern University.

★ ★ ★ **Louise B. Popkin** is a lecturer in Spanish at Harvard. Her translations of Latin-American poetry and fiction have appeared in a number of literary magazines, including *TriQuarterly*. ★ ★ ★ **Tim Richards** and **Judith Richards** have translated a number of stories by Luis Alberto Ramos. They teach in the Department of Foreign Languages and Literatures at the University of Missouri-Kansas City. ★ ★ ★ **Amy Schildhouse**'s "Crazy Guggenheim," translated by Juan Villoro, recently appeared in the literary supplement of the newspaper *El Nacional* in Mexico City. She lives in Columbus, Ohio, where she is working on a collection of short stories.

Mark Schafer has published translations of Virgilio Piñera's *Cold Tales* and *René's Flesh* (both from Eridanos Press), has co-translated Eduardo Galeano's *The Book of Embraces* with Cedric Belfrage (W. W. Norton), and this fall will publish his translation of Alberto Ruy Sánchez's novel *The Names of the Air* (City Lights). ★ ★ ★ **Cynthia Steele**'s critical study, *Politics, Gender and the Mexican Novel, 1968–88: Beyond the Pyramid*, was published earlier this year by University of Texas Press. She has published translations of fiction and poetry by Elena Garro, José Emilio Pacheco, Elena Poniatowska and Edgar O'Hara. Her versions of Inés Arredondo's *Underground River and Other Stories* will be published by the University of Nebraska Press. She has also completed a version of Pacheco's *City of Memory*, and is currently translating short stories by Sergio Pitol.

PUBLICACIONES LITERARIAS DEL
GOBIERNO DEL ESTADO DE CHIAPAS

NUEVO RECUENTO DE POEMAS
Jaime Sabines

EN MEMORIA DE NADIE
Oscar Palacios

MUSICA LUNAR
Efraín Bartolomé

OTRAS DESPUES DE EVA
Jorge Eliécer Rothschuh

ERGUIDO A PENAS
Joaquín Vázquez Aguilar

PARA DECIR MAÑANA
Socorro Trejo Sirvent

ROJO QUE MIDE EL TIEMPO
Marisa Trejo Sirvent

INSTITUTO CHIAPANECO DE CULTURA
Av. Central Poniente 1460, 2900 Tuxtla
Tel: (961) 207 84
Fax: (961) 306 78

Artes de México is a quarterly art magazine devoted to the rich gamut of art in México. Featuring over 100 pages of full-color reproductions, each issue addresses a specific topic among the almost unlimited aspects, both past and present, of Mexican art. Published in Spanish and English, the range of writing is at once informative, literary and scholarly. Each issue also includes a supplement featuring reviews of current shows and recent publications in Mexico, as well as a quaterly museum and gallery guide.

With a tradition of over 40 years, *Artes de México* resumed its briefly interrupted publication in the autumn of 1988 under the innovative editorship of Alberto Ruy Sánchez. Since then, and for four consecutive years, *Artes de Mérxico's* has been awarded three of Mexico's most prestigous awards: Premio al Arte Editorial, Premio Nacional de las Artes Gráficas and Premio Quorum de Diseño.

Artes de México features first-rate writers and art historians among its many contributors, including Octavio Paz, Dore Ashton, Carlos Fuentes, Damián Bayón, Leonor Cortina, Carlos Monsiváis, Fernando Gamboa, Gabriel García Márquez, Eduardo Matos Moctezuma, Severo Sarduy, Edward J. Sullivan and Elisa Vargas Lugo, Beatriz de la Fuente to name only a few. Our issues to date include:

D E M E X I C O

• •

S U B S C R I P T I O N S

I am enclosing a check (#_____) for the amount of
$100 US dollars to Artes de México. Please begin
my one-year subscription (4 issues) with issue No._____

Plaza Rio de Janeiro 52
Colonia Roma 06700 México D.F.
Telephone: 208 3205 Fax: 525 5925

_____

Name

_____

Address   City

_____

Country & Postal Code   Telephone

JOAQUÍN MORTIZ

CONTEMPORARY MEXICAN WRITING

Sealtiel Alatriste ♦ Federico Arana ♦ Homero Aridjis
Inés Arredondo ♦ Juan José Arreola

Efraín Bartolomé ♦ Rafael Bernal ♦ Joaquín Bestard

Federico Campbell ♦ Rosario Castellanos
Martha Cerda ♦ Elsa Cross ♦ Francisco Cuevas Cancino

Leonardo da Jandra ♦ Óscar de la Borbolla
Margarita de Orellana

Carlos Fuentes ♦ Vilma Fuentes

Jaime García Terrés ♦ Ricardo Garibay ♦ Elena Garro

Jorge Ibargüengoitia

José Agustín

Hernán Lara Zavala ♦ Vicente Leñero
Jorge López Páez

Francisco Martín Moreno ♦ David Martín del Campo
Marco Antonio Montes de Oca
Angelina Muñiz-Huberman

José Emilio Pacheco ♦ Octavio Paz ♦ Aline Pettersson
Elena Poniatowska ♦ Francisco Prieto

Abel Quezada

Rafael Ramírez Heredia ♦ Bernardo Ruiz
Carlos Ruiz Mejía ♦ Alberto Ruy Sánchez

Jaime Sabines ♦ Ignacio Solares ♦ Ilán Stavans

Paco Ignacio Taibo II ♦ Carletto Tibón

Edmundo Valadez ♦ Juan Villoro

Agustín Yáñez

MICHIGAN QUARTERLY REVIEW

presents a special issue

THE MIDDLE EAST

edited by Anton Shammas

This oversize issue will explore questions of cultural identity as well as social and political dynamics in countries throughout the Middle East. With the 500th anniversary of Columbus's voyage as a context, the issue will emphasize the interrelations of Middle Eastern, European, and American cultures.

* Sidra Ezrahi, "Exile and Homecoming in the Modern Jewish Imagination"
* Ammiel Alcalay on Jerusalem and the interconnectedness of the Levantine world
* Ted Swedenburg, "Palestinian/American Histories of the *Kufiya*"
* The Lessons of 1492: Essays by Juan Goytisolo and Roger Abdul Wahhab Boase on Spain and "The Morisco Problem"
* An Interview with the Lebanese novelist Hanan Al-Shaykh
* Fiction by Salwa Bakr (Egyptian), Saleem Barakat (Kurdish), Deborah Najor (Chaldean/American), and Salma Matar Sayf (United Arab Emirates)
* Poetry by Adonis, Meena Alexander, Pauline Kaldas, Khaled Mattawa, Haas Mroue, David Williams--and a sequence of prose poems by Naomi Shihab Nye
* Also: an essay and portfolio of works by Kamal Boullata; an essay on Egyptian cinema by Walter Armbrust; a review-essay on Arab and Israeli fiction by Muhammed Siddiq; a memoir by Aziz Shihab; and more

---

Recent and forthcoming in MQR: Stephen Brockmann, "The Cultural Meaning of the Gulf War"; Richard Ford, "What We Write, Why We Write It, And Who Cares"; Robert Hayden, "A Selection of Letters"; An Interview with Medbh McGuckian; Suzi Gabler on environmental art; Lee Bollinger on free speech; Tobin Siebers on ethnocentrism; Adrienne Donald on The Silence of the Lambs
And a double issue for fall of 1993 on "The Male Body"

For the Fall 1992 issue send a check for $8 to *MQR*, 3032 Rackham Building, University of Michigan, Ann Arbor, MI 48109-1070
A year's subscription is $18; two years, $33

MISSOURI

WHAT A PIECE OF WORK
Stories by Will Baker
From a hilarious parody
of conceptual art to a
bitter, elegiac tragedy of
the poor people of the
Andean highlands, this is
a collection of astonishing
stories by a highly
original writer.
200 pages, $19.95

ADJUSTING TO THE LIGHT
Poems by Miller Williams
"There is no voice like Miller
Williams'. . . . Who else after all
could speak in the voice of the
Almighty and make us believe it, just before we
laugh."—Betty Adcock. 64 pages, $16.95 cloth, $9.95 paper

WHAT A
PIECE
OF WORK

STORIES BY
WILL BAKER

A CIRCUS OF WANT
Poems by Kevin Stein
"These are enormously
compelling poems. As a
reader I am swept up in
their process, as they move
from place to unexpected
place, from connection to
surprising conection. . . .
A Circus of Want is a
moving, honest book."
—Lisel Mueller. 64 pages,
$16.95 cloth, $9.95 paper

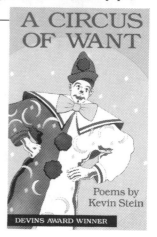

A CIRCUS
OF WANT

Poems by
Kevin Stein

DEVINS AWARD WINNER

UNIVERSITY
OF
MISSOURI
PRESS

*2910 LeMone
Boulevard
Columbia, MO
65201
1–800–828–1894*

THIEF OF LIVES
Stories by Kit Reed
Small triumphs and bittersweet
defeats make *Thief of Lives* a wise
and haunting look at people
very much like ourselves. From the author of the
critically acclaimed psychological thriller *Gone.*
192 pages, $19.95

Between The Lines

LETTERS BETWEEN UNDOCUMENTED LATIN AMERICAN IMMIGRANTS & THEIR FAMILIES & FRIENDS

EDITED AND WITH AN INTRODUCTION BY LARRY SIEMS
WITH A PREFACE BY JIMMY SANTIAGO BACA

"These letters stand as invaluable testimonies to the lives of countless invisible, unheard beings that the media, the U.S. Government would have remain anonymous. In other centuries they would have arrived in the hulls of ships— in shackles or in third-class steerage. Here, remarkably, is history as told by the participants themselves to lend a reality to the unreality of statistics and counter the 'official' story. By allowing these voices to speak, Mr. Siems has restored them their humanity."
—Sandra Cisneros

"Here is the uprootedness, the tenacity, the nostalgia, and the hope that accompanies hundreds of thousands of people who walk, run, or crawl to what they believe will be a better life."
—Margaret Randall, author of *Sandino's Daughters* and *Christians in the Nicaraguan Revolution*

Bilingual $24.95   cloth   336 pages   ISBN: 0-88001-277-3

The Ecco Press
(609) 466-4748

M A N D O R L A

NUEVA ESCRITURA DE LAS AMÉRICAS • NEW WRITING FROM THE AMERICAS

Edited by Roberto Tejada

Apartado postal 5-366 • 06500 México D.F.• México

P.O. Box 117 • Cooper Station • New York, New York 10003 • USA

❦

• Mandorla is a semi-annual literary magazine devoted to new writing and translation from the Americas. The format of the dialogue is "bilingual," but not in the conventional sense of the word. In English and Spanish, translated work appears only in its surrogate tongue. Previously unpublished material is featured only in its original language. French or Portuguese writing will appear in its original, including translation into both Spanish and English. • While the focus of the magazine is primarily early to present 20th-century poetry and poetics, Mandorla also publishes work on the visual arts, ethnography and other fields of cultural interest for the Americas.

• Issue 2 includes work by the following writers and translators: César Vallejo, Clayton Eshleman, Sylvia Navarrete, Gertrude Stein, Magali Tercero, Michael Davidson, Xavier Villaurrutia, Eliot Weinberger, Octavio Paz, Esther Allen, Guy Davenport, Gabriela Montes de Oca, Severo Sarduy, Paul Metcalf, Rossana Reyes, Salvador Elizondo, Kurt Hollander, Hugo Gola, Jan William, Coral Bracho, Lorna Scott Fox, Alfonso Alfaro, Eduardo Milán, Horacio Costa, Eduardo Vázquez Martín, Roberto Tejada, Ana Belén López, David Huerta, La Vonne Poteet, Thad Ziolkowski, Cuauhtémoc Medina; artwork by Fernando Leal Audirac, Cindy Sherman, Melanie Smith, Francis Alÿs, Eugenia Vargas, Thomas Glassford, Diego Toledo, Abraham Cruzvillegas.

❦

• •

I am enclosing 20 dollars in check or money order for a one-year subscription to Mandorla.

Name

Address

Subscription rate for libraries and institutions is 30 dollars.

Taking Note:
From Poets' Notebooks

Philip Booth
Sharon Bryan
Douglas Crase
Guy Davenport
Rita Dove
Stephen Dunn
Carolyn Forché
Reginald Gibbons
Allen Grossman
Donald Hall
Anselm Hollo
Garrett Hongo
Donald Justice
X.J. Kennedy
William Matthews
Mekeel McBride

J.D. McClatchy
Heather McHugh
Jane Miller
Robert Morgan
Lisel Mueller
Mary Oliver
Gregory Orr
Alicia Ostriker
Michael J. Rosen
Liz Rosenberg
Vern Rutsala
Peter Sacks
Laurie Sheck
William Stafford
Eleanor Ross Taylor
Rosanna Warren

Excerpts from the Notebooks of 32 American Poets
A Special Edition of *Seneca Review*

AMERICAN SHORT FICTION

Editor: Laura Furman
University of Texas at Austin

American Short Fiction has established itself as the quarterly of choice for readers who want at their fingertips strong and beautifully narrated stories. **American Short Fiction** publishes original stories by the masters of today—from Reynolds Price to William Humphrey to Joyce Carol Oates—and the new voices of tomorrow.

Contents of Number 8, Winter 1992

Special offer to subscribers:

Special 25% discount on gift subscriptions—introduce someone special to the newest stories from today's best writers. Subscribers to **American Short Fiction** can give one-year gift subscriptions for $18, a 25% discount. Send your name and address along with the recipient's name and address and $18 for each gift subscription. We will notify each recipient of your gift.

Please send gift subscription renewal notices to: ☐ subscriber
☐ gift recipient

American Short Fiction is published in
Spring (March), Summer (June), Fall (September), and Winter (December)
Subscriptions: Individual $24, Institution $36
Outside USA, add $5.50/subscription
Single Copy Rates:
Individual $7.95, Institution $9, Outside USA, add $2/copy
Prepayment only, please.

To subscribe, or for more information, write:

**University of Texas Press, Journals Department,
Box 7819, Austin, Texas 78713**

Recent Chicano titles from

ʘilingual ʘeview/ʘress

1990 Western States Book Award for fiction

The Devil in Texas/El diablo en Texas, by Aristeo Brito
Bilingual edition of the classic Chicano novel. "Brito has a serious and resonant talent and is a writer of impressive range and possibility."
—*Western States Book Awards Jury Citation*
224 pp.   cloth, $21.00   paper, $13.00

Peregrinos de Aztlán
by Miguel Méndez
New edition of the enduring Chicano novel that presents a contemporary version of the ancient Aztec myth of Aztlán. Clásicos Chicanos edition, with introduction by Francisco Lomelí.
200 pp.   paper only, $12.00

Distant Journeys, by Rafael Castillo
Rich and invigorating contemporary fables and complex allegories that depict the existential angst and crises in identity of characters trapped in the nightmare of the American dream.
112 pp.   paper only, $9.00

Three Times a Woman: Chicana Poetry, by Alicia Gaspar de Alba, María Herrera-Sobek, and Demetria Martínez
Full-length collections of poetry by three outstanding Chicana poets. "Each has a separate voice, but they produce a splendid harmony."
—*Albuquerque Journal*
168 pp.   paper only, $13.00

The Dream of Santa María de las Piedras, by Miguel Méndez
English translation by David William Foster of the acclaimed novel. "Reflects an impassioned world with effective mastery." —Camilo José Cela
194 pp.   cloth, $22.00   paper, $12.00

1991 American Book Award winner

Southern Front, by Alejandro Murguía
A fictionalized account, written by a Chicano participant, of the experiences of the international volunteers who fought with the Sandinistas against the Somoza regime in Nicaragua.
128 pp.   paper only, $10.00

1989 American Book Award winner

The Ultraviolet Sky
by Alma Luz Villanueva
The prize-winning first novel by the well-known Chicana writer. ". . . a vivid exploration of human relationships and change." —*Santa Cruz Sun*
379 pp.   cloth, $26.00   paper, $16.00

Tristealegría, by Francisco Santana
Deeply personal poetry rooted in popular culture and the oral tradition of the *poeta del pueblo.*
104 pp.   paper only, $8.00

Police Make House Calls
by Armand Hernández
Highly original, aphoristic poetry exploring the ironies and contradictions of the justice system.
80 pp.   paper only, $7.00

Sapogonia, by Ana Castillo
The new novel by the highly praised author of *The Mixquiahuala Letters.* "Ana Castillo at her best, a literary triumph." —Rudolfo A. Anaya
320 pp.   cloth, $24.00   paper, $14.00

Voice-Haunted Journey
by Eliud Martínez
A novel about social and psychic realities that explores the transformation of those realities into literary creation.
264 pp.   cloth, $22.00   paper, $13.00

Order through your bookstore, or direct from BILINGUAL REVIEW/PRESS, Hispanic Research Center, Arizona State University, Tempe, AZ 85287-2702. (602) 965-3867. Make check or money order payable to Bilingual Review/Press; add 5% shipping and handling ($1.00 minimum). Orders from individuals must be prepaid unless accompanied by an institutional purchase order.

The ANTIOCH REVIEW
50th Anniversary Issue

Over 450 pages

Volume 50, numbers 1 & 2 • Winter/Spring 1992 • $12.95, plus $2.00 postage

Daniel Bell	Elizabeth Fox-Genovese	Sylvia Plath
Jorge Luis Borges	Clifford Geertz	David Riesman
T. Coraghessan Boyle	Allen Ginsberg	Anne Sexton
Raymond Carver	Andrew Greeley	Elaine Showalter
Robert Creeley	Denise Levertov	Mark Strand
William Dickey	Philip Levine	William Trevor
Annie Dillard	Gordon Lish	Richard Wilbur
Ralph Ellison	Cynthia Ozick	Joy Williams

The Antioch Review, P.O. Box 148, Yellow Springs, OH 45387

PUT *TriQuarterly*
ON YOUR HOLIDAY GIFT LIST
BEFORE OUR RATES INCREASE!

For anyone interested in contemporary writing, there is no better present than a gift subscription to *TriQuarterly*. In addition to regular issues, our famous special issues (like the one you're holding now) bring *TQ*'s readers large and very attractive books focused on new writing from abroad or important contemporary literary topics.

What better way to share your own pleasure in reading, and to support the art of writing?

Gift subscriptions are **still only $16** if you yourself already subscribe. Take advantage of this offer before our rates go up on January 1, 1993, and we'll send *you* a gift as well—choose a paperback copy of *TriQuarterly*'s landmark anthology, *Fiction of the Eighties*, or a clothbound first edition of William Goyen's selected stories, *Had I a Hundred Mouths*.

Let us hear from you soon. If we receive orders by December 5, we can guarantee that the recipient of the gift subscription will receive it by December 25—and we'll notify them of your gift with an attractive card.

(If you don't presently subscribe, but would like to, fill out and mail us the form below—we'll *still* send you a free book, even if your order is not for a gift!)

Remember to act before January 1, 1993—and save!!

The
Threepenny
Review

TriQuarterly thanks the following life subscribers:

David C. Abercrombie
Amin Alimard
Lois Ames
Richard H. Anderson
Roger Anderson
Sandy Anderson
I. N. C. Aniebo
University of Arizona Poetry Center
Gayle Arnzen
Michael Attas
Asa Baber
Tom G. Bell
Carol Bly
Susan DeWitt Bodemer
Kay Bonetti
Robert Boruch
Van K. Brock
Gwendolyn Brooks
Timothy Browne
Paul Bundy
Eric O. Cahn
David Cassak
Stephen Chapman
Anthony Chase
Freda Check
Michael Chwe
Andrew Cyr
Doreen Davie
Kenneth Day
Mark W. DeBree
Alan Distler
Anstiss Drake
J. A. Dufresne
John B. Elliott
Christopher English
Carol Erickson
Steven Finch
David R. Fine
Paul Fjelstad
Torrence Fossland
Helen and C. Dwight Foster
Jeffrey Franklin
Peter S. Fritz
Mrs. Angela M. Gannon
Kathy M. Garness
Lawrence J. Gorman
Maxine Groffsky
Rev. Dr. Elliott Hagle
Jack Hagstrom
Ross B. Heath
Charles Hedde
Gene Helton
Donald Hey
Donald A. Hillel

Craig V. Hodson
Irwin L. Hoffman
Irwin T. Holtzman
P. Hosier
Charles Huss
Curtis Imrie
Helen Jacob
Del Ivan Janik
Gary Michael Katz
Dr. Alfred D. Klinger
Loy E. Knapp
Sydney Knowlton
Mr. and Mrs. Carl A. Kroch
Judy Kunz
Conrad A. Langenberg
John Larroquette
Isaac Lassiter
Dorothy Latiak
Elizabeth Leibik
Patrick A. Lezark
Patricia W. Linton
Philip Lister
Mr. and Mrs. W. J. Lorentz de Haas
Prof. Kubet Luchterhand
Ellen L. Marks
Richard Marmulstein
James Marquardt
Kevin McCanna
Robert D. McChesney
Charles Gene McDaniel
Robert McMillan
Michael Meaney
George Meredith
Lois Adele Meyer
Cliff Michel Gallery
University of Michigan Hopwood Room
Ralph Miller
Kenneth Monroe
James E. Morrison IV
Max Nathan
Dean Neprud
Catherine Ohs
Paul Peters and Rosemarie Kozdron
Scott Peters
Jane Petro
Evelyn Pine
Doyle Pitman
Barbara Polikoff
Alex T. Primm
Richard Prinz, M.D.
Honora Rankine-Galloway
Anne Katheryn Ream
J. M. Reese
Peter Reich